THIRD EDITION

3

GRAMMAR
IN CONTEXT

SANDRA N. ELBAUM

HEINLE & HEINLE

THOMSON LEARNING™

United States · Australia · Canada · Mexico · Singapore · Spain · United Kingdom

Vice President, Editorial Director ESL/EFL: Nancy Leonhardt
Production Editor: Michael Burggren
Marketing Manager: Charlotte Sturdy
Manufacturing Coordinator: Mary Beth Hennebury
Project Management: Michael Granger; Modern Graphics, Inc.
Composition: Modern Graphics, Inc.

Photo Research: Susan Van Etten
Illustration: Outlook/Anco
Cover/Text Designer: Linda Dana Willis
Cover Photography: Vladimir Pcholkin/FPG
Printer: Von Hoffman Graphics

For permission to use material in this text, contact us:

web   www.thomsonrights.com
fax   1-800-730-2215
phone   1-800-730-2214

Heinle
25 Thomson Place
Boston, MA 02210

UK/EUROPE/MIDDLE EAST:
Thomson Learning
Berkshire House
168-173 High Holborn
London, WC1V 7AA, United Kingdom

AUSTRALIA/NEW ZEALAND:
Nelson/Thomson Learning
102 Dodds Street
South Melbourne
Victoria 3205 Australia

CANADA:
Nelson/Thomson Learning
1120 Birchmount Road
Scarborough, Ontario
Canada M1K 5G4

LATIN AMERICA:
Thomson Learning
Seneca, 53
Colonia Polanco
11560 México D.F. México

ASIA (excluding Japan):
Thomson Learning
60 Albert Street #15-01
Albert Complex
Singapore 189969

JAPAN:
Thomson Learning
Palaceside Building, 5F
1-1-1 Hitotsubashi, Chiyoda-ku
Tokyo 100 0003, Japan

SPAIN:
Thomson Learning
Calle Magallanes, 25
28015-Madrid, España

Photo & Illustration Credits:
p. 31 © Lee White/Corbis, **p. 44** © Susan Van Etten, **p. 77** © Bettmann/Corbis, **p. 92** © TheWhite House, **p. 92** © Archive Photos, **p. 97** © Bettmann/Corbis, **p. 117** © Bettman/Corbis, **p. 149** © Kevin Fleming/Corbis, **p. 158** © Susan Van Etten, **p. 189** © Corbis, **p. 195** © Reuters Newsmedia,Inc./Corbis, **p. 195** © Bettmann/Corbis, **p. 219** © Owen Franken/Corbis, **p. 219** © Susan Van Etten, **p. 245** © Susan Van Etten, **p. 259**, © D. Robert Franz/Corbis, **p. 260** © Underwood&Underwood/Corbis, **p. 266,** ©   Bob Rowan; Progressive Image/Corbis, **p. 276** © AP/Wide World/Paul Warner, **p. 313** © Bettmann/Corbis, **p. 317** © Corbis, **p. 321** © Susan Van Etten, **p. 325** © Susan Van Etten, **p. 343** © Susan Van Etten, **p. 350** © Jacques M. Chenet/Corbis, **p. 387** © Raymond Gehmann/Corbis, **p. 407** © Susan Van Etten

Library of Congress Cataloging-in-Publication Data

Elbaum, Sandra N.
    Grammar in context / Sandra Elbaum.—3rd ed.
        p. cm.
    Includes index.
    ISBN 0-8384-1268-8 (bk. 1 : pbk. : alk. paper)—ISBN 0-8384-1270-X (bk. 2: pbk. :
alk. paper)—ISBN 0-8384-1272-6 (bk. 3: pbk. : alk. paper)
    1. English language—Grammar—Problems, exercises, etc.   2. English
language—Textbooks for foreign speakers.   I. Title.

PE1112.E3642000
428.2'4—dc21
                                                        00-040822

ISBN 0-8384-1272-6

Printed in the United States of America
4 5 6 7 8 9   05 04 03 02

Contents

Lesson 2

Lesson 3

Lesson 4

Lesson 5

Lesson 6

Lesson 7

Lesson **8**

Lesson 9

Lesson 10

Appendices

**In memory of Meyer Shisler
Teacher, Scholar, Inspiration**

Acknowledgments

I would also like to show my appreciation for the following teachers who reviewed **Grammar in Context:**

Caroline Cochran	Northern Virginia Community College, VA
Carol Dent	City College of San Francisco, Alemany Center, CA
Bill Griffith	Georgia Institute of Technology, GA
Kathi Jordan	Contra Costa College, CA
Ed Rosen	City College of San Francisco, CA
Rebecca Suarez	University of Texas, El Paso, TX
Ethel Tiersky	Truman College, IL
Karen Tucker	Georgia Institute of Technology, GA
Andrea Woyt	Truman College, IL
Anita Zednik	Northern Virginia Community College, VA

A special thanks to my family of friends for helping me get through it all: Jim M. Curran, Cornelius Hassell, Chay Lustig, Hal Mead, Alison Montgomery, Marilyn Orleans, Meg Tripoli, and Lydia York.

And many thanks to my students at Truman College, who have increased my understanding of my own language and taught me to see life from another point of view. By sharing their observations, questions, and life stories, they have enriched my life enormously.

A word from the author

It seems to me that I was born to be an ESL teacher. My parents immigrated to the U.S. from Poland as adults and were confused not only by the English language but by American culture as well. Born in the U.S., I often had the task as a child to explain the intricacies of the language and allay my parents' fears about the culture. It is no wonder to me that I became an ESL teacher, and later, an ESL writer who focuses on explanations of American culture in order to illustrate grammar. My life growing up in an immigrant neighborhood was very similar to the lives of my students, so I have a feel for what confuses them and what they need to know about American life.

ESL teachers often find themselves explaining confusing customs and providing practical information about life in the U.S. Often, teachers are a student's only source of information about American life. With **Grammar in Context, Third Edition,** I enjoy sharing my experiences with you.

Grammar in Context, Third Edition connects grammar with American cultural context, providing learners of English with a useful and meaningful skill and knowledge base. Students learn the grammar necessary to communicate verbally and in writing, and learn how American culture plays a role in language, beliefs, and everyday situations.

Enjoy the new edition of **Grammar in Context!**

Sandra N. Elbaum

Grammar in Context Unites Learners and Language

Students learn language in context, increasing their understanding and ability to use new structures.

Learning a language through meaningful themes and practicing in a contextualized setting promotes both linguistic and cognitive development. In **Grammar in Context,** grammar is presented in interesting and informative readings, and the language is subsequently practiced throughout the chapter. Students learn more, remember more and can use language more effectively when they learn grammar in context.

Students expand their knowledge of American topics and culture.

American themes add a historical and cultural dimension to students' learning. The readings in **Grammar in Context** help students gain insight into American culture and the way many Americans think and feel about various topics. Students gain ample exposure to and practice in dealing with situations such as finding an apartment, holiday traditions, and shopping, as well as practicing the language that goes with these situations. Their new knowledge helps them enjoy their stay or life in the U.S.

Students are prepared for academic assignments and everyday language tasks.

Discussions, readings, compositions and exercises involving higher level critical thinking skills develop overall language and communication skills. In addition to the numerous exercises in the student text and workbook, teachers will find a wealth of ideas in **Grammar in Context.** Students will have interesting, fulfilling, and successful experiences that they will take with them as they complete their ESL classes.

Students learn to use their new skills to communicate.

The exercises and Expansion Activities in **Grammar in Context** help students learn English while practicing their writing and speaking skills. Students work together in pairs and groups to find more information about topics, to make presentations, to play games, and to role-play. Their confidence to use English increases, as does their ability to communicate effectively.

Students enjoy learning.

If learning is meaningful, it is motivational and fun. Places, famous people, trends, customs, and everyday American activities all have an impact on our students' lives, and having a better understanding of these things helps them function successfully in the U.S. By combining rich, cultural content with clear grammar presentation and practice, **Grammar in Context** engages the student's attention and provides guidance in grammar usage and writing. And whatever is enjoyable will be more readily learned and retained.

Welcome to
Grammar in Context, Third Edition
Spanning language and culture

Students learn more, remember more and can use grammar more effectively when they learn language in context. **Grammar in Context, Third Edition** connects grammar with rich, American cultural context, providing learners of English with a useful and meaningful skill and knowledge base.

Grammar charts use simple and clear language taken from the readings to explain structures in context.

Language Notes refine students' understanding of the target structure.

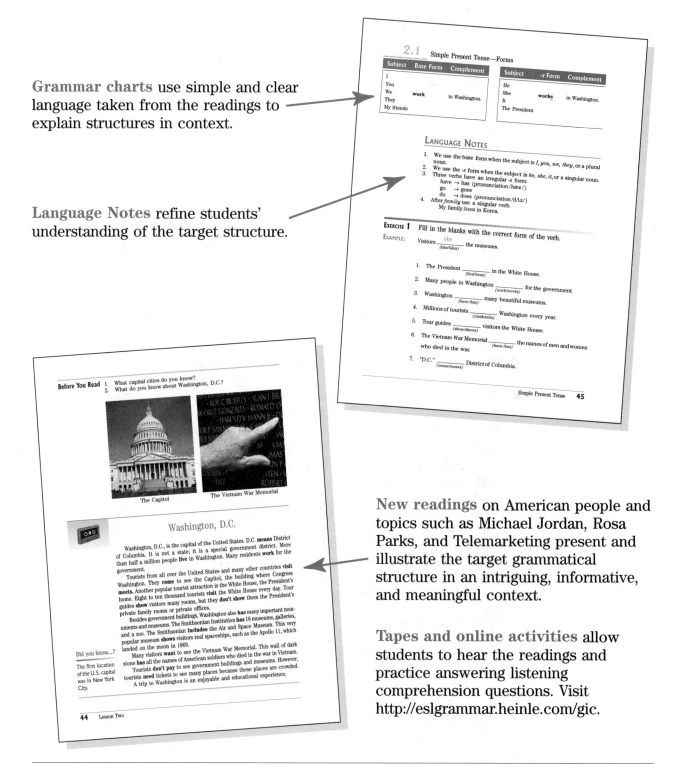

New readings on American people and topics such as Michael Jordan, Rosa Parks, and Telemarketing present and illustrate the target grammatical structure in an intriguing, informative, and meaningful context.

Tapes and online activities allow students to hear the readings and practice answering listening comprehension questions. Visit http://eslgrammar.heinle.com/gic.

A wide array of exercises keeps the classroom lively and targets a variety of learning styles.

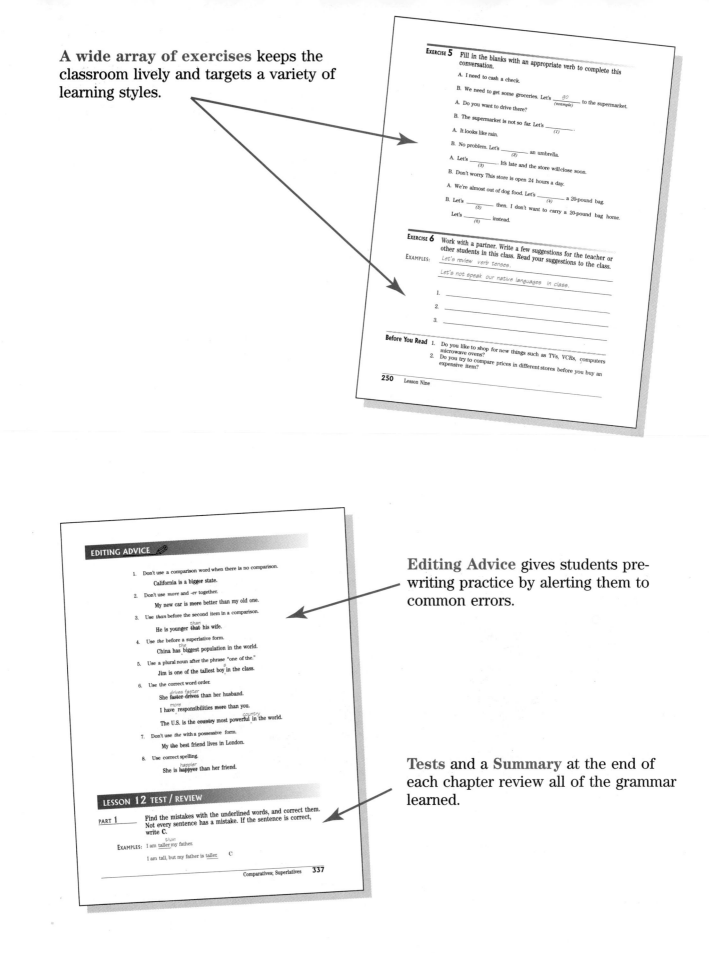

EXERCISE 5 Fill in the blanks with an appropriate verb to complete this conversation.

A. I need to cash a check.

B. We need to get some groceries. Let's ___go___ to the supermarket.
(example)

A. Do you want to drive there?

B. The supermarket is not so far. Let's _____.
(1)

A. It looks like rain.

B. No problem. Let's _____ an umbrella.
(2)

A. Let's _____. It's late and the store will close soon.
(3)

B. Don't worry. This store is open 24 hours a day.

A. We're almost out of dog food. Let's _____ a 20-pound bag.
(4)

B. Let's _____ then. I don't want to carry a 20-pound bag home.
(5)
Let's _____ instead.
(6)

EXERCISE 6 Work with a partner. Write a few suggestions for the teacher or other students in this class. Read your suggestions to the class.

EXAMPLES: Let's review verb tenses.

Let's not speak our native languages in class.

1. _____

2. _____

3. _____

Before You Read 1. Do you like to shop for new things such as TVs, VCRs, computers microwave ovens?
2. Do you try to compare prices in different stores before you buy an expensive item?

250 Lesson Nine

Editing Advice gives students pre-writing practice by alerting them to common errors.

EDITING ADVICE

1. Don't use a comparison word when there is no comparison.
California is a bigger state.

2. Don't use *more* and *-er* together.
My new car is more better than my old one.

3. Use *than* before the second item in a comparison.
He is younger ~~that~~ *than* his wife.

4. Use *the* before a superlative form.
China has *the* biggest population in the world.

5. Use a plural noun after the phrase "one of the."
Jim is one of the tallest boy in the class.

6. Use the correct word order.
She ~~faster drives~~ *drives faster* than her husband.
I have responsibilities *more* than you.
The U.S. is the ~~country~~ most powerful *country* in the world.

7. Don't use *the* with a possessive form.
My the best friend lives in London.

8. Use correct spelling.
She is ~~happyer~~ *happier* than her friend.

LESSON 12 TEST / REVIEW

PART 1 Find the mistakes with the underlined words, and correct them. Not every sentence has a mistake. If the sentence is correct, write C.

EXAMPLES: I am taller *than* my father.

I am tall, but my father is taller.   C

Tests and a **Summary** at the end of each chapter review all of the grammar learned.

Comparatives; Superlatives 337

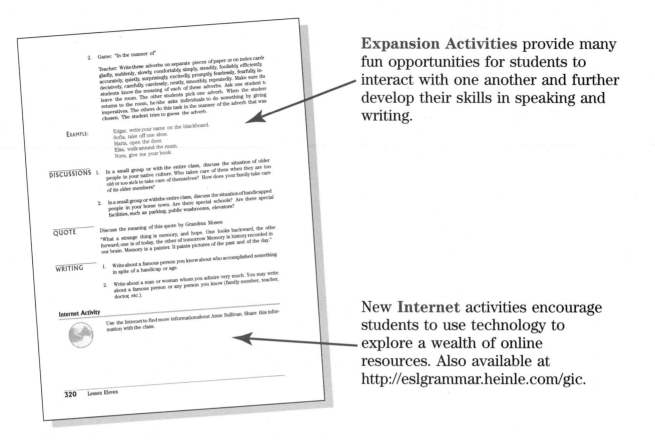

Expansion Activities provide many fun opportunities for students to interact with one another and further develop their skills in speaking and writing.

New **Internet** activities encourage students to use technology to explore a wealth of online resources. Also available at http://eslgrammar.heinle.com/gic.

More Grammar Practice Workbooks

Used in conjunction with **Grammar in Context** or as a companion to any reading, writing, or listening skills text, **More Grammar Practice** helps students learn and review the essential grammar skills to make language learning comprehensive and ongoing.

- Clear grammar charts

- Extensive exercises

- Great for in-class practice or homework

- Follows the same scope and sequence as **Grammar in Context, Third Edition**

Review Lesson

PART 1
VERBS

A. Study Charts:

	Affirmative	**Negative**
Be	He is tired.	He isn't tired.
	I'm afraid.	I'm not afraid.
	He was absent.	He wasn't absent.
Simple present tense	I work.	I don't work.
	He works.	He doesn't work.
Simple past	I worked.	I didn't work.
	I ate.	I didn't eat.
	I fell.	I didn't fall.
	I studied.	I didn't study.
Future	I am going to study.	I am not going to study.
	I will study.	I won't study.
Present continuous	He is sleeping.	He isn't sleeping.
Past continuous	He was sleeping.	He wasn't sleeping.
Present perfect	You have broken the mirror.	You haven't broken the mirror.
Present perfect continuous	We have been studying for two hours.	We haven't been studying for two hours.
Modals	He can study.	He cannot study.

Be—Present	*Be*—Past
I → am You, We, They → are He, She, It → is	I, He, She, It → was You, We, They → were

B. Rules and Examples:

Rules and Examples	Find the mistakes and correct them. Not every sentence has a mistake.
1. For the simple present tense, use the **s** form for *he*, *she*, *it*, singular subjects, gerund subjects, and subjects beginning with *every* and *no*. He **lives** in New York. My father **has** a new car. Learning a new language **takes** time. Everyone **needs** love. Nobody **wants** to get old.	• My brother work*s* in a restaurant. • My best friend lives in Australia. • Raising children are a hard job. • Nobody know how I feel. • No one has time for me now. • Every child deserves love. • Everybody want respect.
2. Use the base form for *I*, *you*, *we*, *they*, and plural subjects. You **live** near me. We **walk** to school. EDITING NOTE: *People* is a plural subject. *have* Some people ~~has~~ a hard life.	• They has free time now. • People complains a lot. • My parents lives in Germany. • The students want more practice.
3. To form the negative of the simple present tense, use *don't* or *doesn't* + the base form. *I*, *you*, *we*, *they*, plural subjects + *don't* *He*, *she*, *it*, singular subjects + *doesn't* He **has** a car. He **doesn't have** an American car. I **speak** Italian. I **don't speak** German.	• He don't know your name. • We doesn't speak French. • The classroom doesn't have a telephone. • He doesn't has a car.
4. Use the correct form of *be*. My parents **are** very kind. I **am** busy. You **were** late yesterday.	• My friends is always good to me. • We was in Canada last summer. • You were in class yesterday. • Most people is kind.

Rules and Examples	Find the mistakes and correct them. Not every sentence has a mistake.
5. Many past tense verbs are irregular. Use the correct form. (For a list of irregular past tenses, see Appendix M). He **found** a job. She **drove** the car. EDITING NOTE: Do not use *be* to form a simple past tense verb. I ~~was~~ bought a car last month.	• They went home early last night. • She heared the news on the radio. • He saw the accident. • She was opened the present. • They wrote a composition.
6. Use *was/were* with *born*. Do not put an ending on *born*. Where **were** you **born**? I **was born** in Mexico.	• They were born in Guatemala. • I borned in July. • Where was your parents born?
7. Continuous tenses = *be* + verb *-ing* They **are eating** now. He **was washing** the dishes when he dropped a glass.	• He eating lunch now. • He's work now. • I sleeping when the phone rang. • They are driving home now.
8. Present perfect tense = *have/ has* + past participle She **has seen** the movie. I **have eaten** lunch. We **have cooked** dinner five times this week. EDITING NOTE: Don't confuse the *-ing* form with the *-en* form. been I've ~~being~~ in the U.S. for ten months.	• I have made many mistakes. • They been here for two hours. • I've look at the clock five times. • She has eating dinner already.
9. Present perfect continuous = *have/has* + *been* + verb-*ing* I **have been studying** English for three years. She **has been sleeping** for six hours. EDITING NOTE: Don't confuse the *-ing* form with the *-en* form. driving I've been ~~driven~~ for three hours, and I'm tired.	• You have been worked for two hours. • I've living in Chicago for three months. • She's been taken English classes for three years.

Rules and Examples	Find the mistakes and correct them. Not every sentence has a mistake.
10. Use an infinitive (*to* + base form) after certain verbs (*want, need, expect, try*). He wants **to find** a job. I need **to learn** new words. NOTE: If two infinitives are connected with *and*, don't repeat *to*. The second verb is an infinitive without *to*. She wants **to get** married and **have** children.	• She needs buy a new car. • I tried called you yesterday. • She wanted to left early last night. • She wants to finish college and finding a job. • She expected to receive a letter yesterday.
11. Include *be* and *to* with the following verbs: *be supposed to, be allowed to, be permitted to, be able to*. I **was** able **to** pass my driving test. You **are** supposed **to** take a test.	• You are able to speak English well. • We not supposed to talk during a test. • You're not allowed park on this side of the street.
12. Future = *will/be going to* + base form I **will help** you later. She **is going to study** tonight. EDITING NOTE: Don't use *be* together with a simple future tense verb. I will ~~be~~ have more time later.	• He will coming home later. • She will become a doctor. • I going to visit my parents on Saturday. • Will you be get married next year?
13. When talking about the future, use the simple present tense in a time clause or an *if* clause. I will help you if I **have** time. When she **visits** her country, she will see her cousins.	• When I will return to my country, I will visit my parents. • He will go to the movies if he will have time. • If I'm home before 10 p.m., I'll call you. • She will visit the Eiffel Tower when she is in Paris.
14. Use *didn't* + the base form to make the negative of regular and irregular verbs. She **saw** the movie. She **didn't see** the play. She **studied** French. She **didn't study** German.	• He didn't went to the party last Saturday. • I don't watched the news last night. • She didn't find a job last week.

Rules and Examples	Find the mistakes and correct them. Not every sentence has a mistake.
15. To show purpose, use *to* + the base form. I came to this school **to learn** English. He saved his money **to buy** a TV.	• I turned on the TV for watch the weather. • What is the best way to learn English? • He came to the U.S. for improving his skills.
16. In American English, the negative of *have* as a main verb is *don't have*. The negative of *has* is *doesn't have*. The negative of *had* is *didn't have*. He **has** time, but he **doesn't have** money. We **had** a review, but we **didn't have** a test.	• She doesn't have any paper. • She hadn't time to do her homework last night. • I haven't money for the bus. • He has not a car.
17. After a modal, use the base form. He **should clean** the house. You **must wear** a seat belt.	• I can't to help you. • You shouldn't driving so fast. • It may rain tonight. • You must to leave immediately.

EXERCISE 1   Find the mistakes with the underlined words, and correct them. Not every sentence has a mistake. If the sentence is correct, write **C**.

EXAMPLES: He <u>drink</u>^s coffee every day.

You <u>were</u> late yesterday.   C

1. She <u>going to buy</u> a new computer next month.

2. She <u>goes</u> to the library once a week.

3. My brother <u>works</u> very hard.

4. She <u>didn't go</u> home after work yesterday.

5. My father <u>have</u> a new car.

6. My cousin <u>lives</u> in New York.

7. I <u>watching</u> TV last night when the telephone rang.

8. My sister <u>likes</u> dogs. She <u>doesn't likes</u> cats.

9. I'll be know a lot of grammar at the end of the semester.

10. He speaks Ukrainian. He doesn't speak Russian.

11. She will take a vacation next month.

12. He's a doctor. He been a doctor since 1997.

13. Nobody know how to fix the problem.

14. I have saw a lot of good movies lately.

15. He was driving to work when he had a flat tire.

16. Last week, she was lost her gloves.

17. I have eating Mexican food many times.

18. She forgot to turned off the oven.

19. If we will have time next week, we will go to the zoo.

20. You should to buy a faster computer.

21. I want eat lunch now.

22. Every student need a textbook.

23. She hasn't a computer.

24. I not want to go outside now.

25. We seen a good movie last Saturday.

26. She quitted her job two months ago.

27. My father was borned in 1945.

28. She's been talking on the phone for two hours.

29. I need a pen for write the composition.

30. She can't understand the lesson.

31. I finded a job yesterday.

32. She didn't understood the explanation.

33. Some people is very friendly.

34. She will become a teacher when she graduates.

35. I'm not able find a good job.

36. Most people want to be rich.

37. You wasn't in class yesterday.

38. He has already taking care of the problem.

39. She came to the U.S. for find a better job.

40. They didn't <u>driving</u> to Canada. They <u>flew</u> there.

41. Be quiet. The baby <u>sleeping</u>.

42. I want <u>to go</u> back to my native country and <u>visiting</u> my parents.

43. You <u>not supposed to talk</u> in the library.

44. She expected <u>received</u> a letter, but she didn't.

PART 2
Adjectives, Adverbs, and Noun Modifiers

A. Study Chart:

Adjectives	Adverbs	Noun Modifiers
He is a **careful** driver.	He drives **carefully**.	He has a **driver's** license.
He is a **good** cook.	He cooks **well**.	He uses a **gas** stove.
She is a **hard** worker.	She works **hard**.	She is a **city** worker.

B. Rules and Examples:

Rules and Examples	Find the mistakes and correct them. Not every sentence has a mistake.

1. A descriptive adjective has no plural form.
    She has a **wonderful** son.
    She has two **wonderful** daughters.
	• Her children are beautiful̸s.
	• You have pretty eyes.
	• Boston and Philadelphia are Americans cities.

2. Use an adverb of manner to describe a verb phrase. Most adverbs of manner are formed by adding -ly to the adjective.
    He speaks English **fluently**.
    I type very **quickly**.
	• You should drive careful.
	• He spoke very quiet.
	• Please speak more softly.

3. Some adverbs have the same form as the adjective: *fast, hard, late, early*.
    He is a **fast** worker. He works **fast**.
    She has an **early** class. She arrives **early**.
	• She worked very hardly last week.
	• She talks very fastly.
	• I'm trying hard to find a job.

Rules and Examples	Find the mistakes and correct them. Not every sentence has a mistake.
4. *Good* is an adjective. The adverb is *well*. She's a **good** cook. She cooks **well**.	• He writes English very good. • He is a good writer.

5. Use an adjective, not an adverb, after *be* or other linking verbs (*seem, look, smell, sound, taste, feel*).
 	
  I am very **proud** of you.
 	
  The coffee smells **fresh**.
 	
  The pie tastes **good**.
	• She seems responsible.
	• She is very carefully when she drives.
	• That music sounds beautifully.

6. Use *too* before an adjective or adverb only if there is a problem presented. If there is no problem, use *very*.
 	
  My brother is a **very** good student.
 	
  He's 14. He's **too** young to drive.
	• I found a wonderful job. I'm too happy.
	• My grandparents are too healthy.
	• Joe and Mary are only 17. They're too young to get married.

7. Use *too much* and *too many* before nouns. Use *too* before adjectives and adverbs.
 	
  That car is **too** expensive. I can't buy it.
 	
  That car costs **too much** money for me.
	• He's too young to retire.
	• He drives too slowly on the highway. He can get a ticket.
	• It's too much hot in here. Let's turn on the air-conditioner.

8. When a noun describes a noun, the first noun is always singular.
 	
  She had a two-**week** vacation.
 	
  I need a five-**dollar** bill.
	• There is a sale at the shoes store.
	• We have a three-days weekend next week.
	• I need an eye exam.

9. *This* and *that* are singular. *These* and *those* are plural.
 	
  This watermelon is big.
 	
  That watermelon is small.
 	
  These grapes are delicious.
 	
  Those cherries are good.
	• That shoes are mine.
	• Those are beautiful boots.
	• This are my English books.

Rules and Examples	Find the mistakes and correct them. Not every sentence has a mistake.
10. Use *too* with affirmative statements. Use *either* with negative statements. I exercise every day, and my sister does **too**. I don't play tennis, and my sister doesn't **either**. EDITING NOTE: Include an auxiliary verb before *too* and *either*. My friend has a dog, and I *do* ^ too.	• My mother doesn't like sports. My sister doesn't too. • She can't speak Spanish, and I can't either. • My mother likes classical music, and I too.
11. Some *-ed* words are adjectives: *concerned, located, situated, married, divorced, crowded, allowed, permitted, worried, tired*. Don't omit the *-ed* for these words. My sister isn't **married**. My college is **located** downtown.	• Are you tire? • I'm not worried about my grades. • She's concern about her daughter. • The elevator isn't crowded.
12. You can put *very* before adjectives and adverbs. You have a **very** good accent. You speak English **very** well. I like this novel **very** much. EDITING NOTE: You cannot put *very* before verbs. I ~~very~~ want to meet your *very much* parents. ^	• I very like your new suit. • His new suit is very expensive. • He dresses very stylishly.

EXERCISE 2 Find the mistakes with the underlined words, and correct them. Not every sentence has a mistake. If the sentence is correct, write **C**.

EXAMPLES: He drives very careful. *ly* ^

He speaks English <u>fluently</u>.　　C

1. Her daughters are very <u>intelligents</u>.

2. He is very <u>proudly</u> because his daughter graduated from college.

3. The bread tastes <u>fresh</u>.

4. I'm <u>too much</u> busy today. I don't have time for you.

5. She <u>very</u> likes her new job.

6. <u>This</u> books are mine.

7. We had a <u>three-weeks</u> vacation.

8. I don't type very <u>fast</u> or very <u>well</u>.

9. I can't speak Italian, and my husband can't <u>too</u>.

10. She studied <u>hard</u> for the test.

11. You are not <u>allow</u> to talk during a test.

12. Where is your house <u>located</u>?

13. I'm <u>concerned</u> about learning English.

14. My sister has a Japanese car, and <u>I too</u>.

15. They speak English <u>perfectly</u>.

16. She doesn't know him very <u>good</u>.

17. My husband likes tennis. My daughter <u>does too</u>.

18. He's always <u>tire</u> because he works so <u>hardly</u>.

19. She gets up <u>early</u> every day.

20. The bus is very <u>crowd</u> in the morning.

PART 3
Comparatives and Superlatives

A. Study Chart:

Examples	Explanation
He is **tall**. He is **taller** than his father. He is the **tallest** person in his family.	Use *-er* and *-est* with short adjectives and adverbs.
Golf is a **popular** sport. Baseball is **more popular** than golf. Soccer is the **most popular** sport in the world.	Use *more* and *most* with longer adjectives.

Examples	Explanation
Your first composition is **good**. Your second composition is **better**. Your last composition is the **best**.	Some adjectives and adverbs have an irregular form. good/well—better—best bad/badly—worse—worst far—farther—farthest little—less—least a lot—more—most
He is **as tall as** his brother. She doesn't dance **as well as** her husband.	*as* adjective/adverb *as*
He has **as much money as** you do. I don't have **as many friends as** you do. You don't drive **as much as** I do.	*as much/many* noun *as* *as much as*
He is **the same height as** his brother. She is **the same age as** her teacher. My mother and father are **the same height**.	*the same* noun *as*
She **looks like** her father. Lemons **don't taste like** oranges. A CD **sounds like** live music.	Use *look like* for a visual similarity. Use *taste like*, *sound like*, *feel like*, and *smell like* for similarities of the other senses.
She **is like** her mother. They're both very talented.	Use *be like* for a character similarity.
The new dollar bills are not **the same as** the old dollar bills. The new dollar bills are **different from** the old dollar bills.	Use *the same as* and *different from* to make statements of equality or inequality.

B. Rules and Examples:

Rules and Examples	Find the mistakes and correct them. Not every sentence has a mistake.

1. Use the comparative form when comparing two things or people. Use *than* before the second item.
 	
    Calculus is **more difficult than** algebra.
 	
    Calculus is **harder than** algebra.
 	
EDITING NOTE: Omit *than* if you omit the second item of comparison.
 	
    Los Angeles is big, but New York is bigger ~~than~~.
 	
EDITING NOTE: Don't use *more* and *-er* together.
 	
    You are ~~more~~ older than I am.
	• She is ~~tallest~~ *taller* than her brother.
	• Los Angeles is bigger Chicago.
	• My class is harder than your class.
	• My aunt is intelligent, but my uncle is even more intelligent than.
	• Books in the U.S. are more expensive books in my country.
	• You drive more better than I do.

2. Use the superlative form when you are comparing one thing to two or more other things. Use *the* before a superlative form.
 	
    New York is **the biggest** city in the U.S.
 	
    California is **the most populated** state in the U.S.
 	
EDITING NOTE: Don't use *most* and *-est* together.
 	
    You are the ~~most~~ tallest person in your family.
	• She thinks her baby is the most beautiful baby in the world.
	• The Sears Tower is the taller building in the U.S.
	• Alaska is largest state in the U.S.
	• You are the most youngest person in the class.
	• Leaving my country was the more important decision in my life.

3. Use *more* and *most* with long adjectives and *-ly* adverbs.
 	
    My sister is **the most intelligent** person in the family.
 	
    You sing **more beautifully** than I do.
	• She works quicklier than her boss.
	• She speaks English more fluently than I do.

4. After *one of the*, use the superlative form and a plural noun. San Francisco is **one of the most beautiful cities** in the U.S.	• New York is one of the big cities in the world. • Philadelphia is one of the oldest cities in the U.S. • The Sears Tower is one of the tallest building in the world.

Rules and Examples	Find the mistakes and correct them. Not every sentence has a mistake.

5. Use *the same . . . as* with nouns. Use *as . . . as* with adjectives and adverbs.
 	
    She is **the same age as** her husband.
 	
    She is **as old as** her husband.
	• I am the same tall as my brother.
	• I'm not as athletic as you are.
	• A nickel is the same shape like a quarter.
	• She isn't as strong than her husband.
	• Her shoes are the same color as her dress.

6. Use *look like, sound like, feel like*, etc. for sense similarities.
 	
    She **looks like** her mother. They have almost the same face.
 	
Use *be like* for other similarities.
 	
    The weather in Cuba **is like** the weather in Puerto Rico. Both islands are tropical.
 	
EDITING NOTE: Don't use *be* with a sense-perception verb.
 	
    They ~~are~~ look like their mother.
	• I am look like my twin brother.
	• You are look like your father. You both love sports.
	• She's beautiful. She looks like a movie star.

7. Use *don't* or *doesn't* to make the negative of sense perception verbs.
 	
    My photo ID **doesn't look like** me at all.
 	
Use *not* to make the negative of *be like*.
 	
    The weather in Los Angeles **isn't like** the weather in San Francisco.
	• Polyester doesn't feel like silk.
	• He has an accent. He isn't sound like an American.
	• I'm not like my brother at all. We have completely different characters.

EXERCISE **3**   Find the mistakes with the underlined words, and correct them.
Not every sentence has a mistake. If the sentence is correct,
write **C**.

EXAMPLES: I am the ~~most~~ oldest of all my cousins.

She is <u>older than</u> her husband.   C

1. He's <u>taller than</u> his brother.

2. He speaks English <u>more better than</u> his brother.

3. He's <u>as smart as</u> his brother.

4. Alaska is <u>the biggest</u> state in the U.S.

5. January is <u>the colder</u> month of the year.

6. New York is <u>one of the most interesting cities</u> in the world.

7. She is <u>funniest</u> girl in the class.

8. He's not <u>as old as</u> his wife.

9. She is beautiful, but her sister is even <u>more beautiful</u>.

10. He's not <u>the same tall as</u> his son.

11. He and his wife are <u>the same age</u>.

12. Oranges don't <u>taste as</u> tangerines.

13. She <u>looks like</u> her mother. They are both pretty.

14. She <u>isn't look like</u> her father. She has her mother's eyes and smile.

15. Asian music <u>doesn't look like</u> American music.

16. Decaf coffee <u>tastes like</u> regular coffee to me.

17. My house in this city is very <u>different than</u> my house in my hometown.

18. A quarter is <u>the same</u> twenty-five cents.

19. He doesn't have <u>as many problems as</u> I do.

20. I don't drink <u>as much coffee</u> my brother.

PART 4

Count and Noncount Nouns[1]

A. Study Chart:

Singular count	Plural count	Noncount
a peach	some peaches	some milk
one peach	two peaches	two glasses of milk
	a couple of peaches	a couple of glasses of milk
	no peaches	no milk
	any peaches (in questions and negatives)	any milk (in questions and negatives)
	a lot of peaches lots of peaches plenty of peaches	a lot of milk lots of milk plenty of milk
	many peaches	much milk (in questions and negatives)
	too many peaches	too much milk
	a few peaches	a little milk
	several peaches	several glasses of milk
	How many peaches?	How much milk?

B. Rules and Examples:

Rules and Examples	Find the mistakes and correct them. Not every sentence has a mistake.
1. Use *much* and *little* with noncount nouns. Use *many* and *few* with count nouns. I don't have **much** time. I don't have **many** friends. She drank **a little** water. She ate **a few** cookies. EDITING NOTE: Don't use *much* in affirmative statements. Use *a lot of*. *a lot of* He drinks ~~much~~ milk. EDITING NOTE: Don't use *of* after *a little*. I drink a little ~~of~~ juice every morning.	*a lot of* • I have ~~much~~ experience with computers. • I don't have much trouble with this lesson. • I bought a lot of sugar. • We saw a little good movies. • Much people came to the party. • He put a little of sugar in his tea. • I get a little help from my friends. • He drinks much water every day.

[1] For a list of noncount nouns, see Appendix A.

Rules and Examples	Find the mistakes and correct them. Not every sentence has a mistake.
2. Use *too much/too many* only if there is a problem presented. If there is no problem, use *a lot of* or *many*. I have **a lot of** friends. I drank **too much** coffee. Now I can't sleep.	• He has too many cousins. He's always happy to see them. • I love music. I have too many CDs. • This coffee has too much sugar. I can't drink it.
3. Use *a few* and *a little* to emphasize a positive quantity. Use *(very) few* and *(very) little* to emphasize a negative quantity. I saw **a few** good movies last week. I rarely see movies in my language because there are **very few** available here. I have **a little** money. Let's go to the movies. I have **very little** money. I can't even buy a cup of coffee.	• He's a lucky man. He has few good friends. • I can't help you today. I have a little time. • I called you a few times last night, but you weren't home.
4. Use *of* with a unit of measure. I drank a cup **of** tea. She bought a loaf **of** bread.	• He bought a jar olive oil. • I need a gallon of milk. • Put a spoonful sugar in my tea.
5. Some unexpected words that are noncount nouns are: *advice, information, equipment,* and *homework*. They are always singular. I want to give you some **advice**. The teacher gave us a lot of **homework**.	• My mother gave me a lot of advices. • Do you have any informations about the new biology course? • I finished all my homework. • He works with a lot of heavy equipments.
6. Use an affirmative verb followed by *no* + noun, or a negative verb followed by *any* + noun. He has **no** time. He doesn't have **any** time. There are **no** elevators in this building. There aren't **any** elevators in this building. EDITING NOTE: Don't use a double negative. I don't have ~~no~~ *any* money today.	• There aren't no Korean students in my class. • I have no time for television. • I don't want no milk in my coffee. • She doesn't have any children. • Nobody doesn't know how I feel.

Rules and Examples	Find the mistakes and correct them. Not every sentence has a mistake.
7. If you omit the noun, use *a lot*, not *a lot of*. He has **a lot of** friends in Mexico, but he doesn't have **a lot** here.	• I have a lot of free time on Monday, but I don't have a lot of on Tuesday. • I have a lot of grammar books. Do you have a lot?

EXERCISE 4 Find the mistakes with the underlined words, and correct them. Not every sentence has a mistake. If the sentence is correct, write **C**.

EXAMPLES: My counselor gave me a lot of informations about colleges.

The teacher gave us a lot of homework last week.   C

1. He has many money.

2. He has many credit cards.

3. He has too much money. He can buy an expensive car.

4. There were a lot of people at the party. Everyone had a great time.

5. I can't talk to you now. I have very little time.

6. She drank three glasses of water today.

7. She put a little of milk in her coffee.

8. The soup has no taste. There is no salt in the soup.

9. He has a lot of mistakes on his test, but he doesn't have a lot on his composition.

10. There are some people from Guatemala in my class.

11. I have much work to do, so I don't have any free time today.

12. The teacher gave me a lot of advices about how to study.

13. You can get a lot of information from the Internet.

14. Do we have a lot of homeworks today?

15. I ate a little of rice with dinner.

16. A little students were absent today.

17. We didn't have no problems.

18. I sent a couple letters to my friends.

PART 5
Nouns and Possessive Forms

A. Study Charts:

Irregular Plural Forms

Singular	Plural
man	men
woman	women
mouse	mice
tooth	teeth
foot	feet
goose	geese
child	children
person	people (OR persons)

Possessive Forms of Nouns

Noun	Ending	Examples
Singular nouns: teacher mother	Add apostrophe + *s*	The **teacher's** office is on the third floor. My **mother's** name is Elena.
Plural nouns ending in *-s*: parents students ladies	Add apostrophe only	My **parents'** house has three bedrooms. Do you know the **students'** names? Where's the **ladies'** room?
Irregular plural nouns: men women	Add apostrophe + *s*	Thomas and Robert are **men's** names. Mary and Susan are **women's** names.

B. Rules and Examples:

Rules and Examples	Find the mistakes and correct them. Not every sentence has a mistake.
1. Put the person who possesses before the thing possessed. My **sister's** car is new.	• ~~Books the students~~ are blue. *The students' books* • My parents' house is near mine. • Car my friend is new.

2. Use the plural form to talk about more than one thing.
 	
    A lot of **people** in the world speak English.
    She has many **friends**.
    One of my **brothers** lives in Boston.
 	
EDITING NOTE: Don't use an apostrophe for a plural ending.
    Two ~~girl's~~ are crying. *girls*
 	
EDITING NOTE: Don't put an *s* ending on an irregular plural.
    They have beautiful children~~s~~.
	• She bought a lot of book.
	• Some of my teacher speak Spanish.
	• One of the classrooms has carpeting.
	• How many cousin's do you have?
	• Do your two brothers live in the U.S.?
	• Do you see the childrens in the park?
	• Five people in my class speak Polish.

3. Use the singular form after *every*. Use the plural form after *all*.
 	
    Every **child** needs love.
    All **children** need love.
	• Every students passed the test.
	• All students have homework.

EXERCISE 5   Find the mistakes with the underlined words and correct them. Not every sentence has a mistake. If the sentence is correct, write **C**.

EXAMPLES: Three ~~woman~~ came late to the meeting.   *women*

My <u>sister's son</u> lives in Los Angeles.   C

1. They have four <u>childrens</u>.

2. There were two <u>men</u> in the office.

3. <u>One of my friend</u> has twin sons.

4. <u>My parents' house</u> is not very big.

5. <u>Car of my father</u> is not very good.

6. What is <u>name your sister</u>?

7. Do you have any <u>brother's</u>?

8. William and Henry are <u>men's</u> names.

9. <u>My sister husband</u> is a very nice man.

10. All <u>student</u> in this class can speak English.

11. Every <u>student</u> in this class can speak English.

12. All the <u>teachers</u> have offices. The <u>teachers' offices</u> are on the second floor.

PART 6
Pronouns and Possessive Adjectives

A. Study Chart:

Subject pronoun	Object pronoun	Possessive adjective	Possessive pronoun	Reflexive pronoun
I	me	my	mine	myself
you	you	your	yours	yourself
he	him	his	his	himself
she	her	her	hers	herself
it	it	its	—	itself
we	us	our	ours	ourselves
you	you	your	yours	yourselves
they	them	their	theirs	themselves
who	whom	whose	whose	—

B. Rules and Examples:

Rules and Examples	Find the mistakes and correct them. Not every sentence has a mistake.
1. Use the object pronoun after a verb or a preposition. I saw **him** at the park. They always talk about **us**.	• Where did you meet your husband? I met ~~he~~ *him* in my math class. • You know my parents. You met they at the party. • I want to know about your sister. Tell me about she.

Rules and Examples	Find the mistakes and correct them. Not every sentence has a mistake.
2. Use the possessive adjective before a noun. Use the possessive pronoun when the noun is omitted. I have **my** books. Do you have **your** books? She doesn't have **her** dictionary. She can borrow **mine**.	• Theirs parents don't speak English. • They give their children all their love. • My textbook is new. Yours is used.
3. After *want, need, expect, would like*, use the object form, plus an infinitive. Do you want **me to mail** the package? I expect **them to answer** my question. EDITING NOTE: Don't use *that* + subject pronoun. She wants ~~that I~~ ^{me to} help her.	• My son watches too much TV. I want that he read more. • The teacher wanted me to correct my mistakes. • The teacher expects we write five compositions.
4. You *say* something. You *tell* someone something. He **said** the wrong thing. He **told me** his problem.	• He told the answer. • She said something, but I didn't hear it. • She told her name, but I forgot it.
5. Don't confuse *her* and *his*. She loves **her** son. He loves **his** wife.	• My husband invited his mother to live with us. • My sister loves his husband.
6. Don't confuse *there, they're,* and *their*. **They're** my friends. **Their** names are Bob and Alice. They live over **there**.	• These are my brothers. They're names are Peter and Tim. • They take their kids to that park over there.
7. Don't confuse *its* and *it's*. The elephant is an interesting animal. **Its** trunk is long. **It's** very big.	• This is a grammar book. It's interesting. • Its review lesson is helpful.
8. Don't confuse *your* and *you're*. **You're** my best friend. I like **your** personality.	• I don't know you're name. • Your a good student. • You're late for class.
9. Don't confuse *who's* and *whose*. **Who's** your English teacher? **Whose** book is this?	• Who's coat is that? • Who's your best friend?

EXERCISE 6 Find the mistakes with the underlined words, and correct them. Not every sentence has a mistake. If the sentence is correct, write **C**.

EXAMPLES: I don't know <u>yours</u> parents.

Who's that man over there? C

1. Do you like dogs? Yes, I like <u>it</u> very much.

2. Where's your sister? I want to talk to <u>she</u>.

3. <u>They're</u> very lonely because <u>they</u> parents live far away.

4. You didn't bring your book today. You can use <u>mine</u>.

5. My brother and sister-in-law take <u>theirs</u> children to a museum once a week.

6. He didn't wash <u>him</u> hands before dinner.

7. My parents wanted <u>that I become</u> a teacher.

8. I didn't see my friends at school, but I saw <u>them</u> at the library.

9. Mary speaks English well, but <u>his</u> husband doesn't.

10. I have two cats. I got <u>them</u> from my friend.

11. They lost <u>there</u> suitcases at the airport.

12. I know what movie you're talking about, but I can't remember <u>it's</u> name.

13. That boy is making a lot of noise. I want <u>he be</u> quiet.

14. The teacher expects <u>us</u> to write five compositions.

15. <u>Who's</u> book is this?

16. We lost <u>ours</u> books.

17. They always look at <u>themself</u> in the mirror.

18. I <u>told them</u> the answer.

19. I don't even know <u>you're</u> name.

20. She <u>said me</u> the secret.

PART 7

Sentence Structure and Word Order

A. Study Chart:

Subject	Verb	Complement
She	speaks	English.
I	went	home.
Jack	didn't come	to work.
You	are	early.

B. Rules and Examples:

Rules and Examples	Find the mistakes and correct them. Not every sentence has a mistake.
1. Every sentence must have a verb. My teacher **is** very patient. The college **is** located downtown. REMEMBER: Many *-ed* words are adjectives (*married, worried, tired,* etc.)	• I *am* very tired today. • My sister is married. • The bus crowded in the morning. • I concerned about your health.
2. Every verb must have a subject. **It** is important to have a good job. **I** didn't understand the lesson because **it** was too hard for me. EDITING NOTE: Don't repeat the subject with a pronoun. My sister ~~she~~ plays the piano.	• Let's stay inside. Is cold today. • Is impossible to learn English in a month. • My parents they have a new house. • I don't like birds as pets because make a lot of noise.
3. Sometimes we need *there + be* to introduce the subject. **There were** a lot of people at the party. **There will be** an election in 2012. EDITING NOTE: Use *there,* not *it,* to introduce a new subject. *There's* ~~It's~~ a map on the wall.	• It's a telephone in the kitchen. • In the park a beautiful garden. • There will be a concert tonight. • Are some Puerto Rican students in my class.

Rules and Examples	Find the mistakes and correct them. Not every sentence has a mistake.

4. The basic sentence word order is Subject + Verb + Complement. Put the subject before the verb in all clauses.
 	
    S   V   S
  She cooks when **her son**
      V
  comes home from school.
 	
      S   V
  The book was very long.
	• The workers began to work when arrived the boss.
	• I didn't go to work because the office was closed.
	• Everything that said the teacher is important.
	• Was very interesting the movie.

5. If a compound subject includes **I**, put **I** after the other subject.[2] **My friend and I** need help.	• I and my husband went for a walk. • My friend and I like to dance. • Me and my cousin will go to the movies.
6. Put *together* after the complement. We went to the movies **together**.	• We went home together. • My friend and I together ate lunch.

7. You can put *maybe* at the beginning of the sentence, or you can use *may* as a modal verb after the subject.
 	
  Maybe he is sick.
  He **may** be sick.
  Maybe it will rain tomorrow.
  It **may** rain tomorrow.
	• You maybe will find a good job.
	• He maybe is angry.
	• He may drive to Wisconsin.
	• Maybe he will drive to Wisconsin.

8. Do not separate the verb from the object.
 	
  She **typed the report** very slowly.
  They **opened the window** carefully.
	• She likes very much her new apartment.
	• He looks all the time at the clock.
	• She opened her eyes slowly.
	• You drove very quickly the car.

9. A phrase of time or place can come before the subject or at the end of the verb phrase.
 	
  Once in a while, she eats meat.
  She eats meat **once in a while**.
	• We every day practice grammar.
	• Every other day I visit my parents.
	• He in the kitchen eats breakfast.

[2] You often hear people say "My friend and me" or "Me and my friend" in the subject position, but they are very informal.

Rules and Examples	Find the mistakes and correct them. Not every sentence has a mistake.

10. Put a one-word adverb (*always, never, probably, even, just, especially,* etc.):
 	
 • between the subject and the verb.
 	
   I **always** watch TV at night.
 	
   She **probably** received the letter.
 	
 • after the verb *be*.
 	
   I am **never** late.
 	
   You are **especially** kind.
 	
 • between the auxiliary verb and the main verb.
 	
   I will **probably** call you later.
 	
   I have **never** gone to Paris.
	• She always is late to class.
	 • I have wanted always to visit London.
	 • You have never seen my vacation pictures.
	 • We are making probably progress.
	 • He can study with noise. He even can study with loud rock music.
	 • They are probably right.
	 • I don't have much money. Just I have three dollars.

11. Most frequency words can come at the beginning of the sentence. However, *always* and *never* don't come at the beginning of the sentence.
 	
   We **never** speak Spanish in class.
 	
   You **always** have the right answer.
 	
   You are **always** right.
	• Never he walks to work.
	 • You always tell the truth.
	 • Always I have coffee with breakfast.
	 • She is never on time.

12. Put an adjective before, not after, a noun. She has a very **interesting** job.	• I saw a very long movie. • The U.S. is a country very powerful.

13. *Enough* follows an adjective or adverb.
 	
   I am **old enough** to make my own decisions.
 	
   He speaks English **fluently enough** to be a receptionist.
	• The little girl is enough smart to read the book.
	 • He drives well enough now to get his driver's license.

14. In a comparative statement, put *more* before a noun. Seattle has **more rain** than San Diego.	• He has money more than I do. • I have more time than you do.

Rules and Examples	Find the mistakes and correct them. Not every sentence has a mistake.
15. In a comparative statement, put the comparative adverb after the verb phrase. I **read English faster** than you do. You **cook better** than your wife.	• I more quickly finished the homework than you did. • She writes English more beautifully than we do.
16. If two nouns come together, put the specific noun before the general noun. She has a **winter coat.** I need a **coat hanger.**	• Can I borrow your hair drier? • This wig is made of hair human.

EXERCISE 7 Find the mistakes with word order, and correct them. If the subject or verb is missing, add it. Take out any extra words. Not every sentence has a mistake. If the sentence is correct, write C.

EXAMPLES: We did (at night) the homework.

It i
I̸s necessary to have a good dictionary.

On Monday and Wednesday, the teacher is usually in her office.   C

1. Came in late the student and took a seat in the back.

2. She always has problems with spelling.

3. Because she has a full-time job, she has a lot of responsibilities.

4. Is very important to know your rights.

5. I have always wanted to visit Paris.

6. Began registration on August 18.

7. I don't like very much my biology class.

8. I found on the desk a dictionary.

9. Whenever I have a problem, I talk to my father.

10. She doesn't know anything about your problem.

11. There's in my class a Japanese woman.

12. She can't always come to class on time.

13. He usually eats cereal for breakfast.

14. Never he eats eggs for breakfast.

15. He usually is sleepy in the afternoon.

16. San Francisco a very beautiful city.

17. Are a lot of closets in my new apartment.

18. She's almost finished with her composition. Just she has to write a title.

19. She opened carefully the package.

20. Once in a while, Mary and Tom eat dinner together.

21. I don't have enough money to buy the book. Only I have ten dollars on me.

22. I and my brother went to Toronto.

23. The counselor maybe knows the answer to your question.

24. After arrived the teacher, the lesson began.

25. After my brother found a job, bought a car.

26. He doesn't want to eat for dinner chicken.

27. Came to the U.S. my father last year.

28. Me and my friend saw a good movie last night.

29. She left angrily the room.

30. At nine o'clock starts the second part of the movie.

31. Is very good the story you wrote.

32. I may go to a movie this weekend.

33. The teacher isn't here today. She maybe is sick.

34. He will probably go to Mexico for vacation.

35. I will be probably absent next week.

36. Is he enough old to drive?

37. She has a wonderful family.

38. He earns money more than his wife.

39. My parents they live in Montreal.

40. I run faster than you do.

41. Do you have a license fishing?

42. I always listen to the news on the radio.

43. I can't quickly run.

44. There's a good movie on TV at 6 o'clock.

PART 8
Question Word Order

A. Study Charts:

Be

Wh- Word	*Be*	Subject	*Be*	Complement
		She	is	in California.
	Is	she		in Los Angeles?
Where	is	she?		
Why	isn't	she		in Los Angeles?
		Who	is	in Los Angeles?

Simple Present Tense

Wh- Word	*Do/Does*	Subject	Verb	Complement
		She	watches	TV.
	Does	she	watch	TV at night?
When	does	she	watch	TV?
Why	doesn't	she	watch	TV at night?
		Who	watches	TV at night?
		How many people	watch	TV at night?

Simple Past Tense

Wh- Word	*Did*	Subject	Verb	Complement
		He	bought	a TV.
	Did	he	buy	a VCR?
When	did	he	buy	a TV?
Why	didn't	he	buy	a VCR?
		Who	bought	a VCR?

Modal

Wh- Word	Modal	Subject	Aux. verb	Modal	Complement
		She	can	play	the piano.
	Can	she		play	the guitar?
When	can	she		play	the piano?
Why	can't	she		play	the guitar?
	Who		can	play	the guitar?

Continuous Tense

Wh- Word	Aux. verb	Subject	Aux. verb	Main verb	Complement
		They	are	eating	lunch.
	Are	they		eating	rice?
What	are	they		eating?	
Why	aren't	they		eating	rice?
	Who		is	eating	rice?

B. Rules and Examples:

Rules and Examples	Find the mistakes and correct them. Not every sentence has a mistake.
1. Use normal question word order for cost, spelling, and meaning. How much **did** your book **cost**? What **does** "VCR" **mean**? How **do** you **spell** your name? How **do** you **say** "teacher" in your language?	• How ^*do you* spell "Minnesota"? • What does "friendship" mean? • How much cost your trip to the U.S.? • How do you spell the name of your country? • How say "hello" in your language?
2. Do not use *do/does/did* with questions about the subject. Who **came** to the party? How many people **came** to the party? Which people **came** to the party? What kind of people **came** to the party?	• How many students brought a dictionary today? • Who did come late to the meeting? • Who has my keys?

Find the mistakes with question formation and correct them. Not every sentence has a mistake. If the sentence is correct, write **C**.

EXAMPLES: Why ~~you didn't~~ *didn't you* call me last night?

Who called you last night?   C

1. What means "invent"?

2. Who lives in the White House?

3. When were you buy your books?

4. What kind of car your brother bought?

5. How much money do you have?

6. Where does live your teacher?

7. What time you go to bed every night?

8. Do you ever drink coffee at night?

9. Why don't you buy a new computer?

10. How many states has the U.S.?

11. How many students in the class speak Spanish?

GRAMMAR

The Present Perfect
The Present Perfect Continuous

CONTEXT

Job Résumé and Cover Letter
My Job as a Pilot

LESSON FOCUS

We form the present perfect with *have/has* + past participle.

I *have had* my job since March.
He *has been* a pilot for many years.

We form the present perfect continuous with *have/ has* + *been* + verb *-ing*.

They *have been living* in this city since 1998.
She *has been working* in a hotel for three years.

1. What was your first job? How did you find it?
2. Do you have a job now? What do you do? How did you find your job?

Read the following job résumé and cover letter on the next two pages. In the cover letter, pay special attention to the present perfect and present perfect continuous tenses.

Daniel Mendoza
6965 North Troy Avenue
Chicago, Illinois 60659
(773) 555-1946
Email: dmendoza@srv.com

Objective: A managerial position in a small to mid-size hotel

PROFESSIONAL EXPERIENCE

1998–Present	Town and Country Hotel	Chicago, Illinois
	Front office manager	
	Personnel management; guest relations; reservations	
1996–1998	Mid-Town Hotel	Evanston, Illinois
	Bookkeeper (part-time)	
	Accounts payable; accounts receivable; payroll	
1992–1996	Travel Time Hotel	Champaign, Illinois
	Front desk clerk (part-time)	
	Guest relations; handling check-ins and guest requests	
1988–1992	Hotel Mendoza	Mexico City, Mexico
	Front desk clerk	
	Guest relations; housekeeping; front reception	

EDUCATION

Northwestern University   Evanston, Illinois
Master of Science Degree: Business Administration, 1998

University of Illinois   Urbana, Illinois
Bachelor of Science Degree: Business Administration, 1996

National University of Mexico   Mexico City
Degree in Hotel Management, 1992

SKILLS

Software
Experience with Word, Powerpoint, Excel, Access, Quicken

Internet Skills
Experience with searching for information; basic web page design

REFERENCES AVAILABLE UPON REQUEST

6965 North Troy Avenue
Chicago, Illinois 60659
June 4, 2000

Mr. Ray Johnson, General Manager
Paradise Hotel
226 West Jackson Boulevard
Chicago, Illinois 60606

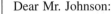

Dear Mr. Johnson:

I would like to apply for the job of hotel office manager at the Paradise Hotel.

I come from Mexico City, where my family owns a hotel. I worked in the family business part-time when I was in high school. After high school, I studied hotel and restaurant management at the National University of Mexico. I came to the U.S. in 1992 because I wanted to continue my education and learn about managing larger hotels. Since I came to the U.S., I **have worked** in several American hotels. Over the years my English **has improved**, and I now consider myself bilingual, fluent in both Spanish and English, which is a plus in the hotel business. I **have** also **studied** French and can speak it fairly well. I **have been** a U.S. citizen for the past two years.

I received my bachelor's degree from the University of Illinois in 1996 and my master's degree from Northwestern University in 1998. For the past few years, I **have been working** at the Town and Country Hotel. As you can see from my résumé, I **have had** a lot of experience in various aspects of the hotel business. Now that I have my degree in business administration, I am ready to assume[1] more responsibilities.

If you **have** already **filled** the manager's position, I would like you to consider me for any other position at your hotel. I **have** always **loved** the hotel business, and I know I can be an asset[2] to your hotel.

Thank you for considering my application. I look forward to meeting with you soon.

Sincerely,

Daniel Mendoza

Daniel Mendoza

1.1   The Present Perfect Tense—Forms

Examples	Explanation
I **have had** a lot of experience. My English **has improved** a lot.	*I, you, we, they* + *have* + past participle *He, she, it* + *has* + past participle
My family has **always** had a hotel. I have **never** worked in a restaurant.	*have/has* + adverb + past participle

(continued)

---

[1] *Assume* means *take on* or *accept.*
[2] To be an *asset* to a company means to have a talent or ability that will help the company.

Examples	Explanation
I've had a lot of experience. **It's** been hard to find a job. **There's** been a change in my plans.	Contractions: I have = I've He has = He's You have = You've She has = She's We have = We've It has = It's They have = They've There has = There's
My father**'s** taught me a lot about the hotel business.	Most singular nouns can contract with *has*.

I **haven't** had experience in the restaurant business.
 Mr. Johnson **hasn't** called me.
	Negatives =
	     have not + past participle
	     has not + past participle
	 Negative contractions = *haven't, hasn't*

LANGUAGE NOTES

1. The **'s** in *he's, she's, it's* can mean *has* or *is*. The word following the contraction will tell you what the contraction means.
    He's working. = He *is* working.
    He's worked. = He *has* worked.
2. The past participle of regular verbs ends in *-ed*. The past form and the past participle are the same for regular verbs.
    He *worked* yesterday. He *has worked* in several hotels.
3. Many irregular past tense verbs have the same form for the past participle.
    He *told* the truth.   He *has told* the truth.
    He *bought* a car.   He *has bought* a car.
4. Some verbs have a past participle that is different from the past tense.
    I *saw* the résumé.   I *have seen* the résumé.
    He *wrote* a letter.   He *has written* a letter.
5. For an alphabetical list of irregular past tenses and past participles, see Appendix M.

EXERCISE 1   Fill in the blanks with the correct form of the verb in parentheses to form the present perfect tense.

EXAMPLE: Daniel ___*has sent*___ three résumés this week.

                              (send)

     1. He _____ in Chicago for a few years.

                     (be)

     2. You _____ his résumé.

                     (see)

3. He _____ several interviews.
   (have)

4. Mr. Johnson _____ a letter from Daniel.
   (get)

5. There _____ many applicants for the job.
   (be)

6. Daniel's parents _____ in the hotel business.
   (always/be)

7. Daniel _____ from college.
   (recently/graduate)

8. I _____ Daniel's résumé.
   (read)

9. Daniel _____ as a programmer.
   (never/work)

10. Daniel _____ many letters.
    (write)

11. He _____ his résumé to many companies.
    (send)

12. The company _____ 20 applicants so far.
    (interview)

1.2 The Present Perfect—Question Formation

Examples	Explanation
He has worked in the hotel business.	In a question, reverse the subject and *have* or *has*.
Has he worked in Chicago? Yes, **he has**.	Don't use a contraction for a short *yes* answer.
Has he worked in New York? No, he hasn't.	
Where **has he** worked?	The word order for *wh-* questions is: *WH-* word + *have/has* + subject + past participle
How long **has he** worked in the hotel business?	

EXERCISE 2 Read the job interview with Daniel. Write the missing words in the blanks.

A. I've ___*looked at*___ your résumé. I see you work in a hotel.
   (look at)

B. Yes, I do.

A. How long _____ you _____ this job?
   (1)   *(2)*

B. I'_____ had this job for only a short time. But I _____ a
   (3)   *(4)*
   lot of experience in the hotel business. In fact, my parents own a
   hotel in Mexico.

A. How long _____ your parents _____ a hotel?
  (5)   (6)

B. Most of their lives.

A. _____ you seen your parents recently?
  (7)

B. Yes, I _____ . My mother _____ _____ to the U.S. a
       (8)   (9)   (10)

few times to see me. But my father _____ never _____
                                     (11)   (12)

here because someone has to stay at the hotel all the time. He's

_____ me many times, "When you are an owner of a business,
  (13)

you don't have time for vacations." But I don't want to be an owner

now. I just want a job as a manager. _____ you filled the position
                                        (14)

yet?

A. No, I haven't. I'_____ already _____ several people
         (15)   (16)

and will interview a few more this week. When we make our decision,
we'll let you know.

1.3 Uses of the Present Perfect Tense—Overview

Examples	Explanation
Daniel **has been** in the U.S. since 1992. He **has had** his present job for a short time. He **has** always **loved** the hotel business.	The action started in the past and continues to the present.
He **has sent** out 20 résumés so far. He **has had** three interviews this month.	The action repeats during a period of time that started in the past and continues to the present.
Mr. Johnson **has received** Daniel's letter. He **hasn't made** his decision yet. **Has** Daniel ever **worked** in a restaurant? Daniel **has studied** French, and he speaks it fairly well.	The action occurred at an indefinite time in the past. It still has importance to a present situation.

EXERCISE 3 Fill in the blanks with appropriate words to complete each statement. (Refer to the résumé and cover letter on pages 32–33.)

EXAMPLE: Daniel has included ___*his phone number*___ in his résumé.

1. Daniel has been _____ since 1992.

2. He has had his job at the Town and Country Hotel for _____.

3. He has studied in _____ universities.

4. He has never worked in _____.

5. He has had a lot of experience in _____.

6. In his cover letter, he has not included _____.

7. So far, he has worked in _____ hotels.

8. He hasn't _____ a job yet.

1.4 The Present Perfect with Continuation from Past to Present

We use the present perfect tense to show that an action or state started in the past and continues to the present.

Examples	Explanation
Daniel has been a U.S. citizen **for two years**. His parents have been in the hotel business **all their lives**. He has had his job **for the past few years**.	Use *for* + amount of time to show when the action began. Omit *for* with an expression beginning with *all*. You can say *for the past/last* + time period.
Daniel has been in the U.S. **since 1992**. I have been a citizen **since last March**.	Use *since* + date, month, year, etc. to show when the action began.
He has wanted to manage hotels **(ever) since he *was* a teenager**. I have had my car **since I *came* to the U.S.**	Use *since* or *ever since* + to begin a clause that shows the start of a continuous action. The verb in the *since*-clause is in the simple past tense.

(continued)

Examples	Explanation
Daniel went to Chicago in 1998. He has been there **ever since**. My grandfather gave me a watch when I was five years old. I have had it **ever since**.	You can put *ever since* at the end of the sentence. It means "from the past time mentioned to the present."
How long has he been in the U.S.? **How long** have you known your best friend?	Use *how long* to ask an information question about length of time.
Daniel has **always** loved the hotel business. I have **always** wanted to start my own business. Daniel has **never** written to Mr. Johnson before. I have **never** liked cold weather.	We use the present perfect with *always* and *never* to show that an action began in the past and continues to the present. We often use *before* at the end of a *never* statement.

EXERCISE 4   Fill in the blanks with the missing word. (Not every sentence needs a word.)

EXAMPLE: I ___*have*___ been in the U.S. for three years.

1. He has been in Chicago _____ 1996.

2. How _____ have you been married?

3. She found a good job in 1990. She has worked at the same job ever _____ .

4. He has worked at a hotel ever since he _____ from high school.

5. They have been in the U.S. _____ all their lives.

6. She has had her apartment for the _____ ten months.

7. _____ you lived here all your life?

8. I've been at this college for three years. _____ have you been at this college?

9. He'_____ been sick _____ Monday.

10. We'_____ known each other for many years.

EXERCISE 5   Make statements with *always*.

EXAMPLE: Name something you've always thought about.
I've always thought about my future.

1. Name something you've always disliked.

2. Name something you've always liked.

3. Name something you've always wanted to own.

4. Name something you've always wanted to do.

5. Name something you've always believed in.

EXERCISE 6   Write four **true** sentences telling about things you've always done or ways you've always been. Share your answers with the class.

EXAMPLES:
I've always worked very hard.

I've always been very thin.

1. _____

2. _____

3. _____

4. _____

EXERCISE 7   Make statements with *never*.

EXAMPLE: Name a machine you've never used.
I've never used a fax machine.

1. Name a food you've never tried.

2. Name something you've never drunk.

3. Name something you've never owned.

4. Name something you've never done.

5. Name something the teacher has never done in class.

EXERCISE 8 Write four **true** sentences telling about things you've never done but would like to. Share your answers with the class.

EXAMPLES: I've never gone to Paris, but I'd like to.

I've never flown in a helicopter, but I'd like to.

1. _____

2. _____

3. _____

4. _____

1.5 *For* and *Since* in Negative Statements

Examples	Explanation
Daniel hasn't worked in Mexico **since** 1992.	He worked in Mexico until 1992. He stopped in 1992.
Daniel hasn't seen his parents **for** three years. OR Daniel hasn't seen his parents **in** three years.	He saw his parents three years ago. That was the last time. In negative statements, you can use either *for* or *in*.
Hi Martha! I haven't seen you **in ages**.	*In ages* means "in a long time."

EXERCISE 9 Name something.

EXAMPLE: Name something you haven't eaten in a long time.
I haven't eaten fish in a long time.

1. Name someone you haven't seen in a long time.

2. Name a place you haven't visited in a long time.

3. Name a food you haven't eaten in a long time.

4. Name a subject you haven't studied since you were in high school.

5. Name a game you haven't played since you were a child.

6. Name something you haven't had time to do since you started to study English.

1.6 The Present Perfect vs. the Simple Present

Examples	Explanation
I **am** in the U.S. now. I **have been** in the U.S. for two years. She **has** a car. She **has had** her car since March. I **love** my job. I **have** always **loved** my job. I **don't like** tomatoes. I **have** never **liked** tomatoes.	The simple present refers only to the present time. The present perfect with *for*, *since*, *always*, or *never* connects the past to the present.

EXERCISE 10 Fill in the blanks to complete the following conversations.

EXAMPLE:
A. Do you have a computer?

B. Yes, I do.

A. How long ____*have you*____ had your computer?

B. I ____*have had*____ my computer for three years.

1. A. Do you have a car?

   B. Yes, I do.

   A. How long _____ your car?

   B. I _____ my car for six months.

2. A. Are you married?

   B. Yes, I am.

   A. How long _____ married?

   B. I _____ since 1995.

3. A. Do you have a computer?

   B. Yes, I _____.

   A. How long _____ your computer?

   B. I _____ my computer _____ the past _____.

4. A. Do you want to learn English?

   B. Of course, I do.

   A. _____ long _____ to learn English?

   B. I _____ to learn English ever since I _____ a child.

5. A. Does your mother have a driver's license?

   B. Yes, she _____.

   A. How _____ her driver's license?

   B. She _____ her driver's license since _____.

6. A. _____ Ms. Foster your teacher?

   B. Yes, she is.

   A. How long _____ your teacher?

   B. For _____.

7. A. Does your school have a computer lab?

   B. Yes, it _____.

   A. _____ long _____ a computer lab?

   B. It _____ a computer lab since _____.

8. A. Do you know your friend Mark very well?

   B. Yes, I _____.

   A. How long _____ each other?

   B. We _____ each other ever _____ we _____ in elementary school.

9. A. _____ your son _____ a cell phone?

   B. Yes, he _____.

   A. How long _____?

   B. He bought one when he started going to college and he _____ it ever _____.

10. A. Do you like to dance?

   B. Yes, I _____.

   A. _____ you always _____ to dance?

   B. Yes. I've always liked to dance. But my husband _____ never _____ to dance.

EXERCISE 11 Read each statement about your teacher. Then ask your teacher a question beginning with the words given. Include *always* in your question. Your teacher will answer.

EXAMPLE: You're a teacher. Have you __*always been a teacher?*__

No. I was a nurse before I became a teacher. I've only been a teacher for five years.

1. You teach adults. Have you _____

2. You work with ESL students. Have you _____

3. You're a teacher at this college. Have you _____

4. You think about grammar. Have you _____

5. English is easy for you. Has English _____

6. Your last name is _____. Has your last

   name _____

7. You live in this city. Have you _____

8. You like teaching. Have you _____

EXERCISE 12 Ask a present tense question. Another student will answer. If the answer is *yes*, ask *Have you always . . .*?

EXAMPLE: A. Are you interested in learning English?
B. Yes, I am.
A. Have you always been interested in learning English?
B. Yes. I've been interested in learning English since I was a small child.

1. Are you a good student?

2. Do you wear glasses?

3. Do you like to travel?

4. Are you interested in politics?

5. Do you like American movies?

6. Are you an optimist?

7. Do you think about your future?

8. Do you live in an apartment?

9. Are you a friendly person?

10. Do you use credit cards?

1. What are some professions you think are interesting?
2. What are some jobs you wouldn't want to have?

Read the following article. Pay special attention to the present perfect and the present perfect continuous.

My Job as a Pilot

My name is Robert Arthur. I work as a pilot for a major commercial airline. I **have been working** as a pilot for over 30 years. After college I went into the U.S. Air Force, where I served for ten years. After I left the Air Force, I got a job with a major commercial airline and **have been flying** commercially ever since. Lately I **have been thinking** about retirement because pilots have to retire at the age of 60.

People **have** often **asked** me how I became interested in flying. Like most pilots, my interest in aviation goes back to my childhood, when I watched birds and airplanes fly through the sky.

My job **has taken** me away from my home and my family much of the time. I**'ve lived** in many locations. For the past few years, however, I**'ve been living** in Pittsburgh. To be a pilot, I **have had** to make many sacrifices. But there is nothing else I'd rather do. For me, flying presents a perspective of how one fits in with the rest of the world.

Did you know...?

The average American stays with one employer for about five years.

1.7 The Present Perfect Continuous

Examples	Explanation
I **have been working** as a pilot for over 30 years.	The present perfect continuous = *have* or *has* + *been* + verb *-ing*.
I **have been thinking** about retirement for the past few years.	

(continued)

Examples	Explanation
He **has been living** in Pittsburgh for the past few years. He **has lived** in Pittsburgh for the past few years.	With some verbs, we can use either the present perfect or the present perfect continuous with actions that began in the past and continue to the present. There is very little difference in meaning.
He's working now. He **has been working** for the past eight hours.	If the action is happening right now, at this minute, use the present perfect continuous.
I have **always** loved to fly. I have **never** had another career.	Do not use the continuous form with *always* and *never*.

LANGUAGE NOTES

1. We do not use a continuous tense with nonaction verbs.
    > He *has had* a lot of experience as a pilot. (NOT: He *has been having* a lot of experience.)

    The following verbs are nonaction verbs:

believe	have	like	mean	prefer	seem
care	hear	love	need	remember	understand
cost	know	matter	own	see	want

2. *Have* and *think* can be action or nonaction verbs, depending on their meaning. COMPARE:
    > I *have been thinking* about retirement. (*Think about* = action verb)
    >
    > I *have* always *thought* that flying is exciting. (*Think that* = nonaction verb)
    >
    > Daniel *has been having* problems finding a job.
    >
    > Daniel *has had* a lot of experience in hotels.

EXERCISE 13 Fill in the blanks in the following conversations.

EXAMPLE:
A. Do you ___play___ a musical instrument?

B. Yes. I play the guitar.

A. How long ___have___ you ___been playing___ the guitar?

B. I ___'ve been playing___ the guitar since I ___was___ ten years old.

1. A. Do you work with computers?

    B. Yes, I do.

    A. How long _____ you _____ with computers?

    B. I _____ with computers since 1998.

---

2. A. _____ your father study English?

   B. Yes, he does.

   A. How long _____ he been _____?

   B. He _____ since he _____ to this city.

3. A. Does your teacher have a lot of experience?

   B. Yes, she _____.

   A. How long _____ teaching English?

   B. She _____ English for 20 years.

4. A. Do you wear glasses?

   B. Yes, I _____.

   A. How _____ glasses?

   B. I _____ glasses since I _____ in high school.

5. A. _____ your parents live in this city?

   B. Yes, they _____.

   A. How _____ in this city?

   B. For _____.

6. A. Is your roommate preparing to take the TOEFL[3] test?

   B. Yes, he _____.

   A. How long _____ to take this test?

   B. Since _____.

7. A. _____ you studying for your chemistry test?

   B. Yes, I _____.

   A. How _____ for your chemistry test?

   B. I _____ all week.

8. A. _____ your roommate using the computer now?

   B. Yes, he _____.

   A. How long _____ it?

   B. He started to use it when he woke up and _____

      it ever _____.

[3] The *TOEFL* is the Test of English as a Foreign Language. Many U.S. colleges and universities require foreign students to take this test.

9. A. _____ it raining now?

   B. Yes, it _____ .

   A. How long _____?

   B. It _____ since _____ .

10. A. _____ she talking about her children again?

    B. Yes, she _____ .

    A. How long _____ about them?

    B. For the past _____ .

EXERCISE 14 Fill in the blanks to make a **true** statement about the present. Then make a statement that includes the past by changing to the present perfect continuous with *for* or *since*.

EXAMPLE: I'm studying _____*French*_____ .

I've been studying French for two semesters.

1. I work in/as _____

   _____

2. I live _____

   _____

3. I attend _____

   _____

4. I'm trying to _____

   _____

5. I'm wearing _____

   _____

6. The teacher is explaining _____

   _____

7. I'm thinking about _____

   _____

8. I'm using _____

   _____

1.8 The Present Perfect vs. the Simple Past

Examples	Explanation
How long **have** you **had** your present car? I**'ve had** my present car for three months. How long **have** you **been working** at your present job? I**'ve been working** at my present job for two years.	Use *how long* and *for* with the present perfect or present perfect continuous to include the present.
How long **did** you **work** at your last job? I **worked** at my last job for five years. How long **did** you **have** your last car? I **had** my last car for six years.	Use *how long* and *for* with the simple past tense when you are not including the present.
When did you **come** to the U.S.? I **came** to the U.S. a few months **ago**.	A question that asks *when* uses the simple past. A sentence that uses *ago* uses the simple past.
I **came** to this city on January 15. I **have been** in this city since January 15. I **have been living** in this city since January 15.	Use the past tense to refer to a past action that does not continue. Use the present perfect (continuous) to show the continuation of an action from past to present.

EXERCISE 15 Fill in the blanks with the simple past, the present perfect, or the present perfect continuous, using the words in parentheses.

EXAMPLES: How long ___*has she had*___ her computer?
(she/have)

When ___*did she buy*___ her computer?
(she/buy)

1. How long _____ president of the U.S.?
(be/Bill Clinton)

2. He _____ president from 1993 to 2001.
(be)

3. How long _____ president of the U.S.?
(be/use the name of the current president)

4. He _____ president since _____.
(be)

5. I _____ English since I was in high school.
   (study)

6. When I was a child, I _____ German.
   (study)

7. Albert Einstein died in 1955. He _____ in the U.S. for 22 years.
   (live)

8. I _____ in this city for _____ years.
   (live)

9. When _____ your car?
   (you/buy)

10. I _____ my car two years ago.
    (buy)

11. How long _____ your driver's license?
    (you/have)

12. I _____ my driver's license since May.
    (have)

13. How long _____ our English teacher?
    (you/know)

14. I _____ our teacher for six months.
    (know)

15. When _____ the English teacher?
    (you/meet)

16. I _____ her in September.
    (meet)

17. How long _____ English in your previous school?
    (you/study)

18. How long _____ English in this school?
    (you/study)

1.9   The Present Perfect with Repetition from Past to Present

```
                        now
past ←┌ ----/---/---/-----------┼------------→ future
      │ He has had three        ↓
      │ interviews this month.
      └──────────────────────────
```

Examples	Explanation
Daniel **has had** three interviews this month. I **have made** two phone calls today. We **have had** one test this semester.	We use the present perfect to talk about the repetition of an action in a time period that includes the present. The time period is open, and there is a possibility for more repetition to occur. Open time periods include: *today, this week, this month, this year, this semester.*

(continued)

Examples	Explanation
Daniel **has sent** out 100 résumés up to now. So far, he **hasn't found** a job. He **has worked** in several hotels.	We sometimes use *so far* and *up to now* to mean "including this moment." We can use *several, many, a lot of,* or a number to show repetition from past to present.
How many interviews **has** he **had** this year? How much money **has** he **spent** on career counseling so far? He **hasn't spent** any money at all on career counseling.	We can ask a question about repetition with *how many* and *how much.* A negative statement with "any . . . at all" means the number is zero.

LANGUAGE NOTES

Do not use the continuous form for repetition.
> She *has gone* to the dentist three times this year.
> NOT: She *has been going* to the dentist three times this year.

EXERCISE 16 Write a statement to tell how many times you have done something in this city. (If you don't know the exact number, you may use *a few, several,* or *many*.)

EXAMPLES:

live in/apartment(s)
I've lived in one apartment in this city.

get lost/time(s)
I've gotten lost a few times in this city.

1. have/job(s)

   _____

2. have/job interview(s)

   _____

3. have/traffic ticket(s)

   _____

4. buy/car(s)

   _____

5. attend/school(s)

   _____

6. live in/apartment(s)

   _____

7. go downtown/time(s)

   _____

EXERCISE 17 Ask a question with *How much . . . ?* or *How many . . . ?* and the words given. Talk about today. Another student will answer.

EXAMPLES:
coffee/have
A. How much coffee have you had today?
B. I've had three cups of coffee today.

glasses of water/drink
A. How many glasses of water have you drunk today?
B. I haven't drunk any water at all today.

1. tea/have
2. glasses of water/have
3. cookies/eat
4. glasses of cola/have

5. e-mails/send
6. miles/walk or drive
7. money/spend
8. coffee/have

1.10 Present Perfect vs. Simple Past with Repetition

Examples	Explanation
How many interviews **have** you **had** this month? I **have had** two interviews so far this month.	This month is not finished. Using the present perfect with *so far* shows that there is possibility for more.
How many interviews **did** you **have** last month? I **had** four interviews last month.	When we use a past time expression (*yesterday, last week, last year*), the number is final. We must use the simple past tense.
I **have been** absent twice this semester.	This semester is not finished. There's a possibility to be absent more times this semester.
I **was** absent four times last semester.	Last semester is finished. The number four is final. We must use the simple past.
a) I **have eaten** two pieces of bread today. b) I **ate** two pieces of bread today. a) I **have made** five phone calls today. b) I **made** five phone calls today.	With a present time expression (such as *today, this week*), you may use either the present perfect or the simple past. In sentences (a), the number may not be final. In sentences (b), the number may be final.

LANGUAGE NOTES

1. If you refer to the experiences of a dead person, you must use the simple past tense because nothing more can be added to that person's experience.

    Marilyn Monroe *starred* in many movies. She died in 1962.
    Julia Roberts *has starred* in many American movies.

2. If you have moved here and do not plan to live in your hometown again, use the simple past tense to talk about your experiences in your hometown.

    In my hometown, I *had* five jobs.
    In this city, I *have had* two jobs.

EXERCISE 18 In the conversation below, fill in the blanks with the present perfect or the simple past of the verb in parentheses.

A. I'm very frustrated about finding a job. I ___*have sent*___ out 100
    (example: send)

    résumés so far. And I _____ dozens of phone calls to companies.
    (1 make)

B. Have you _____ any answers to your letters and calls?
    (2 have)

A. Yes. Last week I _____ six interviews. But so far, nobody
    (3 have)

    _____ me a job.
    (4 offer)

B. You should call those companies.

A. I know I should. But this week, I _____ very busy getting career
    (5 be)

    counseling. I _____ my counselor several times in the
    (6 see)

    past few weeks.

B. Has your counselor _____ you any advice about looking for a
    (7 give)

    job?

A. Yes. Last week she _____ me a lot of advice. But looking for a
    (8 give)

    job is so strange in the U.S. I feel like I have to sell myself.

B. Don't worry. You _____ much work experience in
    (9 not/have)

    the U.S. so far. I'm sure you'll get used to the process of finding a
    job.

A. I don't know. I _____ to a lot of other people looking
    (10 talk)

    for work. Even though English is their native language, they

    _____ much luck either.
    (11 not/have)

B. _____ easy for you to find a job when you lived in
    (12 it/be)

    your native country?

A. In my native country, I _____ this problem. After I
                                  (13 never/have)

    _____ from college, I _____ a job immediately
         (14 graduate)   *(15 find)*

    and _____ in the same place for many years.
              (16 work)

B. In the U.S., people change jobs often. Take me, for example.

    I _____ six jobs, and I'm only 28 years old.
          (17 have)

A. I'm 40 years old. But when I lived in my native country, I _____
                                                                      (18 have)

    the same job for ten years. And I _____ in the same apartment
                                            (19 live)

    for many years until I came to the U.S. My parents _____ in the
                                                              (20 live)

    same apartment from the time they got married until the time they
    died.

B. Get used to it! Life today is about constant change.

1.11   The Present Perfect with Indefinite Past Time—Overview

We use the present perfect to refer to an action that occurred at an
indefinite time in the past that still has importance to the present situation.

                                    now
    past ←⌐----------?-------------│------------------→ future
          │ Have you ever worked │
          │ in a hospital?   │
          └──────────────────────→┘

Examples	Explanation
Has Daniel **ever** worked in a restaurant? No, he hasn't. Have you **ever** seen a job counselor? Yes, I have.	A question with *ever* asks about any time between the past and the present. Put *ever* between the subject and the main verb.
Has he found a job **yet**? No, not **yet**. Has his wife found a job **yet**? Yes, she has **already** found a job.	*Yet* and *already* refer to an indefinite time in the near past. There is an expectation that an activity took place a short time ago.
Has he had a lot of interviews **lately**? Has he seen a career counselor **recently**?	*Lately* and *recently* refer to an indefinite time in the near past.
He has **just** finished writing a new résumé.	*Just* means a short time ago.

EXERCISE 19 Read the following conversation. Underline the present perfect and present perfect continuous tenses.

A. There's going to be a job fair at the college next week. <u>Have you ever gone</u> to one?

B. What's a job fair?

A. Representatives from different companies come to one place. You can meet these people, find out about their companies, and give them your résumé. Lately I've been going to a lot of job fairs. And I've been looking for jobs online. I've just rewritten my résumé too. I haven't found a job yet, but I'm hopeful.

B. But you have a good job as a secretary.

A. I'm going to quit in two weeks. I've already given my employer notice. I've worked there for two years, and I haven't had a raise yet. I've realized that I can make more money doing something else. I've talked to a career counselor and I've taken a test to see what I'm good at. I've also taken more courses to upgrade my skills.

B. Have you decided what you want to do?

A. Yes. I've decided to be a legal secretary.

1.12   Questions with *Ever*

Answering with Present Perfect	Answering with Simple Past
Have you ever **been** a desk clerk? Yes. **I've been** a desk clerk many times.	**Have** you ever **been** a desk clerk? Yes. I **was** a desk clerk from 1994 to 1998.
Have you ever **taken** a French course? Yes. **I've** taken a French course.	**Have** you ever **taken** a French course? Yes. I **took** a French course in high school.
Have you ever **written** a letter to Mr. Harris? No. **I've** never **written** a letter to Mr. Harris.	**Have** you ever **written** a letter to Mr. Johnson? Yes, I **wrote** to him last week.

EXERCISE 20 Ask a question with *Have you ever . . . ?* and the words given. Use the past participle of the verb. Another student will answer. To answer with a specific time, use the simple past tense. To answer with a frequency response, use the present perfect tense.

EXAMPLES: go to the zoo
A. Have you ever gone to the zoo?
B. Yes, I've gone there many times.

go to Disneyland
A. Have you ever gone to Disneyland?
B. Yes, I went there last summer.

1. find money on the street
2. go to a garage sale
3. meet a famous person
4. study art history
5. get a ticket for speeding
6. be on television
7. win a contest or a prize
8. lend money to a friend
9. lose your keys
10. break an arm or a leg
11. get lost in this city
12. go to court
13. hear of[4] Martin Luther King, Jr.
14. eat in a Vietnamese restaurant
15. order products over the Internet

EXERCISE 21 Find a partner. Ask your partner a question with *Have you ever . . . ?* and the words given. If the answer is *yes*, ask for more specific information. Report something interesting about your partner to the class.

EXAMPLE: eat a hot dog
A. Have you ever eaten a hot dog?
B. Yes, I have.
A. When did you eat a hot dog?
B. I ate one at a picnic last summer.

1. go to a football game

2. tell a lie

3. go to Canada

4. travel by train

5. eat pizza

6. go to Disneyworld

[4] *Hear of* means to recognize a name.

7. be on a roller coaster

8. see a play in this city

9. eat Chinese food

10. use a fax machine

11. buy a lottery ticket

12. go camping

13. use a scanner

14. take pictures of buildings in this city

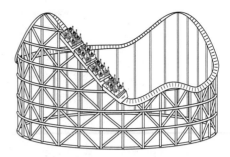

roller coaster

EXERCISE 22 Work with a partner. Use *ever* to write four questions to ask your teacher. Your teacher will answer.

EXAMPLES: *Have you ever eaten raw fish?*

Have you ever written a poem?

1. _____

2. _____

3. _____

4. _____

EXERCISE 23 Fill in the blanks with the present perfect or the simple past to complete each dialog.

1.   A. Have you ever ___*studied*___ algebra?

B. Yes. I studied it in high school.

A. I like math a lot. Do you?

B. No, I _____ never _____ math.

2.   A. Have you ever _____ to Canada?

B. No, I never have. But I would like to go there some day.

A. _____ you ever gone to Mexico?

B. Yes. I _____ there two years ago.

3.   A. Have you ever broken your arm or leg?

B. Yes. I _____ my leg when I was ten years old. I was climbing

a tree when I _____ .
$\qquad$ *(fall)*

A. Which leg _____ you _____?

B. I broke my left leg.

4. A. _____ your parents ever come here to visit you?

   B. No, they never _____. But last year my brother _____ to visit me for three weeks.

5. A. _____ you ever _____ an Italian movie?

   B. No, I haven't. But I _____ seen many French movies.

   A. I _____ never _____ a French movie.

6. A. _____ you ever _____ to the public library in this city?

   B. Yes. I _____ gone there many times. Last week I _____ there on Monday and checked out a novel by Mark Twain. I have never _____ Mark Twain's books in English.

   A. _____ you ever _____ his books in translation?

   B. Oh, yes. In high school, I _____ two of his novels in Spanish.

EXERCISE **24** Ask a question with *Have you ever . . . ?* and the words given. Another student will answer.

EXAMPLE: ask your boss for a raise
A. Have you ever asked your boss for a raise?
B. No, I never have.

1. fill out a job application

2. have an interview

3. use the Occupational Outlook Handbook[5]

4. see a job counselor

5. attend a job fair

6. use a résumé writing service

7. take courses to train for a job

8. use the Internet to find a job

9. go to a state employment office

10. read a book about finding a job

---

[5] The *Occupational Outlook Handbook* is a government publication that gives lists of jobs. For each job, the handbook gives information about the nature of the work, the salary, the training needed, the future of this job, and more.

---

11. quit a job

12. have your own business

1.13 *Yet, Already,* and *Just*

We use *yet* to ask if an expected activity took place a short time ago.

Answering with Present Perfect	Answering with Simple Past
Has he **eaten** dinner yet? Yes, he **has eaten** dinner already. Yes, he **has** just **eaten** dinner.	**Has** he **eaten** dinner yet? Yes, he **ate** dinner an hour ago.
Has he **washed** the dishes yet? No, he **hasn't washed** the dishes yet. OR No, not yet.	**Has** he **washed** the dishes yet? Yes, he just **washed** the dishes.

LANGUAGE NOTES

1. For an affirmative statement, use *already*. You can put *already* at the end of the sentence or between the auxiliary verb and the main verb.
    I have found a job *already*.
    I have *already* found a job.
2. For a negative statement, use *yet*.
    I haven't found a job *yet*.
3. Use *just* to show that an activity happened immediately before the present. We can use the simple past or the present perfect with *just*.
    He *just wrote* his résumé.
    He *has just written* his résumé.

EXERCISE 25 Ask a student who has recently moved here questions with the words given and *yet* or *already*. The student who answers should use the simple past tense if the answer has a specific time.

EXAMPLE: go downtown
A. Have you gone downtown yet?
B. Yes, I went downtown three weeks ago.

1. buy a car
2. find an apartment
3. get a library card
4. use public transportation
5. visit any museums
6. meet any of your neighbors

EXERCISE 26 Ask a question with the words given and *yet*. The student who answers should use the simple past tense if the answer has a specific time.

EXAMPLES: the teacher/take attendance
A. Has the teacher taken attendance yet?
B. Yes, he has. He took attendance at the beginning of the class.

the teacher/return the homework
A. Has the teacher returned the homework yet?
B. No, he hasn't. OR No, not yet.

1. we/have an exam

2. we/study modals

3. you/learn the irregular past tenses

4. the teacher/learn the students' names

5. you/learn the other students' names

6. the teacher/teach the past perfect

EXERCISE 27 Daniel is preparing for his job interview. He made a list of things to do. He has checked those things he has already done. Make sentences about Daniel's list using the present perfect with *yet* or *already*.

EXAMPLE: √ prepare résumé
He has already prepared his résumé.

____ send suit to cleaner's
He hasn't sent his suit to the cleaner's yet.

1. √ buy a new tie

2. √ wash white shirt

3. ____ iron white shirt

4. √ get a haircut

5. √ rewrite résumé

6. ____ take résumé to copy center

7. √ see a job counselor

8. ____ put papers in briefcase

9. ____ send for transcripts

10. √ get letters of recommendation

EXERCISE 28 Fill in the blanks to complete each conversation.

EXAMPLE: A. Have you bought your textbook yet?

B. No, I _____*haven't*_____ bought it _____*yet.*_____

1. A. Have you _____ dinner yet?

    B. No, I haven't. I _____ lunch at 2:30, so I'm not hungry now.

2. A. _____ your sister gotten married yet?

    B. Yes. She _____ married two weeks ago. She _____ a beautiful wedding.

    A. Has she _____ back from her honeymoon yet?

    B. Yes. She _____ back last Thursday.

3. A. Have your parents _____ an apartment yet?

    B. No. They _____ found one yet. They're still looking.

4. A. I'm going to rent the movie *Titanic*. Have you _____ it yet?

    B. Yes, I _____ it a couple of years ago, but I'd like to see it again.

5. A. What are you going to do during summer vacation?

    B. I haven't _____ about it yet. It's only April.

    A. I've already _____ plans. I'm going to Disneyworld. I _____ my ticket last week.

6. A. Has the movie _____ yet? I want to buy some popcorn before it begins.

    B. Shhh! It _____ ten minutes ago.

7. A. Do you want to go to the museum with me on Saturday?

    B. Sorry. I _____ already _____ other plans for Saturday.

8. A. _____ your brother _____ from Mexico yet?

    B. No, he hasn't. We're expecting him to arrive on Tuesday.

9. A. I'd like to talk to the teacher, please.

    B. I'm sorry. She's already _____ for the day.

    A. But she told me to call her before 4 o'clock and it's only 3:30.

    B. She _____ at 2 o'clock because her son was sick.

10. A. Is that a good book?

    B. Yes, it is. I haven't _____ it yet, but when I finish it, you can have it.

1.14   Questions with *Lately* and *Recently*

A question with *lately* and *recently* asks about an indefinite time in the near past.

Answering with Present Perfect	Answering with Simple Past
Have you **seen** any good movies lately?	**Have** you **seen** any good movies lately?
No, I **haven't seen** any good movies lately.	Yes. I **saw** a great movie last week.
Have we **had** any tests recently?	**Have** we **had** a test recently?
No, we **haven't had** any tests recently.	Yes. We **had** a test two days ago.

LANGUAGE NOTES

An affirmative answer usually uses the simple past tense and a specific time. A negative answer usually uses *lately* or *recently* and the present perfect.

EXERCISE 29 Ask a *yes/no* question with the words given. Another student will answer. A past-tense statement may be added to a *yes* answer.

EXAMPLE: go swimming recently
A. Have you gone swimming recently?
B. Yes, I have. I went swimming yesterday.

1. write to your family lately

2. go to the library recently

3. go to the zoo lately

4. see any good movies lately

5. receive any letters lately

6. be absent lately

7. have a job interview lately

8. read any good books recently

9. make any long-distance calls lately

10. take any tests recently

EXERCISE 30 Work with a partner. Write four questions to ask your teacher about what he or she has done lately. Your teacher will answer.

EXAMPLE: _Have you taken a vacation lately (or recently)?_

1. _____

2. _____

3. _____

4. _____

EXERCISE 31 Fill in the blanks with the simple past or the present perfect.

EXAMPLE: A. Have you ___gotten___ a letter from your parents lately?
(get)

B. Yes. I ___got___ a letter from them yesterday.

1. A. Have you _____ any pictures lately?
(take)

   B. No. I _____. My camera is broken.

2. A. Have you _____ any good movies lately?
(see)

   B. Yes. I _____ a great movie last weekend.

3. A. Have you _____ for a walk lately?
(go)

   B. Yes. I _____ for a walk yesterday.

4. A. Have you _____ yourself a gift lately?
(buy)

   B. Yes. I _____ myself a new CD player last week.

5. A. Have you _____ a good conversation with a friend lately?
(have)

   B. No. I _____ time to talk with my friends lately.

6. A. Have you _____ a massage lately?
(have)

   B. No. I _____ never _____ a massage.

7. A. Have you _____ the laundry lately?
(do)

   B. Yes. I _____ it this morning.

8.   A. Have you _____ to any parties lately?
            (go)

     B. No, I _____ . I've been too busy lately.

1.15   The Present Perfect Continuous with Ongoing Activities

Examples	Explanation
Daniel **has been sending** out a lot of résumés lately. Robert **has been thinking** about retirement lately. I **have been learning** a lot about American culture. My English **has been improving**.	We use the present perfect continuous to show that an activity has been ongoing or repeated from a time in the near past to the present.

LANGUAGE NOTES

Remember, do not use the continuous form with nonaction verbs.
     She *has been* absent a lot lately.

EXERCISE 32 Fill in the blanks with *have* or *haven't* to tell about your experiences lately. (You may add a sentence telling why.)

EXAMPLE: I __*haven't*__ been reading a lot lately. *I haven't had much time.*

1. I _____ been getting a lot of sleep recently.

2. I _____ been getting together with my friends lately.

3. I _____ been watching the news a lot lately.

4. I _____ been studying a lot lately.

5. I _____ been learning a lot about English grammar lately.

6. I _____ been worrying a lot lately.

7. I _____ been looking for a job recently.

8. I _____ been watching a lot of TV recently.

9. I _____ been having a lot of problems with my car lately.

10. I _____ been spending a lot of money recently.

11. I _____ been absent a lot lately.

12. I _____ been using a computer a lot lately.

Fill in the blanks to make **true** statements about yourself.

EXAMPLES: _My pronunciation_____ has been getting better.

   _My eyesight_____ has been getting worse.

1. _____ has been improving.

2. _____ has been getting worse.

3. _____ has been increasing.

4. _____ has been helping me with my studies.

1.16   The Present Perfect with No Time Mentioned

Examples	Explanation
I'm a pilot. People **have** often **asked** me how I became interested in flying. I **have lived** in many locations. I **have flown** to many cities. To be a pilot, I **have had** to make a lot of personal sacrifices.	Sometimes we use the present perfect to talk about the past without any reference to time. The time is not important or not known or imprecise.
I have studied French and can use it in the hotel business. If you **have filled** the position, please consider me for any other position in your hotel.	We use the present perfect without reference to time to show that the past is relevant to a present situation.

EXERCISE 34 Fill in the blanks to make a **true** statement about yourself.

EXAMPLE: I've eaten ___*pizza*___, and I like this food a lot.

1. I've visited _____, and I would recommend this place to other people.

2. I've tried _____, and I like this food a lot.

3. I've seen the movie _____, and I would recommend it to others.

4. The teacher has said that _____, but some of us forget.

5. I've studied _____, and it has really helped me in my life.

6. I've had a lot of experience with _____ and can help you with it, if you need me to.

EXERCISE 35 Check to tell which of these work-related experiences you've had. Then at the bottom, write three more things you've done at your present or former job. Write things that would impress a job interviewer.

1. ___ I've worked on a team.

2. ___ I've taken programming courses.

3. ___ I've had experience talking with customers on the phone.

4. ___ I've worked overtime when necessary to finish a project.

5. ___ I've worked and gone to school at the same time.

6. ___ I've helped my family financially.

7. ___ I've given oral presentations.

8. ___ I've done research.

9. ___ I've created a Web site.

10. ___ I've done physical labor.

11. ___ I've been in charge of a group of workers.

12. ___ I've traveled as part of my job.

13. _____

14. _____

15. _____

EXERCISE 36 Fill in the blanks with the present perfect (for no time mentioned) or the simple past (if the time is mentioned) of the verb in parentheses.

I ___*have had*___ many new experiences since I moved here. I
     (have)

_____ some foods for the first time in my life. I _____
     (1 try)   *(2 eat)*

pizza, but I don't like it much. Yesterday, I _____ Chinese food for the
                                                      (3 try)

first time and thought it was delicious.

I _____ (4 meet) a lot of new people and have some new friends.

I _____ (5 see) some behaviors I _____ (6 never/see) before. For example, there's a guy in my math class who wears torn jeans every day. Yesterday I _____ (7 ask) him if he needs money for new clothes, but he just laughed and said, "Torn clothes are in style."

I _____ (8 visit) some interesting places. I _____ (9 go) to the art museum and the science museum. I _____ (10 take) a boat ride on a nearby river. I _____ (11 even/go) to the top of the tallest building.

I _____ (12 learn) about looking for a job. I _____ (13 write) résumés and _____ (14 have) job interviews. I _____ (15 go) to job fairs. I _____ (16 even/use) the Internet for my job search. Last week I _____ (17 go) to see a job counselor at my college, and she _____ (18 give) me some help with interviewing techniques.

1.17 The Present Perfect vs. the Present Perfect Continuous with No Time Mentioned

Examples	Explanation
a) My counselor **has helped** me with my résumé. b) My family **has been helping** me a lot. a) I **have applied** for a job in New York. b) I **have been applying** for jobs all over the U.S. a) **Have** you **eaten** in a restaurant lately? b) **I've been eating** in restaurants a lot lately.	Examples (a) refer to a singular occurrence at an indefinite time in the past. Examples (b) refer to an ongoing activity.

EXERCISE 37 Check the sentence or clause that best completes the idea.

EXAMPLE: I can't sleep. The people in the next apartment . . .

_____ have made a lot of noise.

_✓_ have been making a lot of noise.

1. He's been sick all week.

    _____ He's stayed in bed.

    _____ He's been staying in bed.

2. She is unhappy.

    _____ She has just lost her job.

    _____ He has been losing her job.

3. She lost her job three weeks ago. She hasn't had much free time lately because . . .

    _____ she has looked for a new job.

    _____ she has been looking for a new job.

4. My writing has been improving a lot because . . .

    _____ I have written a composition.

    _____ I have been writing compositions.

5. At first she planned to move, but now she doesn't want to.

    _____ She has changed her mind.

    _____ She has been changing her mind.

6. I meet new people everywhere: in my neighborhood, at my job, at school.

    _____ I have met new people.

    _____ I have been meeting new people.

7. Now I can pay for my car repair because I . . .

    _____ have received a check from my insurance company.

    _____ have been receiving a check from my insurance company.

8. Every week I put 20 percent of my salary in the bank. I plan to buy a house as soon as I can.

    _____ I have saved my money.

    _____ I have been saving my money.

9. I'm going to become an engineer.

___ I have made my decision.

___ I have been making my decision.

10. I didn't have time to watch TV today because . . .

___ I have worked on my composition.

___ I have been working on my composition.

EXERCISE 38 Fill in the blanks with the present perfect, the present perfect continuous, or the simple past of the verb in parentheses.

A. How's your mother?

B. She ___*hasn't been feeling*___ well lately. She _____
    (not/feel)   (1 have)

a lot of problems with her back lately. I _____ her to the doctor
                                            (2 take)

yesterday.

A. What happened to her?

B. Last month she _____ down and _____ her back.
                    (3 fall)   (4 hurt)

A. Why _____ she _____ to the doctor when it _____ ?
        (5 not/go)   (6 happen)

B. At that time, she _____ her back would get better. But little
                      (7 think)

by little it _____ worse.
              (8 get)

EXERCISE 39 Fill in the blanks with the simple past, the present perfect, or the present perfect continuous of the verb in parentheses. (In some cases, more than one answer is possible.)

EXAMPLE: I ___*worked*___ as a cashier when I was in high school.
                 (work)

1. I think I'm qualified for the job of driver because I _____ as
                                                         (work)
   a driver before.

2. I _____ a pilot many years ago. My job as a pilot _____
       (become)   (take)
   me away from home much of the time.

3. I don't like the sight of blood, so I _____ about
                                          (never/think)
   becoming a doctor.

4. I'm a hair stylist. I _____ people's hair for 15 years.
   (cut)

5. I'm afraid of the interview process because I _____ a
   (never/have)
   job interview before.

6. Many years ago, I _____ as a kindergarten teacher. Now I
   (work)
   have my own day care center.

7. I'm a car mechanic. I _____ a mechanic for three years. I
   (be)
   _____ a lot of experience working with American cars, but
   (have)
   I _____ much experience with foreign cars.
   (not/have)

8. I'm 62 years old and I like my job as a lab technician, but I _____
   _____ about retiring soon.
   (think)

9. When I was in my native country, I _____ an engineer, but now
   (be)
   I'm a salesperson.

10. People _____ me why I want to be a funeral
    (often/ask)
    director when I graduate.

11. Lately I _____ the Internet a lot to get information about jobs.
    (use)

12. I _____ several interviews already, but I _____
    (have)   (not/find)
    a job yet.

13. I _____ an actor, but I would like to try it.
    (never/be)

14. I _____ to be a nurse, so I'm going to apply to the
    (always/want)
    nursing program next year.

15. I'm not happy with my present job, so I _____ for a new
    (look)
    one.

16. Last year I _____ my own accounting business.
    (start)

17. Two years ago, I retired. I _____ a taxi for 25 years.
    (drive)

18. I need to hire someone with experience in selling shoes. _____
    _____ shoes?
    (you/ever/sell)

19. I _____ computers, so I've decided to become a
    (always/like)
    programmer.

20. After I graduated from high school, I _____ a soldier for two
    (be)
    years.

Compare the Simple Present and the Present Perfect

Simple Present	Present Perfect
She **has** a job.	She **has had** her job for six months.
She **is** a lab technician.	She **has been** a lab technician since May.

Compare the Present Continuous and the Present Perfect Continuous

Present Continuous	Present Perfect Continuous
He **is working** now.	He **has been working** for three hours.
She **is sleeping** now.	She **has been sleeping** for 20 minutes.

Compare the Simple Past and the Present Perfect

Simple Past	Present Perfect
Daniel **worked** in Mexico City from 1988 to 1992.	He **has worked** in Chicago since 1998.
He **found** a job in 2000.	He **has had** his present job since January, 2000.
He **bought** his car when he came to Chicago.	He **has had** his car since he came to Chicago.
When **did** he **come** to Chicago?	How long **has** he **been** in Chicago?
He **wrote** three letters last month.	He **has written** five letters this month.
He **studied** business in college.	He **has studied** French and speaks it well.
He **went** to New York in July.	He **has gone** to Los Angeles many times.
Did you **eat** a hamburger last night?	**Have** you ever **eaten** a hot dog?

Compare the Present Perfect and the Present Perfect Continuous

Present Perfect	Present Perfect Continuous
Robert **has worked** as a pilot for 30 years.	Robert **has been working** as a pilot for 30 years. (Both sentences have the same meaning.)
Robert **has lived** in many different locations.	Robert **has been living** in Pittsburgh for several years.
How many apartments **have** you **had** in this city?	How long **have** you **been living** in your present apartment?
I **have sent** out 25 résumés.	I **have been sending** out a lot of résumés lately.
He **has slept** well and is ready for his interview.	He **has been sleeping** for six hours (and he's still asleep).

EDITING ADVICE

1. Don't confuse the *-ing* form and the past participle.

    I've been ~~taken~~ _taking_ English courses for several years.

    Have you ever ~~being~~ _been_ in Texas?

2. Don't confuse *for* and *since*.

    He's been in Chicago ~~since~~ _for_ three years.

3. Use the simple past, not the present perfect, with a specific past time and in questions and statements with *when*.

    He ~~has written~~ _wrote_ a book five years ago.

    She ~~has~~ bought a car when she ~~has~~ found a job.

    When ~~has he gotten~~ _did he get_ his driver's license?

4. Use the present perfect (continuous), not the present tense, if the action started in the past and continues to the present.

    I'~~m~~ _have been_ working in a factory for six months.

    How long ~~do~~ _have_ you ~~have~~ _had_ your computer?

---

5. Don't use the continuous form for repetition.

eaten
How many times have you <s>been eating</s> pizza?

6. Use the simple past in a *since* clause.

came
He's had three jobs since he <s>has come</s> to the U.S.

7. Use correct word order.

never been
He has <s>been never</s> in New York.

ever eaten
Have you <s>eaten ever</s> Chinese food?

8. Use *yet* in negative statements. Use *already* in affirmative statements.

yet
I haven't finished the book <s>already</s>.

already
I've finished the book <s>yet</s>.

9. Use *how long* for a question about length of time. Don't include the word *time*.

How long <s>time</s> have they been working in a restaurant?

10. If the main verb is *have*, be sure to include the auxiliary verb *have* for the present perfect.

has
He had his job since March.

LESSON 1 TEST / REVIEW

PART 1 Find the mistakes with the underlined words, and correct them. Not every sentence has a mistake. If the sentence is correct, write C.

EXAMPLES:

seen
How many times have you <u>seeing</u> the movie?

Have you ever <u>traveled</u> by train?   C

1. <u>How long time</u> have you known your husband?

2. <u>Has</u> your mother <u>been</u> sick lately?

3. She's worked in a restaurant <u>since</u> five months.

4. Have you <u>gone ever</u> to the art museum?

5. How long <u>does</u> our teacher <u>work</u> at this school?

6. I'm <u>studying</u> English <u>for</u> three years.

7. How long <u>you've been living</u> in your present apartment?

8. He's had three jobs since <u>he's come</u> to this city.

9. How many times <u>have you calling</u> your parents this month?

10. When <u>have you come</u> to this city?

11. She <u>bought</u> a car when she <u>found</u> a job.

12. Have you ever <u>giving</u> your sister a present?

13. When her dog <u>died</u>, she felt sad.

14. She <u>has</u> her car since she graduated.

PART 2

Fill in the blanks with the simple present, simple past, present perfect, or present perfect continuous tense of the verb in parentheses.

I ___*am*___ in the U.S. now. I _____ here for one year. My
   (be)   (1 live)

life _____ a lot since I _____ to the U.S. For example, in
   (2 change)   (3 come)

my country I _____ as an engineer, but I _____ a job now.
          (4 work)   (5 not/have)

All this month, I _____ for a job, but I _____ one
              (6 look)   (7 not/find)

yet. I know it takes time.

   In my country, I _____ a lot of contact with my friends, but here I
                (8 have)

am alone. So far I _____ several nice people, but I don't consider
              (9 meet)

any of them my friends. It takes time to make friends. I suppose I

_____ these people long enough.
   (10 not/know)

   Here everybody has a car. I _____ to own a car.
                          (11 always/want)

I _____ my driver's license three months ago, but I _____
   (12 get)   (13 not/buy)

a car yet because I don't have enough money. I plan to buy one in the near
future.

   Since I _____ here, my life _____ easy, but I know
          (14 come)   (15 not/be)

that I will succeed in this country in time.

EXPANSION ACTIVITIES

CLASSROOM ACTIVITIES

1. Walk around the room. Find one person who has done each of these things. Write that person's name in the blank.

    a. _____ has been exercising a lot lately.

    b. _____ has been losing weight lately.

    c. _____ has never gone downtown in this city.

    d. _____ has traveled to more than ten countries.

    e. _____ has never owned a car.

    f. _____ has always wanted to be in a movie.

    g. _____ hasn't bought the textbook yet.

    h. _____ has been in this city for less than six months.

    i. _____ has just found a job.

    j. _____ has worked in a restaurant.

    k. _____ has never used public transportation in this city.

    l. _____ has eaten raw fish.

    m. _____ has worked out in a gym several times this month.

    n. _____ has never eaten an avocado.

    o. _____ has never used a cell phone.

    p. _____ has been looking for a job.

2. Role Play: Find a partner. Pretend that one of you is looking for a job and the other one is the interviewer. Ask and answer questions about your experience, education, interests, talents, etc. Below are some sample questions that interviewers sometimes ask:

    *   Why did you leave your last job?
    *   Why did you apply for this position?
    *   Where would you like to be five years from now?
    *   What are your strengths?
    *   What are your weaknesses?
    *   Why should we hire you?

3. Game—True-True-False: Form a small group. On a piece of paper, write two unusual things you have done in your past. Write one false statement about your past. (Use the present perfect with no mention of time.) Read your statements to the other members of your group. The other members have to guess which is the false statement.

EXAMPLES: I've flown in a helicopter.
              I've worked on a farm.
              I've met the president of my native country.

4. Fill in the blanks and discuss your answers.

a) I've learned _____ from my experiences in the U.S.

b) I've thought a lot about _____

c) Most people in my native country have never _____

d) In the U.S., it's been hard for me to _____

DISCUSSION

1. How is looking for a job in the U.S. different from looking for a job in your native country?

2. How is the work environment in your present job different from the work environment in a previous job you had?

3. In your native country, how do people usually select a career? Are there career counselors to help people make a decision?

4. Have you ever used the Internet to search for jobs? Has it been helpful?

5. Look at the list of jobs below. Which ones do you think are interesting and why? What do you think are some good or bad things about these jobs?

airplane pilot	funeral director	librarian
architect	gardener	musician
bus driver	immigration officer	newspaper reporter
circus clown	lawyer	police officer
firefighter	letter carrier	veterinarian

WRITING

1. Write about your past work experiences.

2. Write about a career that you think is interesting. Explain why you think this career is interesting.

3. Write about two or three things that your life experience has taught you.

4. Write an article giving advice to somebody looking for a job.

OUTSIDE ACTIVITIES

Interview an American about his or her job. Find out the following information and report it to the class.

- how long he or she has been working at this job
- what his/her job responsibilities are
- if he/she likes this job
- how he/she found this job

NOTE: It is not polite to ask about salary.

Internet Activities

1. Type "career" or "jobs" in a search engine. See how many "hits" come up.

2. Find some career counseling Web sites. Find a sample résumé in your field or close to your field. Print it out and bring it to class. What's the difference between a chronological résumé and a functional résumé?

3. From one of the Web sites you found, get information on one or more of the following topics:

    - how to write a cover letter
    - how to find a career counselor
    - how to plan for your interview
    - how to network
    - what questions to ask the interviewer

4. See if your local newspaper has a Web site. If it does, find the "help wanted" section of this newspaper.

5. Type in "job fair." Are there any jobs fairs near you?

6. Type in "Campbell Interest and Skills Survey." Answer the questions in this survey to find out what career you are suited for.

7. Type in "Occupational Outlook Handbook." Find information about a job that interests you.

8. Many businesses have pages on the Internet that give information about the company and offer job listings. Find information about a company that interests you.

GRAMMAR

Passive Voice
Participles Used as Adjectives
Get + Participles and Adjectives

CONTEXT

The Oscars
Movie Ratings
The Actor President
Charlie Chaplin

LESSON FOCUS

The verb in some sentences is in the active voice.
The verb in some sentences is in the passive voice.

> Thomas Edison *invented* motion pictures. (ACTIVE VOICE)
> Motion pictures *were invented* by Thomas Edison. (PASSIVE VOICE)

Participles can be used as adjectives.

> We saw an *interesting* movie. (PRESENT PARTICIPLE)
> I'm *interested* in American movies. (PAST PARTICIPLE)

We use *get* with certain past participles and other adjectives.

> She *got married* five years ago.
> I *got hungry* and ate dinner without you.

Examples	Explanation
American films **are made** in Hollywood.	Passive = a form of *be* + past participle
An award **will be given** to the best movie director.	
Popcorn **is sold** in movie theaters.	
Star Wars **was directed** by George Lucas.	If the performer of the action is mentioned, it follows *by*.

Before You Read
1. Who is your favorite actor? Who is your favorite actress?
2. What movies have you seen recently?

Read the following article. Pay special attention to verbs in the passive voice.

The Oscars

The Academy Awards **are given** out every year to recognize outstanding work of movie actors, directors, and others who are part of the movie-making industry. These awards, called Oscars, **are presented** in a formal ceremony in Hollywood in the spring. Several people **are nominated** in specific categories, such as Best Movie, Best Actor, Best Music, Best Costumes. One person **is chosen** to receive an award. The winner's name **is placed** in a sealed envelope, and the envelope **is** not **opened** until the night of the ceremony. In the weeks before the ceremony, movie reviewers make predictions about which movies and actors **will be picked**, but the winners' names **are** not **known** ahead of time.

When the awards ceremony started in 1927, 15 awards **were presented** and the ceremony **was attended** by only 250 people. Anyone who could afford a ticket could attend. Today about two dozen Oscars **are presented**. Tickets **are** no longer **sold** to the general public; invitations **are** only **sent** to people involved in making the movies and to their guests. Today the awards **are presented** in a 6,000-seat auditorium. An even bigger auditorium **is being built**.

Since 1952, Oscar night **has been televised** and **broadcast** in the U.S. as well as in hundreds of other countries. This show **is seen** by hundreds of millions of people. Viewers watch as their favorite movie stars arrive looking beautiful and hopeful.

Did you know...?

Walt Disney won the most Oscars ever: 26.

When the winner's name **is announced**, he or she comes to the stage to receive the award and thank everyone who helped make winning possible. The ceremony is very long. In fact, in 1997 the ceremony lasted longer than the movie that won the most awards: *Titanic*.

2.2 Passive and Active Voice

Active	Passive
I **saw** the Academy Awards ceremony last year.	The Academy Awards ceremony **was seen** by millions.
Federico Fellini **made** many movies.	His movies **were made** in Italy.
Do you **know** the winners' names?	The winners' names **are not known** until the night of the ceremony.
The Academy **gives** awards to the best actors and movies.	The awards **are given** every spring.

LANGUAGE NOTES

1. The passive voice is formed by using a form of *be* + past participle. It is sometimes followed with a *by* phrase.

SUBJECT	BE	PAST PARTICIPLE	BY PERFORMER OF ACTION
Hamlet	was	written	by Shakespeare.

2. The active voice focuses on the person who performs the action. The passive voice focuses on the receiver of the action.

   My brother saw *Star Wars* six times. (The emphasis is on *my brother*.)

   Star Wars has been seen by millions of people. (The emphasis is on *Star Wars*.)

3. When the verb is in the active voice, the subject performs the action. When the verb is in the passive voice, the subject receives the action.

   ACTIVE: The man *ate* the fish.

   PASSIVE: The man *was eaten* by the fish.

EXERCISE 1   Read the following sentences. Decide if the underlined verb is active (A) or passive (P).

EXAMPLES: The actress <u>received</u> an Oscar.   *A*

The actress <u>was given</u> an Oscar.   *P*

1. The actress <u>wore</u> a beautiful gown.
2. The gown <u>was designed</u> by Anne Klein.
3. Steven Spielberg <u>presented</u> an Oscar.
4. Spielberg <u>was presented</u> an Oscar.
5. The director <u>has been nominated</u> many times.
6. The movie <u>was filmed</u> in black and white.
7. Many actors <u>live</u> in California.
8. *Gone with the Wind* <u>was made</u> in 1939.
9. *It's a Wonderful Life* <u>has been shown</u> on TV many times.
10. The names of the winners <u>will be printed</u> in tomorrow's newspaper.
11. The actress <u>thanked</u> all the people who helped her win.
12. The actress <u>was driven</u> to the ceremony in a white limousine.
13. Hollywood <u>was built</u> at the beginning of the twentieth century.
14. Hollywood <u>has become</u> the movie capital of the U.S.
15. Movie reviewers <u>make</u> predictions about the winners.

2.3   Passive—Form

Tense	Active	Passive = *Be* + Past Participle
Simple Present	A committee **chooses** the best actor.	The best actor **is chosen** by a committee.
Present Continuous	They **are giving** an award now.	An award **is being given** now.
Future	They **will pick** the best movie. They **are going to pick** the best movie.	The best movie **will be picked**. The best movie **is going to be picked**.
Simple Past	They **announced** the winner's name.	The winner's name **was announced**.
Past Continuous	They **were taking** photographs.	Photographs **were being taken**.
Present Perfect	They **have chosen** the best movie.	The best movie **has been chosen**.
Modal	They **should announce** the winner's name.	The winner's name **should be announced**.

Observe negatives and questions with the passive voice:

AFFIRMATIVE:	The movie **was filmed** in the U.S.
NEGATIVE:	It **wasn't filmed** in Canada.
QUESTION:	**Was** it **filmed** in Hollywood? No, it **wasn't**.
WH- QUESTION:	Where **was** it **filmed**?

LANGUAGE NOTES

1. Passive voice can be used with different tenses and with modals. The tense of the sentence is shown by the verb *be*. Use the past participle with every tense.

    The auditorium *was built* in 1968.
    A new auditorium *is being built* now.
2. An adverb can be placed between the auxiliary verb and the main verb.

    The ceremony is *usually* held in March.
    The winners are *never* announced ahead of time.
3. Never use *do, does,* or *did* with the passive voice.

    The movie *wasn't* made in the U.S. (NOT: The movie didn't made in the U.S.)
    When *was* the movie made? (NOT: When did the movie made?)
4. If two verbs in the passive voice are connected with *and,* do not repeat *be.*

    The Oscar ceremony *is televised and seen* by millions of people.
5. Notice the difference in pronouns in an active sentence and a passive sentence. After *by,* the object pronoun is used.

    ACTIVE: **She** saw **him**.   ACTIVE: **They** helped **us**.

    PASSIVE: **He** was seen by **her**.   PASSIVE: **We** were helped by **them**.

EXERCISE 2 Fill in the blanks with the passive voice of the verb, using the tense given.

EXAMPLE: (simple present: *give*)

The best actor ___*is given*___ an Oscar.

1. (simple present: *see*)

    The awards ceremony _____ _____ by millions of people.

2. (future: *choose*)

    Which actor _____ _____ _____ next year?

---

3. (modal: *can/see*)

The movie _____ _____ _____ at many theaters.

4. (present perfect: *make*)

Many movies _____ _____ _____ about World War II.

5. (simple present: *print*)

A movie guide _____ _____ in the daily newspapers.

6. (simple past: *give*)

James Cameron _____ _____ an award in 1997 for Best Director, for *Titanic*.

7. (present continuous: *show*)

A good movie _____ _____ _____ at a theater near my house.

8. (simple past: *make*)

Gone with the Wind _____ _____ in 1939.

9. (present perfect: *show*)

It's a Wonderful Life _____ _____ _____ on TV many times.

10. (present perfect: *give*)

Over 2,000 Academy Awards _____ _____ _____ out since 1927.

11. (simple past: *give*)

In 1927, only one award _____ _____ to a woman.

12. (simple past: *add*)

Sound _____ _____ to movies in 1927.

13. (simple present: *often/make*)

Movies _____ _____ _____ in Hollywood.

14. (simple past: *choose*)

_____ *The Godfather* _____ as best picture? Yes, it

_____ .

2.4 Passive Voice with a Performer

Active	Passive
Billy Crystal **presented** the Oscar.	The Oscar **was presented** by Billy Crystal.
Spielberg **directed** *Jurassic Park*.	*Jurassic Park* **was directed** by Spielberg.
Mozart **composed** *The Magic Flute*.	*The Magic Flute* **was composed** by Mozart.
Shakespeare **wrote** *Romeo and Juliet*.	*Romeo and Juliet* **was written** by Shakespeare.

LANGUAGE NOTES

1. When the sentence has a strong performer (a specific person: Shakespeare, Mozart, etc.), we can use either the active or passive voice. The active voice puts more emphasis on the person who performs the action. The passive voice puts more emphasis on the action. In general, the active voice is more common than the passive voice.
2. We often use the passive voice when the performer *made, discovered, invented, built, wrote, painted,* or *composed* something. Using the passive voice emphasizes the result more than the performer.
    Spielberg *directed* the movie. (emphasis on Spielberg)
    The movie *was directed* by Spielberg. (emphasis on the movie)
3. We can use the passive voice to shift the emphasis to the object of the preceding sentence.
    Steven Spielberg **directed** *Star Wars*, didn't he?

    No. *Star Wars* **was directed** by George Lucas.
4. When the performer is included, use *by* + noun or object pronoun.
    Romeo and Juliet was written **by Shakespeare**.
    Hamlet was written **by him** too.

EXERCISE 3   Change these sentences from active to passive voice.

EXAMPLE: Alexander Graham Bell invented the telephone.
The telephone was invented by Alexander Graham Bell.

1. Mark Twain wrote *Tom Sawyer*.

   _____

2. He wrote *Huckleberry Finn* too.

   _____

---

3. Henry Mancini composed *Moon River*.

_____

4. Thomas Edison invented the light bulb.

_____

5. Leonardo Da Vinci painted *The Mona Lisa*.

_____

6. Ernest Hemingway wrote *The Old Man and the Sea*.

_____

7. The Wright brothers invented the airplane.

_____

8. Albert Einstein developed the theory of relativity.

_____

9. George Lucas directed *Star Wars*.

_____

10. Barbra Streisand sang *People*.

_____

11. George Gershwin composed *Porgy and Bess*.

_____

12. Anthony Hopkins played President Nixon in a 1995 movie.

_____

EXERCISE 4   Change these sentences from passive to active. Use the same tense.

EXAMPLE: Several Oscar presentations have been hosted by Billy Crystal.
Billy Crystal has hosted several Oscar presentations.

1. *E.T.* was made by Steven Spielberg.

_____

2. *Jurassic Park* was directed by him too.

_____

3. Shakespeare was played by Joseph Fiennes in a 1998 movie.

_____

4. Many novels have been written by Stephen King.

_____

5. Novels <u>are rewritten</u> by screenwriters to make them into movies.

6. Many great movies <u>have been made</u> by Steven Spielberg.

7. Spielberg <u>was given</u> an award by the Academy for *Schindler's List*.

8. The costumes <u>will be designed</u> by Calvin Klein.

9. The Oscar <u>was being presented</u> by Robin Williams.

10. A new movie <u>is being made</u> by Spielberg.

Before You Read
1. Do you like American movies? What kinds of movies do you like?
2. Do you think some movies shouldn't be seen by children? Explain your answer.

Read the following article. Pay special attention to sentences that contain the passive voice.

Movie Ratings

Movies in the U.S. **are rated** according to their appropriateness for different viewers. These ratings **can be found** in movie listings in newspapers or on the Internet. The following chart shows the abbreviations that **are used** and what they mean.

Rating	Meaning	Explanation
G	GENERAL AUDIENCES	All ages **are admitted**.
PG	PARENTAL GUIDANCE SUGGESTED	Some material may not be suitable for children.
PG-13	PARENTAL GUIDANCE OF CHILDREN UNDER 13	Some material may not be suitable for children under 13.
R	RESTRICTED	Children under 17 **will not be admitted** without a parent or adult guardian.
NC-17	NO CHILDREN UNDER 17	No one under 17 **will be admitted**.

Usually the rating **is posted** at the box office[1] of the movie theater. If you rent movies, the rating **can be found** on the box of the video and on the video itself.

2.5 Using Passive Voice without a Performer

Examples	The passive voice is used when:
Parental guidance **is suggested** for many movies. Children under 17 **will not be admitted** to a movie that is rated NC-17.	It is not important to mention who performed the action.
My purse **was stolen** while I was at the movies. It **was found** and **returned** to the manager.	We do not know who performed the action. NOTE: In conversation, we can use the active voice with *someone*: Someone **stole** my purse.
Children **are not allowed** to enter some movies. *Titanic* **was nominated** for 14 awards in 1997.	The performer of the action is obvious and doesn't need to be mentioned. In the first example, it is obvious that the theater manager doesn't allow children to enter. In the second example, it is obvious that the Academy nominated the movie.
The Academy presents awards. The awards **are** usually **presented** in March. A committee chooses the winners. The winners **are chosen** weeks before the ceremony. Parents should supervise their children. Children **shouldn't be allowed** to see some movies.	We shift the attention to the object of the preceding sentence.

(continued)

[1] The *box office* is where tickets are sold, usually just outside the theater.

Examples	The passive voice is used when:
American movies **are seen** in many countries. Videos **can be rented** at many stores. Movie listings **can be found** in the newspaper. Spanish **is spoken** in Mexico.	The performer is not a specific person. The action is done by people in general. NOTE: In conversation, the active voice is often used with the impersonal subjects *people, you, we,* or *they.* People *see* American movies in many countries. You *can rent* videos at many stores. We *can find* movie listings in the newspaper. They *speak* Spanish in Mexico.
I **was told** that you love movies.	We prefer not to mention the performer.
An award **is given** to the best actor. Subtitles **are used** in foreign movies.	We want to give the sentence an impersonal tone.

LANGUAGE NOTES

1. The passive voice is used more frequently without a performer than with a performer.
2. In signs, captions, or headlines, you will often see the verb *be* omitted from a passive construction.
   No one under 17 admitted
   Parental guidance suggested
   No parking allowed

EXERCISE 5   The following sentences would be better in passive voice because the performer is not important or not known. Change the sentences to passive voice, removing the performer.

EXAMPLE: People built Hollywood in the early 1900s.
Hollywood was built in the early 1900s.

1. They <u>make</u> many American movies in Hollywood.

   _____

2. They <u>suggest</u> parental guidance for many movies.

   _____

3. The popcorn is fresh. They are making it now.

   _____

4. They have colorized some old movies.

   _____

5. You can find movie ratings in the newspaper.

   _____

6. They don't allow children to see some movies.

   _____

7. You can rent most older movies at a video store.

   _____

8. They will announce the winners soon.

   _____

9. In 1927, they presented only 15 Oscars.

   _____

10. Who did they invite to the Oscar presentation?

    _____

11. People didn't see the Academy Awards on TV until 1952.

    _____

12. They are building a new theater near my house.

    _____

13. They filmed the movie in Canada.

    _____

14. They are filming a new movie now.

    _____

15. They have sold all the tickets.

    _____

16. You can find the video in the sci-fi[2] section of the video store.

    _____

17. I went to buy popcorn, and someone took my seat.

    _____

18. We call a videocassette recorder a "VCR."

    _____

19. People should return videos before midnight.

    _____

[2] *Sci-fi* means science fiction. Sci-fi movies show fantasies about the future.

20. You <u>can see</u> old movies on TV.

_____

21. They <u>chose</u> *Rain Man* as the best film of 1988.

_____

22. Every year they <u>give</u> awards for the best movies.

_____

23. They <u>televise</u> the Oscar ceremony each year.

_____

24. In a movie theater, they <u>show</u> coming attractions before the main movie begins.

_____

25. An accident happened while they <u>were filming</u> the movie.

_____

26. We <u>use</u> passive voice in technical writing.

_____

27. They <u>added</u> sound to movies in 1927.

_____

28. They <u>don't speak</u> English in Cuba.

_____

EXERCISE 6 Fill in the blanks with the passive voice of the verb in parentheses, using the tense given.

A. What kind of movies do you like?

B. I love sci-fi. My favorite movie of all time was *Star Wars*.

A. Steven Spielberg directed *Star Wars*, didn't he?

B. No. It ___*was directed*___ by George Lucas. He _____ for
    (past: *direct*)   (*1 present: know*)
    making movies with special effects.

A. That movie _____ in the 1970s. You were just a child at
              (*2 past: make*)
    that time.

B. I didn't see *Star Wars* when I was a child. I saw it about five

    years ago. *Star Wars* is so popular. It _____ in movie
                                            (*3 present perfect: show*)
    theaters many times.

A. Where _____?
(4 past: *it/film*)

B. In Hollywood. Most American movies _____ in Hollywood
(5 present: *make*)
But there were a lot of special effects. Those _____
(6 past: *probably/do*)
by computer.

A. How many *Star Wars* movies _____?
(7 present perfect: *make*)

B. Four, so far. The first one came out in 1977. When the last one
was released, tickets _____ out immediately. They're all terrific
(8 past: *sell*)
movies.

A. I saw the earlier ones, but I didn't see the last one. I _____
(9 past: *tell*)
it wasn't very good. It didn't get good reviews in the newspapers.

B. Don't believe everything you read. You should see it.

A. I suppose I can rent the video.

B. I think a movie like that _____ on a large screen, not on
(10 should/see)
a TV screen.

A. You know, I'm not much of a sci-fi fan. I prefer the old classic movies
that _____ in the 1940s.
(11 past: *make*)

B. I can't believe it! With all the high technology that _____
(12 present continuous: *use*)
in today's films, you prefer old movies that _____ in
(13 past: *film*)
black and white!

A. I'm old-fashioned, I guess.

EXERCISE **7** Finish these sentences using the passive voice of one of the
verbs from the box below. Choose an appropriate tense.

pay	order	give	repair
drive	tow	call	✓ hit

EXAMPLE: My brother's car _____*was hit*_____ by another car last week.

1. A police officer _____ to the scene of the accident.

2. Both drivers _____ tickets for not stopping at a stop sign.

3. My brother's car couldn't _____, so his car _____ to a repair shop after the accident.

4. My brother is borrowing my car until his car _____.

5. The mechanic doesn't have the parts he needs to fix the car. Parts _____ last week, but they still haven't come in.

6. Luckily my brother has good insurance. He won't have to pay very much. The repair shop _____ by the insurance company.

EXERCISE 8   The following sentences would be better in active voice because the performer is a specific person. Change these sentences to active voice. Use the same tense.

EXAMPLE: Lucy is loved by me.
   I love Lucy.
   _____

1. A video will be rented by my brother.
   _____

2. The video should be returned by him.
   _____

3. The winner was predicted by the reviewer.
   _____

4. The winner's name is being announced by Steven Spielberg.
   _____

5. The Oscar presentation was being watched by me when the phone rang.
   _____

6. The movie is being discussed by the viewers.
   _____

7. Good movies have been made by George Lucas.
   _____

8. Many beautiful dresses are designed by Calvin Klein.
   _____

---

9. An Academy Award <u>was won</u> by Dustin Hoffman.

_____

10. A black dress <u>wasn't worn</u> by the actress.

_____

11. <u>Was</u> the music <u>written</u> by Randy Newman?

_____

12. A good time <u>was had</u> by everyone at the Oscar presentations.

_____

13. Relatives <u>are usually thanked</u> by the winner.

_____

14. <u>Were</u> the tickets <u>bought</u> by your brother?

_____

15. The children <u>will be shown</u> a movie by the teacher.

_____

Before You Read 1. Have you ever heard of Ronald Reagan?
2. Have you ever seen Reagan in an old movie?

President Reagan

Reagan acting in *Knute Rockne,*
All American

Read the following article. Pay special attention to verbs. Some verbs are
active and some are passive.

The Actor President

The Academy Awards ceremony has been postponed only three times. The last time was in 1981, when there was an assassination attempt on U.S. President Ronald Reagan.

Ronald Reagan **was** the president of the U.S. from 1981 to 1989. Before he **became** president, he was governor of California. Even before that, he was a Hollywood actor. He **worked** as an actor in the 1930s and the 1940s.

On March 20, 1981, the day of the Oscar presentation, something terrible **happened**. Reagan's car **stopped**, and as he **was getting** out, he **was shot** in an assassination attempt. He **didn't die** from the gunshot wounds and soon **recovered**. However, one of his aides, Jim Brady, **was** badly **wounded**.

Brady **remained** paralyzed as a result of his wounds. Brady **worked** hard to change laws about guns in America. Because of his efforts, laws **were changed**, making it harder to buy a handgun.

2.6 Using Active Voice Only

Examples	Explanation
Reagan **lived** in California for many years. He **became** President in 1981. Something terrible **happened** on March 20, 1981. What **happened**? Reagan **recovered** from his wounds. He **didn't die** from his wounds.	Some verbs are not used with the passive voice. These are verbs that have no object. Verbs of this kind are: happen go fall become live sleep come look die seem work recover be remain These are called *intransitive* verbs.
My brother **changed** as he got older. Laws **were changed** as a result of the shooting. The leaves on the tree **moved** in the wind. The dead leaves **were moved** by the janitor.	The active voice is used with *change* and *move* when the action happens by itself, in a natural way. The passive voice is used with these verbs if someone causes the action to happen.

(continued)

Examples	Explanation
The car **stopped** at the corner. The car **was stopped** by the police. The store **opens** at 8 a.m. The store **is opened** by the manager. The movie **started** at 8:10. The movie **was started** by the projectionist.	The active voice is used with *start*, *stop*, *open*, and *close* even though the subject is not really the performer. The passive voice is used with these verbs if the performer is mentioned.

LANGUAGE NOTES

1. Even though *have* is followed by an object, it is not usually used in the passive voice.
    > He *has* a car. NOT: A car is had by him.
2. Notice that we say *was/were born*. (This is a passive construction.) However, *die* is always an active verb.
    > President Nixon *was born* in 1913. He *died* in 1994.
    > President Reagan *wasn't born* in California. He *didn't die* in the shooting.
3. *Leave* can be intransitive or transitive, depending on its meaning.
    > He *left* class early. (*Leave* means "go out." It's an intransitive verb.)
    > His books *were left* on the floor. (*Leave* means "not take." It's a transitive verb.)

EXERCISE 9 Which of the following sentences can be changed to passive voice? Change those sentences. If the sentences cannot be changed, write *No Change*.

EXAMPLES: The assassin <u>didn't kill</u> Reagan. _____*Reagan wasn't killed.*_____

When <u>did</u> this terrible event <u>happen</u>? _____*No change.*_____

1. In 1981, something terrible <u>happened</u>. _____

2. Someone <u>shot</u> Reagan. _____

3. Reagan <u>fell</u> when the assassin <u>shot</u> him. _____

4. Brady's experience in 1981 <u>changed</u> him. _____

5. Someone <u>stopped</u> the assassin before he could run away. _____

_____

6. Movie stars <u>live</u> in California. _____

7. We <u>had</u> fun at the movie. _____

8. Marilyn Monroe <u>died</u> in 1962. _____

9. The video store <u>opens</u> at 9 a.m. _____

10. It <u>closes</u> at 11 p.m. _____

11. I <u>slept</u> during the movie. _____

12. After hours, you <u>can return</u> videos through the slot. _____

_____

EXERCISE 10 Circle the correct words to complete this story.

I (*example: gave,* (*was given*)) a book of free movie passes for my birthday. I (*1 invited, was invited*) one of my friends to go with me. We (*2 went, were gone*) to a new movie theater downtown. We (*3 saw, were seen*) a movie that (*4 directed, was directed*) by Steven Spielberg. This was my first time in an American movie theater, and several things (*5 happened, were happened*) that were unusual for me.

First, I was surprised that people (*6 were eating, were eaten*) during the movie. Popcorn, candy, and soda (*7 sell, are sold*) in the theater lobby. I don't understand why people (*8 buy, are bought*) food to eat during the movie. Also, coming attractions (*9 show, are shown*) before the movie. During the coming attractions, a lot of people (*10 were talking, were being talked*). But as soon as the movie (*11 started, was started*), everyone (*12 became, was become*) quiet. Another unusual thing was that at the end of the movie, nobody (*13 applauded, was applauded*). While the credits³ (*14 were showing, were being shown*), people (*15 were leaving, were being left*). While I (*16 was reading, was being read*) the credits, people started to walk in front of me. It was also strange for me that popcorn boxes and candy wrappers (*17 left, were left*) on the floor of the theater.

I was also surprised that the movie theater was so small and narrow. I (*18 told, was told*) by my American friend that the theater was big at one

³ The *credits* means the list of people who made the movie.

---

time but that it (*19 divided, was divided*) into several small theaters so that several movies (*20 can show, can be shown*) at one time. Theaters (*21 make, are made*) more money that way.

Anyway, in spite of all these surprises, I (*22 enjoyed, was enjoyed*) the movie very much.

2.7 Passive with *Get*

Passive with *Be*	Passive with *Get*
Reagan **was shot** by John Hinckley.	Reagan **got shot** on the day of the Oscars.
Brady **was injured** by a bullet.	Brady **got injured** when he was with the President.
I **was laid** off by my company.	I **got laid** off because production was slow.

LANGUAGE NOTES

1. In conversation, we sometimes use *get* instead of *be* with the passive. We usually omit the performer after *get*.
2. *Get* is frequently used with: *killed, injured, wounded, paid, hired, fired, laid off*.

EXERCISE 11 Fill in the blanks with *get* + past participle of the verb in parentheses.

EXAMPLE: Who _____*got chosen*_____ for the part in the movie?
                         (*choose*)

1. Reagan _____ in 1980.
           (*elect*)

2. President Carter _____ in 1980.
                     (*not/reelect*)

3. Reagan _____ on the day of the Oscars.
           (*shoot*)

4. Brady _____.
          (*wound*)

5. No one _____.
           (*kill*)

6. Did you _____ for the job?
            (*hire*)

7. How often do you _____?
                     (*pay*)

8. His car _____ last night from in front of his house.
            (*steal*)

9. The little boy told a lie, and he _____.
                                      (*punish*)

10. We have so much to do, but I'm not worried. Everything will
_____ little by little.
   (do)

11. The results of the exam _____ to the wrong person by
   (send)
mistake.

12. When I went to the lobby to buy popcorn, my seat _____.
   (take)

13. One student _____ cheating on the exam.
   (catch)

14. If you leave your car in a no-parking zone, it might _____.
   (tow)

2.8 Participles Used as Adjectives

A present participle is verb + *-ing*. A past participle is the third form of
the verb (usually *-ed* or *-en*). Both present participles and past participles
can be used as adjectives.

Present Participles	Past Participles
We saw an **entertaining** movie. *Star Wars* is an **exciting** movie. *Star Wars* has **amazing** visual effects.	The winners' names are placed in **sealed** envelopes. I wasn't **bored** during the movie. Are you **interested** in sci-fi movies?

Before You Read
1. Have you ever heard of Charlie Chaplin?
2. Have you ever seen a silent movie? Do you think a silent movie can be interesting today?

Read the following article. Pay special attention to participles used as adjectives.

Charlie Chaplin

Charlie Chaplin was one of the greatest actors in the world. His **entertaining** silent movies are still popular today. His **charming** character "Little Tramp" is well **known** to people throughout the world. His idea for this poor character in **worn**-out shoes, round hat, and cane probably came from his childhood experiences.

Born in poverty in London in 1889, Chaplin was abandoned by his father and left in an orphanage by his mother. He became **interested** in acting at the age of five. At ten, he left school to travel with a British acting company. In 1910, he made his first trip to America. He was talented, athletic, and hard-**working**, and by 1916 he was earning $10,000 a week. He was the highest-**paid** person in the world at that time. He produced, directed, and wrote the movies he starred in.

Even though "talkies" came out in 1927, he didn't make a movie with sound until 1940, when he played a comic version of the **terrifying** dictator, Adolph Hitler.

As Chaplin got older, he faced **declining** popularity as a result of his politics and personal relationships. After he left the U.S. in 1952, Chaplin was not allowed to re-enter because of his political views. He didn't return to the U.S. until 1972, when he was given a special Oscar for his lifetime of **outstanding** work.

Did you know...?

Ronald Reagan did not want Chaplin to be allowed back into the U.S.

2.9 Participles Used as Adjectives to Show Feelings

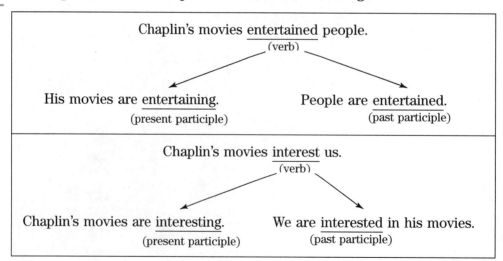

Chaplin's movies <u>entertained</u> people.
(verb)

His movies are <u>entertaining</u>.
(present participle)

People are <u>entertained</u>.
(past participle)

Chaplin's movies <u>interest</u> us.
(verb)

Chaplin's movies are <u>interesting</u>.
(present participle)

We are <u>interested</u> in his movies.
(past participle)

LANGUAGE NOTES

1. In some cases, both the present participle and the past participle of the same verb can be used as adjectives. Common paired participles are:

amazing	amazed	exhausting	exhausted
amusing	amused	frightening	frightened
annoying	annoyed	frustrating	frustrated
boring	bored	interesting	interested
convincing	convinced	puzzling	puzzled
disappointing	disappointed	satisfying	satisfied
embarrassing	embarrassed	surprising	surprised
exciting	excited	terrifying	terrified
		tiring	tired

2. A present participle shows the cause of a feeling.
    > The movie bored me. → The movie was *boring*.
    >
    > → I left the *boring* movie before it was over.

    The movie *actively* caused the feeling of boredom.

3. A past participle describes the receiver of a feeling.
    > The movie bored the audience. → Some people were *bored*.
    >
    > The *bored* people got up and left.

    The audience *passively* received the feeling of boredom.

4. A person can cause a feeling in others, or he can receive a feeling. Therefore, a person can be both *interesting* and *interested*, *frightening* and *frightened*.
    > Chaplin had an *interesting* life. He was poor and then became very rich.
    >
    > I am *interested* in Chaplin. I would like to know more about him.

5. An object (like a book or a movie) doesn't have feelings, so a past participle cannot be used to describe an object.
    > The book is interesting. (never *interested*)
    >
    > The movie is entertaining. (never *entertained*)

6. The following pictures show the difference between a *frightening* man and a *frightened* man.

A. The man is frightening the children. = He's a *frightening man*.

B. The man is frightened by the robber. = He's a *frightened man*.

EXERCISE 12 Use the verb in each sentence to make two new sentences. In one sentence, use the present participle. In the other, use the past participle.

EXAMPLE:
The game entertains the children.
1. The game is entertaining.
2. The children are entertained.

1. The movie frightened the children.

2. The book interests the children.

3. The children are amusing the adults.

4. The trip tired the children.

5. The game excited the children.

6. The vacation exhausted the adults.

7. The movie bored the adults.

8. Chaplin interests me.

EXERCISE 13 Fill in the blanks with the correct participle (present or past) of the verb in parentheses.

EXAMPLE:
I was _____*bored*_____ during the lecture and fell asleep.
(bore)

1. After walking for two hours, I felt _____ and had to rest.
(tire)

2. Last night I saw an _____ movie. I enjoyed it a lot.
(interest)

3. He felt _____ when he misunderstood his boss.
(embarrass)

4. I didn't enjoy watching *Psycho*. It was a _____ movie. I

felt _____ for the rest of the week.
(frighten)

5. I have some _____ neighbors. They always make a lot of
(annoy)
noise when I'm trying to sleep.

6. My cousin was _____ when he came to the U.S. and saw
(surprise)
so many poor people.

7. Learning a new language is sometimes very _____ .
(frustrate)

8. I was _____ when I didn't get the job.
   (disappoint)

9. When we saw a Charlie Chaplin movie for the first time, we were

   _____ .
   (amuse)

10. We had a _____ afternoon. We went to the beach.
    (relax)

11. We took the children to the circus. The circus was _____
    (excite)

    for them.

12. The children were _____ to see the elephants at the circus.
    (excite)

2.10 Other Past Participles Used as Adjectives

Examples	Explanation
The door is locked by the janitor every day. The door is **locked**.	*Be* + past participle as an adjective looks just like the passive form. However, as an adjective, the past participle shows no action. It is the result of a previous action.
No one knows the winner's name because the envelope is **sealed**.	Previous action: Someone *sealed* the envelope.
Is this seat **taken**?	Previous action: Someone *took* the seat.
Chaplin was **born** in England.	Previous action: His mother *bore* a child.
Many people are **involved** in making a movie. Hollywood is **located** in California. Is Geraldine Chaplin **related** to Charlie Chaplin?	In some cases, there is no previous action.

LANGUAGE NOTES

1. Past participles, when used as adjectives, can be found in phrases such as these:

an air-conditioned room	a known fact
a broken dish	a broken promise
a devoted wife	a locked door
a closed door	a married woman
a crowded bus	an educated person
a deserted building	a spoiled child
a divorced man	a used car
an injured soldier	a sealed envelope
a wounded soldier	

2. The following are some common combinations of *be* + past participle. The past participle is used as an adjective.

be accustomed (to)	be educated	be made (of, in)
be allowed (to)	be filled (with)	be married
be born	be finished	be permitted (to)
be closed	be gone	be pleased
be concerned	be insured	be prepared
(about)	be interested (in)	be related (to)
be crowded	be involved (in)	be taken
be divorced	be located	be used to
be done	be locked	be worried (about)
be dressed	be lost	

3. An adverb can be placed before past participle adjectives:
   a well known actor
   a well educated person
   a well behaved child
   a well dressed woman
   a well fed dog
   a highly paid performer
   a closely watched experiment
   a slightly used book
   closely related languages

EXERCISE 14 Underline the past participle in the following sentences.

EXAMPLE: Movie theaters are <u>crowded</u> on Saturday night.

1. The movie theater is closed in the morning.

2. Where is the movie theater located?

3. Charlie Chaplin got married several times.

4. Children are not allowed to see some movies.

5. Many movies are made in Hollywood.

6. How many people were involved in making *Star Wars*?

7. Chaplin was a well paid actor.

8. Chaplin was born in England.

9. He was well known all over the world.

10. Ronald Reagan was involved in movies before he became a politician.

EXERCISE 15 Fill in the blanks and discuss your answers.

EXAMPLE: I'm interested in _____*sports*_____.

1. _____ is a well known actor.

2. I'm interested in _____ movies.

3. The _____ is always crowded.

4. Now I'm worried about _____.

5. In the past, I was worried about _____.

6. In my opinion, _____ is an amazing
   (*choose one*) actor/athlete/politician.

7. _____ is a very talented musician.

8. Married people _____ than single people.

9. Children shouldn't be allowed to _____.

10. This college is located _____.

EXERCISE 16 Fill in the blanks with an appropriate past participle.

EXAMPLE: We can't get into the library because the door is _____*locked*_____.

1. Last night I slept only four hours. I'm so _____ today.

2. Charlie Chaplin wasn't _____ in the U.S. He came here when
   he was 21 years old.

3. My apartment isn't _____, so it's hot in the summer.

4. The Statue of Liberty is _____ in New York.

5. I have two sisters. One is single. The other is _____.

---

6. Children are not _____ to see R-rated movies without a parent.

7. It is a well _____ fact that women live longer than men.

8. When the chicken is _____, please turn off the oven.

9. I'm in a new city, and I don't have a map. I'm _____ and need to ask for directions.

10. Is the Oscar _____ of gold?

2.11 Past Participles and Other Adjectives with *Get*[4]

Examples	Explanation
My brother **is married** to a wonderful woman. He **got married** in 1992. The child **is lost**. He **got lost** when he left his mother's side. **I'm dressed** and ready to go to work. I **got dressed** after breakfast.	*Be* + past participle is a description of the noun. The noun has this description over a period of time. *Get* + past participle shows a change in a situation.
It's dark outside. It **gets dark** early in winter months. Chaplin **was rich**. He **got rich** in the movie business.	*Get* can be used with some adjectives to show a change. *Get* means *become*.

LANGUAGE NOTES

1. Past participles used with *get* are:

get accustomed to	get dressed	get scared
get acquainted	get engaged	get tired
get bored	get hurt	get used to
get confused	get lost	get worried
get divorced	get married	

2. Adjectives used with *get* are:

| get angry | get hungry | get old | get sleepy | get well |
| get dark | get fat | get nervous | get rich | get upset |

[4] For a list of expressions with *get*, see Appendix C.

EXERCISE 17 Fill in the blanks with *get* or *be* + adjective or past participle of the verb in parentheses. Choose an appropriate tense.

EXAMPLES: I ___*am worried*___ about my grades.
            (worry)

            She ___*got worried*___ when she realized that her son wasn't in his room.
            (worry)

1. I _____. I don't understand this lesson at all.
   (confuse)

2. I understood the explanation about the passive voice, but I _____
   _____ when the teacher started to explain the difference
   (confuse)
   between *interested* and *interesting*.

3. She _____ five years ago.
   (marry)

4. I have two sisters. One sister is single; the other one _____
   (marry)
   and has two children.

5. How's your mother? She _____, thank you.
   (well)

6. I heard your brother is sick. I hope he _____ soon.
   (well)

7. When she broke her favorite vase, she _____ and started
   (upset)
   to cry.

8. He _____ because he hasn't been able to find a job.
   (upset)

9. My grandmother is 90. She _____.
   (old)

10. No one wants to _____. Everyone wants to stay young
    (old)
    forever.

11. Bill Gates _____ and famous.
    (rich)

12. My aunt _____ when the stocks she bought tripled in value.
    (rich)

Part 1—Passive Voice

Passive Voice	Use
Romeo and Juliet **was written** by Shakespeare. *Star Wars* **was directed** by George Lucas.	With a Performer • To emphasize the receiver of the action
Shakespeare wrote *Romeo and Juliet*. *Romeo and Juliet* **was written** in the sixteenth century. *Romeo and Juliet* **was made** into a movie in 1968. Movies **can be rented** at a local video store. Children **are** not **allowed** to see some movies. Hollywood **was built** in the beginning of the twentieth century. I **was told** that you didn't like the movie.	Without a Performer • To shift the attention from the performer to the receiver • When it is not important to mention who performed the action • When the performer is obvious • When the performer is not a specific person. It is people in general. • When we want to give the sentence an impersonal tone • To hide the identity of the performer
Reagan **got shot** in 1981. I **got fired** from my job.	• With *get*, in certain conversational expressions

Part 2—Participles Used as Adjectives

Examples	Explanation
Silent movies are very **interesting**. We are **interested** in the life of Charlie Chaplin.	Use the present participle to show that the noun produced a feeling. Use the past participle to show that the noun received a feeling.
I'm tired of your **broken** promises. Is this seat **taken**?	Use the past participle to show that someone did something to the noun: Someone *broke* the promise. Someone *took* the seat.
She **got confused** when the teacher explained participles. I **got lost** on my way to your house. She **got upset** when she couldn't find her keys.	Use *get* with past participles and other adjectives to mean *become*.

Part 1—Passive Voice

1. Use *be*, not *do/does/did* to make negatives and questions with the passive voice.

   My watch ~~didn't~~ *wasn't* made in Japan.

   When ~~did~~ *was* the movie filmed?

2. Don't use the passive voice with intransitive verbs.

   The accident ~~was~~ happened at 10:30 p.m.

   Her grandfather ~~was~~ died three years ago.

3. Don't confuse the *-ing* form and the past participle.

   The candy was ~~eating~~ *eaten* by the child.

4. Don't forget the *-ed* ending for a regular past participle.

   The floor was wash*ed* by the janitor.

5. Don't forget to use a form of *be* in a passive sentence.

   The movie *was* seen by everyone in my family.

6. Use an object pronoun after *by*.

   My mother prepared the soup. The salad was prepared by ~~she~~ *her* too.

Part 2—Participles and Other Adjectives

1. Don't forget the *-ed* ending for past participles used as adjectives.

   I'm very tire*d* now. I have to go to sleep.

   When did you get marr*ied*?

2. Don't forget to include a verb (usually *be*) before a participle used as an adjective.

   My college *is* located on the corner of Broadway and Wilson Avenues.

3. Participles used as adjectives are used with *be*, not *do*.

$\overset{isn't}{\text{The drugstore }\cancel{\text{doesn't}}\text{ located near my house.}}$

$\overset{Are}{\cancel{\text{Do}}\text{ you bored in your math class?}}$

LESSON 2 TEST / REVIEW

PART 1　　　Find the mistakes with the underlined words, and correct them. Not every sentence has a mistake. If the sentence is correct, write **C**.

EXAMPLES:　The movie $\overset{was}{\underline{\text{filmed}}}$ in Mexico last year.

A good movie <u>is being shown</u> this week in a theater near my house.　　**C**

1. The composition <u>didn't written</u> by Jim. It was written by his brother.

2. The criminal <u>was taking</u> to the police station.

3. A dictionary <u>found</u> on the floor of the classroom.

4. The janitor <u>found</u> a dictionary on the floor of the classroom.

5. Where <u>was</u> the accident <u>happened</u>?

6. Where <u>was</u> the movie <u>filmed</u>?

7. I <u>wasn't given</u> any information about the final exam.

8. The answers <u>can find</u> in the back of the book.

9. Steven Spielberg <u>has made</u> many movies.

10. A new theater <u>is being built</u> this year.

11. When <u>did</u> *Gone with the Wind* <u>made</u>?

12. Reagan <u>was elected</u> President in 1980.

13. He <u>got shot</u> in 1981.

14. Reagan <u>didn't killed</u>.

15. The Oscar ceremony <u>was postponed</u> in 1981.

16. Before the 1950s, movies <u>were usually filmed</u> in black and white.

17. Reagan <u>acted</u> in many movies before he <u>was become</u> a politician.

18. *E.T.* <u>was directed</u> by Spielberg. *Star Wars* wasn't directed by <u>he</u>.

PART 2 Change from active to passive. Do not mention the performer. Use the same tense as the underlined verb.

EXAMPLE: People <u>will see</u> the movie on cable TV.

The movie will be seen on cable TV.

1. They <u>gave</u> Whoopi Goldberg an Oscar for her performance in *Ghost*.

_____

2. Which actor <u>will</u> they <u>choose</u> next year?

_____

3. People <u>have seen</u> Julia Roberts in many movies.

_____

4. You <u>should see</u> *Star Wars* on a big screen.

_____

5. You <u>can find</u> *Star Wars* in the sci-fi section of the video store.

_____

6. They <u>didn't film</u> *Gone With The Wind* in black and white.

_____

7. They <u>are filming</u> a new movie in New York.

_____

8. They <u>don't permit</u> children under 17 to see some movies.

_____

9. Everybody <u>knows</u> John Travolta for his performance in *Saturday Night Fever*.

_____

10. When <u>did</u> they <u>make</u> *Saturday Night Fever*?

_____

PART 3   Change from passive to active. Use the same tense.

EXAMPLE: Movies <u>can be rented</u> by them.
            They can rent movies.

1. *Star Wars* <u>was not seen</u> by me.

   _____

2. The movie <u>is being directed</u> by George Lucas.

   _____

3. She <u>has been taken</u> to the movie by him.

   _____

4. Some movies <u>shouldn't be seen</u> by children.

   _____

5. An Oscar <u>was won</u> by Jodie Foster.

   _____

6. Tootsie <u>was played</u> by Dustin Hoffman.

   _____

7. A movie <u>was being watched</u> by the audience.

   _____

8. When <u>was</u> *Star Wars* <u>made</u> by George Lucas?

   _____

9. Popcorn <u>will be bought</u> by us.

   _____

10. Popcorn <u>isn't eaten</u> by her during a movie.

    _____

PART 4   Fill in the blanks with the passive or active of the verb in
          parentheses. Use an appropriate tense.

EXAMPLE: The teacher ___*usually gives*___ homework in each class.
                        (usually/give)

1. A lot of corrections _____ on my last composition.
                              (make)

2. The compositions _____ at the end of each day.
                          (collect)

3. The teacher _____ the homework during the class.
     (always/return)

4. The students _____ their answers in the book.
     (usually/write)

5. Your name should _____ at the top of the page.
     (write)

6. The students _____ to use their textbook during an exam.
     (not/permit)

7. The teacher _____ the students during a test.
     (always/watch)

8. The test will _____ tomorrow.
     (return)

9. The student should _____ before a test.
     (study)

10. English _____ in this class.
     (always/speak)

11. Our native languages _____ in this class.
     (not/usually/use)

12. Your grade will _____ to your house by mail.
     (send)

PART 5   Find the mistakes with the underlined words, and correct them. Not every sentence has a mistake. If the sentence is correct, write **C**.

EXAMPLES: Are you worr*ied* about your children?

When did they get divorced?   C

1. You look like you don't understand the lesson. Are you confuse?

2. I very tired now. I just want to go to sleep.

3. I come from Miami. I'm not accustomed to cold weather.

4. Last week we saw a very boring movie.

5. My cousin was excited about coming to the U.S.

6. Do you have an interesting job?

7. I was surprised to find out that you are marry.

8. When did you get married?

9. I'm not satisfy with my grade in this course.

10. The teacher's office located on the second floor.

11. The library doesn't crowded at 8 a.m.

12. Do you disappointed with your grade?

PART 6   Fill in the blanks with the present participle or the past participle of the verb in parentheses.

EXAMPLES: The movie wasn't very good. In fact, it was _____boring_____.
(bore)

I had a great meal. I feel very _____satisfied._____
(satisfy)

1. We read an _____ story about Charlie Chaplin.
(interest)

2. He became _____ in acting when he was a child.
(interest)

3. He was well _____ all over the world.
(know)

4. When he left the U.S. in 1952, he was not _____ to re-enter.
(allow)

5. Chaplin was _____ four times.
(marry)

6. He was an _____ actor.
(entertain)

7. I am never _____ during one of his movies.
(bore)

8. There's an _____ new movie at the Fine Arts Theater.
(excite)

9. Are you _____ in seeing it with me?
(interest)

10. The movie theater will be _____ on Saturday night.
(crowd)

11. I was _____ when I saw *Psycho*.
(frighten)

12. It was a very _____ movie.
(frighten)

13. I didn't like the movie I saw last week. I was very _____ in it.
(disappoint)

14. My friend liked the movie. He thought it was a very _____ movie.
(excite)

EXPANSION ACTIVITIES

CLASSROOM ACTIVITIES   1.   Form a group of about five students. Match the event on the left with the name on the right. The answers can be found on page 113.

a) The *Mona Lisa* was painted by   Alexander Fleming

b) Penicillin was discovered by   William Shakespeare

c) Mexico was conquered by   Steven Spielberg

d) DNA was discovered by   Hernán Cortéz

e) Cars were mass-produced by   Mark Twain

f) *MacBeth* was written by   Abraham Lincoln

g) *I Want to Hold Your Hand* was sung by Leonardo Da Vinci

h) The slaves in the U.S. were freed by The Beatles

i) *Bolero* was composed by   Crick and Watson

j) *Guernica* was painted by   Henry Ford

k) *Saving Private Ryan* was directed by Maurice Ravel

l) *Tom Sawyer* was written by   Pablo Picasso

Answers:

l) Mark Twain	f) William Shakespeare
k) Steven Spielberg	e) Henry Ford
j) Pablo Picasso	d) Crick and Watson
i) Maurice Ravel	c) Hernán Cortéz
h) Abraham Lincoln	b) Alexander Fleming
g) The Beatles	a) Leonardo Da Vinci

2. Form a group of about five students. Circle the correct date for each event. Discuss your choices with your group. The answers can be found below.

a) The Golden Gate bridge was built in	1705	1865	1937
b) *Romeo and Juliet* was written in	1261	1403	1594
c) The *Mona Lisa* was painted in	1503	1603	1703
d) The Statue of Liberty was sent to the U.S. from France in	1826	1886	1925
e) The Panama Canal was built in	1812	1914	1948
f) America was discovered in	1281	1345	1492
g) The Taj Mahal was built in	1362	1638	1825
h) Sound was added to movies in	1917	1927	1947

Answers:

h) 1927	g) 1638	f) 1492	e) 1914
d) 1886	c) 1503	b) 1594	a) 1937

3. In a small group of people from your native country (if possible), give your opinions about the best actors and actresses in the U.S. and in your native country.

4. Fill in the blanks. Then find a partner. Discuss your answers with your partner.

a. _____ is an interesting place in this city.

b. _____ is an interesting actress.

c. _____ is a boring topic in our grammar class.

d. A surprising fact about the U.S. is _____

e. _____ is a relaxing activity.

f. I feel relaxed when _____

g. I get bored when I _____

h. I get angry when _____

i. You know you're getting old when _____

j. I get confused when _____

k. People in my native county who _____ can get rich.

l. One of the main reasons people get divorced is _____

DISCUSSION

1. Is it important to give awards to actors and actresses? Why or why not?

2. Have you ever seen an Academy Awards ceremony? What do you think of it?

3. Are movie ratings helpful? Why or why not?

4. How are U.S. films different from films made in other countries?

5. What are some of your favorite movies? What movies have you seen lately?

6. What American movies have been popular in your native country?

WRITING

Write about an entertainment event that you have recently attended (such as a movie in a theater, a concert, an art fair, a museum exhibit). Did you enjoy it? Why or why not? Was there anything surprising or unusual about it?

OUTSIDE ACTIVITIES

1. Look for signs, headlines, and captions that use passive constructions. (Remember, sometimes the verb *be* is omitted in a sign.) Copy the passive sentences and bring them to class.

2. Rent and watch a Charlie Chaplin movie.

Internet Activities

1. Find information about an actor or actress that interests you. Print out this information and bring it to class.

2. Find out who won the Oscars last year in these categories: Best Actor, Best Actress, Best Picture, Best Director.

3. Check to see if your local newspaper has a Web site. If it does, are there movie listings?

4. At a search engine, type in "movies." Find out what movies are playing in a theater near your house. Write down the ratings of three movies. Bring this information to class.

5. Choose two of these famous actors. Find out when they were born and when they died.

Humphrey Bogart	Spencer Tracy	John Wayne
Marilyn Monroe	Henry Fonda	Gary Cooper
Clark Gable	Vivien Leigh	Audrey Hepburn
Cary Grant	Grace Kelly	Mary Pickford

GRAMMAR

The Past Perfect Tense
The Past Perfect Continuous
The Past Continuous
Comparison of Past Tenses

CONTEXT

The Titanic
Survivors of the Titanic

LESSON FOCUS

The past perfect tense is formed with *had* + past participle.

> He *had traveled* by ship before.
> The winter *had been* very mild.

The past perfect continuous is formed with *had* + *been* + verb *-ing*

> The ship *had been traveling* for four days.
> The passengers *had been enjoying* themselves.

The past continuous is formed with *was/were* + verb *-ing*.

> I *was sleeping* when I heard a loud noise.

In this lesson, we will compare all past tenses.

1. Have you ever traveled by ship? Where did you go? What was the trip like?
2. Did you see the 1997 movie *Titanic*? If so, did you enjoy it? Why or why not?

Read the following article. Pay special attention to the past perfect tense.

The Titanic

The year was 1912. The radio **had** already **been invented** in 1901. The Wright Brothers **had** already **made** their first successful flight in 1903. The Titanic—the ship of dreams—**had** just **been built** and was ready to make its first voyage from England to America with its 2,200 passengers.

The Titanic was the most magnificent ship that **had** ever **been built**. It had luxuries that ships **had** never **had** before: electric light and heat, electric elevators, a swimming pool, a Turkish bath, libraries, and much more. It was built to give its first-class passengers all the comforts of the best hotels.

But rich passengers were not the only ones traveling on the Titanic. The passengers in third class were emigrants who **had left** behind a complete way of life and were coming to America with hopes of a better life.

The Titanic began to cross the Atlantic Ocean on April 10. The winter of 1912 **had been** unusually mild, and large blocks of ice **had broken** away from the Arctic region. By the fifth day at sea, the captain **had received** several warnings about ice, but he was not very worried; he didn't realize how much danger the ship was in. On April 14, at 11:40 p.m., an iceberg was spotted[1] straight ahead. The captain tried to reverse the direction of his ship, but he couldn't because the Titanic was traveling too fast and it was too big. It hit the iceberg and started to sink.

The Titanic **had** originally **had** 32 lifeboats, but 12 of them **had been removed** to make the ship look better. While the ship was sinking, rich people were put on lifeboats. Women and children were put on the lifeboats before men. By the time the third-class passengers were allowed to come up from their cabins, most of the lifeboats **had** already **left**.

Several hours later, another ship arrived to help, but the Titanic **had** already **gone** down. Only one third of the passengers survived.

Did you know...?

Only four of the first-class female passengers died. (These women chose to stay with their husbands.) Almost half of the third-class female passengers died.

[1] *To spot* means *to see suddenly.*

3.1 The Past Perfect—Form

Subject	*Had/Hadn't*	Adverb	Past Participle	Complement
The captain	**had**		**received**	several warnings.
He	**hadn't**		**paid**	attention to the warnings.
Passengers	**had**	never	**enjoyed**	so much luxury.
The Titanic	**had**	originally	**had**	32 lifeboats.
It	**had**	already	**gone** down	when help came.

Passive Voice with Past Perfect

Subject	*Had/Hadn't*	Adverb	*Been*	Past Participle	Complement
The radio	**had**	already	**been**	**invented**	in 1912.
The Titanic	**had**	just	**been**	**built**	in 1912.
Twelve lifeboats	**had**		**been**	**removed.**	
Poor men	**hadn't**		**been**	**put**	on lifeboats.

LANGUAGE NOTES

1. Subject pronouns (except *it*) can be contracted with *had: I'd, you'd, he'd, she'd, we'd, they'd.*
    He'd made a mistake.

2. Apostrophe + **d** can be a contraction for both *had* or *would*. The word following the contraction will tell you what the contraction means.
    He'd spoken. = He *had* spoken.
    He'd speak. = He *would* speak.

3. The contraction for *had not* is *hadn't*.

4. Compare statement and question word order.
    STATEMENT: The ship *had gone* down.
    YES/NO QUESTION: *Had* the ship *gone* down quickly?
    WH- QUESTION: When *had* the ship *gone* down?

Fill in the blanks with the past perfect of the verb in parentheses.

EXAMPLE: The Titanic had luxuries that ships _____*had never had*_____ before.
$\qquad\qquad\qquad\qquad\qquad\qquad\qquad\qquad\quad$ *(never/have)*

1. Poor emigrants on the ship _____ behind a way of life.
   $\qquad\qquad\qquad\qquad\quad$ *(leave)*

2. By 1912, the Wright brothers _____ a successful flight.
   $\qquad\qquad\qquad\qquad\qquad\qquad\quad$ *(already/make)*

3. The Titanic _____ 32 lifeboats.
   $\qquad\qquad\qquad\quad$ *(originally/have)*

4. The captain of the Titanic didn't pay attention to the warnings he

   _____ .
   (receive)

5. The winter before April, 1912, _____ unusually mild.
   $\qquad\qquad\qquad\qquad\qquad\qquad\quad$ *(be)*

6. Pieces of ice _____ away from the Arctic region.
   $\qquad\qquad\qquad\quad$ *(break)*

7. Passengers heard a noise but didn't understand what _____

   _____ .
   (happen)

8. For many years, people searched for the Titanic. By 1985, the wreck

   of the Titanic _____ .
   $\qquad\qquad\qquad\qquad\quad$ *(passive: find)*

9. By 1912, the radio _____ .
   $\qquad\qquad\qquad\quad$ *(passive: already/invent)*

10. In 1912, the Titanic was the biggest ship that _____

   _____ .
   (passive: ever/build)

3.2 The Past Perfect—Use

The past perfect is used to show the relationship of one past event to a later past event or time.

```
                                          now
                                           |
past ←--------------------------------------|--------------------------------→ future
                    ↑                      |
          The Titanic went down.     ↑     |
                         A rescue ship arrived.
```

Examples	Uses of the Past Perfect
By the time the rescue ship arrived, the Titanic **had** already **gone** down. By 1912, the Wright brothers **had** already **invented** the airplane. In 1912, the Titanic **had** just **been built**.	To show that something happened before a specific date, time, or event
When people got on the lifeboats, the rescue ship **hadn't** arrived **yet**. When the rescue ship arrived, many passengers **had** already **died**.	To show that something happened or didn't happen before the verb in the *when* clause
There was a lot of ice in the water because the previous winter **had been** unusually mild.	After *because*, to show a prior reason
Many passengers didn't realize that the ship **had hit** an iceberg.	In a noun clause,[2] when the main verb is past
The passengers in third class were emigrants who **had left** behind their old way of life. The Titanic was the most magnificent ship that **had** ever **been built**.	In a *who/that/which* clause, to show a prior action We sometimes use the past perfect with a superlative form.
Many emigrants on the Titanic **had** never **left** their homelands before.	With *never . . . before*, in relation to a past time (in this case, 1912)
The ship **had been** at sea for five days when it hit an iceberg.	With *for*, to show the duration of an earlier past action

LANGUAGE NOTES

1. *Yet, already, just, for* + time period, and *never . . . before* are often used with the past perfect to help show the time relationship of one past time or event to another.

[2] For more about noun clauses, see Lesson 9.

2. The past perfect can be used with *before* and *after*, but it is not necessary because the time relationship is clear.

   Before the Titanic hit the iceberg, the captain *tried* to turn the ship around.

   OR

   Before the Titanic hit the iceberg, the captain *had tried* to turn the ship around.

3. Either the past perfect or the simple past can be used with *because* when the cause and result are close in time. However, if the cause and result are not close in time, usually the past perfect is used for the cause.

   I couldn't call you because I *(had) lost* your phone number.
   There were not enough lifeboats because several *had been removed*.

EXERCISE 2   Fill in the blanks with the past perfect of the verb in parentheses.

EXAMPLE: I couldn't sleep last night because I _____*had drunk*_____ four cups of coffee.
(drink)

1. She understood how to fix the computer problem yesterday because

   she _____ the same problem before.
   (have)

2. I failed the test because I _____ absent for three weeks.
   (be)

3. He couldn't use his credit card because it _____ a long
   (expire)

   time ago.

4. My cousin didn't have to study English when he started college be-

   cause he _____ it as a child.
   (learn)

5. She was nervous when she gave a speech because she _____

   _____ in front of a group of people before.
   (never/speak)

6. Everyone was surprised when you failed the test because you

   _____ good grades before.
   (always/have)

7. The story of the Titanic was not new to me because I _____
   (see)

   the movie.

8. I didn't recognize her because she _____ her hair.
   (cut)

Start with the year 1912. Tell if something had already happened by this year or hadn't yet happened.

EXAMPLE: World War I began in 1914.
           In 1912, World War I had not yet begun.

_____

1.   The Wright brothers flew the first airplane in 1903.

     _____

2.   Henry Ford mass-produced cars in 1913.

     _____

3.   Radio was invented in 1901.

     _____

4.   President McKinley was assassinated in 1901.

     _____

5.   The U.S. declared war on Germany in 1917.

     _____

6.   San Francisco was destroyed by an earthquake in 1906.

     _____

7.   The U.S. government started to collect income tax in 1913.

     _____

EXERCISE **4**   The sentences below tell you which action happened first. Connect these sentences with *by the time* and *already*.

EXAMPLE: First: My wife and children ate dinner.
           Second: I came home.
           By the time I came home, my wife and children had already

           eaten dinner.
           _____

           First: He finished all his reports.
           Second: He left work.

1.   _____

           First: Her husband saw the movie.
           Second: She saw the movie.

2.   _____

_____

The Past Perfect Tense; The Past Perfect Continuous; The Past Continuous   **123**

First: He fell asleep on the sofa.
Second: The late movie was over.

3. _____

First: My parents knew each other for ten years.
Second: My parents got married.

4. _____

First: The building burned down.
Second: The fire department arrived.

5. _____

First: I studied English in high school.
Second: I started college.

6. _____

First: I saw the movie *Titanic*.
Second: I read about the Titanic in my grammar book.

7. _____

First: He found a job.
Second: He graduated from college.

8. _____

EXERCISE 5   Tell if the following had already happened or hadn't happened yet by the time you got to class.

EXAMPLE: the teacher/collect the homework
By the time I got to class, the teacher had already collected the homework.
OR
When I got to class, the teacher hadn't collected the homework yet.

1. the teacher/arrive

2. most of the students/arrive

3. the class/begin

4. the teacher/take attendance

5. I/do the homework

6. the teacher/hand back the last homework

7. the teacher/explain the past perfect

EXERCISE 6   Tell if the following had already happened or hadn't happened yet when you came to this school.

EXAMPLE: study English
When I came to this school, I had already studied English.
OR
When I came to this school, I hadn't studied English yet.

1. buy an English dictionary
2. finish high school
3. know a lot about this school
4. get a college degree
5. study basic English
6. turn 18 years old

EXERCISE 7   Combine the two sentences.

EXAMPLE: First: They made a big mistake.
Second: They realized it later.
They realized that they had made a big mistake.

First: I left my umbrella at work.
Second: I realized this later.

1. _____

First: You studied English when you were a child.
Second: I didn't know this.

2. _____

First: You lost your job.
Second: I didn't know this.

3. _____

First: You lived in Japan when you were a child.
Second: I didn't know this.

4. _____

First: You watered the plants.
Second: I didn't know this.

5. _____,
so I watered them anyway.

First: I locked the keys in the car.
Second: I realized this.

6. _____

First: He lost his wallet.
Second: He thought this.

7. _____,
but it was in his jacket pocket.

First: The captain made a big mistake.
Second: He realized it later.

8. _____

EXERCISE 8   Fill in the blanks with the past perfect of the verb in parentheses. Include the word *ever*.

EXAMPLE: In 1912, the Titanic was the most magnificent ship anybody _had ever seen_.
                                                                   (see)

1. In 1950, television was the most amazing thing many people _____.
                                                              (see)

2. Before she came to the U.S., her trip from Bosnia to Greece was the longest trip she _____.
                                                              (take)

3. My first new car cost $6,000 in 1988. It was the most expensive thing I _____. My present car cost me $15,000.
                          (buy)

4. When he was 18 years old, passing the exam to go to college was the hardest thing he _____.
                                                              (do)

5. When I was 18, choosing a college was the most difficult decision I _____.
                                                                      (make)

6. I thought my first boyfriend was the most handsome man I _____—until I met my future husband.
                          (meet)

7. *Gone with the Wind* was the best movie I _____—until I saw *Titanic*.
                                              (see)

EXERCISE 9   Fill in the blanks with the simple past tense for the more recent past action and the past perfect tense for the earlier past action.

EXAMPLE: When I _got up_, my wife _had already walked_ the dog,
                      (get up)   (already/walk)
so I didn't have to do it.

1. When I _____, the sun _____.
            (get up)   (already/rise)

2. I was going to make a pot of coffee, but I _____ that my
                                               (notice)
wife _____ a pot.
     (already/make)

---

3. I _____ several phone calls by the time I _____
   (make) the house. *(leave)*

4. I _____ take the subway to work because my wife _____
   (have to) *(take)*

   _____ the car.

5. When I _____ to work, my boss _____.
   (get) *(not arrive/yet)*

6. By the time I _____ out to lunch, I _____ to
   (go) *(speak)* ten clients.

7. I took an aspirin before I went home because I _____ a
   (have) headache all day.

8. My children _____ to bed by the time I _____
   (already/go) *(get)* home from work.

9. I _____ asleep right away because I _____ a very hard
   (fall) *(have)* day at work.

3.3 *When* with the Simple Past or the Past Perfect

Sometimes *when* means *before*. Sometimes *when* means *after*.

When = After	When = Before
When the captain saw the iceberg, he **tried** to turn the ship around.	When the captain saw the iceberg, the ship **had been** at sea for five days.
When the Titanic was built, passengers **bought** tickets to go to America.	When the Titanic was built, the radio and airplane **had** already **been** invented.
When I came home, my wife and I **ate** dinner.	When I came home, my wife **had eaten** dinner.

LANGUAGE NOTES

If you use the simple past in the main clause, *when* means *after*. If you use the past perfect in the main clause, *when* means before.

EXERCISE 10 Write numbers to show which action happened first.

EXAMPLES:

When she got home, she took an aspirin.
(1 over "got", 2 over "took")

When she got home, she had already taken an aspirin.
(2 over "got", 1 over "taken")

1. When they came into the room, their son left.

2. When they came into the room, their son had just left.

3. When I got home from school, I did my homework.

4. When I got home from school, I had already done my homework.

5. When she got to my house, she had eaten dinner.

6. When she got to my house, she ate dinner.

7. The teacher gave a test when Linda arrived.

8. The teacher had already given a test when Linda arrived.

EXERCISE 11 Fill in the blanks with the verb in parentheses. Use the simple past to show that *when* means *after*. Use the past perfect to show that *when* means *before*.

EXAMPLES:

When I saw the movie *Titanic*, I ___told___ my friends about it.
(tell)

When I saw the movie *Titanic*, I ___had never heard___ of this ship before.
(never/hear)

1. When the Titanic sank, a rescue ship _____ to pick up the (come) survivors.

2. When the ship hit an iceberg, the captain _____ several (receive) warnings.

3. When the ship was built, many rich people _____ tickets. (buy)

4. When the ship left England, 12 lifeboats _____. (passive: *remove*)

5. When the passengers heard a loud noise, they _____ to get on (run) the lifeboats.

6. When the Arctic ice started to melt, pieces of ice _____ away.
   (break)

7. When people saw the Titanic for the first time, they _____ *(never/see)* such a magnificent ship before.

8. When the rescue ship arrived, many passengers _____ .
   (already/die)

3.4 The Past Perfect Continuous Tense

The Titanic
had been traveling
for 5 days.

now

past ←- → future

↑
It sank.

Examples	Explanation
The Titanic **had been traveling** for five days when it sank.	The past perfect continuous = *had* + *been* + verb *-ing*.
Some people **had been rowing** lifeboats for several hours by the time the rescue ship arrived.	The past perfect continuous tense is used to show the duration of a continuous action that was completed before another past action. We use *for* to show the amount of time.

LANGUAGE NOTES

Remember: Do not use the continuous form with nonaction verbs.

EXERCISE 12 Fill in the blanks with the simple past tense or the past perfect continuous tense of the verb in parentheses.

EXAMPLE: When I ___came___ to the U.S., I ___had been studying___ English for
          (come)   *(study)*
three years.

1. I _____ for two years when I _____ a
      (wait)   *(get)*
   chance to leave my country.

2. I _____ in the same house all my life when I
      (live)
   _____ my city.
      (leave)

3. I _____ very sad when I left my job because I _____
   (feel)   (work)

   _____ with the same people for ten years.

4. I _____ to be a nurse for six months when
      (study)

   a war _____ in my country.
          (break out)

5. When I _____ my country, the war _____
            (leave)   (go on)
   for three years.

6. My family _____ in Germany for three months
               (wait)

   before we _____ permission to come to the U.S.
              (get)

7. By the time I _____ to the U.S., I _____
                  (get)   (travel)

   for four days.

3.5 The Past Perfect (Continuous) or the Present Perfect (Continuous)

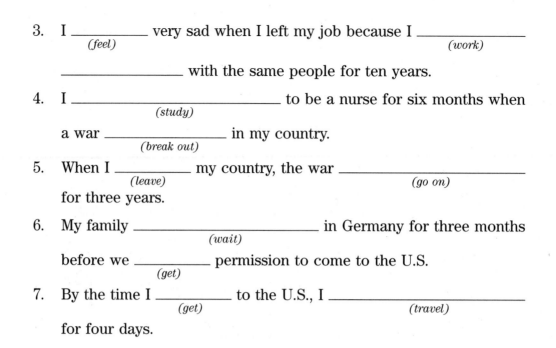

Examples	Explanation
When the passengers were rescued, they **had been rowing** for three hours.	The past perfect continuous is used to show that a continuous past action occurred before another past action.
The captain **had received** several warnings by the time he saw the iceberg.	The past perfect is used to show that a single action or a repeated action occurred before another past action.
We are talking about the Titanic now. We **have been talking** about it for 15 minutes.	The present perfect continuous is used to show that a continuous action occurred before the present time.

(continued)

Examples	Explanation
I **have seen** the movie *Titanic* several times. now past ←-----/--/--/-----┼------------→ future └────────┘ have seen **Have** you ever **seen** the movie? now past ←------?--------┼------------→ future └────────┘ have seen	The present perfect is used to show that a repeated action or a single action occurred before the present time.

LANGUAGE NOTES

The past perfect is used when we look back from a time in the past. The present perfect is used when we look back from the present time. The past perfect and the present perfect cannot be used interchangeably.

EXERCISE 13 Fill in the blanks with the present perfect, the present perfect continuous, the past perfect, or the past perfect continuous of the verb in parentheses.

EXAMPLES: I live in the U.S. now. I _____have been living_____ here for five years.
(live)

I lived in Canada until 1998. I _____had been living_____ in Canada for three
(live)
years when I decided to come to the U.S.

1. My sister quit her job last month. She _____ at
(work)
the same job for five years when she quit.

2. I love my job. I _____ at the same job since
(work)
I graduated from high school.

3. He couldn't pay his rent last month because he _____ all
(spend)
his money on medical bills.

4. This month I _____ $150 on groceries so far.
(spend)

5. She was born in New York. Her cousins were born in Moscow.
She _____ her cousins, but she'd like to.
(never/see)

6. Her father lived in Moscow until he died last year. When he died,
he _____ his grandchildren in the U.S.
(never/see)

The Past Perfect Tense; The Past Perfect Continuous; The Past Continuous **131**

7. He ate a hot dog for the first time at a baseball game last month.

He _____ a hot dog before.
        (never/eat)

8. He loves pizza. He _____ pizza many times.
                          (eat)

3.6 Comparison of Past Tenses—Forms

Examples	Tense
I **lived** in Los Angeles from 1995 to 1998. Then I **moved** to Chicago.	Simple Past
I **have been** in Chicago since 1998.	Present Perfect
I **have been living** in Chicago since 1998.	Present Perfect Continuous
I **was living** in Los Angeles when I met my husband.	Past Continuous
When I met my husband, I **had been** in Los Angeles for 11 months.	Past Perfect
When I met my husband, I **had been living** in Los Angeles for 11 months.	Past Perfect Continuous

Before You Read
1. Why do you think the Titanic disaster is still interesting today?
2. If you could ask a survivor of the Titanic any question, what would you ask him or her?

Read the following article. Pay special attention to past tense verbs (simple past, past continuous, past perfect, past perfect continuous).

Survivors of the Titanic

About 700 people **survived** the Titanic disaster and **lived** to tell their stories to newspapers.

Philip Zanni, an Assyrian emigrant, **was traveling** to the U.S. in third class. He **was sleeping** when he **heard** a crash. He immediately ran to the upper deck[3] where he saw great confusion. Men **were lowering** the lifeboats,

---

[3] A *deck* is a floor of a ship.

and Zanni **tried** to jump into one of them. But an officer with a gun **stopped** him, yelling "Women and children first." Moments later, the officer **turned** away and Zanni **jumped** on. He **was hiding** under one of the seats when the boat **pulled** away. There were 20 women and three men in the boat. They **had** to row quickly because the ship **was sinking**. When they were about two miles away, they **saw** the Titanic sink. It wasn't until five in the morning that they **saw** a rescue ship arrive. Zanni reported that while the survivors **were being raised** to the rescue ship, a woman **begged** Zanni to save her dog, which she **had been carrying** since leaving the Titanic.

Mary Davis, a second-class passenger, **was traveling** to visit her sister in New York. She **had saved** the money for the trip by working as a maid in London. She **was sleeping** when she **heard** a noise. She **was told** that there was no danger, and so she **returned** to bed. A few minutes later, she **was told** to go to the highest deck because the ship **was sinking**. Two men **helped** her get on a lifeboat, and then it **was lowered**. In the morning, the rescue ship **found** her boat and **pulled** the people aboard. When Ms. Davis **died** in 1987 at the age of 104, she **had lived** to be older than any other Titanic survivor.

3.7 The Past Continuous Tense

The past continuous tense is formed with *be* + verb *-ing*.

Examples	Explanation
What **was** Mr. Zanni **doing** at 11:40 p.m.? He **was sleeping**.	The past continuous shows what was in progress at a specific past time.
Mr. Zanni **was traveling** to the U.S. when the ship **sank**. While men **were lowering** the lifeboat, Mr. Zanni **jumped** in. Ms. Davis **was sleeping** when she **heard** a noise.	We use the past continuous together with the simple past tense to show the relationship of a longer past action to a shorter past action.
While rich people **were traveling** in first class, poor people **were traveling** in the lower deck of the ship.	The past continuous can be used in both clauses to show that two past actions were in progress at the same time.
Mr. Zanni **was traveling** to the U.S. in third class. Ms. Davis **was traveling** to meet her sister in New York.	In telling a story, the past continuous is used to describe the scene before the main action occurred. In this case, the main action happened when the Titanic hit an iceberg.

(continued)

Examples	Explanation
Mr. Zanni **was going to** get on the lifeboat, but an officer stopped him. The captain of the Titanic **was going to** turn the ship around, but it was too late.	*Was/were going to* is used to show that a past intention was not carried out.

LANGUAGE NOTES

1. If the time clause precedes the main clause, separate the two clauses with a comma.
    > The Titanic was crossing the Atlantic Ocean when it sank. (No COMMA)
    > When the Titanic sank, it was crossing the Atlantic Ocean. (COMMA)

2. *While* is used with a past continuous verb. *When* is used with the simple past tense. COMPARE:
    > Men were lowering the lifeboat *when* Zanni jumped in.
    > *While* men were lowering the lifeboat, Zanni jumped in.

3. In conversation, many people use *when* in place of *while*.
    > *When* men were lowering the lifeboat, Zanni jumped in.

4. *As* and *while* have the same meaning.
    > *As* the ship was sinking, people started to scream.
    > *While* the ship was sinking, people started to scream.

EXERCISE 14 What were these people doing when the Titanic hit an iceberg?

EXAMPLE: Passenger A: I ____*was sleeping*____ .
                                        (sleep)

1. Passenger B: My husband and I _____ .
                                              (dance)

2. Passenger C: I _____ a walk.
                            (take)

3. Passenger D: My friend and I _____ cards.
                                          (play)

4. Passenger E: I _____ a book.
                          (read)

5. Waiter: I _____ dinner.
                    (serve)

6. Captain: I _____ to turn the ship around.
                      (try)

EXERCISE 15 Fill in the blanks with the simple past or the past continuous of the verb in parentheses.

EXAMPLE: What _was the captain doing_ when the Titanic _hit_ an iceberg?
(the captain/do)   (hit)

1. While Philip Zanni _____ in third class, Mary Davis
(travel)

_____ in second class.
(travel)

2. Zanni _____ to America when this tragedy _____.
(immigrate)   (happen)

3. Many of the passengers _____ or _____ when
(eat)   (dance)

the Titanic _____ an iceberg.
(hit)

4. Mary Davis _____ when she _____ a noise.
(sleep)   (hear)

5. The lifeboats _____ while the ship
(passive: lower)

_____ .
(sink)

6. Zanni _____ on the lifeboat while it _____
(jump)   (passive: lower)
to the water.

7. While people _____, a woman _____
(row)   (carry)
a small dog.

8. Mary Davis _____ in New York when she _____ .
(live)   (die)

EXERCISE 16 Fill in the blanks with the simple past or the past continuous of the verb in parentheses.

A. I'm really upset. My phone bill is so high this month.

B. Why? __Did__ you __make__ a lot of long-distance calls last
(make)
month?

A. No. That's not the problem. While I _____, my 8-year-old
(1 work)

son was home alone. He _____ a 900 number. He
(2 call)

_____ TV when he _____ an offer about a cartoon
(3 watch)   (4 see)

character. He _____ that he could talk to his favorite character.
(5 think)

My son _____ about 900 numbers.
(6 not/understand)

He _____ that they aren't free.
(7 not/know)

B. How much do you have to pay for his call?

A. Sixty dollars. The call was four dollars a minute. He _____ (8 talk)

for about fifteen minutes.

B. Wasn't your wife home at the time?

A. Yes, but she _____ (9 work) in the garden, and she thought that

our son _____ (10 do) his homework.

B. When _____ (11 you/find out) about the call?

A. I _____ (12 find out) when I _____ (13 get) my phone bill. I was shocked.

B. Didn't he tell you that he made the call?

A. No. When I _____ (14 come) home that day, he _____ (15 do) his

homework. So I didn't know about the call until the bill _____ (16 arrive) .

B. What _____ (17 you/do) when you _____ (18 find out)? Did you punish

your son?

A. I _____ (19 go) to punish him, but I _____ (20 realize) that he didn't

understand that he had done anything wrong. So I just _____ (21 explain)

to him about 900 numbers, and he _____ (22 promise) never to do it again.

3.8 Comparison of Past Tenses—Uses

Examples	Explanation
The Titanic **left** England on April 10, 1912. Mary Davis **survived** the Titanic and **lived** until she was 104 years old.	The simple past tense does not show a relationship to another past action. It can be used for a short action or a long action.
Many passengers **were sleeping** at 11:40 p.m. The Titanic **was crossing** the Atlantic when it sank.	The past continuous tense shows that something was in progress at a specific time in the past.
When the rescue ship arrived, 1,500 people **had** already **died**.	The past perfect shows the relationship of a past action to a later past action.

(continued)

Examples	Explanation
The Titanic **had been traveling** for five days when it sank.	The past perfect continuous is used with the amount of time of a continuous action that happened before another past action.
How many movies **have** you **seen** about the Titanic? **Have** you ever **seen** the movie *Titanic*? People **have been** fascinated with the Titanic for almost a hundred years.	The present perfect uses the present time as the starting point and looks back.
We **have been talking** about the Titanic for several days.	The present perfect continuous uses the present time as the starting point and looks back at a continuous action that is still happening.

LANGUAGE NOTES

1. Sometimes the past continuous and the past perfect continuous can be used in the same case.
    The Titanic *had been crossing* the Atlantic when it hit an iceberg.
    The Titanic *was crossing* the Atlantic when it hit an iceberg.
2. Sometimes the simple past or the past perfect can be used in the same case.
    Some lifeboats *were* removed before the Titanic left.
    Some lifeboats *had been* removed before the Titanic left.

EXERCISE 17 Fill in the blanks with the correct past tense. Use the passive voice where indicated. In some cases, more than one answer is possible.

EXAMPLE: The Titanic __*sank*__ in 1912.
(sink)

1. The Titanic _____ in Ireland.
   (passive: *build*)

2. When the captain _____ the iceberg, he _____ to turn the
   (see)   (try)
   ship around.

3. There was a lot of ice in the water in 1912 because the previous

   winter _____ mild.
   (be)

4. The Titanic _____ fast when it _____ an iceberg.
   (travel)   (hit)

---

5. Many people _____ when they _____ a loud
   (sleep)   (hear)
   noise.

6. When they _____ the noise, they _____ up.
             (hear)   (wake)

7. When third-class passengers _____ to the top deck, most of the
                                (go)
   lifeboats _____ .
             (already/leave)

8. A few hours later, another ship _____ , but the Titanic
                                    (arrive)
   _____ .
   (already/sink)

9. The rescue ship _____ up the people in the lifeboats.
                   (pick)

10. The Titanic _____ its first voyage when it _____ .
                (make)   (sink)

11. In 1985, the ship _____ in the North Atlantic.
                      (passive: finally/find)

12. People are still interested in the Titanic. People _____
                                                        (be)
    interested in it for almost a hundred years.

13. Many articles and books _____ about the Titanic
                            (passive: write)
    over the years.

14. Several movies _____ about the Titanic
                   (passive: make)
    over the years.

15. In 1912, the sinking of the Titanic was the worst tragedy that
    _____ .
    (ever/occur)

16. I was going to invite my friends to come over and watch the video
    Titanic, but most of them _____ the movie.
                                (already/see)

EXERCISE **18** Fill in the blanks with the correct past tense of the verb in
parentheses. (In some cases, more than one answer is possible.)

A. I loved the movie *Titanic*. I ___*saw*___ it for the first time when
                                    (see)
   it came out. Since then, I _____ it two more times.
                              (1 rent)
   _____ it?
   (2 you/ever/see)

B. Do you mean the movie with Leonardo DiCaprio? Actually, I
   _____ it. Many years ago, I _____ an old movie
   (3 never/see)   (4 see)
   about the Titanic from the 1950s.

A. The 1997 version was great. You should rent it.

B. You know, I _____ it about six months ago, but I
(5 rent)

only watched about 15 minutes of it. While I _____ it,
(6 watch)

there was a power failure in my area and the electricity _____
(7 go)

out for several hours. I _____ return the video that night. Up
(8 have to)

to now, I _____ all about it—until you mentioned it.
(9 forget)

A. You should rent it again. It was a great story.

B. But everyone knows how the story _____. The ship _____
(10 end)   (11 sink)

and a lot of people _____.
(12 die)

A. But there was also a great love story. It's a story about a woman named

Rose. She _____ to marry a rich man when she _____
(13 plan)   (14 meet)

Jack and _____ in love with him. Jack was a poor man
(15 fall)

who _____ in third class. When Rose was with Jack,
(16 travel)

she _____ freer than she _____ before. But
(17 feel)   (18 ever/feel)

when Rose's fiancé _____ that Rose was in love with
(19 find out)

another man, he _____ very angry.
(20 become)

B. Stop! Don't tell me more. I think I'll rent it this weekend.

A. If you do, let me know. I'd like to see it again.

B. But you _____ it.
(21 already/see)

A. It's so good I could watch it again.

EXERCISE 19 Fill in the blanks with the correct past tense of the verb in
parentheses. In some cases, more than one answer is possible.

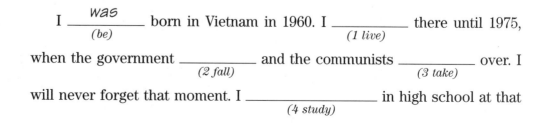

I __was__ born in Vietnam in 1960. I _____ there until 1975,
(be)   (1 live)

when the government _____ and the communists _____ over. I
(2 fall)   (3 take)

will never forget that moment. I _____ in high school at that
(4 study)

time. I _____ (5 take) a math test when the director of our

school _____ (6 come) into the class and announced that the government

_____ (7 fall). Everyone in my class _____ (8 become) silent. The

teacher _____ (9 stop) our test and _____ (10 tell) us to go home. By the time

I _____ (11 get) home from school, my father _____ (12 already/make)

arrangements to leave the country. Our lives _____ (13 be) in great danger

because my father _____ (14 work) for the U.S. military for ten years.

We _____ (15 leave) in a hurry. We _____ (16 have) no time to say good-bye to

our friends or pack our belongings. We _____ (17 take) with us only

the most necessary things. We _____ (18 leave) behind many things that

_____ (19 take) my family years to acquire.

    After we _____ (20 leave) Vietnam, we _____ (21 go) to Thailand. We

_____ (22 stay) there for three years. While we _____ (23 wait)

for permission to come to the U.S., we _____ (24 study) English. We

_____ (25 want) to be prepared for our life in the U.S. I'll never forget

December 5, 1978, one of the happiest days of my life. It was three o'clock,

and I _____ (26 help) my brother practice his English lesson when my

father _____ (27 run) into the room with a letter in his hand. He was so happy

because the U.S. government _____ (28 give) us permission to go to

America. We _____ (29 be) so excited when my father _____ (30 tell) us the news.

    When we _____ (31 arrive) at the Los Angeles airport on February 6, 1979,

our sponsor _____ (32 wait) for us. He _____ (33 hold) a sign that said,

"Welcome to the U.S., Mr. Ly Tran and family." We _____ (34 be) so happy and

excited. My mother _____ (35 start) to cry.

    Now we _____ (36 be) in the U.S. for over 20 years and we are doing

well. My sister plans to become a doctor. She _____ all her courses
(37 finish)

last year, but she _____ her medical exams yet. She
(38 not/take)

_____ for these exams for six months. My
(39 study)

brother _____ as a computer programmer for the last
(40 work)

three years. And I _____ my own restaurant for the past
(41 have)

ten years. Unfortunately, my father died last year, but he was proud that

he _____ his children to safety and that he _____
(42 take)   (43 give)

us the opportunity to study and become Americans.

SUMMARY OF LESSON 3

1.   SHOWING THE RELATIONSHIP BETWEEN TWO PAST ACTIONS

The Past Perfect:

The reference point is past.	Another action is more past.
When the rescue ship **arrived**,	many people **had died**.
In **1912**,	the airplane **had** already **been invented**.

The Past Perfect Continuous:

The reference point is past.	A continuous action preceded it.
A woman wanted to save the dog	that she **had been carrying** since she left the Titanic.
The captain couldn't turn the ship around	because it **had been traveling** so fast.

The Past Continuous:

An action was in progress . . .	. . . at a specific time or when a shorter action occurred.
They **were sleeping**	at 11:40 p.m.
We **were watching** the movie	when the phone rang.

2. RELATING THE PAST TO THE PRESENT

The Present Perfect	The Present Perfect Continuous
Have you ever **seen** the movie *Titanic*? I **have** never **seen** it, but I'd like to. I **have seen** two movies this month.	She is watching the movie now. She **has been watching** it for 45 minutes.

3. DESCRIBING THE PAST WITHOUT RELATING IT TO ANOTHER PAST TIME

The Simple Past Tense
I **rented** a movie last week. I **liked** the movie so much that I **watched** it twice. Mary **lived** in England all her life.

EDITING ADVICE ✎

1. Don't use *be* to form the simple past tense.

    He ~~was~~ *came* ~~come~~ home at 6 o'clock last night.

2. Don't forget *be* in a past continuous sentence.

    was
    I ⌃ walking on the icy sidewalk when I fell and broke my arm.

3. Do not use a present tense for an action that began in the past. Use the present perfect (continuous).

    have been
    I ~~am~~ married for ten years.

    has been
    She ~~is~~ working at her present job for seven months.

4. Don't forget *have* with perfect tenses.

    have
    I ⌃ been living in the U.S. for six months.

5. Don't confuse the present perfect and the past perfect. The past perfect relates to a past event.

   When I started college, I ~~have~~ *had* never used a computer before.

   She's a teacher now. She ~~had~~ *has* been a teacher for 15 years.

6. Use the simple past with *ago*.

   He ~~was coming~~ *came* to the U.S. four years ago.

7. Use *when*, not *while*, for an action that has no continuation.

   I was washing the dishes ~~while~~ *when* I dropped the plate.

8. Use the simple past, not the present perfect, in a *since* clause.

   She has had her car ever since she ~~has come~~ *came* to the U.S.

9. Don't use the continuous form for a repeated action.

   By the time I got to work, I had ~~been drinking~~ *drunk* four cups of coffee.

10. Don't confuse the *-ing* form with the past participle.

    When he moved to Chicago, he had never ~~seeing~~ *seen* a skyscraper before.

11. Be careful to choose the correct past tense in a sentence with *when*.

    When I left my hometown, I ~~had come~~ *came* to New York.

    When I arrived in class, the test ~~began~~ *had begun* already.

12. Don't confuse active and passive.

    In 1985, the Titanic was ~~finding~~ *found*.

PART 1   Find the mistakes with the underlined words, and correct them. Not every sentence has a mistake. If the sentence is correct, write **C.**

EXAMPLES: I couldn't answer the phone when it rang because I ~~took~~ *was taking* a shower.

She <u>found</u> a job last week.   C

1. I <u>was work</u> when the fire <u>started</u>.

2. How long <u>do you live</u> in this city?

3. They <u>were getting</u> married five years ago.

4. When he <u>came</u> to the U.S., he <u>had never studied</u> English before.

5. <u>Have you ever seeing</u> the mayor of this city?

6. He is divorced now. He <u>was</u> married for ten years.

7. She <u>left</u> her dictionary in the library yesterday.

8. When she <u>came</u> to the U.S., she <u>has never spoken</u> English before.

9. My sister is in medical school. She <u>has wanted</u> to be a doctor ever since she <u>has been</u> a little girl.

10. My grandparents <u>were living</u> in Germany when World War II <u>started</u>.

11. I <u>been working</u> as a computer programmer for five years. I love my job.

12. My sister is a nurse. She <u>had been</u> a nurse for ten years.

13. When we <u>finished</u> dinner, we <u>washed</u> the dishes.

14. An accident <u>was happened</u> in front of my house early this morning.

15. Last year when the landlord <u>raised</u> my rent, I <u>decided</u> to move.

16. I wasn't injured in the car accident because I <u>had been wearing</u> my seat belt.

17. By the time my sister <u>came</u> to the U.S., our father <u>had</u> already <u>died</u>.

18. We <u>had been driven</u> for three hours when we had a flat tire.

19. When he came to the U.S., he <u>had</u> never <u>met</u> an American before.

20. Fifteen hundred people <u>died</u> on the Titanic.

21. <u>Have</u> you ever <u>traveled</u> by ship? No, I never <u>have</u>.

22. When they <u>came</u> to the U.S., they <u>saw</u> the Statue of Liberty.

PART **2**

Fill in the blanks with the simple past or the past perfect of the verb in parentheses.

EXAMPLE: When Mary Davis ___*came*___ to America, she ___*had never left*___ England
                                 (come)   (never/leave)
before.

1. I registered late for this class. The class _____ a test on the
                                                                    (already/have)
   review lesson by the time I _____ .
                                           (register)

2. She _____ to go to Paris for vacation last year because she
                (want)

   _____ there before.
        (never/go)

3. I got to class late. By the time I _____ to class, the teacher _____
                                                  (get)

   _____ the homework.
        (already/explain)

4. When she got to work, she _____ that she _____
                                               (realize)   (leave)
   the stove on and had to go back home.

5. When my mother came to the U.S., she _____ afraid to speak English
                                                              (be)

   because she _____ English with an American before.
                        (never/speak)

6. When I _____ English lessons, I _____ a
                 (start)   (never/study)
   foreign language before.

7. Many people _____ when they _____ into the water
                        (die)   (jump)
   because the water was so cold.

8. Many of the survivors of the Titanic _____ of old age
                                                          (already/die)

   when the ship _____ .
                       (passive: *find*)

9. He _____ the fire department when the fire _____ .
          (call)   (start)

10. When the fire department came, the house _____ down.
                                                         (already/burn)

Fill in the blanks with one of the past tenses: simple past, past continuous, present perfect (continuous), or past perfect (continuous). In some cases, more than one answer is possible.

A. What _____*happened*_____ to your car?
   (happen)

B. I _____ an accident yesterday.
   (1 have)

A. How _____ it _____?
   (2 happen)

B. I _____ to work when a dog _____ in front of my car.
   (3 drive)   *(4 run)*

   I _____ my car suddenly, and the car behind me _____
   (5 stop)   *(6 hit)*

   my car because the driver _____ me too closely.
                              (7 follow)

A. _____ a ticket?
   (8 you/get)

B. No, but the driver who hit me did.

A. Who will pay to have your car fixed?

B. The other driver. When he _____ me, he _____ out of his car
                              (9 hit)   *(10 get)*

   and _____ me his insurance card. He's a new driver. He _____
       (11 give)

   _____ his driver's license for two months.
   (12 only/have)

A. You're a new driver too, aren't you?

B. Oh, no. I _____ for twenty years.
             (13 drive)

A. I thought you _____ your driver's license a few months ago.
                 (14 get)

B. In this state, I have a new license. But I _____ a driver's license
                                             (15 have)

   for many years before I _____ here.
                            (16 move)

A. _____ you ever _____ a ticket?
                        (17 get)

B. One time. I _____ about 65 miles an hour on the highway
               (18 drive)

   when a police officer _____ me. She said that the speed limit was
                         (19 stop)

   only 55. She _____ me a ticket for speeding. She also gave me a ticket
                (20 give)

   because I _____ my seat belt.
             (21 not/wear)

CLASSROOM ACTIVITIES

1. Form a small group. Look at the facts below. Find the year that is closest to the year you were born. Tell if this event had already happened or hadn't happened yet when you were born.

   EXAMPLE:

   1975: Bill Gates started Microsoft.
   When I was born, Bill Gates had not yet started Microsoft.

   a. 1944: The first computers were made.

   b. 1954: The war in Vietnam started.

   c. 1957: The first rocket went into space.

   d. 1959: Fidel Castro took power over Cuba.

   e. 1963: President Kennedy was assassinated.

   f. 1969: Men landed on the moon.

   g. 1975: Bill Gates started Microsoft.

   h. 1976: The U.S. celebrated its 200th birthday.

   i. 1979: Sony introduced the first Walkman.

   j. 1981: IBM sold the first personal computer.

2. In a small group or with the entire class, turn to the person next to you and say a year. The person next to you has to tell a short story about his/her life at or before that time.

   EXAMPLE:

   1996
   I had just graduated from high school. I was living with my parents. I hadn't thought about coming to the U.S. at that time.

   1963
   I hadn't been born yet.

   1997
   I had just had my second child. I was living with my wife's parents.

3. On an index card, write the following sentence, filling in the blank to make a **true** statement about yourself. The teacher will collect the cards and read the sentences. Try to guess who wrote the sentences.

   When I came to this school, I had never _____ before.

   EXAMPLE:

   When I came to this school, I had never paid so much for a textbook before.

DISCUSSION   Why do you think that women and children were put on lifeboats before men?

WRITING   Choose one of the following topics and write a short composition.

1.   An accident or unusual experience that happened to you

2.   How you met your spouse or a new friend

3.   An important event in the history of your native country

4.   A famous person who died in an accident, assassination, or other unusual way

OUTSIDE ACTIVITY   Rent the movie *Titanic* (1997) and/or *A Night to Remember* (1957). Write a summary of one of these movies.

Internet Activity

   Find Web sites that tell about the Titanic. Find personal accounts of survivors. Report one of these to the class.

Lesson Four

GRAMMAR

Modals—Present and Future
Related Expressions

CONTEXT

Sweepstakes or Scam?
Marketing to Children
Responding to Telemarketing Calls
Don't Believe Everything You See
Game Shows and Talk Shows

LESSON FOCUS

The modal auxiliaries are: *can, could, shall, should, will, would, may, might, must, ought to.*

She *should* enter the contest.
She *might* win a prize.

Related expressions are: *have to, have got to, be supposed to, be able to, be allowed to, be permitted to, had better.*

She *is able to* understand the rules.
He *has to* mail a postcard.

Examples	Explanation
She **should** leave. (advice) She **must** leave. (necessity) She **might** leave. (possibility)	Modals add meaning to the verb that follows it.
You **must pay** your rent.	The base form follows a modal.
You **should not** leave now.	To form the negative, put *not* after the modal.
A pen **should be used** for the test.	A modal can be used in passive voice: modal + *be* + past participle
He **must** go to court. = He **has to** go to court. You **must not** park your car there. = You **are not supposed to** park your car there. He **can** speak English well. = He **is able to** speak English well.	The following expressions are like modals in meaning: *have to, have got to, be able to, be supposed to, be allowed to, had better.*

LANGUAGE NOTES

1. Use a base form after a modal.
    > He *should leave* now. (NOT: should to leave; NOT: should leaving)
2. Modals never have an *-s, -ed,* or *-ing* ending.
    > She *can* speak well. (NOT: She *cans*)
3. Don't use two modals together.
    > You *will have to* go to court. NOT: You will must go to court.
    > She *might have to* leave early. NOT: She might must leave early.
4. *Shall* is more common in British English than in American English.
    > BRITISH: We *shall* study modals.
    > AMERICAN: We *will* study modals.
    > NOTE: Americans sometimes use *shall* in a question for suggestions or invitations.
    > *Shall* we dance?
5. Observe affirmatives, negatives, and questions with modals.

AFFIRMATIVE	He *can* speak German.
NEGATIVE	He *can't* speak French.
YES/NO QUESTION	*Can* he speak English?
SHORT ANSWERS	Yes, he *can.* / No, he *can't.*
WH- QUESTION	Why *can't* he speak French?
SUBJECT QUESTION	Who *can* speak French?

Read the following article. Pay special attention to *have to, must, should* and *ought to.*

Sweepstakes or Scam?

Did you ever get a letter with your name printed on it telling you that you have won a prize or a large amount of money? Most Americans get these letters. Are these offers for real?

Some companies offer legitimate sweepstakes, or chances to win. In most cases, you **have to** mail a postcard to enter. You may win, but keep in mind that the chances are very, very small. Many people enter anyway because they feel they've got nothing to lose and might even win something.

However, the Federal Trade Commission (FTC) estimates that Americans lose more than one billion dollars each year through sweepstakes scams (tricks to take your money). Yes, you might win a prize or money, but it could be a check for 50¢ or a cheap, worthless ring. You **should** learn the difference between a legitimate company and a company that is just trying to take your money. Be careful of companies that tell you the following:

- You **must** act now or the offer will expire.
- You can't afford to miss this offer.
- You've already won a free gift. All you **have to** do is pay postage and handling.
- You've won. You **must** call a 900 number to claim your prize.
- You've won a free vacation. All you **have to** do is pay a service fee.

Also, be careful of companies that ask you for your credit card number. You **should** never give out your credit card number to companies that you are unfamiliar with.

What about the legitimate companies? Why do they give away money and prizes? Sweepstakes are a way for a company to call your attention to its products. One company, for example, wants you to subscribe to magazines. Some people think they **have to** order magazines to win. However, in a legitimate sweepstakes, you **don't have to** buy anything or send any money to enter. According to the law, these companies **must** make it clear to you that you **don't have to** buy anything.

If you are suspicious of an offer, you can check out the company with an organization called the Better Business Bureau.[1] If you think that you have been a victim of a scam, you **should** report it to the National Fraud[2] Information Center, the Federal Trade Commission, or the Attorney General in your state.

How can you avoid these scams before you become a victim? If you receive a letter saying you are a guaranteed winner, you **ought to** throw it in the garbage.

4.2 Necessity

Modal	Alternate	Explanation
Sweepstakes companies **must** obey the law. They **must** make their conditions clear to you.	Sweepstakes companies **have to** obey the law. They **are supposed to** make their conditions clear to you.	Legal obligation
You **must** act now! Don't wait or you will lose this fabulous offer!	You**'ve got to** act now! You **have to** act now!	Urgency
	I **have got to** go to the post office. I **have to** mail a package. I**'ve got to** buy some stamps too.	Personal obligation

LANGUAGE NOTES

1. Avoid using *must* for personal obligations. It sounds very official and is too strong for most situations. *Have to* and *have got to* are more common.

2. Avoid using *must* for reporting rules that come from an outside source (the law, the teacher, your boss, etc.) *Be supposed to* is much more common in reporting a rule. The law says, "You must wear a seat belt in a car." However, if you see that your passenger isn't wearing her seat belt, you say, "You're supposed to wear your seat belt." You are reminding your passenger of the law. It is not your law.

[1] The Better Business Bureau cannot tell you if a company is good. It can only tell you the history of complaints against a company.
[2] *Fraud* is a method of tricking someone to get money.

3. *Be supposed to* is also more common than *must* when reporting on a law that is broken.

> This sweepstakes offer says I won a prize. It's *supposed to* tell me exactly what I won, but it doesn't.
>
> Why are those students talking in the library? They're *supposed to* be quiet.

4. In fast, informal speech, *have to* is often pronounced "hafta." *Has to* is pronounced "hasta." *Have got to* is often pronounced "gotta." (*Have* is often not pronounced before "gotta.") Listen to your teacher pronounce the sentences in the preceding box.

5. We don't usually use *have got to* for questions and negatives.

> I've *got to* leave now. Do you *have to* leave too?

EXERCISE 1 Fill in the blanks with an appropriate verb.

EXAMPLE: Drivers must _____*stop*_____ at a red light.

1. To drive a car, you must _____ a license.

2. In a car, people must _____ babies in a special car seat.

3. To become an American citizen, you must _____ a citizenship test.

4. To rent an R-rated movie, a person must _____ at least 17 years old.

5. In many cities, a landlord must _____ a smoke detector in every apartment.

6. If the sweepstakes company tells you that you must _____ something, it's not a legitimate company.

7. Airplane passengers must _____ a seat belt.

EXERCISE 2 Finish these sentences to talk about personal obligations.

EXAMPLE: I have to _____*call my parents*_____ once a month.

1. I can't go to the movies tonight. I've got to _____.

2. The teacher can't talk to you now. She has to _____.

3. I have a headache. I have to _____.

4. My English isn't perfect. I've got to _____.

5. I'm gaining too much weight. I've got to _____.

6. I'm not sure of the spelling of a word. I have to _____.

7. I have to _____ every day.

EXERCISE 3 Make a list of personal obligations you have on the weekends.

EXAMPLE: _On Saturdays, I have to take my daughter to ballet lessons._

_____

_____

_____

EXERCISE 4 Make a list of obligations you have at your job.

EXAMPLE: _I've got to answer the phone and fill out orders._

_____

_____

_____

EXERCISE 5 A teenager is talking about all the rules his parents gave him and his sister. Fill in the blanks with *be supposed to* + an appropriate verb.

EXAMPLE: I _'m supposed to babysit_ for my little sister when my parents aren't home.

1. I _____ my homework before I watch TV.

2. I (not) _____ on the phone with my friends for more than 30 minutes.

3. I _____ my room once a week. My mother gets mad when I leave it dirty.

4. If I go to a friend's house, I _____ my parents where I am so they won't worry.

5. I _____ my parents with jobs around the house.

   For example, I _____ the dishes once a week.

   I _____ the garbage every day.

6. I have a part-time job. I _____ some of my

   money in the bank. I (not) _____ my money on foolish things.

7. My sister _____ her toys away when she's finished playing.

8. She (not) _____ the stove.

9. She (not) _____ TV after 8 p.m.

10. She _____ to bed at 8:30.

EXERCISE 6 Report some rules in one of the following places: in your apartment, in court, in traffic, in a library, on an airplane, or in the airport.

EXAMPLES:

In my apartment, the landlord is supposed to provide heat

in the winter.

I'm supposed to pay my rent by the fifth of the month.

_____

_____

_____

4.3 *Must Not* and *Not Have To*

Examples	Explanation
Sweepstakes companies **must not** ask you to send money. You **must not** lie in court. You **must not** cheat on a test.	Prohibition: This is against the law.
You **don't have to** buy magazines to enter a sweepstakes. In a legitimate sweepstakes, you **don't have to** spend any money. You **don't have to** be present when the winner's name is chosen.	It is not necessary, not required, or not expected.

LANGUAGE NOTES

In affirmative statements, *have to* and *must* have a similar meaning. Remember, *must* sounds more formal and is used more for legal and urgent situations. In negative statements, *must not* and *not have to* are very different.

EXERCISE 7 Fill in the blanks with *not have to* or *must not.*

EXAMPLE: If you receive a sweepstakes postcard, you _____*don't have to*_____ send it back.

1. You _____ buy something to win. No purchase is necessary.

2. Sweepstakes companies _____ break the law.

3. In a legitimate sweepstakes, you _____ call a 900 number to win a prize.

4. Passengers on an airplane _____ use a computer while the plane is taking off and landing.

5. Passengers on an airplane _____ pay for their meal. It's included in the price of the ticket.

6. Passengers on an airplane _____ carry a weapon.

7. Passengers on an airplane _____ walk around when the airplane is taking off or landing.

8. Passengers on an airplane _____ wear their seat belt after the seat belt sign is turned off.

9. Students _____ copy answers from each other during a test.

10. The students in this class _____ bring their dictionaries to class.

11. Teachers _____ teach in the summer if they don't want to.

12. Teachers in American schools _____ hit children. It is prohibited.

EXERCISE 8 Fill in the blanks with *don't have to* or *must not* to describe situations in a public library.

EXAMPLES: You _____*must not*_____ write in a library book.
You _____*don't have to*_____ know the name of the author to find a book. You can find the book by the title.

1. You _____ wait until the due date to return a book. You can return it early.

2. You _____ eat in the library.

3. You _____ study in the library. You can study at home.

4. You _____ return your books to the circulation desk. You can leave them in the book drop.

book drop

---

5. You _____ tear a page out of a book.

6. You _____ make noise in the library.

EXERCISE 9 Tell if you have to or don't have to do the following.

EXAMPLES: work on Saturdays
I have to work on Saturdays.

wear a suit to work
I don't have to wear a suit to work.

1. pay rent on the first of the month

2. study English

3. get up early on Sundays

4. cook every day

5. wear formal clothes (a suit, a dress) to work/school

6. come to school on Saturdays

EXERCISE 10 Tell if students in your school have to or don't have to do the following.

EXAMPLES: wear a uniform
Students in my school don't have to wear a uniform.

take final exams
Students in my school have to take final exams.

1. stand up to answer a question

2. go to the chalkboard to answer a question

3. call the teacher by his or her title (for example, "Professor")

4. buy their own textbooks

5. pay tuition

6. attend classes every day

7. have a written excuse for an absence

8. get permission to leave the classroom

1. What kind of programs do children like to watch?
2. What kind of advertising do they see on these programs?

Read the following article. Pay special attention to modals.

Marketing to Children

When children watch TV, they often see ads for toys they might want their parents to buy for them. Or they may be given a 900 number to call to talk to their favorite cartoon character. It is easy for small children to believe what they see and hear on television. For this reason, the law restricts advertising to children under 12. When the audience of a TV show is more than 50 percent children, pay-per-call services (services that require you to call a 900 number) **cannot** place ads during or immediately before or after these shows. Ads **cannot** be placed in books, comic books, or magazines if more than 50 percent of the readers are children under 12. There is only one exception to this rule: educational services, such as homework help, **may** offer pay-per-call numbers.

The best protection for children comes from parents. Parents **should** talk with their children. They **should** tell their kids not to call a 900 number without their permission. But many parents are not home or are busy while their children watch TV. To avoid this problem, parents can have the phone company block 900 calls from their phone. But they must pay for this service.

Permission and Prohibition

Examples	Explanation
Educational services **may** advertise to small children. These services **can** charge for homework help.	Use *may* or *can* to show that something is permitted.
Advertisers **cannot** place ads in magazines for children under 12. Pay-per-call services **may not** show an ad during a children's TV program.	Use *may not* or *cannot (can't)* to show that something is prohibited.

LANGUAGE NOTES

1. Alternate forms are *be allowed to* and *be permitted to*.
   Advertisers *are not allowed to* place ads in comic books.
   Advertisers *are not permitted to* place ads in comic books.
2. The meaning of *cannot* (not permitted) is very similar to the meaning of *must not* (prohibited).
   You *can't* park at a bus stop. = You *must not* park at a bus stop.

EXERCISE 11 Fill in the blanks with an appropriate permission word to talk about what is or isn't permitted in your native country.

EXAMPLES: A man ___*isn't permitted*___ to have more than one wife.

Teachers ___*can*___ talk about religion in public schools.

1. People _____ own a gun.

2. People under 18 _____ get married.

3. Children _____ work.

4. Children _____ see any movie they want.

5. A man _____ have more than one wife.

6. A married woman _____ get a passport without her husband's permission.

7. Teachers _____ talk about religion in public schools.

8. Teachers _____ hit children.

9. People _____ travel freely.

10. People _____ live anywhere they want.

Examples	Explanation
Children **should** obey their parents. Children **shouldn't** call 900 numbers without their parents' permission. You **shouldn't** give out your credit card number to people you don't know.	*Should* is used for advice, to say that something is a good idea. *Shouldn't* means that something is a bad idea.
If you receive a letter saying you are already a winner, you **ought to** throw it in the garbage.	*Ought to* has the same meaning as *should*.
A. Someone is ringing my doorbell. B. You**'d better not** open the door if you don't know who it is.	*Had better (not)* is used to give a warning. There may be a bad result if the advice is not followed.

LANGUAGE NOTES

1. *Ought* is the only modal followed by *to*. *Ought to* is pronounced /ɔtə/. Don't use *ought to* for negatives and questions. Use *should*.
2. *Had better (not)* is often used in conversation to give a warning. Use *'d* to contract *had* with a pronoun. In some fast speech, *'d* is omitted completely.
   > *You had better* be careful.→ *You'd better* be careful. → *You better* be careful.

EXERCISE 12 Give advice to people who are saying the following.

EXAMPLES: I'm lonely. I don't have any friends.

You should get a dog or a cat for companionship.

I'm so tired. I've been working hard all day.

You ought to get some rest.

1. I've had a headache all day.

_____

2. The teacher wrote something on my paper, but I can't read it.

_____

3. Every time I write a composition and the teacher finds mistakes, I have to write it all over again.

_____

4. I got a letter telling me that I won a million dollars.

_____

5. My old TV doesn't work well anymore. It's too expensive to repair.

_____

6. I received an offer for a new job. It pays double what I get now.

_____

7. My car is making a strange noise. I wonder what it is.

_____

8. I sit at a desk all day. I don't get enough exercise. I'm gaining weight.

_____

9. Whenever I tell my personal problems to my coworker, he tells other people.

_____

10. I have to write a résumé, but I don't have any experience with this.

_____

EXERCISE 13 Tell what people should do or say in the following social situations in your native culture. Share your answers with the class.

EXAMPLE: If you are invited to someone's house for dinner, _you should bring a small gift._

1. If you invite a friend to eat in a restaurant, _____

_____

2. If you bump into someone, _____

_____

3. If you don't hear or understand what someone says, _____

_____

4. If someone asks, "How are you?" _____

_____

5. If you want to leave the dinner table while others are still eating, _____

_____

6. If a woman with a small child gets on a crowded bus, _____

_____

7. If you're invited to someone's house for dinner, _____

_____

8. If you meet someone for the first time, _____

_____

EXERCISE 14 Give a warning by using *you'd better (not)* in the following job situations.

EXAMPLE: You've been late three times this week. *You'd better come on time* , or the boss will fire you.

1. You usually take five extra minutes for lunch. _____

_____, or you will lose pay.

2. You work too slowly. _____,
or the boss will find someone else.

3. You just typed up a report. _____
save it on disk.

4. You are the only person who wears jeans to the office. _____

_____ if you want to look appropriate.

5. You've been using the phone for your personal calls. _____

_____, or your boss will get angry.

6. One of the men in the office is a big gossip. He tells whatever you

say to the boss. _____,
or you'll be sorry later.

4.6 Comparing Negative Modals

Examples	Explanation
You **don't have to** buy magazines to enter a sweepstakes.	It's not necessary.
You **shouldn't** give strange callers your credit card number.	It's a bad idea.
Advertisers **cannot** place ads in magazines for children under 12. They **may not** place ads in magazines for children under 12.	It's prohibited.
You **must not** talk during the test.	It's prohibited. (official tone)
You **are not supposed to** talk during the test. A legitimate sweepstakes company **is not supposed to** ask you for your credit card number.	This is a reminder of a rule. (unofficial tone)
You**'d better not** arrive late for the exam, or you won't have time to finish it.	This is a warning. A negative consequence is stated or implied.

EXERCISE 15 Work with a partner. Use *be supposed to* to write a list of rules the teacher has for this class. Use affirmative and negative statements.

EXAMPLES:
We're not supposed to use our books during a test.

We're supposed to write five compositions this semester.

_____

_____

_____

_____

_____

_____

_____

EXERCISE 16 Work with a partner. Name some things you must not do while driving a car. (Use *you* in the impersonal sense.)

EXAMPLE: You must not pass a car when you're going up a hill.

_____

_____

_____

_____

_____

EXERCISE 17 Choose the correct words to complete these sentences.

EXAMPLES: We (shouldn't, don't have to) talk loudly in the library.

We (shouldn't, don't have to) bring our dictionaries to class.

1. The teacher says we (can't, don't have to) use our books during a test.

2. The teacher says we (shouldn't, don't have to) sit in a specific seat in class. We can sit wherever we want.

3. We (can't, don't have to) talk to each other during a test. It's not permitted.

4. We (must not, don't have to) type our compositions. We can write them by hand.

5. We (shouldn't, can't) speak our native language in class. It's not a good idea.

6. We (don't have to, aren't supposed to) come back after the final exam, but we can in order to pick up our tests.

7. Parents often tell children, "You (shouldn't, don't have to) talk to strangers."

8. Children (may not, don't have to) enter an R-rated movie without an adult.

9. Parents (aren't supposed to, don't have to) send their kids to public schools. They can send them to private schools.

10. Teachers (aren't supposed to, don't have to) teach summer school if they don't want to.

11. English teachers (shouldn't, don't have to) talk fast to foreign students.

12. A driver who is involved in an accident must report it to the police. He (must not, doesn't have to) leave the scene of the accident.

13. I'm warning you. You (don't have to, 'd better not) spend so much time talking to your co-workers, or you might lose your job.

14. Drivers (don't have to, must not) go through red lights.

EXERCISE 18 Fill in the blanks to make true statements.

EXAMPLE: I don't have to _make an appointment to see the teacher._

1. In this class, we aren't supposed to _____.

2. In this class, we don't have to _____.

3. The teacher doesn't have to _____, but he/she does it anyway.

4. In this building, we must not _____.

5. You'd better not _____, or the teacher will get angry.

6. We're going to have a test next week, so you'd better _____ _____.

7. When another student doesn't know the answer, you shouldn't _____. You should let him try to find it himself.

8. You can't _____ in the computer lab. It's not permitted.

9. Teachers should be patient. They shouldn't _____ when students don't understand.

10. You don't have to _____ to win a sweepstakes prize.

Before You Read
1. Do you ever buy anything by catalog or by telephone?
2. Do you ever get calls from people who want to sell you something?

Read the following article. Pay special attention to *can, could,* and *should.*

Responding to Telemarketing Calls

Do you get phone calls telling you about special offers? Most people do. Most companies that call you are legitimate companies that are trying to sell you something. But these calls are very annoying. If you don't want to listen to a sales pitch,[3] here are some suggestions:

- You **could** politely say you don't need anything and then quickly hang up.
- You **can** tell the caller to mail you the information about the product or service.
- You **could** ask to have your name taken off the list.
- You **can** tell the caller not to call you anymore.
- You **could** get a caller ID and pick up the phone only when you get calls from people you know.

Remember that the people calling you are not the cause of the problem. They didn't decide to call you; their employers did. So you **shouldn't** get angry at them.

If you do decide to listen and buy a product or service, remember, you **should** never give out your credit card number to companies you don't know about. If you want more information about a company, you **could** contact the Better Business Bureau or the Attorney General in your state.

4.7 Making Suggestions

Examples	Explanation
You **could** use a caller ID to see who's calling. You **can** tell the caller to send you information by mail.	*Can* and *could* are used to offer suggestions. More than one choice is acceptable.
You **should** always be careful of strange callers. You **shouldn't** give out your credit card number.	*Should* is used when you feel that there is only one right way.

[3] A *sales pitch* is a talk that tries to persuade you to buy something.

LANGUAGE NOTES

Can and *could* have the same meaning in offering suggestions. *Could* does not have a past meaning in offering suggestions.

EXERCISE 19 Offer at least two suggestions to a person who says each of the following statements. (You may work with a partner.)

EXAMPLE: I need to find a book about American history.

You could go to a bookstore. You can get one at the public library.

You could try an online bookstore.

1. I'm leaving for vacation tomorrow, and I need to find out about the weather in the city where I'm going.

2. I need to lose ten pounds.

3. My landlord is raising my rent by $50, and I can't afford the increase.

4. I'd like to learn English faster.

5. I want to know the price of an airline ticket to my country.

6. I need to buy a new computer, and I want to compare prices.

7. I'm going to a party. The hostess asked each guest to bring something to eat.

8. I type so slowly. I need to learn to type faster.

4.8 *Have To, Can, Could,* and *Should*

Examples	Explanation
Do I have to listen to the caller? No, you don't have to. You **could** just hang up.	*Could* offers one of several possible ways of responding.
Do I have to be polite? No, you don't have to, but you **should**.	*Should* suggests that there is a right way to respond.
Do they have to take my name off their list if I ask them to? Yes, they **have to**.	*Have to* shows that something is necessary or obligatory.
Do I have to buy something to enter a sweepstakes? No, you don't have to, but you **can**.	*Can* shows that something is acceptable, but not necessary. You have a choice.

EXERCISE 20 Ask your teacher if he or she has to do these things. Your teacher can answer with "Yes, I do," "No, I don't have to, but I can," or "No, I don't have to, but I should."

EXAMPLES: correct the homework
A. Do you have to correct the homework?
B. Yes, I do.

work in the summer
A. Do you have to work in the summer?
B. No, I don't have to, but I can.

help students after class
A. Do you have to help students after class?
B. I don't have to, but I should.

1. work during the summer

2. give a final exam

3. teach reading

4. take more courses in the teaching of English

5. call the school when you're going to be absent

6. work in the evenings

7. have office hours

8. write lesson plans

9. take attendance

10. call the students by their last names

11. know another language in order to teach English

12. attend teachers' meetings

Before You Read
1. Do you think TV commercials are interesting?
2. Do you believe what you see in commercials?

Read the following conversation. Pay special attention to *be supposed to*.

Don't Believe Everything You See

A. Last week I saw an informative TV show about a new product that**'s supposed to** make you look younger. And I saw information about a business deal that**'s supposed to** make you rich in six months. There were experts and celebrities[4] on the show.

B. You can't believe everything you see on TV. Those "experts" and celebrities **are supposed to** say those things because they're paid a lot of money to make you believe that what they're saying is true.

A. But these seemed like very informative TV shows.

B. Those aren't shows at all. They're "infomercials."

A. What's an infomercial?

B. It's a commercial that looks like a TV show. You**'re supposed to** think that you're watching an informative TV show and getting advice from experts and celebrities. These "shows" last 30 minutes, like regular TV shows. And they have commercial breaks, like regular TV shows, to make you believe they're real shows. These "shows" tell you that their products

---

[4] *Celebrities* are famous people, such as actors or athletes.

are **supposed to** make you thin, young, rich, and beautiful. You're **supposed to** believe them and spend your money on useless products.

A. But the results look so real.
B. They're **supposed to** look real. But don't believe everything you see on TV.

4.9 Expectations

Examples	Explanation
This product **is supposed to** grow hair in 30 days. Another product **is supposed to** make you look younger. Let's rent *Titanic* this weekend. It's **supposed to** be a good movie. It's **supposed to** rain this weekend.	*Be supposed to* is used to show that we have an expectation about a product, a movie, a restaurant, the weather, etc., based on information we were given. The information may be true or false.
You're **supposed to** believe you are watching an informative show. I'm **supposed to** write a paper for my class. The teacher **is supposed to** give us a grade at the end of the semester.	In these examples, the subject of *be supposed to* is expected to do something.

LANGUAGE NOTE

Remember that *be supposed to* is also used for rules and laws:
  Drivers *are supposed to* wear a seat belt.
  We're *not supposed to* talk during the test.

EXERCISE 21 Write a sentence telling what this new product is supposed to do.

EXAMPLE: Are you starting to look old? Try Youth Cream.
It's supposed to make you look younger.

1. Are you bald? Use Hair Today, a new cream.

_____

2. Do you look weak? Use Muscle Power, a new cream.

_____

3. Do you forget things? Try Memory Builder, a new pill.

_____

4. Is English hard for you? Try QuickEnglish, a new video cassette.

_____

5. Do you have stained teeth? Try WhiteBright Toothpaste.

_____

6. Do you want to make money in 30 days? Try FastMoney, a new book.

_____

7. Are you overweight? Try SlimTrim, a new diet drink.

_____

8. Do you want to make your work in the kitchen easier? Buy Quick-Chop, a new device for chopping vegetables.

_____

EXERCISE 22 Fill in the blanks with *be supposed to* plus a verb to complete these statements.

EXAMPLE: We _'re supposed to have_ a test soon on modals. The teacher mentioned it yesterday.

1. Let's take an umbrella. It _____ today.

2. Let's eat at Maxwell's Restaurant tonight. The food _____ _____. My friend ate there last week and really liked it.

3. I have to go to the airport to pick up my brother. His plane _____ _____ at 5:45.

4. I won't be able to go to the movies with you tonight. My cousin in Peru _____ at 8 p.m., so I have to be home to receive his call.

5. My boss _____ a raise soon. We talked about it a few months ago.

6. How many compositions _____ for this course?

7. How many tests _____ in this course?

8. Do you know anything about registration? When _____ registration for next semester _____?

9. I can't go to the museum with you on Friday. I _____

_____ my mother to the doctor. She doesn't drive.

10. I'm moving next month. My friends _____.
I always help them when they move.

EXERCISE 23 Work with a partner. Write a list of three things the teacher expects from the students in this class or at this school. Begin with *we*.

EXAMPLE: *We're supposed to come to class every day.* _____

1. _____

2. _____

3. _____

EXERCISE 24 Work with a partner. Write a list of three things that you expect from the teacher in this class. Begin with *he* or *she*.

EXAMPLE: *She's supposed to correct us when we make a mistake.* _____

1. _____

2. _____

3. _____

4.10 Possibilities

Examples	Explanation
"You **may** already be a winner, Mr. Goldman!" "This **could** be your lucky day!" Some promises **might** not be true.	Use *may, might, could* to show possibilities about the present.
"If you enter, you **could** win a fabulous prize." If you enter a sweepstakes, you **may** win, but the chances are very small. You **might** win a cheap, useless prize.	We use *may, might, could* to show possibilities about the future. The outcome is not certain.

LANGUAGE NOTES

1. Compare certainty and uncertainty about the present.
   You *are* a winner. (certain)
   You *may be* a winner. (uncertain)
2. Compare certainty and uncertainty about the future.
   You *will win* a prize. (certain)
   You *may win* a prize. (uncertain)
3. For negative possibility, we use *may not* or *might not*. (Don't use *could not*; it means *was not able to*). We do not make a contraction with *may not* or *might not*.
   You *may not* win anything. (future possibility)
   I *couldn't* call you last night. (past inability)
4. For questions about possibility, we usually say, "Do you think . . . *may, might, could* . . . ?"
   Do you think I *might* win? Do you think I *could* get lucky?
   NOTE: The clause after *Do you think* uses statement word order.
5. *Maybe*, written as one word, is an adverb. It is usually put before the subject. *May be*, written as two words, is a modal + verb. COMPARE:
   Maybe you are right. = You *may be* right.
   Maybe we will get a prize. = We *may get* a prize.
   Maybe he needs help. = He *may need* help.

EXERCISE 25 Answer these questions by using the word in parentheses for uncertainty.

EXAMPLE: Is the company legitimate? (*might*)
It might be legitimate.

1. Does the company give out prizes? (*may*)

2. Are the prizes cheap? (*could*)

3. Will I be chosen as a winner? (*might*)

4. Will this company take my money and give me nothing? (*might*)

5. Will I win a cheap prize? (*could*)

EXERCISE 26 Fill in the blanks with the possible results of the following situations.

EXAMPLE: If I pass this course, *I might take a computer course next semester.*

1. If I don't pay my rent, _____

2. If I save a lot of money, _____

---

3. If I drink a lot of coffee tonight, _____

4. If I eat a lot of sugar, _____

5. If I drive too fast, _____

6. If I exercise regularly, _____

7. If I increase my computer skills, _____

8. If children don't learn about computers in school, _____

_____

9. If sweepstakes companies don't obey the law, _____

_____

10. If I win a lot of money, _____

11. If parents don't set a good example for their children, _____

_____

12. If you come late to work every day, _____

13. If you don't do your homework, _____

14. If I enter a sweepstakes, _____

EXERCISE 27 Fill in the blanks with an appropriate verb.

EXAMPLE: My friend may ____*stay*____ here, or he might go back to his hometown.

1. I don't like to live alone. I may _____ a roommate.

2. She might _____ to graduate school next year. She's not sure yet.

3. My brother needs a job. He might _____ for our uncle.

4. My parents might _____ here to visit next year. I'm not sure yet.

5. We may _____ a vacation if we have enough money.

6. I'm saving my money. I may _____ a house next year.

7. You think the next president will be a woman? You may _____ right.

8. You're looking for a good dentist? Ask the teacher for a recommendation. She might _____ of a good dentist.

9. You might _____ I'm crazy, but I'm going to marry a woman I've known for only two months.

10. If your mother-in-law comes to live with you, it could _____ problems between you and your wife.

Before You Read

1. Have you seen game shows on TV? Do you like any of them?
2. Have you seen shows on TV where people talk about their personal problems? What do you think of these shows?

Read the following conversation. Pay special attention to *must*.

Game Shows and Talk Shows

A. I'm confused about some TV shows. For example, on game shows, how do people know all the answers? Somebody **must give** the contestants the answers ahead of time.

B. That's not true. It's illegal to give the contestants the answers ahead of time.

A. Then they **must be** very intelligent.

B. Oh, yes. They are.

A. What about the prize money? Do the winners really win all that money?

B. Yes, they do.

A. It **must feel** great to win so much money.

B. I agree.

A. What about those strange talk shows that are on in the afternoon? Those people who are yelling and screaming at each other **must be** actors.

B. They're not actors. They're real people.

A. They **must not value** their privacy. Those people tell all the personal details of their lives.

B. I think they're not typical people. The people on those shows **must be** crazy to go on TV with all their problems.

4.11 Logical Conclusions

Examples	Explanation
She knows all the answers to the questions. She **must be** smart. He won $10,000. He **must feel** great. People who talk about their personal problems on TV **must not value** their privacy.	*Must* has two completely different uses. In section 4.2, we studied *must* as an expression of necessity. In the above reading and in the examples to the left, *must* shows a conclusion based on information we have or observations we make.

Modals—Present and Future; Related Expressions   **175**

LANGUAGE NOTES

1. For a negative conclusion, use *must not*. Do not use a contraction.
2. *Must* in the preceding cases talks about the present only, not the future.

EXERCISE 28 In each of the conversations below, fill in the blanks with an appropriate verb to make a logical conclusion.

EXAMPLE:

A. Have you ever visited Japan?

B. I lived there when I was a child.

A. Then you must *know how to speak* _____ Japanese.

B. I used to, but I've forgotten it.

1. This is a conversation between two female students.

   A. Would you introduce me to Lee?

   B. Who's Lee?

   A. You must _____ who I'm talking about. He's in your speech class. He sits next to you.

   B. You mean Mr. Song?

   A. Yes, Lee Song. The tall handsome guy with glasses. He doesn't wear a wedding ring. He must _____ single.

   B. I'm not so sure about that. Not all married men wear a wedding ring.

2. This is a conversation between a married woman (M) and a single woman (S).

   M. My husband spends all his free time with our children.

   S. He must _____ kids very much.

   M. He does.

   S. How many kids do you have?

   M. We have four.

   S. Raising kids must _____ the hardest job in the world.

   M. It is, but it's also the most rewarding.

3. This is a conversation between a teacher (T) and a student (S).

   T. Take out the paper I gave you last Monday.

S. I don't have it. Could you give me one, please?

T. Were you in class last Monday?

S. Yes, I was.

T. Then you must _____ it.

S. Oh, yes. You're right. Here it is.

4. This is a conversation between an American (A) and an immigrant (I).

A. It must _____ hard to start your life in a new country.

I. Yes, it is.

A. You must _____ lonely at times.

I. Yes. You must _____ how it feels. You went to live in Japan for a few years, didn't you?

A. Yes, I did. It took me a long time to get used to it.

5. A. I saw some experts on TV talking about a cure for baldness.

They must _____ what they're talking about because they're experts.

B. You must _____ that if you see it on TV it's true. But don't believe everything you see.

EXERCISE 29 Use *must* + base form to make a conclusion.

EXAMPLE: Her children live far away. She never sees them. She _____*must be*_____ very lonely.

1. Look at that ring. It _____ expensive. It's a diamond.

2. Look at that ring. It looks like a diamond. It (not) _____ a diamond because it costs only $10.99.

3. Do they have children? They _____ children. They're buying diapers.

4. Look at those people. They're carrying maps and cameras. They _____ tourists.

5. Does the teacher always know which modal to use? She _____ _____. She's the teacher.

6. I keep calling my friend, but there's no answer. He (not) _____ _____ home.

7. Your sister has six children. She _____ busy. She (not) _____ any free time at all.

8. Jane wears something blue every day. She _____ the color blue.

9. She has cat hairs on her clothes. She _____ a cat.

10. It's starting to get dark outside. It _____ late.

11. Susan has a new boyfriend. She talks about him all the time. She _____ in love.

12. My friend has a lot of sports magazines at home. He _____ _____ sports.

13. One game show contestant won $50,000. He _____ happy.

14. The man is buying dog food. He _____ a dog.

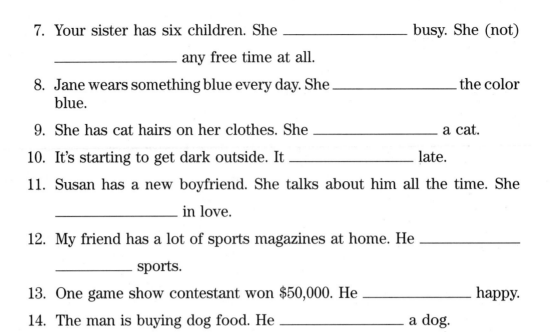

4.12 Probability vs. Possibility in the Present

Degrees of Certainty	Explanation
a) The first word is "better." b) The second word **must be** "or." c) The third word **might be** "worse" or it **could be** "force" or it **may be** "horse."	a) We are certain that the information is true. b) We conclude that the information is correct based on information we have. c) Something is possible. We don't have enough evidence or information to really know.
a) She **knows** the answer. She is giving the correct answer now. b) She **must know** the answer. She has a smile on her face and looks excited. c) She **might know** the answer. There is no expression on her face.	

LANGUAGE NOTES

For negative possibility, use *may not* or *might not*. Don't use *could not* for negative possibility. (*Could not* means past inability: I *could not* work yesterday because I was sick.)

EXERCISE 30 Decide if the situation is probable or possible. Fill in the blanks with *must* for probability or *may/might/could* for possibility.

EXAMPLES:
A. Where is Linda Ramirez from?

B. Ramirez is a Spanish name. She ___*might*___ be from Mexico.

She ___*may*___ be from Colombia. There are so many countries where Spanish is spoken that it's hard to know for sure.

A. She ___*could*___ be from the Philippines. Filipinos have Spanish names, too.

B. Where is Tran Nguyen from?

A. I know that's a Vietnamese name. He ___*must*___ be from Vietnam.

1. A. What time is it?

   B. I don't have a watch. The sun is directly overhead, so it _____ be about noon.

2. A. Where's the teacher today?

   B. No one knows. She _____ be sick.

3. A. Does Yoko speak Japanese?

   B. She _____ speak Japanese. She's from Japan.

4. A. Where's Washington Avenue?

   B. I don't know. We're lost. There's a woman over there. Let's ask her. She _____ know.

5. A. Why is that student sneezing so much?

   B. I don't know. She _____ have a cold, or it _____ be an allergy.

6. A. Is Susan married?

   B. She _____ be married. She's wearing a wedding ring.

7. A. Why didn't Joe come to the party?

   B. Who knows? He _____ not like parties.

8. A. I need to make some copies, and I don't have change for the copy machine.

   B. I _____ have some change. Let me look in my pocket.

9. A. I've never lived far from my parents before.

   B. You _____ miss them very much.

   A. I do.

---

10. A. Look at that young couple. They're always holding hands, **smiling** at each other, and kissing.

    B. They _____ be in love.

11. A. Linda never answers any questions in class.

    B. She _____ be shy or she _____ not know the **answer** to the questions.

12. A. I have a question about grammar.

    B. Let's ask the teacher. She _____ know the answer.

13. A. I have a question about American history.

    B. Why don't you ask our grammar teacher? He _____ know the answer.

4.13 Modals with Continuous Verbs

Examples	Explanation
The child **should be sleeping**. She **shouldn't be watching** TV now.	Use modal + *be* + verb *-ing* for a continuous meaning.
I can't reach my friend. His line is always busy. He **might be using** the Internet now.	
We **are supposed to be listening** to the teacher.	

EXERCISE 31 A student is home sick today. She looks at her watch and knows that her English class is going on right now. She knows what usually happens in class. Read the following statements and tell what *may, must,* or *should* be happening now.

EXAMPLE: The teacher usually asks questions. (must)
He must be asking questions now.

1. The teacher sometimes sits at the desk. (may)

2. The teacher always does the exercises. (must)

3. The teacher explains the grammar. (should)

4. The teacher always helps the students. (must)

5. The teacher sometimes reviews. (might)

6. Sometimes the students don't pay attention. (be supposed to)

7. The students are probably wondering where I am. (must)

8. The teacher sometimes passes back papers. (might)

Examples	Explanation
You **must** take a test to get a driver's license.	Law or rule (official tone)
You**'re supposed to** wear your seat belt.	Law or rule (unofficial tone)
I **have to** mail a letter. I**'ve got to** mail a letter.	Personal obligation
You**'d better** study tonight, or you might fail the test on modals.	Warning; negative consequences stated or implied
You **should** throw that letter in the garbage. You **ought to** throw that letter in the garbage.	Advice
You **may/can** write the test with a pencil. You **may not/cannot** talk during a test.	Permission/Prohibition
I get annoying calls from telemarketers. What **can** I do? You **could** be polite to the caller and listen, or you **can** say you're not interested and hang up.	Suggestions
You **may** win a prize. You **might** win a prize. You **could** win a prize.	Possibility about the future
It**'s supposed to** rain tomorrow. This face cream **is supposed to** make you look younger. My brother **is supposed to** call me this weekend.	Expectation
She won a lot of money. She **must** be happy.	Conclusion about the present
I can't find my keys. They **might** be in your pocket. Did you look there? Or they **could** be on the kitchen table. They **may** be in your car.	Possibility about the present

Review the meanings of negative modals on page 163.

1. Don't use *to* after a modal. (Exception: *ought to*)

    You should ~~to~~ buy a new car.

2. Use the base form after a modal.

    She can't ~~goes~~ *go* with you.

    You should ~~studying~~ *study* now.

3. Don't forget **d** in *supposed to, permitted to, allowed to.*

    He's not suppose*d* to drive. He's too young.

    You're not allow*ed* to talk during the test.

4. Don't forget **'d** to express *had better*.

    You*'d* better take the bus to work. Your car isn't working well.

5. Use *have/has* before *got to* in writing.

    We*'ve* got to leave now.

6. Don't put two modals together.

    You must ~~can~~ *be able to* drive well before you can get your license.

7. Don't forget *be* or *to* in these expressions: *be supposed to, be able to, be permitted to, be allowed to.*

    They *are* supposed to leave at 6 o'clock.

    I'm able *to* work on Saturday.

8. Use correct word order in a question with a modal.

    What ~~I should~~ *should I* do?

PART 1
Find the mistakes with the underlined words, and correct them. Not every sentence has a mistake. If the sentence is correct, write C.

EXAMPLES: He ~~got to~~ talk to you. *'s*

You <u>ought to</u> come to class earlier.   C

1. You <u>must to</u> leave the building immediately.

2. We <u>not allowed to</u> use our books during a test.

3. To become a U.S. citizen, you <u>must be able to</u> speak simple English.

4. She <u>can't find</u> a job.

5. You're almost out of gas. <u>You better</u> fill up your gas tank.

6. The boss expects everyone to be on time. <u>You'd better don't</u> come late to the meeting.

7. She <u>cans type</u> very fast.

8. Where <u>I can</u> find information about museums in this city?

9. You're <u>not allowed to</u> talk during a test.

10. It's cold outside. <u>You'd better</u> take a sweater.

11. <u>We're supposed to</u> write a composition about our parents.

12. I <u>got to buy</u> a new car.

13. When <u>is your brother supposed to</u> arrive?

14. It's <u>suppose to rain</u> tomorrow.

Look at the job application. Circle the best words to complete each sentence. (The numbers on the application refer to each one of the sentences on the next page.)

---

① Fill out the following form. Print in black ink or type. Bring it to the personnel office or mail it to:

Ms. Judy Lipton
P.O. Box 324
Tucson, Arizona 85744

Applications must be submitted by November 15.

② Name _____ _____ _____
                (last)   (first)   (middle initial)

Address _____

City _____ State _____ Zip Code _____

③ Telephone ( ) _____

④ Marital status (optional) _____ Sex _____ ⑤

⑥ Date of birth _____ _____ _____ (You must be at least 18.) ⑦
                  (month)   (day) (year)

⑧ Social Security number _____-_____-_____

⑨ Educational background

	Date graduated	Degree or major
High School	_____	_____
College	_____	_____
Graduate School	_____	_____

⑩ Employment History (Please start with your present or last job.)

Company	Position	Dates	Supervisor	Reason for leaving
_____	_____	_____	_____	_____
_____	_____	_____	_____	_____
_____	_____	_____	_____	_____
_____	_____	_____	_____	_____

Do not write in the shaded box. For office use only.

⑪
Rec'd. by _____
Amer. cit. _____
Doc. checked _____
Transcripts received _____

⑫ The Immigration Act of 1986 requires all successful applicants to present documents to prove U.S. citizenship or permanent residence with permission to work in the U.S.

⑬ This company is an Equal Opportunity Employer. Race, religion, nationality, marital status, and physical disability will not influence our decision to hire.

⑭ I certify that these answers are true.

⑮ Signature: _____ Date: _____

EXAMPLE: You (~~aren't supposed to~~, couldn't) use a red pen to fill out the application.

1. You (have to, might) submit the application to Ms. Lipton. Ms. Lipton (must, should) be the person in charge of hiring. She wants the application by November 15. Today is November 14. You ('d better not, mustn't) send it by regular mail. If you use regular mail, it (must not, might not) arrive on time. You (could, are supposed to) send it by overnight express mail, or you (might, can) take it to Ms. Lipton's office.

2. You (could, are supposed to) write your last name before your first name.

3. You (are supposed to, could) include your phone number.

4. You (shouldn't, don't have to) include your marital status.

5. For sex, you (might, are supposed to) write M for male or F for female.

6. To write the date of your birth in the U.S., you (should, can) write the month before the day (June 7, for example). You have several choices in writing the date. You (must, could) write June 7 or 6/7 or 6-7. If you put the day before the month, an American (might, should) think you mean July 6 instead of June 7.

7. To apply for the job, you (might, must) be over 18.

8. People who work in the U.S. (may, must) have a Social Security number.

9. You (may, are supposed to) include the schools you attended.

10. In the employment history section, you are asked why you left your last job. The employer (might, should) want to know if you were fired or if you left on your own.

11. You (can't, aren't supposed to) write in the gray box. "Amer. cit." (must, should) mean American citizen.

12. You (must not, don't have to) be an American citizen to apply for the job. You can be a permanent resident. You (have to, should) prove your citizenship or residency. If you don't have permission to work in the U.S., you (might not, cannot) apply for this job.

13. The company (might not, may not) choose a worker based on race, religion, or nationality.

14. You (don't have to, must not) lie on the application form.

15. You (may, must) sign the application and include the date.

Read the pairs of sentences. If the sentences have the same meaning, write **S**. If the sentences have a different meaning, write **D**.

EXAMPLES: You <u>have to</u> wear your seat belt. / You <u>must</u> wear your seat belt.   **S**

You <u>must</u> open the window. / You <u>should</u> open the window.   **D**

1. She <u>can</u> drive a car. / She <u>is able to</u> drive a car.

2. He <u>can't</u> speak Korean. / He <u>might not</u> speak Korean.

3. I'm <u>supposed to</u> help my sister on Friday. / I <u>might</u> help my sister on Friday.

4. You <u>don't have to</u> drive to work. / You <u>shouldn't</u> drive to work.

5. You're <u>not supposed to</u> write the answer. / You <u>don't have to</u> write the answer.

6. You're <u>not allowed to</u> use a pencil for the test. / You <u>may not</u> use a pencil for the test.

7. We <u>should</u> visit our mother. / We <u>ought to</u> visit our mother.

8. You <u>should</u> make a right turn here. / You <u>must</u> make a right turn here.

9. If you need more help, you <u>could</u> go to a tutor./ If you need more help, you <u>can</u> go to a tutor.

10. You <u>shouldn't</u> wear jeans. / You <u>must not</u> wear jeans.

11. You <u>must not</u> come back after the final exam. / You <u>don't have to</u> come back after the final exam.

12. I <u>have to</u> work tomorrow. / I've <u>got to</u> work tomorrow.

13. You <u>can't</u> eat in the computer lab. / You <u>are not allowed to</u> eat in the computer lab.

14. I <u>may</u> go to New York next week. / I <u>might</u> go to New York next week.

15. The final exam <u>could</u> be hard. / The final exam <u>might</u> be hard.

16. You <u>don't have to</u> call your teacher by her last name./ It is <u>not necessary to</u> call the teacher by her last name.

17. You <u>must not</u> fill out the application with a red pen. / You <u>aren't supposed to</u> fill out the application with a red pen.

18. You'd <u>better</u> wake up early tomorrow morning. / You <u>could</u> wake up early tomorrow morning.

CLASSROOM ACTIVITIES

1. Form a small group. Take something from your purse or pocket that says something about you. Show it to your group. Your group will make deductions about you.

EXAMPLE: car keys
You must have a car.

2. On the left are some American customs. On the right, tell if there is a comparable custom in your native culture. Write what that custom is.

In the U.S.	In my native culture
When someone sneezes, you're supposed to say, "Bless you."	
If you're invited to a party, in most cases you're not supposed to take your children.	
Americans sometimes have potluck parties. Guests are supposed to bring food to the party.	
There are some foods you can eat with your hands. Fried chicken and pizza are examples.	
Students are not supposed to talk to each other during an exam.	
When you're too sick to go to work, you're supposed to call the employer and say you're not coming in that day.	

3. Bring in two copies of an application. It can be an application for a job, driver's license, license plate, apartment rental, address change, check cashing card, rebate, etc. Work with a partner. One person will give instructions. The other person will fill the application out. Use modals to help the other person fill it out correctly.

4. Find a partner and write some sentences to give advice for each of the following problems.

   a) I got permission to come to the U.S. I have a dog. I've had this dog for six years, since she was a puppy, but I can't take her with me. What should I do?

   b) I got a D in my biology class. I think I deserve a C. What should I do?

c) I need a new car, but I don't have enough money right now. What should I do?

d) I found an envelope with $100 in it in front of my apartment building. There is no name on it. What should I do?

e) My husband's brother came to live with us. He never cooks, cleans, or washes the dishes. I have to do everything. I'm very unhappy with the situation. What should I do?

DISCUSSION

1. Do you think drivers should be allowed to talk on a cell phone while driving?

2. Do you ever watch TV talk shows? What do you think of them?

3. Do you ever watch court shows on TV? What do you think of them?

4. How do you respond to telemarketing calls?

5. What do you think of TV commercials?

6. Did you ever win a prize in a contest, sweepstakes, or raffle? What did you win?

7. Did you ever buy a product that claims to do something but doesn't do it?

OUTSIDE ACTIVITIES

1. Call your local phone company to find out how much it costs to block 900 numbers from your phone.

2. Watch a game show on TV. Write several sentences about the game show using modals and related expressions.

EXAMPLE: Contestants have to press a buzzer to answer a question.

Internet Activities

1. Look for the Web sites of the Federal Trade Commission, the Better Business Bureau, or the National Fraud Information Center. Find some interesting consumer information to share with the class.

2. Look for local TV listings on the Web. You will probably have to type in your zip code to get listings in your area.

3. At a search engine, type in "infomercial." Find a report about TV info-mercials. Print it up and bring it to class.

GRAMMAR

Modals in the Past

CONTEXT

The Assassination of President John F. Kennedy
The Death of John Kennedy, Jr.

LESSON FOCUS

To express the past time with most modals, we use
modal + *have* + past participle.

I *should have studied* English when I was younger.
I *might have left* my sweater at work.

President John F. Kennedy (1917–1963)

1. Have you ever heard of President John F. Kennedy?
2. What political leaders have been assassinated?

Read the following article. Pay special attention to the past form of modals.

The Assassination of President John F. Kennedy

On November 22, 1963, President John F. Kennedy, the thirty-fifth President of the United States, was assassinated in Dallas, Texas, while he was riding in an open car. Many people think it was foolish of him to be in an open car. He **should have had** a covered bulletproof car, as most world leaders do today. His death **could have been prevented**.

Immediately after the assassination, a suspect, Lee Harvey Oswald, was arrested. Two days later, as Oswald was being transferred to a jail, he himself was killed by a gunman in the crowd. An investigation took place to find out the truth behind the assassination. After examining a lot of evidence and questioning many people, the investigating committee determined that Lee Oswald **must have been** the person who shot Kennedy. However, many theories have been made about why he did it. Some people think Oswald **might have been** a crazy person who thought he could get attention by killing a famous man. Another theory states that he **might have been** the agent of another government, possibly Russia or Cuba. According to another theory, organized crime (the Mafia) **may have been** behind the assassination.

Some witnesses report gunshots coming from two different directions. If this is true, Oswald **could not have acted** alone; there **must have been** more than one gunman.

Even though the assassination occurred many years ago, people are still fascinated with this event. Books and movies have appeared through the years offering new theories about this mysterious tragedy. Because Oswald was killed before he went to trial, many questions have remained unanswered.

Did you know...?

John F. Kennedy was the fourth American president to be assassinated. The other three were Abraham Lincoln (1865), James Garfield (1881), and William McKinley (1901).

5.1 Modals in the Past: *Have* + Past Participle

Active:

Subject	Modal	*(Not)*	*Have*	Past Participle	Complement
Oswald	might		have	been	crazy.
He	may	not	have	acted	alone.
Kennedy	should		have	used	a bulletproof car.
He	should	not	have	ridden	in an open car.

(continued)

Passive:

Subject	Modal	(Not)	Have Been	Past Participle	Complement
Kennedy	must		have been	killed	by Oswald.
He	should		have been	protected	better.
Oswald	should	not	have been	shot.	

LANGUAGE NOTES

1. The only modal that has a past form is *can*. The past form is *could*.
   Americans *couldn't* understand why the President was assassinated.
2. For past necessity, *had to* is used.
   President Kennedy's children *had to* grow up without a father.
3. For the other modals, we use *have* + past participle to give a past meaning.
4. In informal speech, *have* is often pronounced like *of* or /ə/. Listen to your teacher pronounce the sentences in the preceding charts with fast, informal pronunciation.

EXERCISE 1 Fill in the blanks with the correct form of an appropriate verb.

EXAMPLE: Americans must have ___*been*___ sad when they heard the news.

1. Kennedy should have _____ more protection.

2. He could have _____ in a closed car, but he preferred an open one.

3. Many people thought that Kennedy's death could have been _____ by having more security.

4. Oswald must have _____ the killer.

5. Oswald may have _____ crazy.

6. Why was Oswald killed? Somebody might have _____ to silence him.

7. Oswald might have _____ the agent of another government.

8. The police should have _____ Oswald more protection as they were taking him to jail.

Examples	Explanation
Why did Oswald kill Kennedy? There are several theories: He **could have been** the agent of another government. Organized crime **may have ordered** the assassination. Oswald **might have been** crazy.	Use *may have*, *might have*, or *could have* + past participle to express possibility about the past. The sentences on the left give theories about a past event.

LANGUAGE NOTES

1. Compare possibility with *maybe* and possibility with modals.
   Maybe he was crazy.→ He *might have been* crazy.
   Maybe the Mafia ordered the assassination.→ The Mafia *could have ordered* the assassination.
2. For negative possibility, don't use *could not have* because it has a different meaning. (See section 5.9)

EXERCISE 2   Change these *maybe* statements to statements with *may have, might have*, or *could have*. Situation: A student dropped out of the course after the first few weeks. These are some guesses why he did it.

EXAMPLE: Maybe he registered for the wrong section. (may)
He may have registered for the wrong section.

1. Maybe he preferred an earlier class. (could)

2. Maybe he wanted to be in his friend's class. (might)

3. Maybe the class was too hard for him. (may)

4. Maybe he got sick. (could)

5. Maybe he didn't like the teacher. (may)

6. Maybe he found a full-time job. (might)

7. Maybe he had a lot of problems at home. (could)

8. Maybe he left town. (might)

EXERCISE 3 Fill in the blanks with an appropriate past participle to make statements of possibility about the past.

EXAMPLE: Linda was yawning during the lesson this morning. She might have _____been_____ bored. She might not have _____had_____ enough sleep last night. She may have _____gone_____ to bed late last night.

1. My friend didn't answer the phone when I called last night. She might not have _____ home. She could have _____ in the shower. She might not have _____ the telephone ring. She might have _____ down the volume on her phone.

2. One student didn't come to class all last week. She may have _____ out of town. She might have _____ sick. Sometimes she has to work overtime. She could have _____ to work overtime last week. She may have _____ guests from out-of-town.

3. I asked my boss for a raise three weeks ago, but she hasn't mentioned anything about it. She might have _____ all about it. Maybe I should remind her.

4. I sent a letter to my friend three weeks ago, and I still haven't received an answer. He might have _____ too busy to write back. The letter could have _____ lost. I might not have _____ enough postage on the letter.

5. I can't find my keys. I might have _____ them in my other jacket. They may have _____ out of my pocket because I have a hole in the pocket. I may have _____ them.

6. I had a job interview last week. Someone was supposed to call me this week, but no one did. They might have _____ the job to someone else. They could have _____ my phone number. They may have _____ that I didn't have enough experience for this job.

5.3 Past Conclusion

Examples	Explanation
After examining the evidence, the investigating committee concluded that Oswald **must have killed** Kennedy. Americans **must have felt** a great loss when their president died.	We use *must have* + past participle to make a statement of deduction about a past event based on observations we make and information we have.

EXERCISE 4   Fill in the blanks with an appropriate verb for past probability.

EXAMPLE:

A. I followed your directions to go downtown yesterday. I took the number 60 bus, but it didn't take me downtown.

B. You must _have misunderstood me_. I said "16," not "60."

1. A. I didn't see your sister yesterday.

   B. You must _____ her. She was in your class yesterday.

2. A. I called my friend's house. The person who answered the phone said, "Apex Car Repair."

   B. You must _____ the wrong number. Try again.

3. A. My husband was an orphan. Both of his parents died when he was small.

   B. He must _____ a difficult childhood.

4. A. Didn't we meet at Sue's party last week?

   B. I wasn't there. You must _____ my brother Tom. We're twins. We look alike.

5. A. My family and I lost all our money on our vacation.

   B. It must _____ a terrible trip.

   A. Yes, it was.

6. Charles has a suntan in winter. He must _____ to a warm sunny place for vacation.

7. Maria took her whole family out to a fancy restaurant. She paid for everything for 20 people. She must _____ a lot of money.

8. My grandparents had 11 children and lived on a farm. They must _____ a hard life.

9. I thought I was driving east, but now I realize I'm driving north. I must _____ a wrong turn somewhere.

10. Sara looked at her test paper and started to cry. She must _____ the test.

11. Ben applied to several universities. Today he received a letter from a university and looked so happy. He must _____.

12. Kim was talking about getting a job and dropping out of school. I haven't seen her in school lately. She must _____.

13. Don asked his parents for money to attend college this semester. He hasn't come back. He must not _____.

14. I said, "How are you?" to one of my classmates and he answered, "I'm 34 years old." He must _____ that I asked, "How *old* are you?"

Before You Read
1. Did you hear about the death of John Kennedy, Jr., in 1999? Where were you when you heard the news?
2. Do you know of any plane crashes in which someone famous died?

John Kennedy, Jr. (1960–1999)

John Kennedy, Jr. in 1963

Read the following article. Pay special attention to past forms of modals and other related expressions.

John Kennedy, Jr.

John Kennedy, Jr. could hardly remember his father. Born 17 days before his father was elected 35th president of the U.S., he was three days short of his third birthday when his father was shot and killed. During his lifetime, he witnessed many other family tragedies: the assassination of his uncle Robert, the untimely deaths of various cousins, and the death of his mother, Jacqueline Kennedy Onassis, in 1994 at the age of 65. John seemed to find happiness when he married his beautiful wife, Carolyn Bessette, in 1996.

John Kennedy, Jr. loved to fly. He got his pilot's license and bought a plane. He had only had his license for 15 months when he was planning to fly to his cousin's wedding in Massachusetts. Before driving to a New Jersey airport on July 16, 1999, he picked up his wife's sister. The two of them arrived at the airport late because of bad traffic that day. Kennedy's wife, Carolyn, was waiting for them there. Their plane took off at 8:30 p.m. Kennedy **was supposed to** drop off his sister-in-law and continue to Massachusetts with his wife for the wedding. He **was supposed to** arrive in Massachusetts a few hours later, but he never made it. By the next morning, when suitcases washed up on the shore, searchers concluded that his plane **must have crashed**. The wedding that **was supposed to** take place was canceled as family members gathered to give each other comfort and wait for more news. Six days later, the three bodies were found.

How and why did this accident occur? Other more experienced pilots believe that Kennedy had made several deadly mistakes:

- He flew in darkness over water. As an inexperienced pilot, he **shouldn't have flown** in darkness.
- Because of the weather, visibility was very low that night, and he didn't have much experience using the instruments. He **shouldn't have flown** with such low visibility.
- He flew over water, where it is easy to become disoriented. He **should have stayed** close to the shoreline.
- He didn't leave a flight plan.[1] He **should have left** a flight plan.
- His plane was large and difficult to handle. He **may not have been** able to handle such a large plane in difficulties. As an inexperienced pilot, he **shouldn't have flown** such a big plane.
- He had broken his ankle a few months earlier and **had to** walk with a cane. Because of his injured ankle, he **may not have been able to** handle the foot pedals.

John Kennedy was only 39 years old when he died, seven years younger than his father was when he died. His wife was 33. The tragedy **must have been** difficult not only for the Kennedys but also for John's wife's family, who lost two members of their family.

---

[1] A flight plan gives information about the pilot's name, speed of the airplane, route, estimated flying time, fuel, registration of airplane, etc.

5.4 *Must Have* vs. *Had To*

Examples	Explanation
Kennedy **had to** walk with a cane. He **had to** pick up his sister-in-law after work. He **had to** get permission to take off.	Use *had to* + base form to show necessity (personal or legal) about the past.
When the plane didn't arrive in Massachusetts, his family thought that it **must have crashed**. Kennedy's death **must have been** difficult for his family.	Use *must have* + past participle to make a conclusion about the past.

EXERCISE 5 Write *had to* + base form for a past necessity. Write *must have* + past participle for past deduction.

EXAMPLES: Kennedy ____*had to pick up*____ his sister-in-law after work.
(pick up)

It ____*must have been*____ hard for Kennedy to control the plane.
(be)

1. You were crying when you heard the news. You _____
(be)
_____ sad.

2. Kennedy grew up without a father. He _____
(have)
a difficult childhood.

3. When Kennedy decided to become a lawyer, he failed the law exam
and _____ it again.
(take)

4. Kennedy injured his ankle and _____ with a
(walk)
cane.

5. On Saturday, July 17, 1999, the Kennedy family _____
(cancel)
_____ the wedding.

6. The tragedy _____ especially hard for
(be)
Carolyn Bessette's parents because they lost two daughters.

7. Kennedy's sister _____ very alone because
(feel)
she had lost her father in 1963, her mother in 1994, and her brother
in 1999.

8. When the plane hit the water, the three passengers _____
(die)
_____ immediately.

9. When the bodies were found, a family member _____ *(identify)*

   _____ them.

10. The family and friends _____ when they *(cry)*

    found out that the bodies had been found.

5.5 Past Mistakes

Examples	Explanation
He **should have made** the trip in daylight. Kennedy **should have stayed** above land. He **shouldn't have flown** in such bad weather conditions.	We use *should have* + past participle to comment on a mistake that was made. We are not really giving advice because it is impossible to change the past.

LANGUAGE NOTES

1. Less frequently, for past mistakes we use *ought to have* + past participle.

   He *ought to have made* the trip in daylight.

2. USAGE NOTE: When a person receives an unexpected gift, he may be a little embarrassed. This person sometimes says, "You *shouldn't have*." This means, "You shouldn't have gone to so much trouble or expense" or "You shouldn't have given me a gift. I don't deserve it."

EXERCISE 6 Fill in the blanks with *have* and an appropriate past participle.

EXAMPLE: Kennedy should ___*have flown*___ before dark.

1. He didn't leave until after dark. He should _____ earlier.

2. He bought a large plane that was difficult to handle. He shouldn't _____ such a large plane.

3. He chose to fly over water. He should _____ a better route.

4. He didn't pay much attention to the weather conditions. He should _____ attention to the weather conditions.

5. He didn't have much experience with the instrument panel. He should _____ more experience with the instrument panel if he wanted to fly at night.

6. When he realized it was getting dark, he should _____ until the next morning.

EXERCISE 7   One day a man realizes that his wife has left him because he hadn't been a very good husband. The sentences below tell what he did. Fill in the blanks to tell what he should have done.

EXAMPLE: He didn't pay much attention to his wife. He should ___*have paid*___ more attention to her.

1. He didn't show his wife affection. He should _____ her more affection.

2. He didn't come home to dinner every night. He should _____ home to dinner every night.

3. He didn't listen to his wife's problems. He should _____ to her problems.

4. He never gave his wife a present. He should _____ her presents.

5. He never said, "I love you." He should _____, "I love you."

6. He never helped his wife with the housework. He should _____ _____ her with the housework.

7. He was very jealous. He shouldn't _____ so jealous.

8. He never gave his wife a compliment. He should _____ her compliments.

9. He never paid attention to the children. He should _____ more attention to his children.

10. He wasn't a good husband. He should _____ a better husband.

EXERCISE 8   Jack had a party at his house, and many things went wrong. Make comments with *should have*.

EXAMPLE: He invited a lot of people to his party, and there was no room to move.
He shouldn't have invited so many people.
_____

1. He didn't prepare enough food. Some of the guests didn't get anything to eat.

   _____

2. He invited some of the people from work but not others. When the others found out, they were upset with him.

   _____

3. One couple brought their children to the party, and the children were bored.

_____

4. The party became noisy, and the neighbors called the police.

_____

5. One woman came very late. Most of the guests had already left.

_____

6. He didn't give good directions on how to get to his party. Several people got lost and never found the party.

_____

EXERCISE 9   A family went on vacation by car. Make comments with *should have*.

EXAMPLE: They didn't fill up their gas tank, and they ran out of gas.

They should have filled up their tank before they left.

1. They didn't take a map, and they got lost.

_____

2. They didn't put air in the tires of the car.

_____

3. They didn't check the oil.

_____

4. They drove too fast and got a ticket.

_____

5. They took a lot of cash, and their money was stolen.

_____

flat tire

6. They didn't take a spare tire, and they had a flat tire.

_____

7. They didn't pack any warm clothes, and it was cold at night.

_____

5.6 Be Supposed To in the Past

Examples	Explanation
Kennedy's plane **was supposed to** arrive in Massachusetts on Friday night. His cousin's wedding **was supposed to** take place the next day.	*Was/were supposed to* is used to show that an expected action did not happen.
You **were supposed to** stop at the stop sign, but you didn't. I **was supposed to** pay my rent last month, but I forgot.	*Was/were supposed to* is used for rules that are broken.

EXERCISE 10 A woman has just come home from a business trip. She expected her husband to do certain things while she was gone. When she came home, she saw that he hadn't done most of these things. Fill in the blanks.

EXAMPLE: You were supposed to ___*water*___ the plants, but you didn't and now they're all dead.

1. You were supposed to _____ the bills, but you haven't done it.

2. You were supposed to _____ in the mail, but all the mail is still in the mailbox.

3. You were supposed to _____ dinner for the children, but I see lots of fast-food cartons in the garbage.

4. You were supposed to _____ the laundry, but the dirty clothes are all piled up.

5. You were supposed to _____ the dishes, but the dishes are all piled up in the sink.

6. The kids were supposed to _____ their homework, but they tell me they watched TV every night.

7. You were supposed to _____ groceries, but the refrigerator is almost empty.

8. I was supposed to _____ home on Friday, but I came home a day early.

5.7 Could and Was/Were Able To

Examples	Explanation
John Kennedy, Jr. was rich. He **could buy** anything he wanted.	In affirmative statements, *could* + base form means *used to be able to.* The person had this ability over a period of time.
On his third try, John Kennedy, Jr. **was** finally **able to pass** the exam to become a lawyer.	Use *was/were able to* for success in doing a single action.
John Kennedy, Jr. **couldn't remember** much about his father. He **wasn't able to remember** much about his father.	In negative statements, *could* and *was/were able to* are used interchangeably.

EXERCISE 11 Fill in the blanks with appropriate words to express past inability.

EXAMPLE: Kennedy wasn't *able to handle* such a big plane.

1. Kennedy wasn't _____ the airport before dark because traffic was so heavy.

2. Kennedy injured his ankle and couldn't _____ without a cane.

3. Visibility was low, so Kennedy couldn't _____ out the window of his plane.

4. His family couldn't _____ why his plane hadn't arrived on Friday night.

5. At first, Americans couldn't _____ that tragedy had come again to the Kennedy family.

6. The searchers weren't _____ the three bodies for six days.

Past Direction Not Taken

Examples	Explanation
President Kennedy **could have ridden** in a closed bulletproof car, but he didn't want to. John Kennedy, Jr. **could have been** an actor, but his mother was against it.	*Could have* + past participle is used to express a past opportunity that was not taken.
A. I moved last month. B. Why didn't you tell me? I **could have helped** you. B. I didn't want to bother you.	A person wanted to do something, but missed the opportunity to do it.
I was so hungry I **could have eaten** the whole pie by myself. I was so tired I **could have slept** all day.	A person had the desire to do something, but didn't.
Driver to pedestrian: Watch out, you idiot! I **could have killed** you.	Something almost happened, but didn't.

LANGUAGE NOTES

Compare *could* + base form and *could have* + past participle:
>When I was younger, I *could dance* all night. (I used to be able to dance all night.)
>Last night I had such a good time at the party that I *could have danced* all night. (I had the possibility or the desire, but I didn't do it.)

EXERCISE 12 Fill in the blanks with the correct form of the verb in parentheses to show that something almost happened but didn't.

EXAMPLE: The party was so wonderful that I could ___*have stayed*___ all night.

(stay)

1. I was so tired that I could _____ for 12 hours yesterday.

(sleep)

2. My boss acted so crazy yesterday that I could _____ him.

(kill)

3. You drove so carelessly that you could _____ an accident.

(have)

4. I was so happy when my counselor told me about my scholarship that I could _____ him.

(kiss)

5. The movie was so good that I could _____ it again and again.
   (watch)

6. Your cookies were so good that I could _____ all of them.
   (eat)

7. I enjoyed dancing so much last night that I could _____ all
   (dance)
   night.

8. The librarian is so beautiful that she could _____ a model.
   (be)

EXERCISE 13 Fill in the blanks with an appropriate verb for past opportunity
not realized.

EXAMPLE: We got married at home, but we could __*have gotten*__ married in church.

1. We had a small wedding, but we could _____ a big one.

2. We spent our honeymoon in San Francisco, but we could _____
   _____ it in Florida.

3. We bought a condo, but we could _____ a house.

4. We live in the city, but we could _____ in a suburb.

5. We got married when we were 28, but we could _____
   married right after we graduated from college.

6. We had only one child, but we could _____ more children.

7. I could _____ a lawyer, but I decided to be a stay-at-home mom.

8. Our daughter could _____ to private school, but she
   wanted to go to public school.

EXERCISE 14 Fill in the blanks to tell about an opportunity that you did not
take. Share your answers in a small group or with the entire
class.

EXAMPLE: I could have gone to Germany instead of coming to the U.S., but it's easier
to find a job in my profession in the U.S.

I could have _____ instead of

_____, but
(use verb + -ing)

_____

EXERCISE 15 John Kennedy, Jr. flew his own plane on the night of July 16, 1999. What are some other things he could have done that night? Write two sentences to give opportunities he did not take.

EXAMPLE: _He could have stayed in a hotel that night._

1. _____

2. _____

5.9 Past Impossibility

Examples	Explanation
A. My parents voted for Kennedy in 1964. B. What? They **couldn't have voted** for him in 1964. He died in 1963. A. I think I saw your brother at the library yesterday. B. It **couldn't have been** him. He's in Europe now on vacation.	_Couldn't have_ + past participle is used to show disbelief or to show that someone's statement is absolutely impossible. We are saying that the facts are wrong, that we can't believe this information because it is completely impossible.
Thanks so much for helping me paint my house. I **couldn't have done** it without you.	When we want to show gratitude or appreciation for someone's help, we often say, "_I couldn't have done it without you._"

LANGUAGE NOTES

Compare _couldn't_ + base form and _couldn't have_ + past participle.
A. I thought you were going to help me move last Saturday. Where were you?
B. I _couldn't help_ you last Saturday. I had to work. (_Couldn't help_ = wasn't able to help_)
A. I moved that piano all by myself.
B. What? You _couldn't have moved_ it by yourself. It's impossible. It's too heavy for one person. (_You couldn't have moved it._ = I don't believe you did it by yourself.)

EXERCISE 16 Fill in the blanks to make statements of disbelief.

EXAMPLE: A. When I was a child, I saw President Kennedy.

        B. You *couldn't have seen him!* _____ He died before you were born.

1. A. U.S. athletes won ten gold medals at the 1980 Olympics.

   B. They _____. The U.S. didn't participate in the 1980 Olympics.

2. A. We had an English test on December 25.

   B. You _____. The school was closed for Christmas Day.

3. A. President Kennedy ran for reelection in 1964.

   B. He _____. He died in 1963.

4. A. Oswald went to prison for many years for killing Kennedy.

   B. He _____. He was killed before he went to trial.

5. A. Hi. Don't you remember me?

   B. No, I'm sorry.

   A. We met in a math class last year.

   B. We _____ last year. I just started school two weeks ago.

6. A. I got an A on my math test.

   B. That's impossible. The teacher said that the highest grade was a B+. You _____ an A.

7. A. Was John Kennedy's mother at his wedding in 1996?

   B. She _____ at his wedding. She died in 1994.

8. One student gave the teacher a perfect composition with no mistakes.

   The teacher thinks that the student _____ _____ the composition by himself. Somebody must have helped him.

9. A. Somebody called me last night at midnight and didn't leave a message. Was it you?

   B. It _____ me. I was sleeping at midnight.

10. Teacher: You failed the test.
Student: What? I _____ the test. I studied for it for 5 hours.

11. A. I can't find my house keys.

    B. Maybe you left them at work.

    A. I _____ them at work. I used them to open the door and get into the house a few minutes ago.

12. Thanks for helping me move last Saturday. I _____ _____ without your help.

13. My in-laws came to visit last week. They _____ at a worse time. We were having the house painted.

14. A. Look at the big fish I caught yesterday.

    B. You _____ that fish. It has a price on it. You must have bought it at the store.

15. A. Kennedy knew a lot about politics. Do you think he learned it from his dad?

    B. He couldn't _____ it from his dad. He was less than three years old when his dad died.

EXERCISE 17 *Combination Exercise* A husband (H) and wife (W) are driving to a party and are lost. They are arguing in the car. Fill in the blanks to complete this conversation.

W. We're lost. And we don't even have a map. You should ___*have taken*___

   (example)

   a map.

H. I didn't think we were going to need one. I must _____

   (1)

   _____ a wrong turn.

W. I think you were supposed to make a right turn at the last intersection,

   but you turned left. We should _____ for direc-

   (2)

   tions the last time we stopped for gas.

H. You know I don't like to ask for directions.

W. Let's use the cell phone and call the Allens and ask them how to get to their house.

H. Let's see. I thought I had the cell phone in my pocket. I can't find it.

   I must _____ it at home.

   (3)

W. No, you didn't leave it at home. I've got it here in my purse. Oh, no.

   You forgot to recharge the battery. You should _____

   (4)

   _____ it last night.

H. Why is it my fault? You could _____ (5) too.

W. Well, we'll just have to look for a pay phone. Do you have any change?

H. I just have dollar bills.

W. You should _____ (6) some change with you.

H. Again, it's my fault.

W. Watch out! You could _____ (7) that other car!

H. I wasn't going to hit that car. I didn't come anywhere close to it.

W. I don't know why we're going in our car anyway. The Petersons offered us a ride. We could _____ (8) with them.

H. You should _____ (9) with the Peterson's and I should _____ (10) home. I could _____ (11) the football game today instead of listening to you complain!

SUMMARY OF LESSON 5

Must

Meaning	Present/Future	Past
Legal obligation	I **must go** to court next week.	I **had to go** to court last week.
Urgency	I **must talk** to the doctor right now!	
Strong necessity	I **must study** for the test next week.	I **had to study** for the test last month.
Prohibition	You **must not tell** a lie in court.	
Deduction; Conclusion	He's wearing a coat inside. He **must be** cold.	I can't find my keys. There's a hole in my pocket. I **must have lost** them.

Should

Meaning	Present/Future	Past
Advice	You **should buy** a new car next year. You **shouldn't eat** fatty foods.	You **should have bought** a new car last year. I **shouldn't have eaten** so many potato chips last night.

Can/Could

Meaning	Present/Future	Past
Ability	I **can speak** English now.	I **could speak** German when I was a child.
Acceptability	You **can wear** jeans to class every day.	You **could have worn** jeans to the party last week.
Permission/ Prohibition	We **can use** a dictionary to write a composition. We **can't use** our books during a test.	We **could use** a dictionary to write the last composition. We **couldn't use** a dictionary during the last test.
Suggestion	How **can** I **learn** about computers? You **can take** a course, or you **could buy** a book and teach yourself.	
Possibility	Mary isn't here today. She **could be** sick.	Mary wasn't here yesterday. She **could have been** sick.
Direction not taken		I **could have gone** to Germany, but I decided to come to the U.S.
Impossibility; Disbelief		A: I voted for President Clinton in 1996. B: You **couldn't have voted** for Clinton. You weren't a citizen in 1996.

May/Might

Meaning	Present/Future	Past
Permission	You **may use** a dictionary during the test.	
Possibility	I **may have** a job interview next week. I'm still not sure. I **might have** a job interview next week.	Simon is wearing a suit to class. He **may have had** a job interview this morning. He **might have had** a job interview this morning.

Ought To

Meaning	Present/Future	Past
Advice	She **ought to buy** a new car soon.	She **ought to have bought** a new car last year. (*rare*)

RELATED EXPRESSIONS

Have To

Meaning	Present/Future	Past
Necessity (personal or legal)	I **have to study** now. I **have to go** to court next week.	I **had to study** yesterday. I **had to go** to court last week.
Lack of necessity	My job is close to my home. I **don't have to drive**. I can walk.	My last job was close to my home. I **didn't have to drive**. I could walk.

Have Got To

Meaning	Present/Future	Past
Necessity	I**'ve got to go** to court next week.	——————

Be Able To

Meaning	Present/Future	Past
Ability	She **is able to play** chess now.	She **was able to play** chess when she was a child.

Be Allowed To/Be Permitted To

Meaning	Present/Future	Past
Permission	We **are not allowed to talk** during a test. You **are not permitted to park** at a bus stop.	We **were not allowed to talk** during the last test. You **were not permitted to park** on my street yesterday because the city was cleaning the streets.

Be Supposed To

Meaning	Present/Future	Past
Expectation	My brother **is supposed to arrive** at 10 p.m. The weatherman said it **is supposed to rain** tomorrow. I**'m supposed to help** my brother move on Saturday.	My brother **was supposed to arrive** at 10 p.m., but his plane was delayed. The weatherman said it **was supposed to rain** yesterday, but it didn't. I **was supposed to help** my brother move on Saturday, but I got sick.

Meaning	Present/Future	Past
Reporting rules and customs	You **are supposed to wear** your seat belt. You **are not supposed to talk** during a test.	He **was supposed to wear** his seat belt, but he didn't. They **weren't supposed to talk** during the test, but they did.

Had Better

Meaning	Present/Future	Past
Warning	You**'d better take** an umbrella, or you'll get wet.	————————

EDITING ADVICE

1. After a modal, always use a base form.

   He could ~~has~~ *have* gone to the party.

2. To form the past of a modal, use *have* + past participle.

   I shouldn't ~~ate~~ *have eaten* so much before I went to bed last night.

3. Don't confuse *must have* + past participle and *had to* + base form.

   I was absent last week and ~~must have taken~~ *had to take* the test in the teacher's office.

4. Don't confuse *couldn't have* + past participle and *couldn't* + base form.

   Last night when I got home, I couldn't ~~have found~~ *find* a parking space.

5. Use the correct form for the past participle.

   He should have ~~went~~ *gone* to the doctor when he felt the pain in his chest.

6. Don't forget the **d** in *supposed to*. Don't forget the verb *be*.

   You were suppose*d* to meet me after class yesterday.

   was I supposed to work last Saturday, but I got sick.

7. *Can* is never used for the past.

        couldn't drive

He ~~can't drove~~ his car this morning because the battery was dead.

LESSON 5 TEST / REVIEW

PART 1   Find the mistakes with the underlined words, and correct them. Not every sentence has a mistake. If the sentence is correct, write **C**.

EXAMPLES: When he heard the good news about his scholarship, he must <u>~~has~~ *have* been</u> excited.

I <u>had to go</u> to court last week.   *C*

1. I <u>was supposed to go</u> on vacation last week, but I got sick.

2. You <u>should have seen</u> the movie with us last week. We had a great time.

3. When your son graduated from college last year, you <u>must be</u> proud.

4. Why did you take the bus to work this morning? You <u>could have driven</u> your car.

5. He looked so tired when he got home from work. He <u>must had</u> a hard day today.

6. I <u>could have went</u> to the University of Illinois, but I decided to go to Truman College instead.

7. My wife is angry because I was late. I <u>should had called</u> her to tell her I was going to be late.

8. I didn't have time to call you yesterday because I <u>had to worked</u> all day yesterday.

9. Last week, he <u>should told</u> his mother the truth about his car accident, but he lied to her.

10. Thanks for helping me find a job. I <u>couldn't have found</u> it without your help.

11. Her daughter was sick yesterday, so she <u>had to leave</u> work early.

12. I <u>should studied</u> English when I was a child.

13. I had to work last Saturday, so I <u>couldn't go</u> to the party.

14. Everyone left the party early. They <u>must not have had</u> a very good time.

15. There wasn't enough food at the party. The host <u>should has bought</u> more food.

16. I <u>can't called</u> you last night because I lost your phone number.

PART 2

Fill in the blanks with the correct form of an appropriate verb.

EXAMPLE: The report on President Kennedy's death said that Oswald must ____*have*____ ____*killed*____ Kennedy.

1. President Kennedy might _____ by the government of another country.

2. John Kennedy, Jr. grew up without a father. It must _____ hard to grow up without a father.

3. John Kennedy, Jr. flew in the dark. He shouldn't _____ in the dark.

4. He got lost and couldn't _____ his way because he was flying over water.

5. He must _____ confused because of poor visibility.

6. He went to the airport late that day. He should _____ to the airport earlier.

7. Carolyn Bessette's parents must _____ very sad when they heard that two of their daughters had died.

8. Kennedy and his wife could _____ on a commercial airplane, but Kennedy decided to use his own airplane.

9. The search teams couldn't _____ the bodies for six days.

10. Some experts believe Kennedy didn't have enough experience flying. They think he should _____ more experience.

11. A. I think Kennedy, his wife, and sister-in-law probably survived for a few days.

    B. They couldn't _____ at all. The airplane hit the water with great force. They must _____ instantly.

12. Kennedy's cousin had to _____ her wedding because of the sad news.

Fill out the following form. Print in black ink or type. Bring it to the personnel office or mail it to:

Ms. Judy Lipton
P.O. Box 324
Tucson, Arizona 85744

Applications must be submitted by November 15.

Name _____Wilson_____ (last) _____Jack_____ (first) _____N_____ (middle initial)

Address _____5040 N. Albany Ave._____

City _____Chicago_____ State _____Ill_____ Zip Code _____

Telephone ( ) _____539-2756_____

Marital status (optional) _____divorced_____ Sex _____M_____

Date of birth _____18_____ (month) _____2_____ (day) _____64_____ (year) (You must be at least 18.)

Social Security number _549_ - _62_ _7149_

Educational background

		Date graduated	Degree or major
High School	Roosevelt	1897	
College			
Graduate School			

Employment History (Please start with your present or last job.)

Company	Position	Dates	Supervisor	Reason for leaving
Apex	Stockboy	5/84–3/88	R. Wilmot	personal
Smith, Inc.		5/88–12/92	M Smith	pay
Olson Co.	loading dock	1/93–present	B. Adams	

Do not write in the shaded box. For office use only.

Rec'd. by _____J.W._____
Amer. cit. _____yes_____
Doc. checked _____?_____
Transcripts received _____yes_____

The Immigration Act of 1986 requires all successful applicants to present documents to prove U.S. citizenship or permanent residence with permission to work in the U.S.

This company is an Equal Opportunity Employer. Race, religion, nationality, marital status, and physical disability will not influence our decision to hire.

I certify that these answers are true. Catholic

Signature: _____Jack N. Wilson_____ Date: _____13/11/00_____

PART 3   Look at the job application. Complete each sentence.

EXAMPLE: His didn't print the application. He should _____have printed or typed_____ the application.

1. He wrote his application with a pencil. He was supposed to _____
   _____ .

2. He didn't write his zip code. He should _____
   his zip code.

3. He forgot to include his area code. He should _____
   _____ it.

4. He included his marital status. He didn't have to _____ it.

5. He wrote the day (18) before the month (2). He should _____

   _____ .

6. He wrote that he graduated from high school in 1897. He couldn't

   _____ in 1897. That's more than 100 years

   ago! He must _____ 1987.

7. He didn't fill in any college attended. He might not _____
   college.

8. He said that he left his first job for personal reasons. He might _____

   _____ because he didn't like his boss. Or he could

   _____ because the salary wasn't high

   enough.

9. He didn't fill in his reason for leaving his last job. He should _____

   _____ .

10. He wrote in the shaded box. He wasn't supposed to _____ .

    _____ . He must not _____

    _____ the directions very carefully.

11. He included his religion. He wasn't supposed to _____ .

    He must _____ the sentence about religion.

12. He printed his name on the bottom line. He was supposed to _____

    _____ .

13. He mailed the application by regular mail on November 14. He should

    _____ . It might not _____ on time.

PART **4**

Fill in the blanks with the past of the modal or expression in parentheses.

After Alan (A) has waited for two hours for his friend Bill (B) to arrive for dinner, Bill finally arrives.

A. Why are you so late? You *were supposed to* be here two hours ago.
    <u>(example: be supposed to)</u>

B. I'm sorry. I got lost and I _____ find your house.
    <u>(1 can't)</u>

A. You _____ a road map.
    <u>(2 should/take)</u>

B. I did, but I _____ it while I was driving. I
    <u>(3 can/not/read)</u>

    _____ a wrong turn.
    <u>(4 must/make)</u>

A. Where did you get off the highway?

B. At Madison Street.

A. That's impossible. You _____ off at Madison
(5 can/not/get)
Street. There's no exit there.

B. Oh. It _____ Adams Street, then.
(6 must/be)

A. But Adams Street is not so far from here.

B. I know. But I had a flat tire after I got off the highway.

A. Did you call for a tow truck?

B. I _____ for a tow truck because I'm a
(7 can/call)
member of a motor club. But I thought it would take too long. So I changed
the tire myself.

A. But you're over two hours late. How long did it take you to change the tire?

B. It _____ about 15 minutes, but then I
(8 might/take)
_____ home, take a shower, and change
(9 have to/go)
clothes. I was so dirty.

A. You _____ me.
(10 should/call)

B. I wanted to, but I _____ the paper where I
(11 can/not/find)
had your phone number. I _____ it while
(12 must/lose)
I was changing the tire.

A. Well, thank goodness you're here now. But you'll have to eat dinner alone.

I got hungry and _____ for you.
(13 can/not/wait)

EXPANSION ACTIVITIES

CLASSROOM
ACTIVITIES

1. A student will read one of the following problems out loud to the class.
The student will pretend that this is his or her problem. Other students will
ask for more information and give advice about the problem. Try to use
modals, past and present.

Problem A My mother-in-law came to the U.S. last May. She stayed with
us for three months. I told my husband that he had to find another apartment
for her. He didn't want to. I finally said to my husband, "Tell her to leave,

or I'm leaving." So he helped her move into her own apartment. Now my husband is mad at me. Do you think I did the right thing?

Problem B I had a beautiful piano. I got it from my grandmother, who bought it many years ago. When I moved into my new apartment, I couldn't take the piano because it was too big for the entrance. So I sold it. Do you think I did the right thing?

Problem C My wife gave me a beautiful watch last Christmas. While I was on a business trip in New York last month, I left my watch in my hotel room. A few days later, I called the hotel, but they said that no one reported finding a watch. So far, I haven't told my wife that I lost the watch. What should I do?

Problem D A very nice American family invited me to dinner last night. The wife worked very hard to make a beautiful dinner. But I'm not used to eating American food and thought it tasted awful. But I ate it so I wouldn't hurt their feelings. They invited me to dinner again next week. What can I do about the food?

Problem E *Write your own problem, real or imaginary.*

2. Fill out the application on page 184 of Lesson Four. Make some mistakes on purpose. Find a partner and exchange books with your partner. Tell each other about the mistakes using modals.

EXAMPLE:
> For "sex," you wrote M. You're a woman, so you should have written F.

DISCUSSION

The following excerpt from a poem by John Greenleaf Whittier is about regret. Discuss the meaning of the poem.
> For all sad words of tongue or pen,
> The saddest are these: "It might have been!"

WRITING

1. Write about a mistake you once made. Tell about what you should have done to avoid the problem.

2. Write a short composition about another direction your life could have taken. What made you decide not to go in that direction?

3. Write about a famous person who died tragically.

Internet Activity

1. Look for information about President John F. Kennedy and his son, John Kennedy, Jr. Bring an article about one of these two men to class.

2. Find information about Jacqueline Kennedy Onassis.

3. At a search engine, type in "Kennedy assassination." Look at the different assassination theories.

GRAMMAR

Adjective Clauses
Descriptive Phrases

CONTEXT

Kids and the Media
E-mail and Instant Messages
The Creator of the World Wide Web
Parents Taking Control of the Media

LESSON FOCUS

An adjective clause is a clause that describes a noun.

Did you see the movie *that was on TV last night*?
I have a friend *who doesn't own a TV.*

Descriptive phrases can also describe a noun.

The children *watching TV* should go to bed.
Many programs *shown on TV* are not good for children.

1. Do you watch a lot of TV?
2. Did you watch a lot of TV when you were a child? Did your parents let you choose your own programs?
3. Do you think that some TV shows are bad for children?

Read the following article and facts in the box. Pay special attention to adjective clauses.

Facts About Kids and TV

- Children **who watch four or more hours of TV a day** spend less time on schoolwork and have poorer reading skills.
- Kids can see about five violent acts per hour during prime time[1] and 26 violent acts per hour during Saturday morning children's programs.
- Kids **who watch large amounts of violence** are more likely to use aggression to solve problems.
- Kids see about 20,000 TV commercials a year.
- More than 9 out of 10 food ads on Saturday morning TV are for unhealthy foods, such as candy and fast food.
- Children **who watch four or more hours of TV a day** are more likely to believe advertising claims than children who watch less TV.

Kids and the Media[2]

Before families had TV, most of the information **children got** was from their parents, teachers, and books. But when TV entered American homes in the 1950s, it brought a large variety of information, ideas, and images **that previous generations of children didn't have**. As more mothers entered the workforce, parents controlled fewer and fewer of the programs **that their children watched**.

Today the typical American child spends an average of 5½ hours using some form of media (TV, music, computers, printed material). The average household has 3 TVs, 2 VCRs, 3 radios, 3 tape players, 2 CD players, a video game system, and a computer. A large percentage of children's time is spent watching TV alone or with other kids. In fact, 65 percent of kids over eight have a TV in their bedroom. And parents of children under eight watch TV

---

[1] *Prime time* means the evening hours, generally between 7 and 11 p.m., when the television audience is the largest.
[2] The statistics in this reading come from the Kaiser Family Foundation report *Kids and Media @ The New Millenium* (1999) and the Center for Media Education.

with their kids just 50 percent of the time. Only half of American kids live in households **that have rules about media use**. Mealtime used to be a time **when families could get together** to discuss their daily lives. Now fifty-eight per cent of kids live in homes **where the TV is on during meals**. Forty percent of kids say the TV is on even when no one is watching.

It is clear that parents need to pay more attention to the programs **their kids watch**. They need to set a time limit for using media and help kids make smart TV choices. Above all, they need to model responsible behavior themselves.

6.1 Adjective Clauses—Overview

An adjective clause is a group of words that describes the noun before it.

Examples	Explanation
Children **who watch a lot of TV** have no time for homework.	Use *who* for people.
A woman **whom I met** doesn't allow her kids to watch TV on Saturdays.	Use *whom* for people.
The average child lives in a household **that has three TV sets**.	Use *that* for people or things.
Programs **which show violent behavior** affect kids.	Use *which* for things.
Children **whose parents are at work** often choose their own TV programs.	Use *whose* for possession.
Mealtime is a time **when families can discuss their lives**.	Use *when* for time.
Many kids live in homes **where the TV is on all the time**.	Use *where* for place.
The information **children get from TV** is not always good for them.	*Whom, that,* or *which* can be omitted from some adjective clauses.
Parents should pay attention to the programs **their children watch**.	

EXERCISE 1 Tell if you agree or disagree with each statement. You may discuss your answers.

EXAMPLE: Children who watch a lot of TV can learn a lot about the world.

1. Children who don't watch a lot of TV are more creative than children who watch a lot of TV.

2. Parents should choose the programs their children watch.

3. Parents who watch a lot of TV give a bad example to their children.

4. Parents should ask their kids about the programs they watch.

5. Parents should watch TV with their kids.

6. Children who see violence on TV will become violent.

7. Kids are influenced by the ads for food and candy that they see on TV.

8. Children whose parents read to them when they're small will become good readers.

9. Parents shouldn't let kids watch TV during mealtime.

10. Parents should limit the number of hours that their child watches TV.

11. It is not good for children to spend too much time at the computer.

12. Kids are happy with the limitations their parents give them.

EXERCISE 2 Underline the adjective clauses in Exercise 1. Not every sentence has an adjective clause.

6.2 Relative Pronoun as Subject

Children shouldn't see programs. The programs have violence.

↓

Children shouldn't see programs | **that** / **which** | have violence.

(continued)

Children		don't get enough exercise.
Children		watch TV all day.
Children	**who** **that**	watch TV all day don't get enough exercise.

Language Notes

1. The adjective clause can describe any noun in the sentence.
   Programs *that contain violence* are not good for children. (Adjective clause describes subject.)
   I don't like programs *that contain violence*. (Adjective clause describes object.)
2. Remember, *who* and *that* are for people; *that* and *which* are for things. (*Which* is less common than *that*.)
3. A present-tense verb in the adjective clause must agree in number with the noun it describes.
   Children who *watch* TV all day don't get enough exercise.
   A *child* who *watches* TV all day doesn't get enough exercise.

EXERCISE 3   Each subject below contains an adjective clause. Complete the statement.

EXAMPLE: People who have children ___*have a lot of responsibilities.*___

1. Mothers who work _____

2. Children who are home alone after school _____

3. A child who has a TV in his or her room _____

4. Parents who set a good example for their children _____

5. Children who have a lot of toys _____

6. Children who watch TV all day _____

7. TV shows that have a lot of violence _____

8. Commercials that interrupt a program _____

9. Families that have small children _____

10. People who have cable TV _____

EXERCISE **4**   Fill in the blanks with an adjective clause.

EXAMPLE: I like TV programs ___*that show happy families.*___

1. I don't like TV programs _____

2. Children shouldn't watch TV programs _____

3. TV programs _____ are good for small children.

4. Parents shouldn't give children toys _____

5. Children _____ believe the advertising claims they see over and over again.

6. A good parent is a person _____

7. A good kindergarten teacher is a person _____

8. Small children like books _____

EXERCISE **5**   Fill in the blanks with an adjective clause. Discuss your answers.

EXAMPLE: I don't like people ___*who say one thing but do something else.*___

1. I don't like people _____

2. I don't like apartments _____

3. I don't like movies _____

4. I like movies _____

5. I don't like teachers _____

6. I like teachers _____

7. I don't like teenagers _____

8. I like to have neighbors _____

9. I don't like to have neighbors _____

10. I like to receive mail _____

11. I have never met a person _____

12. I can't understand people _____

13. I like classes _____

14. I like to be around people _____

15. I don't like to be around people _____

16. A good friend is a person _____

17. I have a good friend _____

18. I once had a car _____

EXERCISE 6   Work with a partner. Write a sentence with each of the words given to describe the ideal situation for learning English.

EXAMPLE: classes   *Classes that have fewer than 20 students are better than large classes.*

teachers   *I prefer to have a teacher who doesn't explain things in my language.*

1. teachers _____

2. colleges _____

3. textbooks _____

4. classes _____

5. classrooms _____

6.3   Relative Pronoun as Object

	OBJECT
Parents should pay attention to the programs.	Their kids watch programs.
Parents should pay attention to the programs	**which** / **that** / Ø their kids watch.

	OBJECT	
	I know a woman.	
A woman		doesn't let her kids watch TV.
A woman	**who(m)** / **that** / Ø I know	doesn't let her kids watch TV.

Language Notes

1. The relative pronoun is usually omitted in conversation when it is the object of the adjective clause. However, when it is the subject of the adjective clause, it cannot be omitted.

    I watched a TV program (*that*) I really liked. (*That* can be omitted.)

    I watched a TV program *that* had 15 commercials in an hour. (*That* is necessary.)

2. *Whom* is considered more correct than *who* when used as the object of the adjective clause. However, the relative pronoun is usually omitted altogether in conversation.

    The teacher *whom* I had last semester speaks my language. (FORMAL)

    The teacher *who* I had last semester speaks my language. (LESS FORMAL)

    The teacher I had last semester speaks my language. (INFORMAL)

3. In an adjective clause, omit the object pronoun.

    The TV show that I saw ~~it~~ last night was about computers.

EXERCISE 7 Fill in the blanks to make an appropriate adjective clause.

EXAMPLE: My friend just bought a new dog. The last dog ___*he had*___ died a few weeks ago.

1. I have a hard teacher this semester. The teacher _____ last semester was much easier.

2. I studied British English in my native country. The English _____ _____ now is American English.

3. The teacher gave a test last week. Almost everyone failed the test _____ .

4. When I read English, there are many new words for me. I use my dictionary to look up the words I _____ .

5. I had a big apartment last year. The apartment _____ _____ now is very small.

6. Did you return the wallet _____ on the street?

7. I write poetry. One of the poems _____ won a prize.

8. The last book _____ was very sad. It made me cry.

9. Some of the programs _____ have a lot of violence. Parents shouldn't let their children watch these programs.

10. She has met a lot of people at her job, but she hasn't made any friends.

The people _____ are all too busy to spend time with her.

EXERCISE 8   Tell the class something about one of the following topics.

EXAMPLE: a car I'd like to own
Jaguar is a car I'd like to own.

1. a person I'd like to meet

2. a place I'd like to visit

3. a new activity I'd like to try

4. a restaurant I'd like to try

5. a car I'd like to own

6.4   Relative Pronoun as Object of Preposition

I don't like the music.   My kids listen to the music.

I don't like the music | **that** **∅** **which** | my kids listen to.

I don't like the music **to which** my kids listen.
(VERY FORMAL, ALMOST NEVER USED)

I have never heard of the singer.   My son talks about the singer.

I have never heard of the singer | **that** **who** **∅** **whom** | my son talks about.

I have never heard of the singer **about whom** my son talks.
(VERY FORMAL)

LANGUAGE NOTES

The relative pronoun of an adjective clause can be the object of a preposition. In very formal English, the preposition comes before the relative pronoun, and only *whom* and *which* may be used. Informally, most people put the preposition at the of the adjective clause and the relative pronoun is often omitted.

The college *to which* I applied is in California. (FORMAL)
The college *which/that* I applied *to* is in California. (LESS FORMAL)
The college I applied *to* is in California. (INFORMAL)

The counselor *with whom* I spoke gave me a lot of advice. (FORMAL)
The counselor *whom/who/that* I spoke *to* gave me a lot of advice. (LESS FORMAL)
The counselor I spoke *to* gave me a lot of advice. (INFORMAL)

EXERCISE 9 Complete each statement.

EXAMPLE: The class I was in last semester ___*was very crowded.*___

1. The city I come from _____

2. The school I graduated from _____

3. The house/apartment I used to live in _____

4. The elementary school I went to _____

5. The teacher I studied beginning grammar with _____

   _____

6. Most of the people I went to elementary school with _____

   _____

7. _____ is a subject I'm very interested in.

8. _____ is a topic I don't like to talk about.

EXERCISE 10 This is a conversation between two friends. One just came back from an island vacation where he had a terrible time. Fill in each blank with an adjective clause.

A. How was your trip?

B. Terrible.

A. What happened? Didn't your travel agent choose a good hotel for you?

B. The hotel _(that) he chose for me_ didn't have air conditioning.
   (example)

   It was too hot.

A. What kind of food did they serve?

B. The food _____ made me sick.
   _(1)_

A. Did you meet any interesting travelers?

B. I didn't like the other travelers _____. They were
   _(2)_

   unfriendly.

A. Did you travel with an interesting companion?

B. The person _____ was boring. We weren't
   _(3)_

   interested in the same things. The things _____
   _(4)_

   were different from the things _____.
   _(5)_

A. Did you take pictures?

B. The pictures _____ didn't come out.
   _(6)_

A. Did you find any interesting souvenirs?

B. The souvenirs _____ were cheaply made. I didn't buy any.
   _(7)_

A. Could you communicate with the people on the island? Do they speak
   English?

B. No. I don't understand the language _____.
   _(8)_

A. Did you spend a lot of money?

B. Yes, but the money _____ was wasted.
   _(9)_

A. Why didn't you change your ticket and come home early?

B. The ticket _____ couldn't be changed.
   _(10)_

A. Are you going to have another vacation soon?

B. The next vacation _____ will be in December. I think
   _(11)_

   I'll just stay home.

6.5 *Where* and *When* in Adjective Clauses

Examples	Explanation
Mealtime is a time **(when) families can discuss their problems**. Saturday is the only day **(when) my family eats a meal together**.	*When* means "at that time." *When* can be omitted.
Many kids live in homes **where the TV is on all the time**. I'd like to visit the city **where my parents were born**.	*Where* means "in that place." *Where* cannot be omitted.

EXERCISE 11 Use the sentence in parentheses to add an adjective clause to finish the first sentence.

EXAMPLE: I buy my groceries at a store ___*where I can buy fresh produce.*___
(I can buy fresh produce foods at that store.)

1. The teacher didn't give a test on the day _____

   _____. (Some students celebrated a holiday on that day.)

2. You should study at a time _____

   _____. (The house is quiet at that time.)

3. Saturday is the day _____.
   (I am busiest on this day.)

4. The bookstore _____
   is having a sale this week. (I bought my books at the bookstore.)

5. The bank _____
   is open late on Fridays. (I cash my checks at the bank.)

6. The library _____
   is closed this weekend. (I study in that place.)

Exercise 12 Fill in the blanks to tell about yourself.

Example: _____June_____ is the month when I was born.

1. _____ is a place where I can relax.

2. _____ is a place where I can have fun.

3. _____ is a place where I can be alone and think.

4. _____ is a place where I can meet my friends.

5. _____ is a place where I can study undisturbed.

6. _____ is a time when I can relax.

7. _____ is a time when I like to watch TV.

8. _____ is a day when I have almost no free time.

6.6 Where, That, or Which

Examples	Explanation
a) I miss the apartment **where** I used to live.	a) The preposition *in* is not used after the verb *live*. Introduce the adjective clause with *where*.
b) I miss the apartment (**that**) I used to live **in**.	b) The preposition *in* is used after the verb *live*. Introduce the adjective clause with *that*, *which*, or Ø.
c) I miss the apartment **in which** I used to live.	c) If the preposition is at the beginning of the adjective clause, *which* must be used. This sentence is very formal.
a) She lives in a home **where** people watch a lot of TV.	a) People watch a lot of TV in that home. (*where* = in that home)
b) She lives in a home **that** has three TVs.	b) The home has three TVs. (*that* = *home*)

Exercise 13 Fill in the blanks with *where, that,* or *which*.

Example: The home _____*where*_____ I grew up had a beautiful fireplace.

1. The city _____ I was born has a lot of parks.

2. I don't like cities _____ have a lot of factories.

3. I like to shop at stores _____ have products from different countries.

4. I like to shop at stores _____ I can find products from different countries.

5. A department store is a store in _____ you can find all kinds of goods—clothing, furniture, toys, etc.

6. I have a photograph of the home _____ I grew up.

7. The office _____ you can get your transcripts is closed now.

8. She wants to rent the apartment _____ she saw last Sunday.

9. I would like to visit the city _____ I grew up.

10. The town in _____ she grew up was destroyed by the war.

6.7 When or That

Examples	Explanation
a) Spring is the season (**that**) I love best.	a) I love the season. (*that* = season)
b) Spring is the season **that** gives people hope.	b) The season gives people hope. (*that* = season)
c) Spring is a time (**when**) new things grow.	c) New things grow **during** this season. (*when* = during that time)

LANGUAGE NOTE

When can be omitted.

EXERCISE 14 Fill in the blanks with *when* or *that* or nothing.

EXAMPLE: December 31, 1999 was a time __*when*__ people celebrated the beginning of the new century.

1. New Year's Eve is a time _____ I love.

2. February is the only month _____ has fewer than 30 days.

3. My birthday is a day _____ I think about my past.

4. December is a time _____ a lot of Americans buy gifts.

5. Their anniversary is a date _____ has a lot of meaning for them.

6. Do you give yourself the time _____ you need to write a good composition?

7. She wrote about a time _____ she couldn't speak English well.

8. Their vacation to Paris was the best time _____ they had ever had.

Do you use the Internet? What is your primary reason for using it?

2. What are some of the different ways people use the Internet?

Read the following article. Pay special attention to adjective clauses beginning with *whose*.

E-mail and Instant Messages

Do you like getting a piece of handwritten mail? Are there people **whose letters you've saved for years**? The art of letter-writing seems to be dying for many people as more and more of us are turning to our computers to send a quick e-mail.

You might think the United States is a country of serious Internet users. But there are many people **whose only online activity is sending and receiving e-mail**. In 1999, Americans sent 2.2 billion e-mail messages, compared to 293 million pieces of first class mail. People have become more and more dependent on e-mail for quick communication.

Did you know...?

In an e-mail address, .com is a commercial business, .edu is an educational institution, .gov is the U.S. government, .mil is the military, .org is a non-profit organization.

In addition to the quick communication that e-mail gives us, many people are using instant messages to communicate. How does this work? First, you make a list of your on-line buddies.[3] When you go on-line, your computer tells you if the people **whose names are on the list** are on-line too. If they are, you can send them an instant message and have a real-time chat. Teenagers especially love sending and receiving instant messages. And they love going to chat rooms to "talk" to their Internet buddies.

But when people send e-mail and instant messages, they often don't give much thought to how they write; many people use abbreviations and omit punctuation and capital letters. They simply write the first thing that comes into their head, click, and send it. Even though people are writing more, their writing is usually not something to keep and read again years later.

Common symbols and abbreviations used in e-mail:

:-) Symbol to show you're happy

:-(Symbol to show you're sad

LOL = laughing out loud, to mean that something is funny to you

BTW = by the way

BFN = bye for now

TIA = thanks in advance

R = are

U = you

TTYL = talk to you later

[3] A *buddy* is a casual friend.

6.8 *Whose* + Noun in an Adjective Clause

Whose as Subject of the Adjective Clause:

There are people.
               Their only on-line activity is e-mailing.
                  ↓
There are people **whose** only on-line activity is e-mailing.

Whose as Object of the Adjective Clause:

There are people.
            I've saved their letters for years.
              ↓
There are people **whose** letters I've saved for years.

LANGUAGE NOTES

1. *Whose* is the possessive form of *who*. It stands for *his, her, their,* or the possessive form of the noun.
    > You can send an instant message to people *whose names* are on your buddy list. (*Whose = their*)
    > I have an aunt in Australia *whose name* I put on my buddy list. (*whose = her*)
2. *Whose* is always followed directly by a noun.

EXERCISE 15 Underline each adjective clause.

EXAMPLE: A person <u>whose name is on a list</u> will receive catalogs.

1. The TOEFL is a test for students whose native language isn't English.

2. A student whose homework has a lot of mistakes should do it over.

3. Teachers get angry at students whose homework is always late.

4. The woman whose wallet I found and returned gave me a reward.

5. She doesn't know the person whose car she bought.

Use the sentence in parentheses to form an adjective clause.

EXAMPLES: There are many American children *whose parents are divorced.*
(Their parents are divorced.)

There is one student *whose handwriting the teacher can't read.*
(The teacher can't read her handwriting.)

1.   There are many American children _____
     (Their mothers work.)

2.   Working parents _____ need to find day-care
     centers. (Their children are small.)

3.   People _____ can get food stamps.
     (Their incomes are below a certain level.)

4.   A widow is a woman _____
     (Her husband has died.)

5.   There is one student _____
     (The teacher loves to read her compositions.)

6.   The student _____ is absent today.
     (I borrowed his book.)

7.   There are a few students _____
     (I can't remember their names.)

8.   The teacher _____ can advise you
     on what course to take next semester. (You are taking her class.)

EXERCISE **17**   *Combination Exercise.* Fill in the blanks with the correct
words: *who, whom, whose, that, which, where,* or *when.* In
some cases, you don't need any word to fill in the blank. In
some cases, more than one answer is possible.

Children are always happy on the day ___*(when)*___ the school year ends
                                        (example)

and summer vacation begins. They think about all the plans _____ they
                                                            (1)

have for the summer. Some kids go to a day camp _____ is near the
                                                  (2)

family's home. At the end of the day, the child goes home. Other kids go
away to a camp in the country. Kids are instructed by camp counselors.

These counselors are often college kids _____ are trying to earn a little
                                          (3)

extra money during their summer vacation.

Some kids go to specialized camps, such as a music camp, _____
(4)
they can improve a particular skill or learn a new hobby _____ they
(5)
are interested in.

There are some kids _____ parents take them on a trip in a car.
(6)
Often they visit state and national parks. Sometimes they camp out in a

tent _____ the family has brought from home.
(7)

Kids _____ have failed a grade or course in school sometimes go
(8)
to summer school to catch up with their classmates. These kids don't have

as much fun as their friends _____ go to camp.
(9)

6.9 Adjective Clauses after Indefinite Compounds

An adjective clause can follow an indefinite compound: *someone, some-thing, everyone, everything, nothing, anything.*

Examples	Explanation
Everyone **who received my e-mail** knows about the party. I don't know anyone **who lives in Canada**.	The relative pronoun after an indefinite compound can be the subject of the adjective clause. The relative pronoun cannot be omitted.
Something **(that) he wrote** made me angry. He didn't read over anything **I sent him** by e-mail.	The relative pronoun can be the object of the adjective clause. In this case, it is usually omitted.

LANGUAGE NOTES

1. An indefinite pronoun takes a singular verb.
   Everyone who *drives* a car *needs* insurance.
   I don't know anyone who *speaks* Armenian.
2. An adjective clause does not usually follow a personal pronoun, except in very formal language and in some proverbs.
   He who laughs last laughs best.
   He who hesitates is lost.
   In informal language, we would say "anyone who" or "a person who." The above proverb, in less formal language, would be: *A person who* takes too much time deciding sometimes loses the opportunity to do something.

EXERCISE 18 Fill in the blanks with an adjective clause. Use information from nearby sentences to help you.

A woman (W) is trying to break up with a man (M).

M.   I heard you want to talk to me.

W.   Yes. There's something ___*I want to tell you.*___
                                               (example)

M.   What do you want to tell me?

W.   I want to break up.

M.   Are you angry at me? What did I say?

W.   Nothing _____(1)_____ made me angry.

M.   Did I do something wrong?

W.   Nothing _____(2)_____ made me mad.

M.   Then what's the problem?

W.   I just don't love you anymore.

M.   But I can buy you anything _____(3)_____ .

W.   I don't want anything from you. In fact, I'm going to return every-

thing _____(4)_____ .

M.   But I can take you anywhere _____(5)_____ .

W.   I don't want to go anywhere with you. You haven't heard anything

_____(6)_____ . I said that I just don't love you anymore.
Good-bye.

EXERCISE 19 Fill in the blanks with an adjective clause.

EXAMPLE: I don't send e-mail to everyone ___*I know*___ .

1.   You should read everything _____ in an e-mail before
sending it.

2.   When sending an e-mail, you shouldn't write anything _____

_____ .

3.   I received 20 e-mails today. Nothing _____ was
important. It was all junk.

4. Some people delete everything _____ after they read it.

5. If you have a buddy list, you can send an instant message to someone _____ .

6. People you don't know may send you attachments. You shouldn't open an attachment from anyone _____ . It may contain a virus.

EXERCISE 20 Fill in the blanks with an adjective clause.

EXAMPLE: I know someone *who can help you with your car problem* .

1. I don't know anyone _____ .

2. I know someone _____ .

3. Everyone _____ can go to the next level.

4. Anyone _____ should ask the teacher.

5. Everything _____ is useful.

EXERCISE 21 *Combination Exercise.* Fill in the blanks with an adjective clause by using the sentences in parentheses or the context to give you clues.

A. How was your move last month?

B. It was terrible.

A. Didn't you use the moving company _____*I recommended*_____?
   _____(example)_____
   (I recommended a company.)

B. The company _____(1)_____ was not available on

   the day _____(2)_____ . (I had to move on this day.)

   I used a company _____(3)_____ . (I found their name

   in the yellow pages.)

A. What happened?

B. First of all, it was raining on the day _____(4)_____ . That made the move take longer, so it was more expensive than I thought it would be.

A. It's not the company's fault if it rained.

B. I know. But there are many other things _____.
(5)
(Things were their fault.) The movers broke the mirror _____
_____. (I had just bought the mirror.) And they left
(6)
muddy footprints on the carpet _____.
(7)
(I had just cleaned the carpet.) I thought I was getting professional
movers. But the men (They sent these men to my home.) _____
_____ were college students. They didn't
(8)
have much experience moving. Because the move took them so long,
they charged me much more than I expected to pay. The estimate
(They had given me an estimate.) _____ was for
(9)
$600. But they charged me $800.

A. You should talk to the owner of the company.

B. I called the company several times. The woman (I talked to a woman.)
_____ said that the owner would call me back,
(10)
but he never has.

A. You should keep trying. Make a list of everything _____
_____. (They broke or ruined things.) Their
(11)
insurance will probably pay for these things.

B. I don't know if they have insurance.

A. You should never use a company _____.
(12)

B. Everyone _____ (I've talked to people.) tells me
(13)
the same thing.

A. Don't feel so bad. Everyone makes mistakes. We learn from the mistakes _____. Why didn't you ask your friends to help
(14)
you move?

B. Everyone _____ (I know people.) is so busy. I didn't
(15)
want to bother anyone.

A. By the way, why did you move? You had a lovely apartment.

B. It wasn't mine. The person (I was renting her apartment.) _____
_____ spent a year in China, but when she
(16)
came back last month, I had to leave.

A. How do you like your new place?

B. It's fine. It's across the street from the building _____

_____ (My sister lives in that building.). So now we
       (17)

get to see each other more often. Why don't you come over sometime
and see my new place?

A. I'd love to. How about Saturday after 4 p.m.? That's the only time

_____ (I don't have too much to do
       (18)

at that time.).

B. Saturday would be great.

Before You Read 1. Besides computers, what other inventions have changed the way
people communicate with each other?

2. When you think about computers and the Internet, what famous
names come to mind?

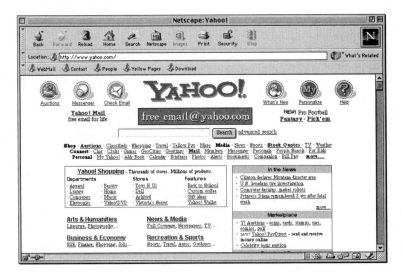

Read the following article. Notice that some adjective clauses are separated from the main clause with a comma.

The Creator of the World Wide Web

Most people have never heard of Tim Berners-Lee. He is not nearly as
rich or famous as Marc Andreessen, who was cofounder of Netscape, or Bill
Gates, whose name has become a household word.

Berners-Lee, who works in a small office at the Massachusetts Institute
of Technology, is the creator of the World Wide Web. The creation of the
Web is so important that some people compare Berners-Lee to Johann
Gutenberg, who invented printing by moveable type in the fifteenth century.

Berners-Lee was born in England in 1955. His parents, who helped design the world's first commercially available computer, gave him a great love of mathematics and learning.

In 1980, Berners-Lee went to work at CERN, a physics laboratory in Geneva, Switzerland, where he had a lot of material to learn quickly. He had a poor memory for facts and wanted to find a way to help him keep track of things he couldn't remember. He devised a software program that allowed him to create a document that had links to other documents. He continued to develop his idea through the 1980s. He wanted to find a way to connect the knowledge and creativity of people all over the world.

In 1991, his project became known as the World Wide Web. The number of Internet users started to grow quickly. However, Berners-Lee is not completely happy with the way the Web has developed. He thinks it has become a passive tool for so many people, not the tool for creativity that he had imagined.

In 1999, Berners-Lee published a book called *Weaving the Web*, in which he answers questions he is often asked: "What were you thinking when you invented the Web?" "What do you think of it now?" "Where is the Web going to take us in the future?"

6.10   Nonessential Adjective Clauses

Examples	Explanation
Berners-Lee, **who was born in England**, now lives in the U.S.	Some adjective clauses are separated by commas from the main part of the sentence.
Bill Gates, **whose name is a household word**, created Microsoft.	Commas are used when the clause is not essential to the meaning of the sentence. The adjective clause adds extra information.
Berners-Lee's parents, **who helped design the first computer**, gave him a love of learning.	A nonessential adjective clause begins with *who, whom, which, where, when,* or *whose. That* is not used in a nonessential adjective clause.
He went to work at CERN, **which is a physics laboratory in Geneva**.	
Berners-Lee was born in 1955, **when personal computers were beyond people's imagination**.	

EXERCISE 22 Put commas in the following sentences to separate the adjective clause from the main part of the sentence.

EXAMPLE: The abacus, which is a wooden rack with beads, was probably the first computer.

abacus

1. The abacus which was created about 2,000 years ago helped people solve arithmetic problems.

2. The first modern computer which was called ENIAC took up a lot of space (1,800 square feet).

3. ENIAC was created in 1942 when the U.S. was involved in World War II.

4. ENIAC which helped the government keep important data was built at the University of Pennsylvania.

5. Personal computers which were introduced in the 1970s are much smaller and faster than previous computers.

6. Bill Gates went to Harvard University where he developed the programming language BASIC.

7. Bill Gates dropped out of Harvard to work with Paul Allen who was his old high school friend.

8. Together Gates and Allen founded Microsoft which has made both of them very rich.

9. In 1984, Apple produced the first Macintosh computer which was easier to use than earlier computers.

10. In 1990, Bill Gates introduced Windows which was Microsoft's version of the popular Macintosh operating system.

6.11 Essential vs. Nonessential Adjective Clauses

Nonessential Clauses (With Commas)	Essential Clauses (Without Commas)
The computer, **which has become part of our everyday lives**, was invented in the 1940s.	The computer **that I bought two years ago** is slow compared to today's computers.
Bill Gates, **who created Microsoft**, never finished college.	The people **who built the first computers** worked at the engineering department of the University of Pennsylvania.
Berners-Lee, **whose parents helped design the first computer**, loved mathematics.	There are many people **whose only on-line activity is sending and receiving e-mail**.

LANGUAGE NOTES

1. A nonessential adjective clause, which is set off by commas, adds extra information to the main clause. Here are some questions to help you decide if the clause needs commas. If the answer to any of these questions is *yes*, then the adjective clause is set off by commas.
    *   Can I put the clause in parentheses?
        Bill Gates (who created Microsoft) never finished college.
    *   Can I write the adjective clause as a separate sentence?
        Bill Gates created Microsoft. He never finished college.
    *   If the adjective clause is deleted, does the sentence still make sense?
        Bill Gates never finished college.
    *   Is the noun a unique person or place?
        Berners-Lee, who invented the Web, is not rich. (Berners-Lee is unique. It is not necessary to explain which Berners-Lee. The adjective clause provides extra information.)
        A person who invents something is very creative and intelligent. (The adjective clause is essential in this sentence to explain which person is creative and intelligent.)
    *   If the noun is plural, am I including all members of a group (all my cousins, all my friends, all Americans, all computers)?
        My friends, who are wonderful people, always help me. (All of my friends are wonderful people.)
        I send e-mail to my friends who have home computers and an Internet service. (Not all of my friends have home computers and an Internet service.)

2. In a nonessential adjective clause, the relative pronoun cannot be omitted. COMPARE:
    The computer *that* she just bought has a big memory. (Essential adjective clause—the pronoun may be included)
    The computer she just bought has a big memory. (Essential adjective clause—the relative pronoun may be omitted.)
    The computer, which was an important invention in the 1940s, was created for military use. (The clause is nonessential. The relative pronoun cannot be omitted.)

EXERCISE 23 Decide which of the following sentences contain a nonessential adjective clause. Put commas in those sentences. If the sentence doesn't need commas, write *NC*.

EXAMPLES: People who send e-mail often use abbreviations.   *NC*
My father, who sent me an e-mail yesterday, is sick.

1. Kids who watch a lot of TV don't spend much time on their homework.

2. My grammar teacher who has been teaching here for 20 years knows a lot about the problems of foreign students.

3. There are many TV programs for children on Saturdays when most kids are home.

4. Children whose parents work are often home alone after school.

5. Berners-Lee whose parents were very educated loved learning new things.

6. Marc Andreesson created Netscape which is a popular Web browser.

7. Berners-Lee worked in Switzerland where the CERN physics laboratory is located.

8. The Instant Message which was a creation of America Online is available to many e-mail users.

9. Did you like the story that we read about Berners-Lee?

10. The computer you bought three years ago doesn't have enough memory.

11. The computer which is one of the most important inventions of the twentieth century has changed the way people process information.

12. Bill Gates who created Microsoft with his friend became a billionaire.

EXERCISE 24 Combine the two sentences into one. The sentence in parentheses is not essential to the main idea of the sentence. It is extra information.

EXAMPLE: John Kennedy was assassinated in 1963. (He was one of the youngest presidents of the U.S.)

John Kennedy, who was one of the youngest presidents of

the U.S., was assassinated in 1963.

1. John Kennedy was the 35th president of the U.S. (We saw his picture on page 189.)

_____

2. The Kennedys became very powerful in Boston. (They were of Irish descent.)

_____

3. Jacqueline Bouvier was a young and beautiful first lady. (John Kennedy married Jacqueline in 1953.)

_____

4. John Kennedy, Jr. could hardly remember his father. (He was only three years old when his father died.)

_____

5. John Kennedy, Jr. died when his plane crashed. (He had had his pilot's license for only a short time.)

_____

6. Kennedy's wife Carolyn died in the plane crash too. (She was only 33 years old.)

_____

7. John and Carolyn died in 1999. (They did not have any children.)

_____

8. John Kennedy, Jr. was seven years younger than his father was when he died. (He was only 39 years old when he died.)

_____

9. John and Carolyn were on their way to Massachusetts. (They were going to attend a cousin's wedding there.)

_____

10. John's cousin's wedding was postponed. (It was supposed to take place on July 17.)

_____

Before You Read
1. Do you ever see some letters and numbers in the corner of your TV screen at the beginning of a program?
2. Should parents control the programs children watch on TV and the Web sites they visit?

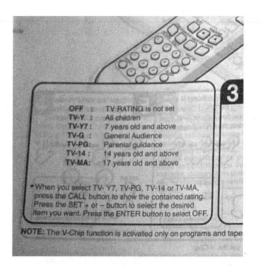

Read the following article. Pay special attention to descriptive phrases.

Parents Taking Control of the Media

An estimated 7 million American kids are home alone after school without adult supervision. They often watch whatever TV shows they want. Parents **concerned about their children's use of the media** can take control. The V-chip, **installed in television sets manufactured after January, 2000,** is a device that allows parents to have control over the programs **watched by their children.** All TVs **with screens 13 inches or larger** must have a V-chip.

How does the V-chip work? Since 1997, TV programs have been rated as to their appropriateness for children of different ages. TV-Y7-FV, for example, is the rating for programs **directed to children over seven**. This kind of program contains "fantasy violence," **found in some cartoons**. By using the V-chip, parents can program their TV to block certain kinds of programs they don't want their kids to watch.

Parents can also block kids from entering certain Web sites. However, many parents don't know how to use the controls **provided by some Internet Service Providers**, such as AOL. Children are often more knowledgeable about computers than their parents.

6.12 Descriptive Phrases

Some adjective clauses can be shortened to descriptive phrases. The phrase follows the noun.

Examples	Explanation
The V-chip is in TVs **manufactured since January, 2000**. Small children shouldn't watch programs **directed to older children**.	Some phrases begin with a past participle.
Kids **watching TV on Saturday mornings** see a lot of commercials. People **buying a TV today** will have the V-chip.	Some phrases begin with a present participle (verb *-ing*).
The V-chip, **a device that allows parents to block certain programs**, does not cost extra. Bill Gates, **the founder of Microsoft**, never finished college.	Some descriptive phrases are noun phrases that give a definition or more information about the preceding noun. This kind of phrase is called an appositive.
TVs **with screens 13 inches or larger** have the V-chip. Children **in elementary school** learn to use computers.	Some phrases begin with a preposition.

LANGUAGE NOTES

1. We can shorten an adjective clause in which the relative pronoun is followed by the verb *be*.

   Parents *who are* concerned about their children's TV habits can use the V-chip.

Parents concerned about their children's TV habits can use the V-chip.

Bill Gates, *who is* the founder of Microsoft, didn't finish college.

Bill Gates, the founder of Microsoft, didn't finish college.

2. Adjective clauses using *who have* can sometimes be changed to phrases using *with*.

People *who have* Internet access can send e-mail.

People *with* Internet access can send e-mail

3. A descriptive phrase can be essential or nonessential. A nonessential phrase is set off by commas.

Children *left alone without supervision* can watch any TV shows they want.

Children, *the future of our country*, need to learn good habits and values.

(NOTE: An appositive is always non-essential.)

EXERCISE 25 Shorten the adjective clause by crossing out the unnecessary words.

EXAMPLE: Televisions ~~which are~~ manufactured today have the V-chip.

1. The TV that is in my bedroom is not very big.

2. The foods that are advertised during Saturday morning TV programs for kids are not usually healthy.

3. Some parents don't know how to use the controls which are provided by their Internet service.

4. TV programs that are directed to children have a lot of commercials for toys.

5. Tim Berners-Lee, who was born in England, now works at M.I.T.

6. M.I.T., which is located in Cambridge, Massachusetts, is an excellent university.

7. Berners-Lee developed the idea for the Web when he was working at CERN, which is a physics lab in Switzerland.

8. Berners-Lee's parents worked on the first computer that was sold commercially.

9. People who are using the Web can shop from their homes.

10. People who are interested in reading newspapers from other cities can find them on the Web.

11. The World Wide Web, which is abbreviated WWW, was first introduced on the Internet in 1991.

12. Computers which are sold today have much more memory and speed than computers which were sold 10 years ago.

13. Marc Andreessen, who was the creator of Netscape, quickly became a billionaire.

14. You can download Netscape, which is a popular Internet browser.

EXERCISE 26 Combine the two sentences. Use a phrase for the sentence in parentheses.

EXAMPLE: Los Angeles is one of the largest American cities. (It is in California.)
Los Angeles, in California, is one of the largest American cities.

1. Alaska is separate from the other states. (It is the largest state.)

   _____

2. Rhode Island is the smallest state. (It is on the east coast.)

   _____

3. Arizona has a dry climate. (It is in the Southwest.)

   _____

4. The White House is in Washington, D.C. (It is the home of the President.)

   _____

5. Puerto Rico is a U.S. territory. (It's a Caribbean island.)

   _____

6. Hawaii is a group of islands. (It is located in the Pacific Ocean.)

   _____

	Essential	Nonessential
Pronoun as subject	Parents **who** (or **that**) **are not home** don't know what their kids are watching on TV. I just bought a computer **that** (or **which**) **has a very big memory**.	My mother, **who works very hard**, comes home late every day. My brother lives in New York City, **which is the biggest city in the U.S.**
Pronoun as object	The first computer **(that** or **which) I bought** didn't have a mouse. The people **(who, whom, that) you meet in chat rooms** are sometimes very silly.	My first computer, **which I bought in 1996**, is much slower than my new computer. My father, **whom you met at the party**, is a programmer.
Pronoun as object of preposition	The person **to whom I sent an e-mail** never answered me. (FORMAL) The person **(whom, who, that) I sent an e-mail to** didn't answer me. (INFORMAL)	Berners-Lee, **about whom we read**, is an interesting person. (FORMAL) Berners-Lee, **whom we read about**, is an interesting person. (INFORMAL)
Where	The store **where I bought my computer** has good prices.	Berners-Lee works at the Massacusetts Institute of Technology, **where he has a small office**.
When	I'll never forget the day **when I arrived in the U.S.**	Kids like to watch TV on Saturdays, **when there are many cartoons**.
Whose + noun as subject	Children **whose parents aren't home** often watch TV.	Berners-Lee, **whose parents worked on computers**, learned a lot in his home.
Whose + noun as object	There are friends **whose letters I've saved for years**.	My mother, **whose letters I've saved**, died two years ago.
Adjective clause after indefinite compound	I don't know anyone **who has a Macintosh computer**. Everything **I learned about computers** is useful.	——————
Descriptive phrase	Home computers **made 20 years ago** didn't have a big memory.	Bill Gates, **the founder of Microsoft**, became a billionaire.

1. Never use *what* as a relative pronoun.

   who
   She married a man ~~what~~ has a lot of money.

   (that)
   Everything ~~what~~ you did was unnecessary.

2. You can't omit a relative pronoun that is the subject of the adjective clause.

   who
   I know a man ᶺ speaks five languages.

3. If the relative pronoun is the object of the adjective clause, don't put an object after the verb.

   The car that I bought ~~it~~ has a stick shift.

4. Make sure you use subject-verb agreement.

   I know several English teachers who speak~~s~~ Spanish.

   has
   A car which ~~have~~ a big engine is not economical.

5. Put a noun before an adjective clause.

   The student w
   ~~Who~~ wants to leave early should sit in the back.

6. Put the adjective clause near the noun it describes.

   The teacher ⟨speaks Spanish ⟨whose class I am taking⟩

7. Don't confuse *whose* with *who's*.

   whose
   A student ~~who's~~ grades are good may get a scholarship.

8. Put the subject before the verb in an adjective clause.

   my cousin bought
   The house which ~~bought my cousin~~ is very beautiful.

PART 1   Find the mistakes with the underlined words, and correct them. Not every sentence has a mistake. If the sentence is correct, write **C.**

EXAMPLES: The students should correct the mistakes that they make ~~them~~.

The students about whom we were speaking entered the room.   *C*

1. The teacher what we have is from Canada.

2. Five students were absent on the day when was given the TOEFL test.

3. The room where we took the test was not air-conditioned.

4. Who missed the test can take it next Friday.

5. Students who knows a lot of English grammar can take a composition course.

6. The teacher whose class I'm taking speaks English clearly.

7. A tutor is a person whom helps students individually.

8. Everyone wants to have a teacher whose pronunciation is clear.

9. The student whose sitting next to me is trying to copy my answers.

10. A teacher helped me at registration who speaks my native language.

11. The teacher gave a test had 25 questions.

12. The student which sits near the door always leaves early.

13. Do you know anyone who has a German car?

14. The textbook we are using has a lot of exercises.

15. The people who live upstairs make a lot of noise in the morning.

PART 2

Fill in the blanks to complete the adjective clause.

EXAMPLES: A. Do you like your new roommate?

B. Not really. The roommate _____*I had last year*_____ was much nicer.

A. Are there any teachers at this school ___*who speak Spanish*___?

B. Yes. Ms. Lopez speaks Spanish.

1. A. I heard you had a car accident. You hit another car.

B. Yes. The woman whose _____ wants me to pay her $700.

2. A. My office uses PC computers.

B. Not mine. The computers _____ are Macintosh.

3. A. Did you buy your textbooks at Berk's Bookstore?

B. No. The store _____ is about ten blocks from school. Books are cheaper there.

4. A. My husband's mother always interferes in our married life.

B. That's terrible. I wouldn't want to be married to a man whose _____

_____

5. A. Do you have a black-and-white TV?

B. Of course not. I don't even know anyone _____ anymore.

6. A. What did the teacher say about registration?

B. I don't know. She spoke very fast. I didn't understand everything

_____

7. A. Do you remember your first day in the U.S.?

B. Of course. I'll always remember the day _____ in my new country.

8. A. The teacher is talking about a very famous American, but I didn't hear his name.

B. The man _____ is John Kennedy.

9. A. Did you buy the dictionary I recommended to you?

B. No. The dictionary _____ is just as good as the one you recommended.

10. A. Do you remember the names of all the students?

B. No. There are some students _____

PART 3

Complete each statement. Every sentence should have an adjective clause.

EXAMPLE: The library is a place ___*where you can read.*___

1. The teacher _____ doesn't teach here anymore.

2. Everything _____ is important to me.

3. Teachers _____ aren't good for foreign students.

4. The teacher will not pass a student whose _____

5. I would like to live in a house _____

6. The classroom _____ is clean and pleasant.

7. I will never forget the day _____

8. I never got an answer to the question _____ about the test.

9. Everyone _____ had a great time.

10. I don't like the dictionary _____, so I'm going to buy a better one.

11. Computers _____ 10 years ago are very slow compared to today's computers.

12. A laboratory is a place where _____

13. There's so much noise in my house. I need to find a place _____

_____

14. Small children whose _____ learn to read faster than children who sit in front of the TV all day.

Combine each pair of sentences into one sentence. Use the words in parentheses to add a nonessential adjective clause to the first sentence.

EXAMPLE: John Kennedy, Jr. died in a plane crash. (He was the son of a president.)

John Kennedy, Jr., who was the son of a president, died in a

plane crash.

1. President Kennedy was killed in 1963. (John Junior was only three years old at that time.)

   _____

2. The television changed the way Americans got their information. (It became popular in the 1950s.)

   _____

3. Berners-Lee studied physics in college. (His parents were programmers.)

   _____

4. Berners-Lee is not a well known person. (We read about him in this lesson.)

   _____

5. Berners-Lee works at M.I.T. (He has a small office there.)

   _____

6. The V-Chip allows parents to control their children's viewing. (It has been installed in all new TVs.)

   _____

PART **5**

Some of these adjective clauses can be shortened. Shorten them by crossing out unnecessary words. Some of the adjective clauses cannot be shortened. Do not change them.

EXAMPLE: Thanksgiving, ~~which is~~ an American holiday, is in November.

1. The English that is spoken in the U.S. is different from British English.

2. A lot of Americans like to eat at McDonald's, which is a fast-food restaurant.

3. Do not disturb the students who are studying in the library.

4. In the U.S. there are many immigrants who are from Mexico.

5. The computer that you bought has a very big memory.

6. She doesn't like the music that her daughter listens to.

7. Everyone who saw the movie liked it a lot.

8. Everyone whom I met at the party was very interesting.

9. Children who watch TV all day don't get enough exercise.

10. Parents whose children are small should control the TV programs that their kids watch.

11. The teacher with whom I studied beginning grammar comes from Canada.

12. The Web, which was introduced only a short time ago, has changed the way many companies do business.

PART **6**   **Some of the following sentences need commas. Put them in. If the sentence doesn't need commas, write "no commas."**

EXAMPLES: The last article we read was about parental control.   *no commas*
Alaska, which is the largest state, has a very small population.

1. Ms. Thomson who was my English teacher last semester retired last year.

2. I don't like teachers who give a lot of homework.

3. I studied engineering at the University of Michigan which is located in Ann Arbor, Michigan.

4. The computer I bought last month has a very big memory.

5. The computer which is one of the most important inventions of the twentieth century can be found in many American homes.

6. A V-chip is a device that lets parents control the programs their children watch.

7. My mother who lives in Miami has a degree in engineering.

8. I have two sisters. My sister who lives in New Jersey has three children.

9. Our parents who live with us now are beginning to study English.

10. The American flag which has 13 stripes and 50 stars is red, white, and blue.

11. The city where I was born has beautiful museums.

12. St. Petersburg where I was born has beautiful museums.

EXPANSION ACTIVITIES

CLASSROOM ACTIVITIES

1. **Yes, but . . . Game.** Work with a partner. One person will finish the sentence giving a point of view. The other person will contradict the first person by saying, "Yes, but . . ." and giving a different point of view.

   EXAMPLE: People who get married when they are young . . .
   A. People who get married when they are young have a lot of energy to raise their children.
   B. Yes, but people who get married when they are young are not very responsible.

   a) Couples who have a lot of children . . .

   b) People who immigrate to the U.S. . . .

   c) English books that have the answers in the back . . .

   d) People who have a lot of money . . .

   e) People who have a car . . .

   f) People who live in the same place all their lives . . .

   g) Teachers who speak fast . . .

   h) People who use credit cards . . .

   i) Cities that have a lot of factories . . .

   j) Movies that have a lot of violence . . .

   k) Parents who do everything for their children . . .

   l) Couples who have children when they're in their 40s . . .

2. Fill in the blanks and discuss your answers in a small group.

   a) People _____ have an easy life.

   b) No one likes or respects people _____

   c) People who _____ want to come to the U.S.

   d) There are a lot of people who _____

3. **Dictionary Game.** Form a small group. One student in the group will look for a hard word in the dictionary. (Choose a noun. Find a word that you think no one will know.) Other students will write definitions of the word.

Students can think of funny definitions or serious ones. The student with the dictionary will write the real definition. Students put all the definitions in a box. The student with the dictionary will read the definitions. The others have to guess which is the real definition.

EXAMPLE: nonagenarian
             Sample definition: A nonagenarian is a person who has none of the characteristics of his generation.
             Real definition: A nonagenarian is a person who is between 90 and 99 years old.

(Alternate: The teacher can provide a list of words and definitions beforehand, writing them on small pieces of paper. A student can choose one of the papers that the teacher has prepared.)

DISCUSSION

1. In what ways does the computer make life better? In what ways does it make life worse?

2. Discuss the differences between using e-mail and paper mail (sometimes called "snail mail," because it's slow). In what cases is it better to use e-mail? In what cases is it better to write a letter, put it in an envelope, and mail it?

snail

WRITING

1. Write a paragraph telling why parents should or shouldn't control the programs children watch and the amount of time they watch TV.

2. Write a composition about your favorite TV program. Tell why you like it.

3. Write a paragraph telling how you use your computer (or the computers at this school).

4. Write about an important person you know about who didn't receive much attention or money for his or her work.

5. Write about an important invention. How did this invention change society?

Internet Activities

1. Find Tim Berners-Lee's Web site. What kind of information can you get from his Web site?

2. Go to a Web site that sells books. Find Berners-Lee's book, *Weaving the Web*. How much is it? Find a review of his book and print it out.

3. If you don't use AOL, type in "AOL Instant Messenger" at a search engine. Find out how to use this service.

GRAMMAR
Infinitives
Gerunds

CONTEXT
Andrew Carnegie, Philanthropist
Charity and Volunteering
Helping Others Get an Education

LESSON FOCUS
An infinitive is *to* + the base form of the verb.
I want *to help* others.
It's important *to think* of other people.
A gerund is formed by adding *-ing* to the verb.
Volunteering makes me feel good.
I enjoy *volunteering*.

Examples	Explanation
I want **to leave**.	An infinitive is used after certain verbs.
I want him **to leave**.	An object can be added before an infinitive.
I'm happy **to see** you.	An infinitive can follow certain adjectives.
It's important **to learn** English.	An infinitive follows certain expressions with *it*.
I'm saving my money in order **to buy** a car.	An infinitive is used to show purpose.
He's old enough **to vote**. She's too young **to get** married.	An infinitive is used after expressions with *too* and *enough*.

Before You Read 1. Who are some of the richest people today?
2. Should rich people help others?

Andrew Carnegie, 1835–1919.

Read the following article. Pay special attention to infinitives.

Andrew Carnegie, Philanthropist[1]

Andrew Carnegie was one of the world's richest men. He made a fortune in the oil and steel industries but spent most of his life giving his money away.

Carnegie was born in Scotland in 1835. When he was 13 years old, his family emigrated to the U.S. A year later, he started **to work** for $1.20 a week. He was intelligent and hard-working, and it didn't take him long **to become** rich. But he always remembered the day he wanted **to use** a library in Pittsburgh but was not permitted **to enter**. He was disappointed **to learn** that the library was for members only.

As Carnegie's fortunes grew, he started **to give** his money away. One of his biggest desires was **to build** free public libraries. He wanted everyone **to have** access to libraries and education. In 1881, there were only a few public libraries. By the time Carnegie died, there were over 2,500 in the English-speaking world.

But building libraries was not his only contribution. In his book, *The Gospel of Wealth*, he tried **to persuade** other wealthy people **to give** away their money. These are some of the ideas he wrote about in his book:

- **To give** away money is the best thing rich people can do.
- It is the moral obligation of the wealthy **to help** others.
- It is important for a rich person **to set** an example for others.
- It is not good **to have** money if your spirit is poor.
- It is the mind that makes the body rich.
- It is a disgrace[2] **to die** rich.

By the time he died in 1919, Carnegie had given away more than $350 million.

7.2 Verbs Followed by an Infinitive

Examples	Explanation
Carnegie wanted **to build** libraries. He started **to work** when he was 14. He decided **to give** away money. Everyone deserves **to have** an education.	Some verbs are followed by an infinitive.

(continued)

[1] A *philanthropist* is a person who gives away money to help other people.
[2] A *disgrace* is something that brings shame or dishonor.

Examples	Explanation
I want **to read and write** English well.	In a sentence with two infinitives connected by *and*, the second *to* is usually omitted.
Everyone wants **to be given** an opportunity to succeed.	To make an infinitive passive, use *to be* + past participle.

LANGUAGE NOTES .

The verbs below can be followed by an infinitive.

agree	deserve	love*	seem
appear	expect	manage	start*
attempt	forget	need	try*
begin*	hate*	offer	want
can('t) afford	hope	plan	wish
can't stand*	intend	prefer*	would like
choose	know how	prepare	refuse
continue*	learn	pretend	
decide	like*	promise	

*These verbs can also be followed by a gerund. See Section 7.14.

EXERCISE 1 Fill in the blanks with an infinitive. Share your answers with the class.

EXAMPLE: I like _to eat Chinese food._

1. I don't like _____, but I have to do it anyway.

2. I can't afford _____

3. I've decided _____

4. I want _____, but I don't have enough time.

5. I don't want _____, but I have to do it.

6. I sometimes forget _____

7. I love _____

8. I need _____ and _____ every day.

9. I don't know how _____, but I'd like to learn.

10. I would like _____.

Answer these questions. You may discuss your answers.

Why did you decide to come to this city?
I decided to come here because I wanted to go to this school.

1.   Why did you decide to come to this college?

2.   What did you need to do to get into this school?

3.   When did you start to study English?

4.   What do you expect to be doing ten years from now?

5.   What do you hope to accomplish in your lifetime?

6.   Do you want to learn any other languages? Which ones? Why?

7.   Do you plan to get a college degree? In what field?

8.   Do you plan to transfer to a different school?

9.   What do you plan to do after you graduate?

EXERCISE **3**   Fill in the blanks with the passive of the verb in parentheses.

EXAMPLE: I prefer _____*to be called*_____ by my first name.
(call)

1. My son doesn't like _____ what to do.
(tell)

2. She has _____ to the doctor immediately.
(take)

3. Children need _____ love.
(give)

4. It is important _____ by our friends and colleagues.
(respect)

5. She doesn't want _____ in that awful dress.
(see)

6. I want _____ for my character, not for my money.
(love)

7. She has _____ the truth about her husband's illness.
(tell)

8. Children have _____ right from wrong.
(teach)

9. He is too young _____ to drive.
   (permit)

10. That actress expects _____ an award for her role in
    (give)
    the movie.

7.3   Object Before Infinitive

Examples	Pattern
Carnegie wanted **everyone to have** educational opportunities. He encouraged **rich people to help** others. He wanted **them to donate** money. The teacher doesn't want **us to talk** during an exam.	Verb + object (noun or pronoun) + infinitive

LANGUAGE NOTES

The verbs below can be followed by a noun or object pronoun + infinitive.

advise	expect	persuade
allow	forbid	remind
appoint	force	teach*
ask	invite	tell
beg	need	urge
convince	order	want
encourage	permit	would like

*After *teach, how* is usually used: He taught me *how to ski.*

EXERCISE 4   Tell if you want or don't want the teacher to do the following.

EXAMPLES: speak fast
I don't want the teacher to speak fast.

answer my questions
I want him to answer my questions.

1. explain the grammar
2. review modals
3. give us a lot of homework
4. give us a test on gerunds and infinitives
5. give a lot of examples
6. speak slowly
7. correct my pronunciation
8. teach us idioms

EXERCISE 5   Tell if the teacher expects or doesn't expect you to do the following.

EXAMPLES: come on time
The teacher expects us to come on time.

wear a suit to class
The teacher doesn't expect us to wear a suit to class.

1. write perfect compositions
2. learn English in six months
3. do the homework
4. stand up to answer a question
5. raise our hands to answer a question
6. ask questions
7. study on Saturdays
8. practice English every day
9. speak English without an accent
10. use the Internet

EXERCISE 6   Change the following imperative statements to statements with an object pronoun plus an infinitive.

EXAMPLE: A woman says to her husband, "Close the door."
She wants _____*him to close the door.*_____

1. A teacher says to the students, "Write a composition."

   She wants _____

2. A mother says to her children, "Turn off the TV."

   She wants _____

3. A woman says to her husband, "Don't come home late."

   She doesn't want _____

4. The father says to his children, "Study hard."

   He encourages _____

5. The man said to the woman, "Let's dance."

   He invited _____

6. The counselor said to the girl, "Go to college."

   He advised _____

7. The student said to the teacher, "Repeat the word, please."

   The student wanted _____

8. The husband told his wife, "Pick up the kids after school."

   The husband reminded _____

9. I said to my brother, "Help me on Saturday."

   I would like _____

10. Carnegie said to rich people, "Give money to the poor."

    He wanted _____

EXERCISE 7 Use the words given to tell what your family wanted from you when you were growing up.

EXAMPLES: want/move away
My parents didn't want me to move away.

expect/get married
My mother expected me to get married when I graduated from college.

1. expect/respect older people
2. allow/stay out late at night
3. want/help them financially
4. expect/get good grades in school
5. encourage/have a lot of friends
6. want/be obedient
7. want/be independent
8. permit/choose my own friends
9. expect/get married
10. encourage/save money
11. advise/be honest
12. encourage/go to college

Before You Read 1. Do you ever receive address labels in the mail with your name and address printed on them?
2. Do you ever see programs on TV that ask you to send money to support the station?

Read the following article. Pay special attention to verbs followed by infinitives and base forms.

Charity and Volunteering

There are over 600,000 charities in the U.S. that you can give to. In addition, there are thousands of volunteer organizations. But it isn't always easy to **get** people **to give** willingly.

One way charities **get** people **to contribute** is by offering a payroll deduction at work. An employee can have a certain amount of each paycheck deducted, so the money goes to charity before he even sees it. If you are asked to give at your job, keep in mind that it is voluntary; no one can **make** you **give**.

Another way to **get** you **to give** is to send you something free in the mail, such as address labels with your name and address printed on them. Some people feel guilty about accepting the gift without giving something. Some charities **have** volunteers **stand** at intersections with a can or box, asking passing drivers for donations. Often they give you something, such as candy, for your donation.

Public TV stations have fundraisers. Several days out of the year, they ask for your money to support the TV programs you like. The station **has** volunteers **answer** phones to take your credit card number.

Besides giving money, people can volunteer their time. Some volunteers **help** kids **learn** to read; others help feed the homeless; others **help** elderly people **get** meals.

Helping others **makes** us **feel** good. To encourage us to give, the government **lets** us **deduct** our contribution, which lowers our taxes.

7.4 Causative Verbs

Some verbs are often called *causative* verbs because one person causes, enables, or allows another to do something.

Examples	Explanation
Carnegie **persuaded** wealthy people **to give** away their money.	*Get, persuade, convince* are followed by an object + infinitive.
You **convinced** me **to help** the poor.	*Get*, in the example on the left, means persuade.
They **got** us **to contribute** to charity.	

(continued)

Examples	Explanation
Carnegie **helped** people **to get** an education. Volunteers **help** kids **learn** to read.	After *help* + object, either the infinitive or the base form can be used. The base form is more common.
The government **lets** you **deduct** your contribution to charity. The teacher doesn't **let** us **talk** during a test.	*Let* means permit. *Let* is followed by an object + base form. (*Permit* and *allow* are followed by an infinitive.)
a) No one can **make** you **give** to charity. b) Volunteering my time **makes** me **feel** good. c) A sad movie **makes** me **cry**.	a) *Make* means force. b) and c) *Make* means to cause something to happen. *Make* is followed by an object + base form.
Public TV stations **have** volunteers **answer** the phones and take donations. The teacher **had** us **write** a composition about charity.	*Have* means to give a job or task to someone. *Have*, in this case, is followed by an object + base form.

EXERCISE 8   Fill in the blanks with the base form and finish the sentence.

EXAMPLE: The teacher lets us ___*talk in groups when we work on a problem.*___

1. When I was a child, my parents didn't let me _____

   _____

2. When I was a child, my parents made me _____

   _____

3. My parents helped me _____

4. The teacher often has us _____

5. During a test, the teacher doesn't let us _____

   _____

6. The government lets you _____

7. If you need me, I can help you _____

8. She never lets her husband _____

9. He never lets his wife _____

10. No one can make me _____

11. I volunteered to work in a school. One teacher had me _____

_____

12. I volunteered to work in a park. They had me _____

_____

EXERCISE 9 Fill in the blanks with the base form or the infinitive of the words in parentheses.

EXAMPLE: She lets her children _____*watch*_____ TV after they finish their homework.
(watch)

1. She had her son _____ the table.
(set)

2. She had her husband _____ the turkey.
(prepare)

3. She made her son _____ his room.
(clean)

4. She got her son _____ the leaves in the backyard.
(rake)

5. Her son convinced her _____ him a new video game.
(buy)

6. She persuaded him _____ harder.
(study)

7. She helped him _____ his math homework.
(do)

8. She made him _____ off the TV at 9 o'clock and go to bed.
(turn)

9. Her husband got her _____.
(relax)

10. She let him _____ most of the housework.
(do)

7.5 Adjective Plus Infinitive

Examples	Explanation
Some people are happy **to help** others. Are you willing **to donate** your time? I am proud **to be** a volunteer.	Certain adjectives can be followed by an infinitive. Many of these adjectives describe a person's emotional or mental state.

LANGUAGE NOTES

1. The following adjectives can be followed by an infinitive.

afraid	eager	pleased*	sad
ashamed*	glad	prepared*	sorry
delighted*	happy	proud	surprised*
disappointed*	lucky	ready	willing

   *NOTE: Many *-ed* words are adjectives.

2. Notice how we respond when we are introduced to someone.
   A. I'd like you to meet my brother.
   B. (I'm) pleased (glad) to meet you.
   C. (I'm) pleased (glad) to meet you, too.

3. Notice how we respond to news of a death.
   A. My father died last week.
   B. I'm (so) sorry to hear about it.

EXERCISE 10 Fill in the blanks with an infinitive (phrase).

EXAMPLE: Before I came here, I was afraid ___to speak English.___

1. When I left my parents' house, I was eager _____

2. When I started college, I was surprised (to see, learn, find out) ____

3. When I was a child, I was afraid _____

4. Now I'm afraid _____

5. I'm happy _____

6. Wealthy people should be willing _____

7. When I left my hometown, I was sorry _____

8. When I was _____ years old, I was ready _____

7.6 Using the Infinitive to Show Purpose

Examples	Explanation
My parents saved their money **in order to send** me to college. Carnegie gave away money **in order to help** others.	*In order to* shows purpose. It answers the question "Why?" or "What for?"
My parents saved their money **to send** me to college.	*In order* can be omitted.

Complete each sentence.

EXAMPLE: Many students have jobs in order __*to pay for their education.*__

1. I want to learn English in order to _____

2. I came to this school to _____

3. We're studying this lesson to _____

4. I use my dictionary to _____

5. Many people use a spellcheck in order to _____

6. Many people use e-mail to _____

7. I _____ in order to relax.

8. I _____ to learn new words.

9. You should register early to _____

10. Many students apply for financial aid to _____

7.7 Infinitive as Subject

Examples	Explanation
It is good **to help** other people. **It** was Carnegie's dream **to build** libraries.	An infinitive phrase can be the subject of a sentence. We usually begin the sentence with *it* and put the infinitive phrase at the end of the sentence.
It is important **for rich people** to set an example. It is a good idea **for you** to save money.	*For* + an object can give the infinitive a specific subject.
It costs a lot of money **to build** a library. **It takes** a long time **to learn** another language.	An infinitive is often used after *cost* + money and *take* + time.
It didn't take **him** long **to become** rich. How much did it cost **you to take** this course?	An indirect object can follow *take* and *cost*.
To build libraries was Carnegie's dream. **To give** money away is the best thing rich people can do.	Sometimes we begin a sentence with an infinitive phrase. A sentence that begins with an infinitive is very formal.

EXERCISE 12 Complete each statement with an infinitive phrase.

EXAMPLE: It isn't polite _to interrupt a conversation._

1. It's dangerous _____
2. It isn't healthy _____
3. It isn't polite _____
4. It's illegal _____
5. It's a good idea _____
6. It's the teacher's responsibility _____
7. It costs a lot of money _____
8. It's important for me _____
9. It's boring for the students _____
10. It's fun for children _____
11. It's easy for Americans _____
12. It took me a long time _____
13. It cost me a lot of money _____
14. It will probably take me a long time _____

EXERCISE 13 Make sentences with the words given.

EXAMPLE: dangerous/children
             It's dangerous for children to play with matches.

1. fun/children

    _____

2. necessary/children

    _____

3. important/a family

    _____

4. difficult/a large family

    _____

5. necessary/working parents

_____

6. difficult/women in my native culture

_____

7. hard/single parents

_____

8. difficult/the teacher

_____

EXERCISE 14 Complete each statement.

EXAMPLES: *It's impossible* _____ to be perfect.

It costs me 50¢ a minute _____ to make a long-distance phone call to my hometown.

1. _____ to work hard.

2. _____ to fall in love.

3. _____ to get married.

4. _____ to make a mistake in English.

5. _____ to be lonely.

6. _____ to help other people.

7. _____ to take a taxi from downtown to my house.

8. _____ to eat lunch in the school cafeteria.

9. _____ to go to college.

10. _____ to buy my textbooks.

11. _____ to learn English.

12. _____ to give away money.

13. _____ to have a lot of friends.

14. _____ to travel.

EXERCISE 15 Change these statements to make them less formal by beginning with *it*.

EXAMPLE: To succeed at one's job requires hard work.
It requires hard work to succeed at one's job.

1. To find a job can be time-consuming.

   _____

2. To graduate from college is my goal.

   _____

3. To raise children requires a lot of patience.

   _____

4. To give away money is the responsibility of rich people.

   _____

5. To make mistakes in English is natural.

   _____

6. To do the same thing every day is boring.

   _____

7.8 Infinitive with *Too* and *Enough*

Examples	Pattern
He was **too poor to go** to college. You drive **too slowly to drive** on the highway.	*Too* + adjective/adverb + infinitive
I have **too much homework to do**, so I can't go out. We have **too many questions to answer** in one day.	*Too much* + noncount noun + infinitive *Too many* + plural noun + infinitive
You are **old enough to understand** life. She speaks English **well enough to attend** an American university.	Adjective/adverb + *enough* + infinitive
Carnegie had **enough money to build** libraries.	*Enough* + noun + infinitive

LANGUAGE NOTES

1. *Too* shows that the adjective or adverb is excessive for a specific purpose.

   This lesson is *too long* to finish in one day.

2. The infinitive phrase can be preceded by *for* + an object.

   This exercise is short enough *for us* to finish in five minutes.

   That book is too hard *for me* to read without a dictionary.

3. The infinitive can sometimes be omitted.

   A. Can you help me this afternoon?

   B. I'm sorry. I can't. I'm *too busy*.

EXERCISE 16 Fill in the blanks with *too* + adjective or adverb, or *too many/much* + noun.

EXAMPLE: It's _____*too late*_____ for a student to register for this semester.

1. This lesson is _____ to finish in one class period.

2. The cafeteria is _____ for me to study there.

3. Some Americans speak English _____ for me to understand.

4. The bus is sometimes _____ for me to get a seat.

5. It's _____ to go swimming today.

6. It's _____ to predict next week's weather.

7. She earns _____ to qualify for a scholarship.

8. I can't go out with you. I have _____ to do this afternoon.

EXERCISE 17 Fill in the blanks with *enough* + noun, or adjective/adverb + *enough*.

EXAMPLE: I don't speak English _____*well enough*_____ to be in a college–credit writing course.

1. This exercise is _____ to finish in a few minutes.

2. I don't type _____ to write my compositions by computer.

3. He doesn't have _____ to do all the things he wants to do.

4. She's only 16 years old. She's not _____ to get married.

5. You didn't run _____ to win the race.

6. He doesn't have _____ to buy a new computer.

Examples	Explanation
Learning a new language is interesting.	A gerund (phrase) can be used as the subject of a sentence.
I enjoy **learning** a new language.	A gerund (phrase) can be used as the object of a sentence.
I'm excited about **learning** a new language.	A gerund (phrase) can be used as the object of a preposition.
I appreciate **being corrected** when I make a mistake.	A gerund can be passive: *being* + past participle

LANGUAGE NOTES

1. A gerund is used as a noun. COMPARE:
   Tennis is fun. I enjoy *conversation*.
   Swimming is fun. I enjoy *talking*.
2. To make a gerund negative, put *not* before the gerund.
   He's afraid of *not* finding a job.
   Not knowing English well makes my life difficult.

Before You Read 1. Do you think that all rich people like to live in luxury?
2. Do you know anyone who is very generous?

Matel Dawson

Read the following article. Pay special attention to gerunds.

Helping Others Get an Education

When we think of philanthropists, we usually think of the very rich and famous, like Andrew Carnegie. However, Matel Dawson, a forklift driver in Michigan, is an ordinary man who has done extraordinary things.

Dawson started **working** at Ford Motor Company in 1940 for $1.15 an hour. By **working** hard, **saving** carefully, and **investing** his money wisely, he has become rich. But he doesn't care about **owning** expensive cars or **taking** fancy vacations. Instead of **spending** his money on himself, he enjoys **giving** it away. Since 1995, he has donated more than $1 million for college scholarships to help poor students who want to get an education.

Why does Dawson insist on **giving** his money away to college students? One reason is that he did not have the opportunity to finish school. He had to drop out of school after the seventh grade to help support his poor family. He has always regretted not **having** an education. "I advise kids to get a good education," he says. Also, he learned about **giving** from his parents. He watched them work hard, save, and help others less fortunate. His mother made Dawson promise to always give something back. He is grateful to his parents for **teaching** him the importance of **helping** others.

Dawson doesn't plan on **changing** his lifestyle. He's used to **driving** his old car and **living** in a one-bedroom apartment. And he doesn't plan to stop **working** as long as he is able. "It keeps me **going, knowing** I'm helping somebody."

Did you know...?

More than half of all charitable giving comes from Americans earning less than $50,000 a year. Eighty percent of Americans who earn at least $1 million a year give nothing to charity.

7.10   Gerund as Subject

Examples	Explanation
Giving away money makes Dawson feel good. **Living** economically is not hard for Dawson.	A gerund (phrase) can be the subject of the sentence.
Not **finishing** school can affect your whole life.	To make a gerund negative, put *not* before the gerund.
Helping others gives Dawson pleasure.	A gerund subject takes a singular verb.

EXERCISE 18 Complete each statement.

EXAMPLE: Leaving home _was the most difficult decision I have ever made._

1. Going to college _____

2. Making new friends _____

3. Changing old habits _____

4. Learning a new language _____

5. Finding an apartment _____

6. Thinking about my future _____

7. Getting a job _____

8. Leaving home _____

EXERCISE 19 Complete each statement with a gerund (phrase) as the subject.

EXAMPLE: _Taking a warm bath_____ relaxes me at the end of the day.

1. _____ is important for everyone.

2. _____ is difficult for people who don't speak English.

3. _____ is an important decision in a person's life.

4. _____ is against the law.

5. _____ is a healthy activity.

6. _____ is not polite.

7. _____ isn't good for you. (is an unhealthy activity)

8. _____ takes a long time.

9. _____ gives me a lot of satisfaction.

10. _____ makes me feel proud.

7.11 Gerund After Prepositions and Nouns

Examples	Pattern
Dawson doesn't care **about owning** fancy things. He believes **in helping** others.	Verb + preposition + gerund
Carnegie was famous **for building** libraries. Dawson is concerned **about helping** poor college students.	Adjective + preposition + gerund
Dawson thanks his parents **for teaching** him to save money.	Verb + object + preposition + gerund
Dawson doesn't spend money **going** on vacations or **eating** in expensive restaurants. He doesn't have a hard time **saving** money.	A gerund is used after the noun in the following expressions: *have a difficult time, have difficulty, have experience, have fun, have a good time, have a hard time, have a problem, have trouble, spend time, spend money*

EXERCISE 20 Complete the questions with a gerund (phrase). Then ask another student these questions.

EXAMPLE: Are you lazy about ___*writing compositions?*___

1. Are you tired of _____
2. Are you worried about _____
3. Do you ever complain about _____
4. Are you interested in _____
5. Do you ever think about _____
6. Were you excited about _____
7. Did anyone try to stop you from _____
8. Do you ever dream about _____

EXERCISE 21 Fill in the blanks with a gerund phrase.

EXAMPLE: I had problems ___*getting a student loan.*___

1. I had a hard time _____
2. I have a lot of experience _____

3. I don't have much experience _____

4. I spent a lot of money _____

5. I don't like to spend my time _____

6. I have a lot of fun _____

7. I don't have a good time _____

8. I don't have a problem _____

7.12   Using the Correct Preposition

These are some common verb + preposition combinations.

Verb + *about*	Verb + *to*	Verb + *on*	Verb + *in*
care about	adjust to	depend on	believe in
complain about	look forward to*	insist on	succeed in
dream about	object to	plan on**	
forget about			
talk about			
think about			
worry about			

Look forward to means "to wait for a future event with pleasure." Example: I look forward to graduating next year.

**Plan* can also be followed by an infinitive: I plan *to go* = I plan *on going*.

These are some common adjective + preposition combinations.

Adj. + *of*	Adj. + *about*	Adj. + *for*	Adj. + *at*	Adj. + *to*	Adj. + *in*
afraid of*	concerned about	responsible for	good at	accustomed to	interested in
capable of	excited about	famous for	successful at	used to	
guilty of	upset about	grateful to . . . for			
proud of*	worried about				
tired of					

Afraid and *proud* can also be followed by an infinitive.

I'm afraid *to go* out at night. I'm afraid *of going* out at night.
I'm proud *to be* an American. I'm proud *of passing* my citizenship test.

Notice that in some expressions, *to* is a preposition followed by a gerund, not part of an infinitive. COMPARE:

I need *to wear* glasses.
I'm not accustomed *to wearing* glasses.

(continued)

These are some common verb + object + preposition combinations.

Verb + obj. + *of*	Verb + obj. + *for*	Verb + obj. + *from*	Verb + obj. + *about*
accuse . . . of	apologize to . . . for	keep . . . from	warn . . . about
suspect . . . of	blame . . . for	prevent . . . from	
	forgive . . . for	prohibit . . . from	
	thank . . . for	stop . . . from	

Example: She *thanked me for taking* care of her children.

These are some other expressions followed by a gerund.

Noun + *of*	Noun + *for*
in danger of	a need for
in favor of	a reason for
the purpose of	an excuse for
	technique for

Example: What is your *reason for going* home early?

EXERCISE 22 Fill in the blanks with a preposition (if necessary) and the gerund of the verb in parentheses. In some cases, no preposition is necessary.

A. I'm worried ___about___ ___losing___ my job. A lot of workers in my
(example: lose)

factory are in danger _____ _____ laid off.
(1 get)

B. I don't blame you _____ _____ worried. Have you thought
(2 be)

_____ _____ a new career?
(3 start)

A. I'd have to go back to school to retrain. I'd have a hard time _____
(4 study)

now that I'm married and have children.

B. Maybe you could take a short course. It doesn't take long to study to be a licensed practical nurse.

A. I'm not interested _____ _____ a nurse.
(5 become)

B. What about medical records?

A. I'm not good _____ _____ with records. Besides, I can't
(6 work)

spend time _____ to school, even for six months. I need a job
(7 go)

right away.

B. Well, I don't know what to tell you. I hope you succeed _____

_____ a job soon.
(8 find)

EXERCISE 23 Ask a question with the words given. Use the correct
preposition (if necessary) and a gerund. Another student will
answer.

EXAMPLES:
fond/read
A. Are you fond of reading?
B. Yes, I am.

care/get a good grade
A. Do you care about getting a good grade?
B. Of course I do.

1. have trouble/understand spoken English

2. lazy/do the homework

3. have a technique/learn new words

4. afraid/fail this course

5. good/spell English words

6. interested/study computer programming

7. have experience/work with computers

8. think/buy a house some day

7.13 Verbs Followed by Gerunds

Examples	Explanation
Dawson enjoys **giving** money away. He can't imagine not **helping** others. He recommends **saving** money. Students appreciate **receiving** financial aid from Dawson.	Many verbs are followed by a gerund.
He doesn't **go shopping** every day. Do you like to **go fishing**?	*Go* + gerund is used in many idiomatic expressions of sport and recreation.

LANGUAGE NOTES

1. The following verbs take a gerund.

admit	delay	finish	permit	recommend
advise	deny	imagine	postpone	resent
appreciate	discuss	keep (on)	practice	risk
avoid	dislike	mind**	put off***	stop
can't help*	enjoy	miss	quit	suggest
consider				

Can't help means to have no control: When I see a sad movie, I *can't help* crying.

**I *mind* means that something bothers me. I *don't mind* means that something is OK with me; it doesn't bother me: Do you *mind* living with your parents? No, I don't *mind*.

***Put off* means postpone: I can't *put off* buying a car. I need one now.

2. Below are expressions with *go* + gerund.

go boating	go fishing	go sailing	go skiing
go bowling	go hiking	go shopping	go swimming
go camping	go hunting	go sightseeing	
go dancing	go jogging	go skating	

EXERCISE 24 Complete the sentences with a gerund (phrase).

EXAMPLE: I avoid ___*walking alone at night.*___

1. The teacher doesn't permit _____

2. I don't mind _____

3. It's difficult to quit _____

4. I enjoy _____

5. I don't enjoy _____

6. I can't imagine _____

7. I don't like to go _____

8. I avoid _____

9. Everyone appreciates _____

10. I often put off _____

EXERCISE 25 Use *being* + past participle to fill in the blanks with the passive form of the gerund.

EXAMPLE: I dislike ___*being told*___ what to do.
(tell)

1. She dislikes _____.
(criticize)

2. I enjoy _____ a compliment.
(give)

3. I'm tired of _____ where I'm from.
(ask)

4. She's afraid of _____ from her job.
(fire)

5. I appreciate _____ when I make a mistake.
(correct)

6. The criminal is in danger of _____ by the police.
(catch)

7. Wearing a seat belt prevented us from _____ when
(injure)
our car was hit.

8. Do you miss _____ by your parents?
(care for)

7.14 Verbs Followed by Gerund or Infinitive

Examples	Explanation
Dawson likes **giving** money away. He likes **to give** money away. He started **working** in 1940. He started **to work** in 1940.	Some verbs can be followed by either a gerund or an infinitive with no difference in meaning.

LANGUAGE NOTES

The verbs below can be followed by either a gerund or an infinitive with no difference in meaning.

begin	continue	like	prefer
can't stand*	hate	love	start

Can't stand means can't tolerate: I *can't stand* living in a cold climate.

EXERCISE 26 In the following sentences, change gerunds to infinitives and infinitives to gerunds.

EXAMPLES: He began to work at 4:30.
He began working at 4:30.

I love sleeping on the beach.
I love to sleep on the beach.

1. Do you prefer to study in the morning?

2. She hates washing the dishes.

3. When did you begin studying English?

4. If you continue talking about politics, I'm going to leave.

5. They can't stand to watch violent movies.

6. I love to get letters, don't you?

EXERCISE 27 Fill in the blanks with the gerund or infinitive of the verb in parentheses. In some cases, either a gerund or an infinitive may be used.

A. When did you begin _____studying/to study_____ English?
(example: study)

B. When I was in high school. I continued _____ it in college,
(1 study)

but I didn't start _____ it until I came to the U.S.
(2 speak)

A. Do you like _____ English now?
(3 study)

B. Yes. But I'm shy, and I avoid _____ in class.
(4 talk)

A. You'll never learn _____ English if you don't practice.
(5 speak)

B. But I'm afraid of making mistakes.

A. You can't help _____ some mistakes. It's only natural. You
(6 make)

can't expect _____ perfect.
(7 be)

B. You're right, of course. How about you? Do you enjoy _____
(8 speak)

English?

A. Yes. My English is not perfect, but I manage _____
   (9 communicate)

   when I need to. But I dislike _____ homework. I don't mind
                                   (10 do)

   _____ in the blanks in a grammar exercise, but I
   (11 fill)

   hate _____ a composition.
        (12 write)

B. Me too. I always put off _____ it until the night before.
                              (13 do)

7.15   Infinitive and Gerund as Subject

Examples	Explanation
It is expensive **to go** to college. **It** is important **to have** a college education. **It** makes me feel good **to give** money to poor people.	An infinitive phrase can be the subject of a sentence. We usually begin the sentence with *it* and put the infinitive phrase at the end of the sentence.
Going to college is expensive. **Having** a college education is important. **Giving** money to poor people makes me feel good.	A gerund phrase can be used as the subject.
To pay for college is difficult for most families. **To build** libraries was Carnegie's dream. **To give** money away is the best thing rich people can do, according to Carnegie.	Sometimes we begin a sentence with an infinitive phrase. A sentence that begins with an infinitive is very formal.

EXERCISE 28 Change these statements. Change the subject to a gerund form.

EXAMPLE: It is a pleasure to watch children grow up.

Watching children grow up is a pleasure.

1. It's fascinating to meet new people.

   _____

2. It can be boring to do the same thing every day.

   _____

3. It is seldom easy to raise children.

_____

4. It takes practice to use the Internet.

_____

5. It costs a lot of money to go to college.

_____

7.16   Gerund or Infinitive After a Verb: Differences in Meaning

After *stop*, *remember*, and *try*, the meaning of the sentence depends on whether you follow the verb with a gerund or an infinitive.

Examples	Explanation
Dawson loves to work. He doesn't plan to **stop working**.	*Stop* + gerund = Quit or discontinue an activity
Dawson wanted to finish school, but he **stopped to get** a job.	*Stop* + infinitive = Quit one activity in order to start another activity
Dawson **remembers earning** $1.15 an hour in 1940.	*Remember* + gerund = Remember that something happened earlier
Dawson's mother said, "Always **remember to help** other people."	*Remember* + infinitive = Remember something and then do it
Dawson has always had a simple lifestyle. When he became rich, he **tried living** a fancier lifestyle, but it didn't bring him satisfaction.	*Try* + gerund = experiment with something new. You do something one way, and then, if that doesn't work, you try a different method.
I always write my compositions by hand. I **tried writing** them on a computer, but I don't type fast enough.	
Carnegie **tried to enter** a library when he was young, but he was told it was for members only.	*Try* + infinitive = Make an effort or an attempt

EXERCISE 29 Fill in the blanks with the gerund or infinitive of the verb in parentheses.

EXAMPLES: Stop _____*bothering*_____ me. I'm trying to study.
(bother)

The teacher always says, "Remember _____*to do*_____ your homework."
(do)

1. When the teacher came in, the students stopped _____.
(talk)

2. When you learn more English, you will stop _____ your
(use)
dictionary so much.

3. When you're tired of studying, stop _____ a break.
(take)

4. I saw my friend in the hall, and I stopped _____ to her.
(speak)

5. My sister and I had a fight, and we stopped _____ to each
(speak)
other. We haven't spoken to each other for two weeks.

6. The teacher usually remembers _____ the homework papers.
(return)

7. You should remember _____ an infinitive after certain verbs.
(use)

8. Will you remember _____ the homework during spring break?
(do)

9. Do you remember _____ the passive voice last month?
(learn)

10. Remember _____ the passive voice when the subject does not
(use)
perform the action of the verb.

11. I remember not _____ much English a few years ago.
(understand)

12. I remember _____ the present perfect tense even though I
(study)
don't always use it correctly.

13. I always try _____ a few new words every day.
(learn)

14. She wanted to be independent from her parents, so she tried
_____ alone. But she didn't like it and moved back home.
(live)

15. I want telemarketers to stop _____ me. At first I tried
(call)
_____ a polite approach. But that didn't work. Then I
(use)
tried _____ them that my English wasn't good. That didn't
(tell)
work. In fact, nothing works, so now I just hang up.

16. I need more money. I'm going to try _____ a part-time job.
(find)

EXERCISE 30 Read the following conversation between a son (S) and his mother (M). Fill in the blanks with the gerund or infinitive of the word in parentheses.

S. Hi, Mom. I'm calling to say good-bye. I'm leaving tomorrow.

M. Where are you going?

S. To California.

M. You didn't tell me.

S. Of course, I did. I remember _____*telling*_____ you about it when I
   (example: tell)
   was at your house for dinner last week.

M. Oh, yes. Now I remember _____ you say something about
   (1 hear)
   it. Why are you going?

S. I have a good friend there, and he invited me to come and live with
   him. Neither one of us likes living alone, so we're going to try
   _____ together. Besides, I've tried _____ a job here but I
   (2 live)   *(3 find)*
   can't. My friend says there are more opportunities where he lives.

M. Have I met your friend?

S. He was here last year at my birthday party. You met him there.

M. I don't remember _____ him. Anyway, how are you getting
   (4 meet)
   to California?

S. I'm driving.

M. Alone?

S. Yes.

M. If you get tired, you should stop _____ at a rest area. And
   (5 rest)
   you can stop _____ a cup of coffee every few hours.
   (6 get)

S. I will.

M. Don't stop _____ strangers. It could be dangerous.
   (7 pick up)

S. Of course, I won't.

M. And remember _____ me as soon as you get there.
   (8 call)

S. I will. Mom, stop _____ so much. And stop _____
   (9 worry)   *(10 give)*
   me so much advice. I'm 24 years old!

M. Try _____. I'm your mother. Of course, I worry.
   (11 understand)

7.17   *Used To/Be Used To/Get Used To*

Used to + base form and *be used to* + gerund have completely different meanings.

Examples	Explanation
Dawson **used to be** poor. Now he's rich. He **used to earn** $1.15 an hour. Now he earns $24 an hour. He **used to be** married. Now he's divorced. I **didn't use to know** any English. Now I know a lot.	*Used to* + base form shows that an activity was repeated or habitual in the past. This activity has been discontinued. For the negative, use *didn't use to*. NOTE: Omit the *d* in the negative.
Dawson **is used to working** long hours. He **is used to a simple lifestyle**. He **is used to driving** an old car. He **isn't used to driving** an expensive car.	*Be used to* + gerund or noun phrase means "be accustomed to." These sentences describe Dawson's habits. They show what is normal and comfortable for him. For the negative, use *be* + *not* + *used* to.
Dawson **can't get used to spending** money on himself. He **can't get used to fancy cars**.	*Get used to* + gerund or noun phrase means "become accustomed to." For the negative, use *can't get used to*.

LANGUAGE NOTE

The *d* in *used to* is not pronounced.

EXERCISE 31 An American is talking to a foreigner. Choose the correct words in parentheses to complete the following conversation.

A. Where are you from?

B. I'm from Latvia.

A. Where's that? I'm embarrassed that I don't know very much about the rest of the world.

B. Don't worry. (I/*I'm*) used to that question. Everyone asks me where it is. It's in Europe. It used to (*1 be/being*) part of the Soviet Union, but now it's an independent country.

A. Do they speak Russian there?

B. Russian *(2 used/use)* to be the official language, but now the official language is Latvian.

A. How do you like living in the U.S.?

B. I like it. But *(3 I'm not/I can't)* get used to the hot summers here. Our summers are much more comfortable over there.

A. Was your life much different there?

B. Oh, yes. In Latvia, *(4 I'm/I)* used to *(5 live/living)* with my wife, my daughter, and my wife's parents—three generations in one apartment. Now her parents live separate from us. And our daughter went away to college. There *(6 use to/used to)* be five of us in two rooms. Now there are two of us in five rooms!

A. What else is different for you?

B. Our food was much fresher. So much of the food here is sold in packages. *(7 I'm/I)* not used to *(8 eat/eating)* packaged food.

A. Are there any other differences?

B. I have a car now. I didn't *(9 used to/use to)* have a car in Latvia. *(10 I'm/I)* used to take public transportation everywhere.

A. Do you like having a car?

B. I love it. Now I'm used to *(11 drive/driving)* everywhere. I can't even imagine not having a car. But my wife doesn't like to drive. She can't get *(12 use/used)* to it.

A. Do you think your life is better here or in your country?

B. In many ways it's better here. But it's still hard to get used to *(13 live/living)* in a new country.

EXERCISE 32 Finish these statements.

EXAMPLE: I used to ___*go everywhere by bus*___, but now I have a car and drive everywhere.

1. Mr. Dawson used to _____, but now he's rich.

2. I used to _____ a stick shift car, but now I drive an automatic.

3. They used to _____ an apartment, but now they have a house.

4. I used to _____, but my dog died last year.

5. When she was younger, she used to _____, but now she stays home on Saturday nights.

6. He used to _____ money on foolish things, but now he saves his money.

7. I used to _____ in my language, but now I read an English newspaper.

8. My college used to _____ Northeast College, but they changed the name. Now it's called Kennedy College.

EXERCISE 33 Write sentences comparing the way you used to live with the way you live now.

EXAMPLES:
I used to live with my whole family. Now I live alone.

I used to work in a restaurant. Now I'm a full-time student.

I didn't use to speak English at all. Now I speak English pretty well.

Ideas for sentences:

school	job	hobbies
apartment/house	family life	friends

1. _____

2. _____

3. _____

4. _____

5. _____

EXERCISE 34 A student wrote about things that are new for her in the U.S. Fill in the blanks with a gerund or a noun.

EXAMPLE: I'm not used to _shopping in large supermarkets_. In my native country, I shopped in small stores.

1. I'm not used to _____ a small apartment. In my native country, we lived in a big house.

2. I'm not used to _____. In my native country, it's warm all year round.

3. I'm not used to _____ a student. I'm 35 years old, and I've been out of school for 15 years.

4. I'm not used to _____. I studied British English in my native country.

5. I'm not used to _____ on Sundays. In my native country, Sunday is a day when people rest, not shop and do laundry.

6. I'm not used to _____ in class. In my native country, the teacher talks and the students only listen and write.

EXERCISE 35 Fill in the blanks with four different answers.

EXAMPLES: When I came to this city, it was hard for me to get used to:
living in a small apartment.

American pronunciation.

When I came to this city, it was hard for me to get used to:

1. _____
2. _____
3. _____
4. _____

7.18   Sense-Perception Verbs

After sense-perception verbs (*hear, listen to, feel, smell, see, watch, observe*), we can use either the *-ing*[3] form or the base form, with a slight difference in meaning.

Examples	Explanation
Dawson **saw** his mother **work** hard. He **heard** his parents **talk** about helping others.	The base form shows that a person sensed (*saw, heard*, etc.) something from start to finish. All through his life, Dawson saw his parents' work habits and heard his parents' conversations.
When I entered the classroom late, I **heard** the teacher **talking** about gerunds. I **saw** the students **working** in small groups.	The *-ing* form shows that something is sensed while it is in progress. I heard the teacher while she was in the process of explaining gerunds, and I saw the students while they were working in groups.

EXERCISE 36 A person sees a hit-and-run accident from the window of his apartment. (In a hit-and-run accident, the person who causes the accident doesn't stop.) Fill in the blanks with the base form of an appropriate verb to describe what this person saw.

EXAMPLE: I saw a car accident ___*happen*___ from the window of my apartment.

1. I saw a driver _____ through a red light.

2. I saw him _____ another car.

---

[3] The *-ing* form after a sense perception verb is a present participle, not a gerund.

3. I saw the driver _____ the scene of the accident.

4. I saw the ambulance _____ .

5. I saw the paramedics _____ the injured driver from her car.

6. I saw them _____ the injured driver into an ambulance.

7. I saw the ambulance _____ away.

8. I saw a tow truck _____ the car away.

EXERCISE 37 The Fourth of July is American Independence Day. A person is at a park writing about what he sees and hears. Fill in the blanks with the *-ing* form of an appropriate verb.

EXAMPLE: I see kids ___*playing*___ with sparklers.

1. I hear parents _____ their kids to be careful.

2. I can hear a band _____ a patriotic tune.

3. I see children _____ with their friends.

4. I see people _____ a barbecue.

5. I see people _____ American flags.

6. I see people _____ volleyball.

7. I see people _____ hot dogs and hamburgers.

8. I see everyone _____ a good time.

Infinitives and Base Forms

Examples	Explanation
Dawson wants **to help** others.	An infinitive is used after certain verbs.
His mother wanted him **to help** others.	An object can be added before an infinitive.
His mother made him **promise** that he would help others. He helps students **pay** for college.	A base form is used after some verbs.
He's happy **to give** away his money.	An infinitive can follow certain adjectives.
Public TV stations have fundraisers **in order to get** money.	An infinitive is used to show purpose.
It's important **to help** others. **To help** others is our moral obligation.	*It* can introduce an infinitive subject. (INFORMAL) The infinitive can be in the subject position. (FORMAL)
It's important **for rich people to help** others. It's fun **for me to volunteer**.	*For* + noun or object pronoun is used to give the infinitive a subject.
Carnegie had enough money **to build** libraries. Dawson was too poor **to finish** school.	An infinitive can be used with *too* and *enough*.
Dawson heard his mother **talk** about helping others. I smell something **burning**.	After the sense perception verbs, a base form or *-ing* form is used.
It is important **to be loved**.	An infinitive can be used in the passive voice.

Gerunds

Examples	Explanation
Going to college is expensive in the U.S.	A gerund can be the subject of the sentence.
Dawson enjoys **giving** money away.	A gerund follows certain verbs.
Dawson learned about **giving** from his parents.	A gerund is used after a preposition.
He had a hard time **supporting** his family.	A gerund is used after certain nouns.
He doesn't like to **go shopping**.	A gerund is used in many idiomatic expressions with *go*.
I dislike **being told** a lie.	A gerund can be used in the passive voice.

Gerund or Infinitive—Differences in Meaning

Examples	Explanation
I **used to live** with my family. Now I live alone.	Past habit, discontinued
He's lived alone all his life. He **is used to living** alone.	Present custom
I met a friend at the library, and I **stopped to talk** to her.	I stopped what I was doing in order to talk to her.
I had a fight with my neighbor, and we **stopped talking** to each other.	We don't talk to each other anymore.
I **try to give** a little money to charity each year.	*Try* = make an attempt or effort
I put 85¢ in the soda machine and nothing came out. I **tried hitting** the machine, but still nothing happened.	*Try* = experiment with something new

For a list of words followed by gerunds or infinitives, see Appendix D.

1. Don't forget *to* when introducing an infinitive.

   to
   He needs ^ leave.

   to
   It's necessary ^ have a job.

2. Don't omit *it* when introducing an infinitive.

   It's
   ~~Is~~ important to know a second language.

   It c
   ~~C~~osts a lot of money to get a college education.

3. With a compound infinitive, use the base form after *and*.

   go
   He needed to finish the letter and ~~went~~ to the post office.

4. After *want*, *need*, and *expect*, use the object pronoun, not the subject pronoun, before the infinitive.

   me to
   She wants ~~that I~~ speak English all the time.

5. Don't use *to* between *cost* or *take* and the indirect object.

   It cost ~~to~~ me $500 to fly to Puerto Rico.

   It took ~~to~~ him three months to find a job.

6. Use *for*, not *to*, when you give a subject to the infinitive.

   for
   It is easy ~~to~~ me to speak Spanish.

7. Use *to* + base form, not *for*, to show purpose.

   to
   He exercises every day ~~for~~ improve his health.

8. Use a gerund or an infinitive, not a base form as a subject.

   ing
   Find ^ a good job takes time. *OR It takes time to find a good job.*

9. Be careful with *used to* and *be used to*.

   My brother ~~is~~ used to live in New York. Now he lives in Boston.

   'm   living
   I've lived alone all my life and I love it. I ^ used to ~~live~~ alone.

10. Be careful to use the correct form after *stop*.

> She told her son to stop <s>to</s> watch^(ing) TV and go to bed.

11. Use a gerund, not an infinitive, after a preposition.

> I thought about <s>to</s> return^(ing) to my hometown.

12. Make sure to choose a gerund after certain verbs and an infinitive after others.

> I enjoy <s>to</s> walk^(ing) in the park.
>
> I like to walk in the park. *Correct*

13. Use *not* to make the negative of a gerund.

> He's worried about <s>don't</s> ^(not) finding a job.

14. Use a base form or an *-ing* form after a sense-perception verb.

> I saw the accident <s>to</s> happen.
>
> I can smell the soup <s>to</s> cook^(ing).

15. Use the gerund, not the infinitive, with *go* + recreational activity.

> I like to go <s>to</s> fish^(ing) at the river.

16. Use the base form, not the infinitive, after causative verbs *let*, *make*, and *have*.

> He let me <s>to</s> borrow his car.
>
> The teacher made me <s>to</s> rewrite my composition.

PART 1   Find the mistakes with the underlined words, and correct them. Not every sentence has a mistake. If the sentence is correct, write **C.**

EXAMPLES: He was surprised ^{to} get the job.

To help other people is our moral obligation.   *C*

1. She let me <u>to use</u> her cell phone.

2. My daughter is out of town. I want <u>that she call</u> me.

3. Do you like <u>to watch</u> TV?

4. She's old enough <u>get</u> married.

5. She wanted <u>me to help</u> her with her homework.

6. He decided <u>to rent</u> a car and <u>drove</u> to San Francisco.

7. It took me five minutes <u>finish</u> the job.

8. My friend helped me <u>move</u> the piano.

9. <u>Live</u> in a foreign country is difficult.

10. The teacher had us <u>come</u> to her office to discuss our grades.

11. It will cost <u>to me</u> a lot of money <u>to replace</u> my old computer.

12. She <u>needs speak</u> with you.

13. She got me <u>to tell</u> her the secret.

14. The teacher made the student <u>take</u> the test a second time.

15. It was hard <u>to me to find</u> a job.

16. She persuaded her son <u>to wash</u> the dishes.

17. <u>Costs</u> a lot of money to buy a house.

18. He turned on the TV <u>for watch</u> the news.

19. He stopped <u>to work</u> at 4:30 and went home.

20. I met my friend in the cafeteria, and I stopped <u>to talk</u> to her for a few minutes.

21. I like to cook, but I dislike to wash the dishes.

22. I had a good time talking with my friends.

23. Do you go shop for groceries every week?

24. I used to living with my parents, but now I live alone.

25. My sister couldn't get used to live in the U.S., so she went back to our native country.

26. When I came into the room, I heard the teacher talking about the final exam.

27. The walls of my apartment are thin, and I can hear my neighbors to fight.

28. I can smell my neighbors' dinner cooking.

29. She thanked me for take care of her dog while she was on vacation.

30. Did you have trouble to find my apartment?

31. Please remember to turn off the lights before you go to bed.

32. I started learning English when I was a child.

33. I thought about don't coming back to this school next semester.

34. She complained about being disturbed while she was trying to study.

35. Your dress needs to be cleaned before you can use it again.

36. He tried to repair the car by himself, but he couldn't.

PART **2**   **Fill in the blanks with the gerund, the infinitive, or the base form of the verb in parentheses. In some cases, more than one answer is possible.**

EXAMPLE: _Answering_ the phone during dinner really bothers me.
            (answer)

1. I started _____ dinner last night and the phone rang.
                (eat)

2. Someone was trying _____ me something.
                     (sell)

3. I don't enjoy _____ during dinner.
               (passive: interrupt)

4. Sometimes they want me _____ money to charity, but I don't
                   (donate)

    like _____ my credit card number to strangers on the phone.
         (give)

5. I tell them I'm not interested in _____ their product.
   (buy)

6. _____ them you're not interested doesn't stop them. They don't
   (tell)

   let you _____ their sales pitch.
   (interrupt)

7. I used to _____ to the caller politely, but I don't do it anymore.
   (listen)

8. I've told them politely that I don't want to _____,
   (passive: bother)

   but they don't listen.

9. I keep _____ these phone calls.
   (get)

10. I've thought about _____ my phone number, but I heard that
    (change)

    they'll get my new number.

11. _____ my phone number is not the answer to the problem.
    (change)

12. It's impossible _____ them from _____ you.
    (stop) *(call)*

13. I finally decided _____ caller ID.
    (get)

14. It's better _____ who's calling before you pick up the phone.
    (see)

15. Now I have the choice of _____ up or _____ up the
    (pick) *(not pick)*

    phone when it rings.

PART **3**   Fill in the blanks with the correct preposition.

EXAMPLE: We must concentrate _____*on*_____ learning English.

1. What is the reason _____ doing this exercise?

2. Your grade in this course depends _____ passing the tests and doing
   the homework.

3. I dreamed _____ climbing a mountain.

4. The teacher insists _____ giving tests.

5. The Wright brothers are famous _____ inventing the airplane.

6. I hope I succeed _____ passing this course.

7. Most students care _____ getting good grades.

8. I'm not accustomed _____ wearing jeans to school.

9. Students are interested _____ improving their pronunciation.

10. Are you afraid _____ getting a bad grade?

11. Are you worried _____ getting a bad grade?

12. I'm not used _____ speaking English all the time.

Tell if these pairs of sentences mean about the same thing or have completely different meanings. Write *same* or *different*.

EXAMPLES: It's important to spell correctly.
To spell correctly is important.

Same

I used to live in New York.
I'm used to living in New York.

Different

1. I can't remember to brush my teeth.
   I can't remember brushing my teeth.

   _____

2. I like to cook.
   I like cooking.

   _____

3. Going to college is expensive.
   It's expensive to go to college.

   _____

4. I plan to buy a computer.
   I plan on buying a computer.

   _____

5. I stopped watching TV.
   I stopped to watch TV.

   _____

6. She started to lose weight.
   She started losing weight.

   _____

EXPANSION ACTIVITIES

CLASSROOM ACTIVITIES

1. Tell about teachers and students in your school. What do students expect from teachers? What do teachers expect from students?

Teachers (don't) expect students to:	Students (don't) expect teachers to:
Teachers expect students to come to class on time.	*Students don't expect teachers to be friendly.*

Find a partner, and compare your lists.

2. Fill in the blanks. Discuss your answers in a small group.

a) I used to worry about _____

b) Now, I worry about _____

c) I used to have difficulty _____

d) Now, I have difficulty _____

e) People in my family are not used to _____

f) Americans are not used to _____

g) I'm used to _____ because I've done it all my life.

h) I'm not used to _____

because _____

i) I often used to _____, but I don't do it anymore. (OR I rarely do it.)

DISCUSSION

1. These words are written on Andrew Carnegie's tombstone: "Here lies a man who was able to surround himself with men far cleverer than himself." What do you think he meant?

2. According to an old saying, "You're never too old to learn." Do you agree?

3. In your native culture, do rich people help poor people?

4. Do you ever give money to people on the street who collect money for charity? Why or why not?

5. If a homeless person asks you for money, do you help this person? Why or why not? Are there a lot of homeless people or beggars in your hometown? Do other people help them?

6. Would you like to volunteer your time to help a cause? What would you like to do?

WRITING

1. Write a paragraph telling if you agree or disagree with any one of the following statements by Andrew Carnegie:

   - It is not good to have money if your spirit is poor.
   - It is the mind that makes the body rich.
   - It is a disgrace to die rich.

2. Write about a belief you used to have that you no longer have. What made you change your belief?

3. Write a paragraph or short essay telling how your lifestyle or habits have changed over the last ten years.

4. Write about an expectation that your parents had for you that you did not meet. Explain why you did not do what they expected.

5. Write about an expectation you have for your children (or future children).

OUTSIDE ACTIVITY

Ask a friend or neighbor to fill in the blanks in these statements. Report this person's answers to the class.

   - I'm worried about _____

   - I'm grateful to my parents for _____

   - I have a good time _____

   - I used to _____, but I don't do it anymore.

Internet Activities

1. At a search engine, type in "charity." Find the names of charitable organizations. What do these organizations do to help people?

2. Type in "volunteer." Find the names of volunteer organizations. Write down three ways people can volunteer to help others.

Lesson Eight

GRAMMAR

Adverbial Clauses and Phrases
Sentence Connectors
So/Such . . . That

CONTEXT

Columbus and the Discovery of America
A Nation of Immigrants
Slavery—An American Paradox
The Changing Face of America
Adopting a Baby from Abroad

LESSON FOCUS

A sentence often has an adverbial clause or phrase that gives information about reason, purpose, time, contrast, or condition.

MAIN CLAUSE	ADVERBIAL CLAUSE
She left her native country	*because the economic situation there was unstable.*
She left her native country	*even though her family wanted her to stay.*

MAIN CLAUSE	ADVERBIAL PHRASE
She left her native country	*because of economic instability.*
She left her native country	*in spite of her family's objections.*

Ideas within paragraphs can be connected by sentence connectors: *in addition, however, therefore,* etc.

She speaks English fluently. *However,* she can't find a job in her field.

Robert will probably find a job. He speaks English fluently. *In addition,* he has a lot of experience with computers.

We use *so/such . . . that* to show result.

His English is *so* good *that* everyone thinks he's a native speaker.

He has *such* good pronunciation *that* everyone thinks he's a native speaker.

Example	Type of Clause
She went to Germany **before she came to the U.S.**	Time clause
She went to Germany first **because she couldn't get a visa for the U.S.**	Reason clause
She came to the U.S. **so that she could be with her relatives**.	Purpose clause
She came to the U.S. **even though she didn't know English**.	Contrast clause
She will go back to her country **if she saves enough money**.	Condition clause

LANGUAGE NOTES

1. An adverbial clause is dependent on the main clause for its meaning. It must be attached to the main clause.
   WRONG: She didn't come to class. Because she was sick.
   RIGHT: She didn't come to class because she was sick.
2. A dependent clause can come before or after the main clause. If the dependent clause comes before the main clause, it is usually separated from the main clause with a comma. COMPARE:
   I went to Germany before I came to the U.S. (NO COMMA)
   Before I came to the U.S., I went to Germany. (COMMA)

Before You Read In your country, is there a holiday that honors an important person? Does everyone agree that he or she was a great person?

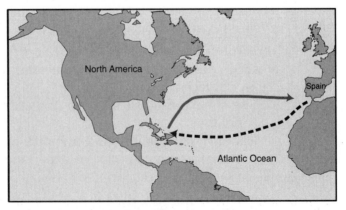

Columbus's First Trip to America

Read the following article. Pay special attention to time words.

Columbus and the Discovery of America

Every American school child knows that on October 12, 1492, Christopher Columbus discovered America. **While** Columbus was looking for a western sea route from Europe to Asia, he arrived in America. **During** this voyage,[1] members of his crew[2] were ready to rebel[3] **after** being at sea **for** over a month without seeing land. Finally, land was spotted, and Columbus became a hero to future generations. **Since** 1892, the 400th anniversary of Columbus's voyage, Americans have been celebrating Columbus Day.

Some people believe that Columbus's arrival was the first step in the creation of the United States and democracy. However, in 1992 **when** Americans were ready to celebrate the 500th anniversary of the discovery of their continent, many minority groups protested saying that this event was not a cause for celebration but an occasion to remember the tragedy suffered by the native peoples[4] who had been living in America **before** Columbus arrived. The arrival of Columbus and other Europeans brought slavery, cruelty, disease, and the destruction of the natural environment.

Until the day he died, Columbus did not realize that he had discovered a new continent. In spite of his mistake, he changed the course of life in America.

Did you know...?

Columbus called the native people of America "Indians" because he thought he was in India.

8.2 Time

Study the meanings and uses of the following time words.

Examples	Explanation
When Columbus arrived in America, he saw native American people.	*When* means "at that time" or "after that time."
Until Columbus arrived in America, certain diseases were unknown there.	*Until* means "up to that time."

(continued)

[1] A *voyage* is a trip.
[2] The *crew* consists of the people working on a ship.
[3] To *rebel* means to go against the orders of a leader.
[4] The plural form *peoples* means *nations* or *tribes*.

Examples	Explanation
Since the fifteenth century, foreigners have been coming to America. **Ever since** Columbus discovered America, foreigners have been coming here.	*Since* or *ever since* means "from that time in the past to the present." Use the present perfect (continuous) in the main clause.
Columbus was at sea **for** 33 days. Americans have been celebrating Columbus Day **for** over 100 years.	Use *for* with the amount of time.
Columbus's men almost rebelled **during** the voyage.	Use *during* with an event (a trip, a vacation, a class, a meeting, a lifetime) or with a specific period of time (the month of August, the week of March 2, the evening of April 3).
While they were traveling to America, Columbus's crew wanted to rebel.	Use *while* with a continuous action.
Whenever we read a story, we learn new words.	*Whenever* means "any time" or "every time."

LANGUAGE NOTES

1. In a negative sentence, you can use either *for* or *in* with the amount of time.
   > I haven't seen my sister *for* three months.
   > I haven't seen my sister *in* three months.
2. In a future sentence, use the present tense after the time word and the future tense in the main clause.
   > I *will call* you when I *get* home.
   > After he *finds* a job, he *will buy* a car.
3. Use *while* with a continuous action. Use *when* with a simple past action. COMPARE:

   While Columbus was looking for Asia, he found America.

   Columbus was looking for Asia *when* he found America.

EXERCISE 1   Fill in the blanks with an appropriate time word. (In some cases, the tense will determine which word to use.)

EXAMPLE: _Until_ Columbus died, he thought he had found a short way to get to Asia.

1. Immigrants have been coming to America _____ many years.

2. _____ his lifetime, Columbus believed that he had found a short way to Asia.

3. _____ Europeans started coming to America, they brought diseases to the native peoples.

4. We have been talking about Columbus _____ about ten minutes.

5. We have been talking about Columbus _____ the class began.

6. Columbus found America _____ he was looking for Asia.

7. _____ Columbus came to America, the Indians didn't have European diseases.

8. _____ Columbus's voyage, members of his crew wanted to rebel.

9. _____ the teacher explained the grammar, he used the text about Columbus to give examples of time words.

10. _____ the teacher explains the grammar, he uses real examples.

11. We haven't had a test _____ over a week.

EXERCISE 2   Fill in the blanks with an appropriate time word. (In some cases, more than one answer is possible.)

When I was a child, I had heard many stories about life in
(example)

America. _____ I saw American movies, I imagined that one day I
(1)

would be in a place like the one I saw. My uncle had lived in the

U.S. _____ many years, and he often came back to visit. _____
(2)   *(3)*

he came back, he used to tell me stories and show me pictures of the U.S.

_____ I was a teenager, I asked my mother if she would let me visit
(4)

my uncle _____ my summer vacation, but she said I was too young
(5)

and the trip was too expensive. _____ I was 20, I finally decided to
(6)

come to the U.S. _____ I was traveling to the U.S., I thought about all
(7)

Adverbial Clauses and Phrases; Sentence Connectors; *So/Such . . . That*   **309**

the stories my uncle had told me. But I really knew nothing about the

U.S. _____ I came here.
        (8)

_____ I came to the U.S., I've been working hard and trying to learn
   (9)

English. I haven't had time to meet Americans or have much fun _____
                                                                (10)

I started my job. I've been here _____ five months now, and I just work
                                    (11)

and go to school. _____ I'm at school, I talk to my classmates
                     (12)

_____ our break, but on the weekends I'm alone most of the time. I
  (13)

won't be able to make American friends _____ I learn more English.
                                          (14)

The American movies I had seen showed me beautiful places, but I never imagined how much I would miss my family and friends.

EXERCISE 3   Fill in the blanks with an appropriate expression.

EXAMPLES: For _____*seven years*_____, she has been working in a bank.

Since _____*1997*_____, she has been working in a bank.

1. During _____, she lived in Poland.

2. For _____, she has lived in England.

3. Since _____, she has lived in England.

4. While _____, she met her future husband.

5. When _____, she was living in Poland.

6. Until _____, she lived with her parents.

7. She hasn't visited Poland in _____

8. While _____, he broke his arm.

9. For _____, he watched TV.

10. During _____, she cried.

11. When _____, she started to laugh.

12. Until _____, she couldn't go out.

13. Whenever _____, she takes a walk in the park.

14. Whenever _____, she uses a dictionary.

15. He's had his driver's license for _____

16. He's had his driver's license since _____

17. He didn't get his driver's license until _____

18. He practiced driving during _____

19. He bought his car when _____

20. While _____, he had an accident.

EXERCISE 4   Complete the statements that apply to you. If the time
expression is at the beginning of the sentence, add a comma
before the main clause.

EXAMPLES: Whenever I have a job interview, _I feel nervous._____

Ever since I found a job, _I haven't had much time to study._____

1. Ever since I was a child _____

2. When I was a child _____

3. _____ ever since I started attending this school.

4. _____ when I started attending this school.

5. _____ until I started attending this school.

6. When the semester began _____

7. Since the semester began _____

8. _____ when I was _____ years old.

9. _____ until I was _____ years old.

10. _____ ever since I was _____ years old.

11. When I got married _____

12. Since I got married _____

13. Until I got married _____

14. _____ when I found a job.

15. _____ since I found a job.

16. _____ until I found a job.

17. When I bought my car, _____

---

18. Until I bought my car, _____

19. Since I bought my car, _____

20. Whenever I drive, _____

8.3 Using the *-ing* Form After Time Words

Columbus returned to Spain after **he discovered** America.

Columbus returned to Spain after **discovering** America.

Before **Jim went** to France, he bought a French dictionary.

Before **going** to France, Jim bought a French dictionary.

LANGUAGE NOTES

If the subject of a time clause and the subject of a main clause are the same, the time clause can be changed to a participial phrase. The subject is omitted, and the present participle (*-ing* form) is used.

EXERCISE 5 Change the time clause to a participial phrase.

EXAMPLE: Before I started ESL classes, I couldn't speak English.
Before starting ESL classes, I couldn't speak English.

1. Before I take a test, I study.

2. Maria will go back to her hometown after she graduates.

3. When Jack traveled through Europe, he learned about Italian architecture.

4. After Susan got married, she moved to London.

5. After Columbus was at sea for many days, he saw land.

6. She always makes a list before she goes shopping.

Before You Read   1.   Why do many emigrants leave one country and move to another?
2.   What do emigrants have to give up? What do they gain?

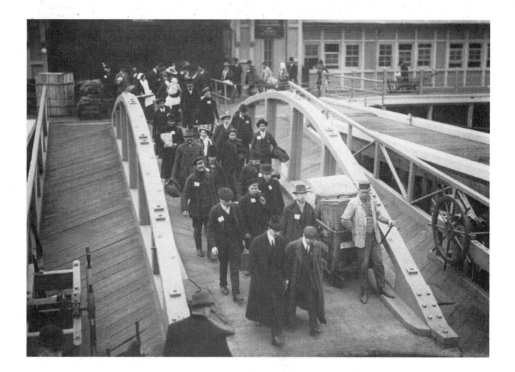

Read the following article. Pay special attention to different ways of giving reasons.

A Nation of Immigrants

The United States is unique in that it is a nation of immigrants, old and new. The U.S. takes in more immigrants than all the rest of the world combined. In 1997, 27 million people, or 10 percent of the population, was foreign born. Between 1995 and 1998, three million people entered the U.S. legally. Why have so many people from other countries left family and friends, jobs, and traditions to start life in a new country? The answer to that question is as diverse as the people who have come to America.

Between 1820 and 1840, many Germans came **because of** political unrest and economic problems in Germany. Between 1840 and 1860, many Irish people came **because of** famine.[5] The potato crop, which they depended on, had failed. Between 1850 and 1882, many Chinese people came to America **because of** famine.

The early group of immigrants came from Northern and Western Europe. In 1881, a large group started arriving from Eastern and Southern Europe. Jews from Eastern Europe came **to** escape religious persecution; Italians came **for** work. Most came **to find** freedom and a better life. The number of immigrants grew; between 1881 and 1920, more than 23.4 million immigrants came. In 1910, 15 percent of the population was foreign born.

[5] *Famine* means extreme hunger because of a shortage of food.

In 1924, Congress passed a law restricting the number of immigrants, and immigration slowed. In 1965, Congress opened the doors again and immigration started to rise. In the 1960s and 1970s, Cubans and Vietnamese people came **to** escape communism. In the 1980s, Jews from the former Soviet Union came **because of** anti-Semitism,[6] and in the 1990s, Bosnians came **because of** war. Many people came **so that** they could be reunited with their families who had come before.

In addition to the legal immigration, about 300,000 come to the U.S. each year illegally. **Since** the U.S. Census cannot count these people, this number is only an estimate.

8.4 Reason and Purpose

Examples	Explanation
Many people come to the U.S. **because** they can have more opportunities here.	*Because* introduces a clause of reason.
Many immigrants came here **because of** war in their countries. Many Irish immigrants came here **because of** the hunger they faced in their country.	*Because of* introduces a noun or a noun phrase.
Since the U.S. Census cannot count illegal immigrants, their number is only an estimate. **Since** the U.S. limits the number of immigrants it will accept, many people cannot get an immigrant visa.	*Since* means *because*. It is used to introduce a fact. The main clause is the result of this fact.
Many people have come to America **in order to** make more money. Cubans came to America **to** escape communism.	*In order to* shows purpose. The short form is *to*.
Many people come to the U.S. **so that** they can be reunited with family members. We left our country **so** we could have a better life.	*So that* shows purpose. The short form is *so*. The purpose clause usually contains a modal: *can*, *will*, or *may* for future; *could*, *would*, or *might* for past.
People come to America **for** freedom. Some people come **for** better jobs.	*For* + noun or noun phrase shows purpose.

[6] *Anti-Semitism* means prejudice or discrimination against Jews.

LANGUAGE NOTES

1. *So* is used to show purpose. *So* is also used to show consequence.
   COMPARE:
   PURPOSE: I came to the U.S. **so** I could be united with my parents.
   CONSEQUENCE: I came to the U.S. when I was 16, **so** I didn't finish high school in my native country.
   NOTE: When *so* is used for consequence, it is usually preceded by a comma. When *so* is used for purpose (shortened from *so that*), a comma isn't used.
2. *Since* is used to show reason. *Since* is also used to show time.
   COMPARE:
   REASON: *Since* he's not a citizen, he can't vote.
   TIME: The U.S. Census has kept records of immigration *since* 1820.
3. Use *for* with a noun. Use *to* with a verb. COMPARE:
   She came here **to** be with her family.
   They came here **for** a better life.
4. Don't follow *so that* with *want*. COMPARE:
   He came to the U.S. *because he wanted to be* reunited with his brother.
   He came to the U.S. *so that he could be* reunited with his brother.

EXERCISE 6 Fill in the blanks with *because, because of, since, (in order) to,* or *so (that)*.

EXAMPLE: Many immigrants came to America ___*to*___ escape famine.

1. Many immigrants came _____ they didn't have enough to eat.

2. Many immigrants came _____ they could feed their families.

3. Many immigrants came _____ they could escape religious persecution.

4. Many immigrants came _____ the political situation was unstable in their countries.

5. Many immigrants came _____ the poor economy in their countries.

6. Many immigrants came _____ be reunited with their relatives.

7. _____ war destroyed many of their homes and towns, many people had to leave their countries.

8. Many immigrants came _____ escape poverty.

9. Many immigrants came _____ freedom.

10. Often immigrants come _____ they can make more money.

11. Often immigrants come _____ make more money.

12. Often immigrants come _____ they see a better future for their children here.

EXERCISE 7 Fill in the blanks with a reason or purpose.

EXAMPLE: Some immigrants come to the U.S. because ___*their native country has*___ *an unstable government.*

1. Some immigrants come to the U.S. because _____
   _____

2. Some immigrants come to the U.S. so that _____
   _____

3. Some immigrants come to the U.S. for _____
   _____

4. Since _____, many immigrants choose
   not to return to their country of origin.

5. Life in the U.S. is sometimes difficult because of _____
   _____

6. I chose to live in this city because _____

7. I chose to study at this school because _____

8. I come to this school for _____

9. I use my dictionary to _____

10. I'm saving money because _____

11. I'm saving money so that _____

12. I'm saving my money for _____

13. I'm saving my money in order to _____

14. Since _____, many immigrants go to big cities.

EXERCISE 8 Fill in the blanks with *because, because of, since, so (that),* or *(in order) to.*

(Two women are talking.)

A. I heard you moved.

B. Yes. We moved last month. We bought a big house ___*so that*___ we
    would have room for my parents. They're coming to the U.S. next
    month _____ they want to be near their children and grand-
                (1)
    children.

A. Where's your new house?

B. It's in Deerfield.

A. Why did you move so far from the city?

B. We prefer the suburbs _____ the schools are much better there.
   (2)

A. But isn't it expensive to live in Deerfield?

B. Yes, it is. We both work _____ pay the mortgage.
   (3)

A. How do you get to work? You have only one car.

B. I take the car _____ it is impossible for me to get to work by
   (4)
   public transportation. But my husband works in the city, so he takes
   the train. He doesn't like to drive downtown _____ the
   (5)
   expense of parking.

A. Maybe I should start to think about buying a house.

B. You really should start saving your money now _____ you will
   (6)
   be able to buy a house soon.

Before You Read
1. What do you know about the history of slavery in the U.S.?
2. Do you think everyone is equal in the U.S.?

Read the following article. Pay special attention to *even though, although,* and *in spite of (the fact that).*

Slavery—An American Paradox[7]

For the first three centuries after Columbus came to America, the largest group of immigrants arrived in America—unwillingly. Ten to twelve million Africans were brought to work as slaves in the rice, sugar, tobacco, and cotton fields of the agricultural south.

In 1776, when America declared its independence from England, Thomas Jefferson, one of the founding fathers of the United States, wrote, "All men are created equal" and that every person has a right to "life, liberty, and the pursuit of happiness." **In spite of** these great words, Jefferson owned 200 slaves at that time.

Even though the importation of slaves finally ended in 1808, the slave population continued to grow as children were born to slave mothers. The country became divided over the issue of slavery. The North wanted to end slavery; the South wanted to continue it. In 1861, Civil War broke out between the North and the South. In 1865, when the North won, slavery was ended. **In spite of the fact that** African-Americans were freed, it took another 100 years for Congress to pass a law prohibiting discrimination because of race, color, religion, sex, or national origin.

Although many new arrivals see the U.S. as the land of equality, it is important to remember this dark period of American history.

8.5 Contrast

Examples	Explanation
Even though slavery ended, African Americans did not get equality. **In spite of the fact that** Jefferson wrote about equality for everyone, he owned 200 slaves. **Although** it was hard to leave family and friends, many people chose to come to America.	For an unexpected result or contrast of ideas, use a clause beginning with *even though*, *although*, and *in spite of the fact that*.
In spite of Jefferson's declaration of liberty for all, he owned slaves. I like the U.S. **in spite of** its problems.	Use *in spite of* + noun or noun phrase.

[7] A *paradox* is a situation that has contradictory aspects.

LANGUAGE NOTES

Anyway and *still* can be used in the main clause to emphasize the contrast. *Anyway* is informal.

> Even though he has a good education, he *still* can't find a job.
>
> Even though he has a good education, he can't find a job *anyway*.

EXERCISE 9 Fill in the blanks with *in spite of* or *in spite of the fact that*.

EXAMPLES: She can't find a job _in spite of the fact that_ she has a good education.

She can't find a job _in spite of_ her high level of education.

1. Many people choose to live in big cities _____ the high crime rate.

2. _____ slavery ended in 1865, African-Americans did not receive equal treatment under the law.

3. Many immigrants come to America _____ the difficulty of starting a new life.

4. I like living in this city _____ I miss my friends and family back home.

5. _____ I speak with an accent, people understand me.

6. _____ my accent, people understand me.

7. _____ life is not perfect in the U.S., many immigrants want to come here.

EXERCISE 10 Complete each statement with an unexpected result.

EXAMPLE: I like the teacher even though _he gives a lot of homework._

1. I like my apartment even though _____

   _____

2. I like this city even though _____

   _____

3. I like this country even though _____

   _____

4. I like this school even though _____

   _____

---

5. I like my job in spite of (the fact that) _____

_____

6. Some students fail tests in spite of (the fact that) _____

_____

7. People celebrate Columbus Day in spite of the fact that _____

_____

8. My uncle passed the citizenship test even though _____

_____

9. The U.S. is a great country in spite of (the fact that) _____

_____

10. Many people want to come to the U.S. even though _____

_____

EXERCISE 11 Complete each statement by making a contrast.

EXAMPLE: Even though Alaska is the biggest state, *it has a small population.*

1. Even though the U.S. is a rich country, _____

_____

2. In spite of the fact that Thomas Jefferson wrote "All men are created equal," _____

3. Even though I don't speak English perfectly, _____

_____

4. In spite of the fact that my teacher doesn't speak my language, ___

_____

5. Even though I miss my friends and family, _____

_____

6. Even though flying conditions were poor on July 16, 1999, John Kennedy, Jr. (*see Lesson 5*), _____

7. Even though Tim Berners-Lee invented the World Wide Web (*see Lesson 6*), _____

8. Even though Matel Dawson has a lot of money (*see Lesson 7*), _____

_____

9. Even though watching a lot of TV isn't good for children, _____

_____

Before You Read

1. What do you think is the largest ethnic minority in the U.S.?
2. Do you ever see signs in public places in Spanish or any other language?

Read the following article. Pay special attention to condition clauses beginning with *if*, *even if*, and *unless*.

The Changing Face of America

The U.S. population is about 275 million. This number is expected to rise to 394 million by 2050. **Unless** there are changes in immigration patterns, 80 million new immigrants will enter the U.S. in the next 50 years.

For most of the nineteenth and twentieth centuries, the majority of immigrants to the U.S. were Europeans. However, since 1970, this trend has changed dramatically. Today most immigrants are Hispanics. Hispanics, who have a high birth rate, are rapidly becoming the largest minority. **Even if** the immigration of Hispanics slows down, their number will increase greatly. But **if** current patterns of immigration continue and **if** the birth rate remains the same, the number of Hispanics will increase from 11% of the total population to 25 percent of the population by 2050. Hispanics are already 31 percent of the population of California and 28 percent of the population of Texas. More than 50 percent of the people who have arrived since 1970 are Spanish speakers. The largest group of Hispanic immigrants comes from Mexico.

Did you know...?

Half of the immigrants in the past 30 years have come from seven countries: Mexico, the Philippines, China, Vietnam, Korea, India, and the Dominican Republic.

Because of their large numbers, Hispanics will have a great influence on the choice of our nation's leaders. Today two-thirds of Hispanic citizens vote Democratic. **If** that continues, the Democratic party will benefit greatly in the coming years.

There are many questions about the future of America. One thing is certain: the face of America is changing and will continue to change.

8.6 Condition

Examples	Explanation
If current immigration patterns and birth rates remain the same, Hispanics will be 25 percent of the population in 2050. **If** Hispanics vote together, they will have a lot of political power.	Use *if* to show that the condition affects the result.
Even if the immigration of Hispanics slows down, their number will increase because of their present birth rate. Children in America learn English **even if** their parents speak another language at home.	Use *even if* to show that the condition doesn't affect the result.
Unless immigration laws change, 80 million new immigrants will come here in the next 50 years. You can't come to the U.S. **unless** you have a visa.	Use *unless* to mean *if not*.

LANGUAGE NOTES

In a future sentence, use the simple present tense in the condition clause.
    If my brother *comes* to the U.S., he *will live* with me.
    Even if the economy of my native country *improves*, I *won't go* back.

EXERCISE 12 Complete each statement.

EXAMPLE: If you speak your native language all the time, *you won't learn English.*

1. If immigrant parents don't educate children about their former country, _____

2. If Hispanics continue to vote for Democrats, _____

3. Many children of immigrants prefer to speak English even if

_____

4. If I make a lot of long distance calls, _____

5. I'll get a good grade if _____

6. If I don't pass this course, _____

7. My English will improve if _____

8. I'll go back to my native country if _____

9. I will become a citizen if _____

10. If I can't come to class next week, _____

EXERCISE 13 Change the sentence from an *if* clause to an *unless* clause.

EXAMPLE: You can't visit France if you don't have a passport.
You can't visit France unless you have a passport.

1. You can't go fishing if you don't have a license.

2. Children cannot see R-rated movies if they're not accompanied by an adult.

3. Children of immigrants will forget their language if they don't use it.

4. Immigrants will continue to come to the U.S. if conditions in their native countries don't improve.

5. You cannot travel to most foreign countries if you don't have a passport.

6. An American citizen can't be President if he or she was not born in the U.S.

7. You shouldn't give friends advice if they don't ask for it.

8. You shouldn't dial 911 if it's not an emergency.

EXERCISE 14 Complete each statement.

EXAMPLE: I don't usually eat fast food _unless I'm in a hurry._

1. I work/study every day unless _____

2. I'm usually in a good mood unless _____

3. I usually answer the phone unless _____

4. I'm going to stay in this city unless _____

5. I will continue to study at this college unless _____

_____

6. Poor students can't afford to go to college unless _____

_____

7. You won't be able to take the next course unless _____

_____

8. You can't get a refund from a store unless _____

_____

EXERCISE 15 Complete each statement.

EXAMPLE: Coffee doesn't affect me. I can sleep even if ___*I drink a cup of coffee*___
at night.

1. Cold weather doesn't bother me. I go out even if _____

_____

2. Making grammar mistakes is OK. People will understand you even if

_____

3. A lot of people in the U.S. have a foreign accent. People will understand you even if _____

4. Will they call off the football game for bad weather? No. They will
play football even if _____

5. He will fail the course because he never does his homework and he's
absent a lot. Even if _____, he will
fail the course.

6. I always do my homework. I may be absent next week, but I'll do
my homework even if _____

7. I may move to a suburb. I will continue to study in the city even if

_____

8. Children of immigrants learn English even if _____

_____

EXERCISE 16 Fill in the blanks in this conversation between two middle-aged men about health. Use *if, even if,* and *unless.*

A. Hi, Joe. You look terrific. In fact, you look like a new man.

B. I've become a vegetarian.

A. Oh, really? Why did you stop eating meat?

B. They say that _____*if*_____ you don't eat meat, you'll live longer. I've
        (example)
also started to exercise every day.

A. I exercise too. I play golf every Sunday in the summer.

B. Golf is a nice sport, but you won't extend your life _____ you do
                                                              (1)
strenuous exercise like playing tennis or running. I get a lot of exercise.
I jog every day. Nothing stops me. I jog _____ it rains or snows.
                                          (2)

A. That's great. I've tried to jog, but I find it boring. I can't do it _____
                                                                        (3)
someone goes with me.

B. _____ you want, we can jog together. Why don't we start tomorrow?
   (4)

A. Uh . . . thanks. I'll call you tomorrow _____ I have time.
                                           (5)

B. Are you really interested in getting more exercise?

A. Let's face it; we're men, so _____ we do all these healthy things,
                                 (6)
we probably won't live as long as most women.

B. But we'll die a lot sooner _____ we take better care of ourselves.
                              (7)

Before You Read 1. Do you know anyone who has adopted a baby?
                     2. Is it important for parents to teach their children about their ancestors?

Read the following article. Pay special attention to sentence connectors.

Adopting a Baby from Abroad

Many American couples want to adopt children. **However**, there is a such a long waiting list and there are so few babies available that people often have to wait years for a child. And the process has become so complicated that people often get discouraged. **As a result**, many Americans are turning to foreign countries for adoption. Americans bring home about 10,000 babies a year from countries such as China, Russia, Ukraine, Korea, Romania, and the Philippines.

However, the process of foreign adoption is not easy or cheap. First, it can cost from $10,000 to $25,000. **In addition**, the Immigration and Naturalization Service (INS) often takes six weeks to four months to process the paperwork. **Furthermore**, parents usually have to travel to the country for a one- to four-week stay.

In spite of all these difficulties, these tiny immigrants bring joy to many American families.

8.7 Sentence Connectors

Ideas within paragraphs can be connected by sentence connectors. These connectors show the relationship of ideas.

Examples	Explanation
Many couples want to adopt American children. **However**, there are very few babies available. The U.S. is not a perfect country. **Nevertheless**, many people want to immigrate to this country.	Sentence connectors that show contrast are *however* and *nevertheless*. These words are similar in meaning to *but*.
Foreign adoption is not for everyone. It can be expensive. **In addition**, it can take a long time. My sister came to the U.S. to earn more money. **Furthermore**, she wanted to be reunited with our family.	Sentence connectors that add more information to the same idea are *in addition, furthermore,* and *moreover.* These words are similar in meaning to *and*.
Many couples are frustrated with the adoption process in the U.S. **Therefore**, they go to other countries to adopt. The North and South did not agree about slavery. **As a result**, a Civil War broke out.	Sentence connectors that show result or conclusion are *therefore, as a result,* and *for this reason.* These words are similar in meaning to *so*.

LANGUAGE NOTES

Use either a period or a semicolon (;) before a connecting word. Use a comma after a connecting word.

EXERCISE 17 Fill in the blanks with an appropriate connecting word.

EXAMPLE: The discovery of America benefited Europeans. _____*However*_____, it brought destruction to the native cultures.

1. The arrival of Columbus and the Europeans who followed brought disease to the native people. _____, a lot of the natural environment was destroyed.

2. The arrival of Columbus brought many problems to the natives of America. _____, Columbus Day is not a time for celebration for Native Americans.

3. Many immigrants came to America at the beginning of the twentieth century. _____, immigration slowed down during World War I.

4. Jews had a hard life in Russia and Poland. Many lived in poor conditions. _____, they were the victims of anti-Semitism.

5. My grandfather immigrated to the U.S. to find a job and make more money. _____, he wanted to be reunited with his relatives.

6. There was a big famine in Ireland. _____, many Irish people left and came to America.

7. In 1924, Congress passed a law restricting the number of immigrants. _____, many people who wanted to come here couldn't.

8. Many Cubans wanted to escape communism in the 1960s. _____, many of them couldn't get permission to leave Cuba.

9. Many Cubans tried to get permission to leave Cuba legally, but couldn't. _____, many people found other ways of leaving. Some built or bought small boats and tried to reach Florida by sea.

10. Close to a million legal immigrants came to the U.S. in 1996. _____, about 275,000 illegal immigrants came that year.

Adverbial Clauses and Phrases; Sentence Connectors; *So/Such . . . That*   **327**

11. A war broke out in Yugoslavia in 1992. _____, many people died or lost their homes.

12. Most immigrants came to the U.S. because they wanted to. _____, Africans were brought here against their will.

13. In 1776, Thomas Jefferson wrote, "All men are created equal." _____, Jefferson had 200 slaves at the time he wrote these words.

14. Africans were brought to the U.S. to work as slaves in different areas of the U.S. _____, many African families were destroyed.

15. Slavery officially ended in 1865. _____, many African-Americans continued to suffer.

16. African-Americans have been the largest minority for many years. _____, this is changing as the Hispanic population increases.

17. Adopting a foreign baby is complicated. People have to pay a lot of money. _____, they have to travel to the foreign country to fill out forms and pick up the baby.

18. There was no future for my family in my native country. _____, we decided to leave and come to America.

EXERCISE 18 Complete each statement.

EXAMPLE: The U.S. is a rich country. However, _it has many poor people._____

1. It is important for me to learn English. Therefore, _____
   _____

2. It is important for me to learn English. However, _____
   _____

3. Living in another country is difficult. Immigrants have to adjust to a new language. In addition, _____

4. Some children speak one language at home and another at school. As a result, _____

5. To learn a new language, you must master the grammar. In addition,
   _____

6. No one wants to leave friends and family. However, _____

   _____

7. If someone wants to come to the U.S. to visit, he or she must have

   a passport. In addition, _____

8. It's important for a new immigrant to know English. Therefore,

   _____

9. I wanted to study English when I was young. However, _____

   _____

10. I may not speak English perfectly. However, _____

   _____

EXERCISE 19 *Combination Exercise.* Choose the correct word to complete this story.

Many people have come to America (*because*/*for*) freedom. But Africans lost their freedom and were brought to America against their will (*1 for/to*) work in the fields. Africans were taken from their homes and put on slave ships (*2 for/to*) cross the Atlantic. (*3 Because of/Since*) hard conditions, many died along the way.

(*4 In spite of/In spite of the fact that*) they worked hard from morning till night, they received no money. In fact, they were often beaten if they didn't obey. They were forced to work hard (*5 so that/in order to*) white plantation owners could become rich. (*6 Although/Unless*) many people in the North were against slavery, slavery continued in the South (*7 because of/since*) Southern slave owners did not want to give up their cheap labor supply.

(*8 Even though/However*) the law prohibited the importation of slaves, slavery continued to increase. (*9 In spite of/In spite of the fact that*) the difficulties of living under slavery, slaves formed strong communities. They tried to keep their African cultural practices, which included music and dance. (*10 Because/For*) people from the same regions in Africa were separated from each other, they lost their native languages, used English, and were given biblical names rather than African names.

Most of the African Americans in the North were free. (*11 In addition/However*), they didn't have an easy life. They couldn't attend public schools. (*12 Furthermore/However*), they weren't allowed to vote. Many slaves from the South tried to run away to the North. (*13 However,/Although*) some were caught and sent back to their "owners."

(*14 Unless/Until*) the slaves were finally freed in 1865, they still faced many difficulties. (*15 In spite of the fact that/In spite of*) the majority of Africans by that time were born in America, they suffered discrimination (*16 because/because of*) the color of their skin.

Discrimination was still legal (*17 when/until*) 1965, when Congress passed a law prohibiting discrimination in jobs and education. (*18 Although/ In spite of*) there has been progress toward equality for all, there are still many inequalities in American life.

8.8 *So . . . That/Such . . . That*

We can show result with *so . . . that* and *such (a) . . . that*.

Examples	Pattern
People have to wait **such a long time** to adopt an American baby **that** many are turning to foreign adoptions. Crossing the Atlantic was **such a hard trip that** Columbus's men wanted to turn back.	*Such* + adjective + noun + *that* NOTE: Use *a* or *an* if the phrase contains a singular count noun.
Foreign adoption is **so expensive that** many people cannot afford it. Small children learn English **so easily that** they become fluent in a short time.	*So* + adjective or adverb + *that*
There are **so many** Spanish-speaking people in Miami **that** you can hear Spanish wherever you go. There are **so few** babies available for adoption **that** many Americans adopt foreign babies.	*So many/few* + plural count noun + *that*
There was **so much** poverty in Ireland in the 1800s **that** Irish people were forced to leave.	*So much/little* + noncount noun + *that*

LANGUAGE NOTES

1. We use *so . . . that* and *such . . . that* to say that a degree of something produces a certain result.
   > The baby is *so* smart *that* she learned to speak when she was ten months old.
   > I had *so much* homework last week *that* I didn't even answer the phone.
2. *That* is often omitted in informal speech.
   > She is *so* nice everyone loves her.
   > It was *such* a good dinner everyone wanted a second helping.
3. The result is not always mentioned.
   > Everyone likes my aunt. She is *so* nice. (*So = very*)
   > I have *so much* homework. (*So much = a lot of*)

EXERCISE 20 Two students are talking about their English class. Fill in the blanks with *so, so much, so many,* or *such (a/an).*

A. How do you like your new English teacher?

B. She's nice, but she gives ___*so much*___ homework that it's impossible
(example)

to do it all. And I work _____ hours that I'm sometimes too
(1)

tired to do my homework. Last week the teacher gave _____
(2)

hard test that almost everyone failed.

A. American teachers are _____ different from teachers in my
(3)

native country that I sometimes don't know what to expect.

B. What do you mean?

A. Well, in my native country they give tests only once a year. The tests

are _____ important that we get one month to study for them.
(4)

B. There is _____ big difference between the American educational
(5)

system and the system in my country that it's hard for me to get used
to it. In my country, students often talk to each other during a test.

But here, the teacher gets _____ mad that she tears up the
(6)

student's test.

A. On the other hand, some teachers here are _____ friendly that
(7)

they let you call them by their first names.

EXERCISE 21 Fill in the blanks with *so, so much/many/little/few,* or *such (a/ an).* Then complete each statement with a result.

EXAMPLES: Michael is ___*such a*___ good student ___*that he gets 100% on all his tests.*___

Learning another language is ___*so*___ hard ___*it can take a lifetime to do it.*___

1. My math class is _____ easy _____

_____

2. Peter is taking _____ classes this semester _____

_____

3. The teacher gives _____ homework _____

_____

4. Sometimes the teacher talks _____ fast _____

_____

---

5. My roommate is from India. She speaks English _____ well
   _____

6. My biology class is _____ boring _____
   _____

7. Ms. Stevens is _____ good teacher _____
   _____

8. English has _____ irregular verbs _____
   _____

9. We had _____ long test _____
   _____

10. I had _____ mistakes on my test _____
    _____

11. The teacher gave _____ confusing explanation _____
    _____

12. I was _____ tired in class yesterday _____
    _____

SUMMARY OF LESSON 8

1.   Adverbial Clauses and Phrases

     Abbreviations: C = Clause, NP = Noun Phrase, VP = Verb Phrase

Time	*when*	**When** I find a job, I'll buy a car.
	whenever	**Whenever** I work overtime, I make extra money.
	until	I worked **until** 8 p.m. I worked **until** the store closed.
	while	**While** I was slicing the bread, I cut my finger.
	since	I've been working **since** 9 a.m.
		I've been working **since** I woke up this morning.
	for	I've been working **for** three hours.
	during	I worked **during** my summer vacation.

(continued)

Reason	because + C	**Because** he doesn't understand English, he can't find a job.
	since + C	**Since** he doesn't understand English, he can't find a job.
	because of + NP	**Because of** his poor English, he can't find a job.
Purpose	(in order) to + VP	He exercises **(in order) to** lose weight.
	so (that) + C	He exercises **so (that)** he can lose weight.
Contrast	even though + C	**Even though** he's rich, he's not happy.
	although + C	**Although** he's rich, he's not happy.
	in spite of the fact that + C	**In spite of the fact that** he's rich, he's not happy.
	in spite of + NP	**In spite of** his wealth, he's not happy.
Condition	if	**If** it snows, we won't drive.
	even if	We'll drive **even if** it rains.
	unless	I won't go **unless** you go with me. I don't want to go alone.

2. Sentence connectors

To add more to the same idea	in addition furthermore moreover	Adopting a baby from another country is not easy. Parents have to pay a lot of money. **In addition,** they have to get permission from the INS.
To add a contrasting idea	however nevertheless	The law says that everyone is equal. **However,** inequalities still exist.
To show a result	therefore as a result for this reason	It is difficult for an uneducated person to find a job that pays well. **Therefore,** I've decided to educate myself and get a degree. Columbus thought he arrived in India. **For this reason,** he called the native people "Indians."

3. Result Clauses

so + adjective + *that*	I was **so tired that** I fell asleep in front of the TV.
so + adverb + *that*	She speaks English **so fluently that** everyone thinks it's her first language.
so many/few + plural noun + *that*	I received **so many letters that** I didn't have time to read them all.
so much/little + noncount noun + *that*	I received **so much mail that** I didn't have time to read it all.
such (a) + adjective + noun + *that*	It was **such a good movie that** I watched it three times.
	These are **such good grapes that** I can't stop eating them.

4. Punctuation

He went home from work early because he was sick. (no comma)

Because he was sick, he went home from work early. (comma)

He was sick. Therefore, he went home from work early. (period before the connecting word, comma after *therefore*)

He had such a bad headache that he had to go to bed. (no comma)

EDITING ADVICE

1. Use *to*, not *for*, with a verb when showing purpose.

   She went to the doctor ~~for~~ *to* get a checkup.

2. Don't combine *so* with *because* or *but* with *even though*.

   Even though she speaks English well, ~~but~~ she can't write it.

   Because he was late, ~~so~~ he didn't hear the explanation.

3. Use *because of* when a noun phrase follows.

   He came late because *of* bad traffic.

4. Don't use *even* without *though* or *if* to introduce a clause.

   Even *though* he's a poor man, he's happy.

   I won't call you even *if* I need your help.

5. Use the *-ing* form, not the base form, after a time word if the subject is deleted.

>   *going*
> Before ~~go~~ home, he bought some groceries.

6. Don't confuse *so that* with *because*.

>   *because*
> He came to the U.S. ~~so that~~ he wanted freedom.

7. After *so that*, use a modal before the verb.

>   *could*
> I bought a VCR so that I ‸watch all my favorite movies at home.

8. Always follow a sentence connector with a complete sentence.

> He came to the U.S. because he wanted more freedom. In
> *he wanted to get a better*
> addition, ‸education.

9. In a future sentence, use the simple present tense in the *if* clause or time clause.

> If I ~~will~~ go back to my hometown, I will visit my best friend.

10. *However* connects two sentences. *Although* connects two parts of the same sentence.

>   *However,*
> She was absent for three weeks. ~~Although~~ she did all the homework.

11. Use *so* + adjective/adverb and *such* when you include a noun.

>   *such a*
> My grandfather is ~~so~~ wise person that everyone goes to him for advice.

LESSON 8 TEST / REVIEW

PART 1　　　Find the mistakes with the underlined words, and correct them. Not every sentence has a mistake. If the sentence is correct, write **C**. (Do not look for punctuation mistakes.)

>   *could be*
> **EXAMPLES:**　I came here so that I <u>~~am~~</u> with my family.
>
> After leaving Greece, I went to Turkey.　　　C

1. <u>Even</u> he is a rich man, he isn't very happy.

2. <u>Since</u> she came to the U.S., she has been living with her sister.

Adverbial Clauses and Phrases; Sentence Connectors; *So/Such . . . That*　　**335**

3. She can't go to the party <u>unless</u> she gets a babysitter **for her baby.**

4. Because he can't find a job, <u>so</u> he doesn't have much **money.**

5. If I <u>will go</u> to the library today, I'll return your books **for you.**

6. Even though she has good qualifications and speaks English well, <u>but</u> she can't find a job.

7. I'm saving my money <u>for buy</u> a new car.

8. <u>Because</u> her health is bad, she is going to quit her job.

9. The children couldn't go out and play <u>because</u> the **rain.**

10. <u>In spite of</u> she has a big family, she feels lonely.

11. The weather won't stop me. I'll drive to New York <u>even</u> it rains.

12. Before <u>prepare</u> dinner, she washed her hands.

13. <u>Since</u> the stores are very crowded on the weekends, I like to shop <u>during</u> the week.

14. She's going to buy a cell phone <u>so that she can</u> make **calls when she's on** the road.

15. He sent his mother a picture of his children <u>so that she sees</u> her grand-children.

16. Alex left his country <u>so that</u> he didn't like the political situation there.

17. You shouldn't open the door <u>unless</u> you know who's there.

18. He uses spell check <u>to</u> check the spelling on his compositions.

19. She is <u>so a bad cook</u> that no one wants to eat dinner at her house.

20. I have <u>so much</u> homework that I don't have time for my **family and friends.**

21. I use e-mail <u>for stay</u> in touch with my friends.

22. I need to get some credits before I enter the university. In addition, <u>the</u> TOEFL test.

Punctuate the following sentences. Some sentences are already complete and need no more punctuation.

EXAMPLE: When he met her, he fell in love with her immediately.

I'll help you if you need me.   C

1. The teacher will help you if you go to her office.

2. She always gets good grades because she studies hard.

3. Even though owning a dog has some disadvantages there are more advantages.

4. Because he didn't study he failed the test.

5. Before he got married his friends made a party for him.

6. She did all the homework and wrote all the compositions however she didn't pass the course.

7. Although I didn't do the homework I understood everything that the teacher said.

8. Even though he worked hard all weekend he wasn't tired.

9. I stayed home last night so that I wouldn't miss a long distance call from my parents.

10. I am unhappy with my job because I don't get paid enough furthermore my boss is an unpleasant person.

11. She was so emotional at her daughter's wedding that she started to cry.

12. My boss never showed any respect for the workers as a result many people quit.

PART **3**   Fill in the blanks with an appropriate time word: *when, whenever, while, for, during, since, until.*

EXAMPLE: My friends were talking ___*during*___ the whole movie. Everyone around them was annoyed.

1. They talk _____ they go to the movies. This happens every time.

2. They were talking _____ everyone else was trying to watch the movie.

3. They started talking _____ they sat down at the beginning of the movie.

4. They talked _____ two hours.

5. They didn't stop talking _____ they left.

6. _____ the movie was over, they left and went their separate ways.

7. I haven't seen them _____ we went to the movies last week.

8. I hate it when people talk to each other _____ a movie.

PART 4 Fill in the blanks with *because, because of, since, for, so that, in order to,* or *therefore*.

EXAMPLE: I come to this school ___*in order to*___ learn English.

1. He came to the U.S. _____ he could learn English.

2. He came to the U.S. _____ find a better job.

3. He came to the U.S. _____ economic problems in his country.

4. He came to the U.S. _____ be with his family.

5. He came to the U.S. _____ a better future.

6. _____ the U.S. is a land of opportunity, many immigrants want to come here.

7. The U.S. is a land of opportunity. _____, many people from other countries want to immigrate here.

8. Irish people came to America in the 1800s _____ they didn't have enough to eat.

PART 5 Fill in the blanks with *even though, in spite of the fact that, in spite of,* or *however*.

EXAMPLE: ___*Even though*___ there are many opportunities in the U.S., my cousin can't find a job.

1. _____ his fluency in English, he can't find a job.

2. He's fluent in English. _____, he can't find a job.

3. _____ he has lived here all his life, he can't find a job.

4. He can't find a job _____ he has good job skills.

PART 6 Fill in the blanks with *if, unless,* or *even if.*

EXAMPLE: _____*If*_____ you're absent, you should call the teacher to let him know.

1. You must do the homework _____ you're absent. Absence is no excuse for not doing the homework.

2. You should come to every class _____ you're sick. If you're sick, stay home.

3. _____ you can't come to class, you need to call the teacher.

4. Some people go to work _____ they have a cold. They don't want to lose a day's pay.

PART 7 Fill in the blanks with *so, so many, so much,* or *such.*

EXAMPLE: I was _____*so*_____ late that I missed the meeting.

1. There were _____ people at the party that there wasn't anywhere to sit down.

2. The food was _____ delicious that I didn't want to stop eating.

3. I had _____ a hard day at work yesterday that I didn't have time for lunch.

4. My son is _____ intelligent that he graduated from high school at the age of 15.

5. She spent _____ a long time on her composition that she didn't have time to do the grammar exercises.

PART 8 Complete each sentence.

EXAMPLE: I didn't learn to drive until ___*I was 25 years old.*___

1. I come to this school for _____

2. I come to this school so that _____

3. People sometimes don't understand me because of _____

4. Since _____, it is necessary for immigrants to learn it.

5. She came to the U.S. to _____

6. I don't watch much TV because _____

7. I like to watch movies even though _____

8. Many people like to live in big cities in spite of the fact that _____
   _____

9. Please don't call me after midnight unless _____

10. I can usually understand the general meaning of a movie even if _____
    _____

11. I didn't speak much English until _____

12. I fell asleep during _____

13. Some students didn't study for the last test. As a result, _____
    _____

14. The teacher expects us to study before a test. However, _____
    _____

15. When applying for a job, you need to write a good résumé. In addition,
    _____

16. My mother has such a hard job that _____

17. There are so many choices of shampoo in the store that _____
    _____

18. It was so cold outside last night that _____

EXPANSION ACTIVITIES

CLASSROOM ACTIVITIES

1. Write the following sentence on a card, filling in the blank with one of your good qualities. The teacher will collect the cards and read them one by one. Other students will guess who wrote the card.

   My friends like me because _____

2. Form a small group. Tell which one of each pair you think is better and why. Practice reason and contrast words.

   • owning a dog or owning a cat
   • driving a big car or driving a small sports car
   • sending an e-mail or writing a letter by hand
   • watching a movie at home on a VCR or watching a movie in a theater
   • writing your compositions by hand or writing them on a computer

- studying at a small community college or studying at a large university
- living in the city or living in a suburb

3. Fill in the blank and discuss your answers in a small group.

    The best time in my life was _____

4. For each of the categories listed below, write a sentence with *even though* in the following pattern:

    I like _____ even though _____.

    Categories: food, exercise, movies, people, places, restaurants, hobbies, animals.

EXAMPLES:

    I like to travel even though it's expensive.
    I like to eat fast food even though I know it's not good for me.

    Find a partner and compare your answers to your partner's answers.

5. Write three sentences to complain about this city. Work with a small group. Practice *so/such . . . that.*

EXAMPLE:

    There is so much traffic in the morning that it takes me over an hour to get to work.

6. Write three sentences about this school. Try to convince someone that this is a good school.

EXAMPLE:

    The teachers are so friendly that you can go to them whenever you need help.

DISCUSSION

1. Frederick Douglass was an ex-slave who became a leader against slavery. In 1852, at a celebration of American Independence Day, Frederick Douglass gave a speech. He said, "This Fourth of July is yours, not mine. You may rejoice, I must mourn." Look up the words "rejoice" and "mourn." Then tell what you think he meant by this.

2. In what ways will America be different when Hispanics make up 25 percent of the population?

3. What are the major reasons people immigrate to the U.S.?

4. Do you think the U.S. is richer or poorer because of its immigrant population?

5. What are other countries you know about with large numbers of immigrants?

6. Does your native country have different ethnic groups, religions, or nationalities? What are they? Do the people get along?

7. When American parents adopt babies from other countries, should they try to teach them about their native country? Why or why not?

WRITING

1. Research and write about a famous person who, like Christopher Columbus, is/was a hero to some people but a bad person to others.

2. Do you think a country is richer or poorer if it has a large number of immigrants? Write a short composition to explain your point of view.

OUTSIDE ACTIVITIES

1. Interview an African-American. Ask him to tell you how slavery has affected his life today. Ask him to tell you about discrimination in America today. Tell the class what you learned about this person.

2. Interview a Hispanic who has been in the U.S. for a long time. Ask him to tell you if Spanish is still used in the home. Ask him if he feels discrimination as a Hispanic American. Tell the class what you learned about this person.

3. Interview an American. Tell him some of the facts you learned in this lesson about immigration. Ask this person to tell you his opinion about immigration.

4. Ask an American where his family was originally from. How many generations has his family lived in the U.S.? Does he have any desire to visit his family's country of origin?

Internet Activity

1. The following people came to America as immigrants. Find information about one of them on the Internet. Who is this person? What country did he/she come from? Print out a page about one of these people.

Madeleine Albright	David Ho	Carlos Santana
Mario Andretti	Henri Kissinger	Sammy Sosa
Liz Claiborne	Yo-Yo Ma	Arnold Schwarzenegger
Gloria Estefan	Zubin Mehta	Elizabeth Taylor
Andy Garcia	Martina Navratilova	Elie Weisel

2. Type in "Ellis Island" at a search engine. What is Ellis Island and why is it important in the history of immigration? Where is it?

3. Find information about one of the following African-Americans: Frederick Douglass, Harriet Tubman, John Brown, Martin Luther King, Jr.

4. Find the Declaration of Independence on the Internet. Print it out and read it.

GRAMMAR

Noun Clauses

CONTEXT

Bringing Up Baby
Pediatricians' Recommendations
Day Care
Dr. Benjamin Spock
What Do Kids Want?

LESSON FOCUS

A noun clause is a group of words that functions as a noun in a sentence.

SENTENCES WITH NOUN OR PRONOUN IN OBJECT POSITION:	SENTENCES WITH NOUN CLAUSE IN OBJECT POSITION:
I believe *the report.*	I believe *that it's important to show kids love.*
He knows *the address.*	He knows *where the school is.*
She asked *a question.*	She asked *if she should pick up the crying baby.*

Examples	Uses of Noun Clause:
I believe **that all people are good.** He's sorry **that he left his country.** It's important **that you understand me.**	After some verbs and adjectives
I don't know **what time it is.** I don't remember **if I left the stove on.**	To include a question in a statement
He said, **"I will return."** He asked, **"Where are you?"**	To repeat someone's exact words
He said **that he would return.** He asked me **what I wanted.**	To report what someone has said or asked

Before You Read

1. Do you think day care for small children should be paid for by the government? Why or why not?
2. Should employers provide maternity leave for new mothers? Why or why not?
3. Do you think grandparents should have a big part in raising children? Why or why not?

Read the following article. Pay special attention to noun clauses.

Bringing Up Baby

Research shows **that a baby's early experiences influence his brain development.** What happens in the first three years of a baby's life affects his emotional development and learning abilities for the rest of his life. It is a well known fact **that talking to infants increases their language ability** and **that reading to them is the most important thing parents can do to raise a good reader.** Some parents even think **that it's important to play Mozart to babies and show them famous works of art.** However, there is no scientific evidence to support this. It is known, however, **that babies whose parents rarely talk to them or hold them can be damaged for life.** One study shows **that kids who hardly play or who aren't touched very much develop brains 20 percent to 50 percent smaller than normal.**

Educators have known for a long time **that kids raised in poverty enter school at a disadvantage.** They are also aware **that early childhood** education can help poor kids succeed in school. A recent study at the University of North Carolina followed children from preschool to young adulthood. The results showed **that children who got high quality preschool education from the time they were infants benefited in later life**. In this study, 35 percent of children who had preschool education graduated from college, compared with only 14 percent of children who did not have preschool education.

While it is important to give babies stimulating activities, experts warn **that parents shouldn't overstimulate them**.

9.2 Noun Clauses After Verbs and Adjectives

Examples	Explanation
Parents know **that kids need a lot of attention**. Some parents think **that babies should listen to Mozart**. Studies shows **that early childhood education is important**.	A noun clause can follow certain verbs.
I am sure **that children need a lot of attention**. Are you surprised **that some parents read to babies?** Parents are worried **that they don't spend enough time with their kids**.	A noun clause can be the complement of the sentence after certain adjectives.
It has been said **that it takes a whole village to raise a child**.	A noun clause can be used after certain verbs in the passive voice.

LANGUAGE NOTES

1. A noun clause often follows one of these verbs:

believe	find out	notice	remember
complain	forget	predict	show
decide	hope	pretend	suppose
dream	know	realize	think
expect	learn	regret	understand
feel*			

    Feel followed by a noun clause means "believe" or "think."
    I *feel* that it's important for a mother to stay home with her baby. =
    I *believe/think* that it's important for a mother to stay home with her baby.

2. A noun clause often follows these adjectives:

be afraid	be clear	be obvious
be amazed	be disappointed	be sure
be aware	be glad	be surprised
be certain	be happy	be worried

3. In conversation, noun clauses can be replaced by *so* after *think, hope, believe, suppose, expect,* and *know.*

A: I hope that our children will be successful.
B: I hope *so* too.
A: Do you think that the children are learning something?
B: Yes, I think *so.*

4. In conversation, *that* before a noun clause is often omitted.

Do you think the children are happy?
I hope my children will be successful.

5. Connect two noun clauses in the same sentence with *and that* or *but that.*

I realize that you are tired *and that* you haven't eaten dinner.
I realize that you are tired *but that* you have to go to work.

EXERCISE 1 Respond to each statistic about American families by beginning with "I'm surprised that . . ." or "I'm not surprised that. . . ."

EXAMPLE: Fifty percent of marriages in the U.S. end in divorce.
I'm not surprised that 50 percent of marriages end in divorce.

1. Only 26 percent of American households are made up of a mother, father, and children.

2. About 7 million American children are home alone after school.

3. About 12 percent of American children don't have health insurance.

4. About 20 percent of American children live in poverty.

5. Sixty-eight percent of married mothers work outside the home.

6. In families where both parents work, women do most of the housework and child care.

7. Thirty-one percent of working wives earn more than their husbands.

8. Fifty-six percent of adults are married.

9. About 10 percent of adults live alone.

10. Sixty-five percent of families own their homes.

EXERCISE 2 Fill in the blanks with a noun clause to talk about your knowledge and impressions of the U.S.

EXAMPLES: I know _that there are fifty states in the U.S._

I'm surprised that _so many people live alone._

1. I think _____

2. I'm disappointed _____

3. I know _____

4. I'm afraid _____

5. It's unfortunate _____

6. I'm surprised _____

7. I've noticed _____

8. Many people think _____

EXERCISE 3 What's your opinion? Answer the questions using *I think* and a noun clause. Discuss your answers.

EXAMPLE: Should mothers of small kids stay home to raise them?

I think mothers of small kids should stay home if their husbands can make enough money. But if they need the money, I think they should work.

1. Should the government pay for child care for all children?

2. Can children get the care and attention they need in day care?

3. Should fathers take a greater part in raising their kids?

4. Should grandparents help more in raising their grandchildren?

5. Should the government give new mothers maternity leave? For how long?

6. Should parents read books to babies before they learn to talk?

7. If children don't behave, do you think it's OK for parents to hit them?

8. Should parents buy a lot of toys for their children?

1. What are some good habits that children should develop? How can their parents encourage these habits?
2. Is television a bad influence on children? Why or why not?

Read the following article. Pay special attention to noun clauses.

Pediatricians' Recommendations

The American Academy of Pediatrics (AAP) is worried that American children spend too much time in front of the TV. The AAP suggests **that pediatricians help parents evaluate their children's entertainment habits**. Doctors are concerned that children who spend too much time in front of the TV don't get enough exercise. At least one in five children is overweight. In the last 20 years, this number has increased more than 50 percent.

The AAP recommends **that children under two not watch any TV at all**. It is essential **that small children have direct interactions with parents for healthy brain growth**. The AAP advises **that parents offer children stimulating activities**.

The AAP recommends **that pediatricians be good role models** by not having TVs in their waiting rooms.

9.3 Noun Clauses After Expressions of Importance

Examples	Explanation
It is essential that babies **have** stimulation. The AAP recommends that pediatricians **be** good role models.	After verbs that show importance or urgency, the base form is used.
Her pediatrician suggested that she **read** to her kids.	Use the subject pronoun before a base form.
The AAP advises that children under two **not watch** any TV at all.	For negatives, put *not* before the base form.

LANGUAGE NOTES

1. Some verbs that express importance or urgency are:

advise*	forbid*	request
ask*	insist	require*
beg*	order*	suggest
demand	recommend	urge*

*The starred verbs can also be followed by an object + infinitive.

I advise *that she stay home with her small children.*

I advise *her to stay home with her small children.*

2. Some expressions that show importance or urgency are:

It is advisable	It is important
It is essential	It is necessary
It is imperative	It is urgent

The above expressions can also be followed by *for* + object + infinitive.

It is essential *that they play* with their children.

It is essential *for them to play* with their children.

EXERCISE 4 Rewrite these sentences as noun clauses.

EXAMPLE: You should see your doctor regularly.

It is important that *you see your doctor regularly.*

1. You should eat a healthy diet.

   It is essential that _____

2. You should exercise regularly.

   It is important that _____

3. A child must receive love.

   It is essential that _____

4. The librarian wants students to be quiet in the library.

   The librarian asks that _____

5. The school wants students to register early for classes.

   The school recommends that _____

6. Universities want foreign students to take the TOEFL®[1] Test.

   Many universities require that _____

7. The teacher wants the students to do the homework.

   The teacher requires that _____

8. The test will begin at 6 o'clock sharp. Don't come late.

   The teacher urges that _____ for the test.

9. The students want the teacher to review modals.

   The students requested that _____

10. The wife wants her husband to help with the children.

    The wife insists that _____

[1] The TOEFL® is the Test of English as a Foreign Language.

Do you think it's OK for mothers of small babies to work outside the home?
2. In your native culture, do women with babies work outside the home? Who takes care of the baby?

Read the following article. Pay special attention to noun clauses.

Day Care

Working parents often put their kids in day care. While most parents interviewed say they are satisfied with the day care they use, experts believe that only about 12 percent of children receive high quality care. Many parents really don't know **how good their day care service is.**

When choosing a day care center, of course parents want to know **how much it costs.** But there are many other questions parents should ask and observations they should make. Parents need to know **if the caregiver is loving and responds to the child's needs.** Does the caregiver hug the child, talk to the child, smile at the child, play with the child?

It is also important to know **if the day care center is clean and safe.** A parent should find out **how the caregiver takes care of sick children.** Is there a nurse or doctor available to help with medical care? Do caregivers know first aid?

Parents should ask **how many children there are per caregiver.** One caregiver for a group of eight four- or five-year-olds may be enough, but babies need much more attention; one caregiver for three babies is recommended.

Experts believe that parents should not put their babies in child care for the first four months. During this time, it is important for babies to form an attachment to their mothers.

Did you know...?

The U.S. Census estimates that two million fathers stay home to take care of small children while the mothers work.

A noun clause is used to include a question in a statement or another question.

Wh- Questions:

Direct Question	Noun Clause as Included Question
QUESTIONS WITH AUXILIARIES OR *BE*: What should working mothers do? Where is the day care center?	I don't know **what working mothers should do**. Can you tell me **where the day care center is**?
QUESTIONS WITH *DO/DOES/DID*: How much training do the caregivers have? What does your child want? When did your child start to talk?	It's important to know **how much training they have**. Do you know **what your child wants**? Do you remember **when your child started to talk**?
QUESTIONS ABOUT THE SUBJECT: Who takes care of the children? How many people take care of the children?	Do you know **who takes care of the children**? You should ask **how many people take care of the children**.

Yes/No Questions:

Direct Question	Noun Clause as Included Question
QUESTIONS WITH AUXILIARIES OR *BE*: Will the children be safe? Is your day care center good? Should she go back to work?	It's important to know **if the children will be safe**. I don't know **whether it is good or not**. She has to decide **if she should go back to work or not**.
QUESTIONS WITH *DO/DOES/DID*: Did your parents leave you with a babysitter? Does the day care center have a lot of toys? Do your children like their teacher?	I can't remember **if my parents left me with a babysitter**. I don't know **whether it has a lot of toys**. I need to know **if my children like their teacher or not**.

LANGUAGE NOTES

1. Statement word order is used for included questions.

   What time is it?

   I don't know what time it is.

2. Remove *do/does/did* from included questions.

   What does she want?

   I don't know what she wants.

3. Introduce a *yes/no* question with *if* or *whether.* You can add *or not* at the end.

   I don't know *if* the child is happy (*or not*). = I don't know *whether* the child is happy (*or not*).

4. An included question is used after phrases such as these:

I don't know	Can you tell me	I wonder
Do you know	I'd like to know	I don't remember
I'm not sure	I can't tell you	Do you remember
Nobody knows	Please tell me	You need to decide
I can't understand	I have no idea	It's important to ask

5. Use a period if the main clause is a statement. Use a question mark if the main clause is a question.

   I don't know what time it is. (statement)

   Do you know what time it is? (question)

6. When asking for information, especially from a stranger, an included question sounds more polite than a direct question.

   DIRECT QUESTION: Who is the director of the day care center?

   MORE POLITE: Can you tell me who the director of the day care center is?

EXERCISE 5 Write these questions as included questions. (These are questions about the subject.)

EXAMPLE: Who wants to leave now?

I don't know ___*who wants to leave now.*___

1. How many students in this class come from South America?

   I don't know _____

2. Who read the article about working mothers?

   I'd like to know _____

3. What happened in the last class?

   Can you tell me _____

4. Who brought a dictionary today?

   I don't know _____

5. Who failed the test?

I wonder _____

Write these questions as included questions. (These are *wh*-questions with *be* or an auxiliary verb.)

EXAMPLE: How many tests have we had?

I don't remember _____*how many tests we have had.*_____

1. When will we have the final exam?

I need to know _____

2. How many lessons are we going to finish?

Can you tell me _____

3. Where is the teacher from?

I wonder _____

4. Where will the final exam be?

You should ask _____

5. When can the teacher see me?

I need to know _____

EXERCISE 7 Write these questions as included questions. (These are *wh*-questions with *do, does,* or *did.*)

EXAMPLE: Where did you buy your books?

Can you tell me _____*where you bought your books?*_____

1. When does the semester end?

Can you tell me _____

2. What grade did I get on the last test?

Can you tell me _____

3. How many mistakes did I make?

I'd like to know _____

4. How many questions does the test have?

It's not important to know _____

5. How many compositions does the teacher want?

You should ask the teacher _____

EXERCISE 8   Write these questions as included questions. (These are *yes/no* questions with an auxiliary verb or *be*.)

EXAMPLE: Is the teacher American?

I'd like to know _if the teacher is American._

1.   Is the test going to be hard?

The teacher knows _____

2.   Will you be our teacher next semester?

I'd like to know _____

3.   Can you help us with registration?

I'd like to know _____

4.   Have you been teaching here for a long time?

Can you tell me _____

5.   Are the students confused?

I have no idea _____

EXERCISE 9   Write these questions as included questions. (These are *yes/no* questions with *do, does,* or *did.*)

EXAMPLE: Does your teacher give a lot of homework?

Can you tell me _if your teacher gives a lot of homework?_

1.   Does the school have a cafeteria?

You should ask _____

2.   Did everyone pass the last test?

I don't know _____

3.   Did you buy a used book?

Please tell me _____

4.   Does the teacher speak Spanish?

I'm not sure _____

5.   Do I need to write a composition?

Can you tell me _____

EXERCISE 10 These are some questions parents can ask before choosing day care for their children. Include each question after "I'd like to know."

EXAMPLE: How much does it cost?

I'd like to know _how much it costs._

1. Do the caregivers have a lot of experience?

   I'd like to know _____

2. How does the caregiver discipline the children?

   I'd like to know _____

3. Can the caregiver handle problems without getting angry or impatient?

   I'd like to know _____

4. Does the caregiver like children?

   I'd like to know _____

5. Am I welcome to drop in and visit?

   I'd like to know _____

6. How does the caregiver take care of sick children?

   I'd like to know _____

7. Is there a nurse or doctor to help with medical care?

   I'd like to know _____

8. Do caregivers know first aid?

   I'd like to know _____

9. Are there smoke alarms in the building?

   I'd like to know _____

10. How many caregivers are there?

    I'd like to know _____

11. Does the caregiver hug the child?

    I'd like to know _____

12. Does the caregiver talk with each child?

    I'd like to know _____

13. How many children are there for each caregiver?

I'd like to know _____

14. Is the place clean and safe?

I'd like to know _____

15. Are there enough toys?

I'd like to know _____

16. Are the toys clean?

I'd like to know _____

17. How long have the caregivers been working there?

I'd like to know _____

18. Is there a high turnover[2] of caregivers?

I'd like to know _____

19. Is the caregiver patient?

I'd like to know _____

20. Is the care center licensed by the state?

I'd like to know _____

21. Does the caregiver enjoy children?

I'd like to know _____

22. Does the child have stimulating activities?

I'd like to know _____

9.5 Question Words Followed by an Infinitive

Direct Question	Included Question as Noun Clause	Included Question Shortened to Infinitive Phrase
What should I do?	I don't know **what I should do.**	I don't know **what to do.**
How can I find a good day care center?	Please tell me **how I can find a good day care center.**	Please tell me **how to find** a good day care center.
Should she work or stay home with her children?	She can't decide **whether (or if) she should work or stay home with her children.**	She can't decide **whether to work or stay** home with her children.

[2] A *high turnover* means that employees change often.

LANGUAGE NOTES

1. Some noun clauses with *can*, *could*, and *should* can be shortened to an infinitive phrase if the subject of the main clause and the noun clause is the same.

She doesn't know what *she* should do. → She doesn't know what *to do.*

2. Use *whether*, not *if*, to introduce an infinitive.

WRONG: I don't know *if* to put my child in day care.

RIGHT: I don't know *whether* to put my child in day care.

3. An infinitive is used after *know how.*

I don't *know how to use* a fax machine.

EXERCISE 11 Complete these sentences with an infinitive phrase.

EXAMPLE: What should I do about my problem?

I don't know ___*what to do about my problem.*___

1. Where can I buy textbooks?

   I don't know _____

2. What classes should I register for?

   I can't decide _____

3. Should I take morning classes or evening classes?

   I don't know _____

4. What else should I do?

   I don't know _____

5. How can I use the computer in the library?

   I don't know _____

6. What could I do about closed classes?

   I don't know _____

7. Who could I ask about graduation?

   I don't know _____

8. Should I take biology or physics?

   I can't decide _____

9. Should I buy new textbooks or used books?

   I'm not sure _____

EXERCISE 12 Complete each statement with an infinitive phrase. Discuss your answers in a small group or with the entire class.

EXAMPLE: I can't decide _whether to stay in this city or move to another city._

1. When I came to this school, I didn't know _____
   _____

2. I can't decide _____

3. When I came to this city, I had to decide _____
   _____

4. A new student at this college needs to know _____
   _____

5. There are so many choices of products in the stores. Sometimes I
   can't decide _____

EXERCISE 13 Two students are talking. Fill in the blanks to complete the included questions. Use correct punctuation (period or question mark).

A. Hi. Where are you going in such a hurry?

B. I need to get to the library before it closes. What time does it close?

A. I'm not sure what time _it closes._
   (example)

B. What time is it now?

A. I don't have my watch, so I don't know what time _____.
   (1)
   But I'm sure it must be after six. Why do you need to use the library?

B. The teacher told us to write a paper. She told us to choose a topic.

   I don't know what topic _____
   (2)

A. Why don't you write about John Kennedy, Jr.? That's an interesting topic. There were a lot of articles written about him when he died.

B. Do you remember when _____
   (3)

A. No. I can't remember _____ in 1998 or 1999. But you
   (4)
   can get that information from the Internet.

B. I don't even know where _____ . And I don't

know how _____ the Internet.

(5)

(6)

A. The computers are on the first floor. Come on. I'll show you how

_____ the Internet.

(7)

(Later)

B. Uh-oh. The library is closed. I wonder what time _____

(8)

tomorrow.

A. The sign says, "Open 9–6."

B. Can you meet me at the library at 10 o'clock?

A. I'm not sure _____ or not. I have an appointment at

(9)

9:30, and I don't know _____ by

(10)

10 o'clock or not. But don't worry. The librarian can show you how

_____ the Internet.

(11)

Before You Read
1. Have you ever heard of Dr. Benjamin Spock? What do you know about him?
2. What are some differences in the ways that children are raised in different cultures?

Read the following article. Pay special attention to the words in quotation marks (". . .") and other noun clauses.

Did you know...?

Dr. Spock's book has been translated into 40 different languages.

Dr. Benjamin Spock

New parents are always worried that they might be making a mistake with their new baby. The baby cries, and they don't know if they should let him cry or pick him up. The baby is sick, and they don't know what to do. **"Trust yourself. You know more than you think you do,"** wrote Benjamin Spock in his famous book *Dr. Spock's Baby and Child Care*, which first appeared in 1946. This book has sold over 50 million copies, making it the biggest-selling book after the Bible. In fact, many parents say **that it is the parents' bible for raising children**.

Before Dr. Spock's book appeared, experts told parents **that they should avoid showing their children affection**. They told parents to break children of bad habits. They also told parents **that they needed to feed children on a rigid schedule**. Spock disagreed with this rigid manner of raising children and decided **that he would write a book**. "I wanted to be supportive of parents rather than scold them," Dr. Spock said. "Every baby needs to be smiled at, talked to, played with . . . gently and lovingly. Be natural and enjoy your baby."

Dr. Spock never imagined **that his book would become so popular**. The last edition came out in 1998, a few months after his death at age 94. He will be remembered for his common-sense advice. **"Respect children because they deserve respect, and they'll grow up to be better people."**

9.6 Exact Quotes

Examples	Explanation
Dr. Spock said, "Trust yourself." President Kennedy said, "Ask not what your country can do for you. Ask what you can do for your country." Martin Luther King, Jr. said, "I have a dream." Andrew Carnegie said, "It is the mind that makes the body rich."	An exact quote is used when we know exactly what a person has said because the speaker's words have been recorded. We put an exact quote between quotation marks.
"Where are you going, little girl?" asked the wolf. "I'm going to my grandmother's house," said the little girl.	An exact quote is used in fiction writing to give words to the characters.

LANGUAGE NOTES

1. The main clause with *said* or *asked* can come at the beginning or the end of a quote. Notice that if it comes at the end, the subject and verb can be inverted.

    "Where are you going?" *the wolf asked.*
    "Where are you going?" *asked the wolf.*

2. Study the punctuation of sentences that contain an exact quote. Note that the first letter of an exact quote is a capital.

Dr. Spock said, "Trust yourself."

The mother asked, "Why is the baby crying?"

"Where are you going?" asked the wolf.

"I'm going to my grandmother's house," said the little girl.

EXERCISE 14 Punctuate the following sentences. Put in capital letters where they are needed.

EXAMPLE: The mother asked "How do I know if the baby is hungry?"

1. The woman asked how often should I feed my baby

2. She said the baby is hungry

3. Dr. Spock said you know more than you think you do

4. Respect children said Dr. Spock

5. Why did you write your book the interviewer asked Spock

6. I wanted to be supportive of parents Spock answered

EXERCISE 15 Read the following folk tale. Add quotation marks.

One day a neighbor passed Nasreddin's house and saw him outside his barn on his hands and knees. He appeared to be looking for something. What are you doing? the neighbor asked.

I'm looking for something, answered Nasreddin.

What are you looking for? the neighbor asked.

I'm looking for my ring. It's very valuable, Nasreddin replied.

I'll help you, said his neighbor. The neighbor got down on his hands and knees and started to help Nasreddin look for his ring. After searching for several hours, the neighbor finally asked, Do you remember where you were when you lost it?

Of course, replied Nasreddin. I was in the barn milking my cow.

If you lost your ring inside the barn, then why are we looking for it outside the barn? asked the neighbor.

Don't be a fool, said Nasreddin. It's too dark in the barn. But out here we have light.

9.7 Reported Speech

Examples	Explanation
Before the 1940s, experts told parents **that they should be strict with their kids**. Before the 1940s, experts told parents **that children needed a rigid schedule for feeding**. They told parents **that too much affection wasn't good for the child**. They said **that too much affection would spoil the child**. I told my mother **that I wanted to marry a man just like my father**.	Reported speech is used to paraphrase or summarize what someone has said. We don't remember the exact words because they weren't recorded. The ideas are more important than the exact words.

Observe the differences between a sentence that has an exact quote and a sentence that uses reported speech:

SENTENCE WITH EXACT QUOTE: She said, "I will help you tomorrow."	SENTENCE WITH REPORTED SPEECH: She said that she would help me the next day.
• quotation marks	• no quotation marks
• comma after *said*	• no comma after *said*
• doesn't contain *that*	• contains *that* (optional)
• pronouns = *I, you*	• pronouns = *she, me*
• verb = *will help*	• verb = *would help*
• time = *tomorrow*	• time = *the next day*

EXERCISE 16 Underline the reported speech in the following paragraph.

Last week my daughter's teacher called me at work and told me that my daughter had a fever and was resting in the nurse's office. I told my boss that I needed to leave work immediately. He said that it would be fine. As I was driving my car on the expressway to the school, a police officer stopped me. She said that I had been driving too fast. She said that I had been driving 10 miles per hour over the limit. I told her that I was in a hurry because my daughter was sick. I said I needed to get to her school quickly. I told the police officer that I was sorry, that I hadn't realized I had been driving so fast. She said she wouldn't give me a ticket that time, but that I should be more careful in the future, whether my daughter was sick or not.

9.8 The Rule of Sequence of Tenses

When reported speech is used after a past tense verb (such as *said* and *told*), we usually follow the rule of sequence of tenses. The tense of the verb(s) in the next clause moves back.

Notice the difference in verb tenses in the following sentences.

Exact Quote	Reported Speech
He said, "I **know** you." (present)	He said (that) he **knew** me. (simple past)
He said, "I **am studying**." (present continuous)	He said (that) he **was studying**. (past continuous)
He said, "She **saw** me yesterday." (simple past)	He said (that) she **had seen** him the day before. (past perfect)
He said, "She **was helping** me." (past continuous)	He said (that) she **had been helping** him. (past perfect continuous)
He said, "I **have taken** the test." (present perfect)	He said (that) he **had taken** the test. (past perfect)
He said, "I **had** never **done** that." (past perfect)	He said (that) he **had** never **done** that. (past perfect)

(continued)

Modals	
He said, "I **can** help you tomorrow."	He said (that) he **could** help me the next day.
He said, "She **may** leave early." (*may* = possibility)	He said (that) she **might** leave early.
He said, "You **may** go." (*may* = permission)	He said (that) I **could** go.
He said, "I **must** go."	He said (that) he **had to** go.
He said, "I **will** stay."	He said (that) he **would** stay.

Modals That Do Not Change Their Form in Reported Speech	
He said, "You **should** leave."	He said (that) I **should** leave.
He said, "You **should have** left this morning."	He said (that) I **should have** left that morning.
He said, "You **could have** come."	He said (that) I **could have** come.
He said, "You **must have** known."	He said (that) I **must have** known.

LANGUAGE NOTES

1. When the main verb is in the present tense, the rule of sequence of tenses is not applied.

    Parents say, "Dr. Spock's book *is* our bible for raising children."

    Parents say that Dr. Spock's book *is* their bible for raising children.

2. In reporting a general truth, the rule of sequence of tenses is often not applied.

    Dr. Spock said, "Children *deserve* respect."

    Dr. Spock said that children *deserve* respect.

3. In reporting something that is still present or true, the rule of sequence is often not applied. However, if there has been a change in circumstances since the statement was made, the rule of sequence of tenses applies. COMPARE:

    My brother said that he *loves* children. (He said this recently. It's still true.)

    When I was a little boy, my grandfather told me that he *loved* to be with his grandchildren. (He said this a long time ago; the grandchildren are grown up and the grandfather may not even be alive now.)

4. In reporting a verb in the future tense, you can use either *will* or *would* if the future action has not happened yet. If the future action has already passed, use *would*. Use *would* for any statement made long ago.

    Our English teacher said that the test on Lesson 9 *will* (or *would*) be next week.

    My kindergarten teacher said that she *would* always remember us.

5. In reporting speech soon after it was said, the rule of sequence of tenses is usually not applied.

  A: I can't find my wallet.
  B: What did you say?
  A: I said I can't find my wallet.

6. In reporting a sentence that has a past tense verb, often the rule of sequence of tenses is not applied.

  My grandmother said, "I *was* born before the war."
  My grandmother told me that she *was* born before the war.
  OR My grandmother told me that she *had been* born before the war.

7. Time words change in reported speech.

  today → that day
  yesterday → the day before
  tomorrow → the next (or following) day
  this morning → that morning

EXERCISE 17   Change each sentence to reported speech. Follow the rule of sequence of tenses.

EXAMPLE: My father said, "I don't believe in giving children a lot of toys."
My father said _that he didn't believe in giving children a lot of toys._

1. My father said, "I hope you will grow up to be President."
 My father said _____

2. My mother said, "You have to make your own decision."
 My mother said _____

3. My mother said, "You can choose your own direction."
 My mother said _____

4. My grandmother said, "I had a difficult childhood."
 My grandmother said _____

5. My grandfather said, "I like to see my grandchildren."
 My grandfather said _____

6. My grandparents said, "Our childhood was very different from yours."
 My grandparents said _____

7. My grandmother said, "I was raised on a farm."
 My grandmother said _____

8. My grandfather said, "I worked on a farm before coming to America."
 My grandfather said _____

9. My grandfather said, "My family left Germany before the war."
 My grandfather said _____

10. My grandmother said, "I am the oldest of 11 children."
 My grandmother said _____

11. My grandparents said, "We want our children to be happy."

My grandparents said _____

12. My grandparents said, "You are living in a new world."

My grandparents said _____

13. My parents said, "We are glad that we came to America."

My parents said _____

14. My mother said, "When you have children of your own, you will understand the difficulties of raising children."

My mother said _____

15. My mother said, "You will always be my baby."

My mother said _____

EXERCISE 18 Go back to Exercise 16. What might have been the exact words of the driver and the police officer?

EXAMPLE: The teacher said, "Your daughter has a fever and is resting in the nurse's office."

9.9 *Say* vs. *Tell*

Examples	Pattern
Dr. Spock **said**, "You know more than you think you do." Dr. Spock **said** to parents, "You know more than you think you do."	EXACT QUOTE: Subject **said**, ". . . ." Subject **said** to someone, ". . . ."
Dr. Spock **said** that parents should trust their instincts. Dr. Spock **told** parents that it was better to feed babies when they wanted to eat.	REPORTED SPEECH: Subject **said** that . . . Subject **told** someone that . . .

LANGUAGE NOTES

1. In reported speech, we *say* something. We *tell* someone something. *Tell* is usually followed by an indirect object.
      He *said* the answer.
      He *told* us the answer.
2. With exact quotes, we usually use *say* or *say to someone*. *Tell* is rare with exact quotes.
      He *said to me*, "I have the answer."
      He *told me* that he had the answer.

3. Other verbs that are used like *say* in reported speech are: *add, admit, agree, announce, answer, claim, comment, complain, confess, declare, explain, reply*. These verbs are not followed by an indirect object.

> He *said* that you should always show children love.
> He *added* that parents needed to be flexible.

4. Other verbs that are used like *tell* in reported speech are: *advise, assure, convince, inform, notify, promise, remind, teach, warn*. These verbs are followed by an indirect object.

> He *told* parents that they knew a lot about their babies.
> He *advised* them that they should trust themselves.

EXERCISE 19 Fill in the blanks with *said* or *told*.

EXAMPLE: He ___*told*___ his children that he loved them.

1. I _____ that I wanted to learn more about raising children.

2. Dr. Spock _____ parents that they knew their baby better than anyone did.

3. The little girl _____ to her mother, "I want to grow up to be just like you."

4. The teacher _____, "Please do your homework."

5. My mother always _____ me that she loved me.

6. The teacher _____ us that we had to write five compositions.

7. I _____ you that I didn't want to buy any more books.

8. When I saw her, I _____ hello.

9.10   Noun Clauses After a Past-Tense Verb

Examples	Explanation
Dr. Spock **decided** that he **would write** a book. He never **imagined** that his book **would become** so popular. He **didn't think** that so many people **were going to buy** his book.	If the main verb is in the past tense (*thought, knew, believed, realized, decided, imagined, understood*, etc.), follow the rule of sequence of tenses on pages 363–364.

Fill in the blanks and discuss your answers. Follow the rule of sequence of tenses.

EXAMPLE: Before I came to this city, I thought that *everybody here was unfriendly*, but it isn't true.

1. Before I came to this city, I thought that _____
   _____ but it isn't true.

2. Before I came to this city, I didn't know that _____
   _____

3. Before I came to this city, I was worried that _____
   _____

4. When I lived in my hometown, I was afraid that _____
   _____

5. When I came to this school, I was surprised to learn that _____
   _____

6. When I came to this school, I realized that _____
   _____

7. When I was younger, I never imagined that _____
   _____

EXERCISE **21** Fill in the blanks to tell about you and your parents when you were a child.

EXAMPLE: When I was a child, I dreamed that *I would be a movie star.*

1. My parents told me that _____

2. My parents hoped that _____

3. My parents thought that _____

4. When I was a child, I dreamed that _____

5. When I was a child, I thought that _____

9.11 Reporting an Imperative

Imperative	Reported Imperative				
	Subject	*Tell/Ask*	**Object**	*(not)*	**Infinitive Phrase**
Trust yourself.	Dr. Spock	told	parents		**to trust** themselves.
Sit down, please.	She	asked	me		**to sit** down.
Don't be late.	The teacher	told	us	**not**	**to be** late.

LANGUAGE NOTES

1. To report an imperative, an infinitive is used after *tell* or *ask* + object.
2. Use *ask* for a request or an invitation. Use *tell* for an instruction or a command. Follow *ask* or *tell* with an object.
   INVITATION: She *asked* me to sit down.
   COMMAND: She *told* me to sit down.
3. Never use *say* to report an imperative.
   WRONG: He *said* to close the door.
   RIGHT: He *told me* to close the door.

EXERCISE 22 Change these imperatives to reported speech. Use *asked* or *told* + object pronoun.

EXAMPLES: The candidate said to us, "Please vote for me."
             The candidate asked us to vote for her.

             The father said to his daughter, "Don't come home late."
             The father told his daughter not to come home late.

1. The thief said to the woman, "Give me your money."

2. The teacher said to us, "Don't be late for class."

3. The teacher said to us, "Give me your tests."

4. The secretary said to the woman, "Sit down, please."

5. The doctor said to the man, "Take two aspirins and call me in the morning."

6. The patient said to the doctor, "Check my blood pressure, please."

7. The woman said to her husband, "Please help me clean the house."

8. The mother said to her children, "Wash your hands before eating."

9. The girl said to her parents, "Please take me to the zoo tomorrow."

_____

10. The father said to his son, "Don't watch so much TV."

_____

11. The dentist said to me, "Brush your teeth after every meal."

_____

12. The wife said to her husband, "Don't open my mail."

_____

13. The father said to his son, "Please bring me the newspaper."

_____

14. The teacher said to us, "Don't open your books during the test."

_____

Before You Read
1. Do you think parents spend enough time with their children?
2. Did your mother work when you were small? Did your parents give you a lot of attention when you were small?

Read the following article. Pay special attention to reported questions.

What Do Kids Want?

Did you know...?

Parents today spend 22 hours a week less with their kids than parents did in 1969.

Mothers who work often feel that they are not giving their kids enough attention. They feel guilty; they think their kids want to spend more time with them.

According to Helen Galinsky, of the Families and Work Institute, working mothers make assumptions about their children, but no one had ever asked kids **what they thought**. So Galinsky interviewed over 1,000 kids of working mothers to find out **what they wanted**. She asked them **if they wanted their working moms to stay home**. Surprisingly, only 10 percent of the children in her study said that they wanted more time with their mothers. However, the kids interviewed said that they wanted their parents to pay more attention to them. They said that their parents were often rushed. When she asked them **what they needed most**, the majority of the kids said that they wanted to feel important and loved.

9.12 Reported Questions

Examples	Explanation
What do children want? Galinsky wanted to find out **what children wanted**. Do they want their mothers to stay home with them? She asked them **if they wanted their mothers to stay home with them**.	When we report an exact question, we follow the rule of sequence of tenses if the main verb is in the past tense (*asked, wanted to know, tried to understand*, etc.). Use statement word order to report a question.

Observe how we report different kinds of questions.

Wh- Questions:

Exact Question	Reported Question
He asked, "What will they do?"	He asked **what they would do**.
He asked, "Where does your friend live?"	He asked **where my friend lived**.
He asked, "Who knows the answer?"	He asked **who knew the answer**.
He asked, "What happened?"	He asked **what had happened**.

Yes/No Questions:

Exact Question	Reported Question
He asked, "Is she a teacher?"	He asked **if she was a teacher**.
He asked, "Have they left?"	He asked **if they had left**.
He asked, "Does he know you?"	He asked **whether he knew me or not**.
He asked, "Did they go home?"	He asked **if they had gone home**.

LANGUAGE NOTES

1. An object can be added after *ask*.
   She asked *them* what they wanted.
2. A reported question ends in a period, not a question mark.
3. For exceptions to the rule of sequence of tenses, see pages 364–365.

EXERCISE 23 Change these questions to reported speech. Follow the rule of sequence of tenses.

EXAMPLE: My grandfather asked me, "Do you want to go fishing with me?"

My grandfather asked me ___*if I wanted to go fishing with him.*___

1. The customs officer asked the tourists, "Are you bringing any fruit into the country?"

   The customs officer asked the tourists _____

2. The registrar asked me, "Do you have your transcripts with you?"

   The registrar asked me _____

3. My mother asked me, "Will you visit me tomorrow?"

   My mother asked me _____

4. I asked the mechanic, "Can you fix my car?"

   I asked the mechanic _____

5. I asked the mechanic, "How much will it cost?"

   I asked the mechanic _____

6. I asked him, "When will the car be ready?"

   I asked him _____

7. I asked my boss, "Can I leave early tomorrow?"

   I asked my boss _____

8. The police officer asked me, "Did you see the accident?"

   The police officer asked me _____

9. I asked the teacher, "Will you return the final exam?"

   I asked the teacher _____

10. The store manager asked the little boy, "Are you lost?"

    The store manager asked the little boy _____

11. The teacher asked us, "Do you want to have a party?"

    The teacher asked us _____

12. My first grade teacher asked me, "What do you want to be when you grow up?"

    My first grade teacher asked me _____

EXERCISE **24** Read the folk tale on pages 361–362 again. Then, without looking at that page, fill in the blanks below with reported speech. Try to paraphrase or summarize. Do not try to remember exactly what was said.

EXAMPLE: Nasreddin's neighbor passed his house and saw that _____*he was looking*_____

*for something.*

1.   His neighbor asked him what _____ .

2.   Nasreddin said that he _____ ring.

3.   His neighbor said that he _____
     Nasreddin to look for the ring.

4.   His neighbor asked him where _____ the ring.

5.   Nasreddin said that _____ in the barn while he
     was milking his cow.

6.   His neighbor asked him why _____

7.   Nasreddin thought that his neighbor _____ for
     asking such a question.

8.   Nasreddin said that he _____ the ring outside

     of the barn because _____

EXERCISE **25** *Combination Exercise.* The author of this book remembers this true story from her childhood. Change the words in parentheses to reported speech.

When I was about 6 years old, I had the measles.[3] My mother told me

(Stay in the bedroom.) _____*to stay in the bedroom*_____ because it was dark
                                        (example)

---

[3] *Measles* is an illness that children often get. The medical name is rubeola.

in there. She said (I don't want the bright light to hurt your eyes.) _____

_____ . My bedroom
_____(1)_____
was near the dining room of the house. My mother told me (You can go

into the dining room.) _____
_____(2)_____
because it was dark in there. She told me (Don't go into the living room.)

_____ because it was too light there.
_____(3)_____
The TV was in the living room and she thought (The brightness of the

TV can hurt your eyes.) _____ .
_____(4)_____
   My sister Micki was three years older than me and liked to bully[4] me.
She had already had the measles, so she wasn't afraid of getting sick. She
came to the door of my bedroom and asked me (Do you know why you

can't go into the living room?) _____
_____(5)_____

_____ . I told her (I don't understand.)

_____ . She said, "The living room is for living
_____(6)_____
people. The dining room is for dying people and you're gonna die." Of
course, I believed her because she was 9 years old and knew much
more than I did. I didn't understand that ("Dining" means "eating," not
"dying.") _____

_____ .
_____(7)_____
   Today we can laugh about this story, but when I had the measles, I

was afraid that (I will die.) _____ .
_____(8)_____

EXERCISE 26 This is a composition about a problem a tenant had with a
landlord. Change direct quotes to reported speech. Remove
quotation marks. Change the punctuation and remove capital
letters where necessary. Use *tell someone* instead of *say to
someone*. (NOTE: It is not necessary to change the tense in a
sentence that has a general truth.)

                                        if he could
   Last January, I called my landlord and asked him/ ~~"Can you~~ turn up the
                                 .
heat?" I said to him, "It's too cold in my apartment." He answered, "None of
_____(1)_____

---

[4] To *bully* means to act cruel to someone who is smaller and more helpless.

the other tenants are complaining about the heat." He said to me, "Put on a
(2)
sweater and stop complaining." I called him many times after that, but I
(3)
always got the same answer. I asked several other tenants, "Are you cold?"
(4)
and all of them said yes. I asked them, "Why don't you complain to the
(5)
landlord?" They said to me, "We have complained many times, but he never
(6)
does anything to solve the problem." Finally, I said to the landlord, "If you
don't turn up the heat, I'll have to move." Of course, he didn't do anything,
(7)
and I moved in March. But that wasn't the end of my problems with him.

Months went by and I still hadn't gotten back my security deposit. Finally
I called him and asked him, "Why haven't you returned my deposit?" He said
(8)
to me, "The carpet is not clean, and one of the windows is broken." I reminded
(9)
him, "The window was already broken before I moved in."
(10)
Yesterday I called the city and asked, "Can the landlord keep my deposit
(11)
for a dirty carpet?" The city worker said to me, "The landlord can't keep
(12)
your deposit for normal wear and tear." I asked the woman, "What does this
(13)
expression mean?" She explained, "A landlord has to expect normal living
(14)
to occur in the apartment, and he can't deduct money from your deposit for
it." Then I told her about the broken window. She asked, "Have you taken
(15)
pictures of the window?" I hadn't, but I said to her, "I have a copy of a letter
(16)
that I wrote to the landlord asking him to fix the broken window." The letter
was dated May 10, 1998. She said to me, "That's good evidence." Then she
(17)
asked me, "Has the landlord sent you a letter with a list of damages?" I said
(18)
to her, "He has told me about these problems by phone." She said, "He must
(19)
put the damages in writing within 30 days after a tenant moves." She said,
(20)
"If he hasn't done that, you can take him to court."
(21)

Reporting information as noun clauses or infinitives:

Direct statement or question	Sentence with included statement or question	Use of noun clause or infinitive
She has a car.	I know **that she has a car.** I'm sure **that she has a car.** It is assumed **that she has a car.**	Noun clause is used after verbs and adjectives.
Talk to your children. Don't be so strict.	It is essential **that you talk to your children.** He recommends **that we not be so strict.**	Noun clause is used after expressions of importance. The base form is used in the noun clause.
Is he married? Where does he live? What should I do?	I don't know **if he's married.** I don't know **where he lives.** I don't know **what to do.**	Noun clause is used as an included question. Infinitive replaces *should* or *can*.
I will leave.	He said, **"I will leave."** He said **that he would leave.**	Noun clause is used in an exact quote or to report what someone has said.
Did you see the movie?	He asked, **"Did you see the movie?"** He asked me **if I had seen the movie or not.**	Noun clause is used in an exact quote or to report a question.
Sit down. Don't be late.	He asked me **to sit down.** He told me **not to be late.**	Infinitive is used to report an imperative.

EDITING ADVICE

1. Use *that* or nothing to introduce an included statement. Don't use *what*.

   I know ~~what~~ *that* she likes to swim.

2. Use statement word order in an indirect question.

   I don't know what time ~~is it~~ *it is*.

3. We *say* something. We *tell* someone something.

   He ~~said~~ *told* me that he wanted to go home.

   He ~~told~~ *said*, "I want to go home."

4. Use *tell* or *ask*, not *say*, to report an imperative. Follow *tell* with an object.

> *told*
> He ~~said~~ me to sit down.
>
> *you*
> I told ^ to wash your hands.

5. Don't use *to* after *tell*.

> He told ~~to~~ me that he wanted to go home.

6. Use *if* or *whether* to introduce an included *yes/no* question.

> *if*
> I can't decide ^ I should buy a car or not.
>
> *whether*
> I don't know ^ it's going to rain or not.

7. Use *would*, not *will*, to report something that is past.

> *would*
> My father said the he ~~will~~ come to the U.S. in 1995.

8. Follow the rule of sequence of tenses when reporting something that happened long ago.

> *wanted*
> When I was a child, my grandmother told me that she ~~wants~~ to travel.

9. Put the subject before the verb in a noun clause.

> I don't know where (lives) your brother?

10. Don't use *so* before a noun clause.

> He thinks ~~so~~ the U.S. is a beautiful country.

11. Use the base form after expressions showing importance or urgency.

> *be*
> It is urgent that you ~~are~~ on time for the meeting.
>
> *review*
> I suggested that the teacher ~~reviewed~~ the last lesson.

12. Use *not* + base form to form the negative after expressions showing importance or urgency.

> *not*
> Doctors recommend that small children ~~don't~~ watch TV.

13. Use a period, not a question mark, if a question is included in a statement.

> I don't know what time it is?

14. Use correct punctuation in an exact quote.

> He said, "I love you."

15. Don't use a comma before a noun clause (EXCEPTION: an exact quote).

> He knows/ that you like him.

LESSON 9 TEST / REVIEW

PART 1   Find the mistakes with the underlined words, and correct them. Not every sentence has a mistake. If the sentence is correct, write **C**.

EXAMPLES: I don't know where <del>does</del> your brother live.

"What do you want?" asked the man.   C

1. I'd like to know <u>what I need to study</u> for the final exam.

2. She is happy <u>what</u> her daughter got married.

3. I don't know <u>what you want</u>.

4. He <u>said</u> me that he wanted my help.

5. I don't know <u>what time is it</u>.

6. The President said, "There <u>will be</u> no new taxes."

7. I don't know <u>what to do</u>.

8. I don't know <u>where should I go</u> for registration.

9. I told you <u>not to leave</u> the room.

10. The weatherman said that it <u>will rain</u> on Sunday, but it didn't.

11. Do you think <u>so</u> New Yorkers are friendly people?

12. Do you think <u>I'm intelligent</u>?

13. I don't know <u>she</u> understands English or not.

14. He asked me <u>where do I live</u>.

15. He told <u>that he wanted</u> to speak with me.

16. He <u>said to his father</u>, "I'm an adult now."

17. I didn't know <u>that learning English would be</u> so hard.

18. Before I started looking for a job, I thought that I <u>will find</u> a job right away, but I didn't.

19. It is important <u>that you be</u> here before 9 o'clock.

20. I recommend <u>that you not give</u> the answers to anyone.

21. He <u>told to me</u> that he wanted to buy a car.

22. He <u>said me</u> to open the window.

23. I suggest <u>that my friend visits</u> me during vacation.

24. My counselor advised <u>that I didn't take</u> so many credit hours.

PART **2** Find the mistakes with **punctuation** in the following sentences. Not every sentence has a mistake. If the sentence is correct, write **C**.

EXAMPLES: He said, "I can't help you."
He said, "I have to leave now."   C

1. I don't know what time it is?

2. Do you know what time it is?

3. I'm sure, that you'll find a job soon.

4. The teacher said I will return your tests on Monday.

5. I didn't realize, that you had seen the movie already.

6. He asked me, "What are you doing here?"

7. "What do you want," he asked.

8. "I want to help you," I said.

9. I told him that I didn't need his help.

10. Can you tell me where I can find the bookstore.

PART 3

Fill in the blanks with an included question.

EXAMPLE: How old is the President?

Do you know _how old the President is?_

1. Where does Jack live?

   I don't know _____

2. Did she go home?

   I don't know _____

3. Why were they late?

   Nobody knows _____

4. Who ate the cake?

   I don't know _____

5. What does "liberty" mean?

   I don't know _____

6. Are they working now?

   Can you tell me _____

7. Should I buy the car?

   I don't know _____

8. Has she ever gone to Paris?

   I'm not sure _____

9. Can we use our books during the test?

   Do you know _____

10. What should I do?

    I don't know _____

Change the following sentences to reported speech. Follow the rule of sequence of tenses.

EXAMPLE: He said, "She is late."

He said that she was late.

1. He said, "Give me the money."

   _____

2. She said, "I can help you."

   _____

3. He said, "Don't go away."

   _____

4. He said, "My mother left yesterday."

   _____

5. She said, "I'm learning a lot."

   _____

6. He said, "I've never heard of Dr. Spock."

   _____

7. They said to me, "We finished the job."

   _____

8. He said to us, "You may need some help."

   _____

9. He said to her, "We were studying."

   _____

10. He said to her, "I have your book."

    _____

11. He said to us, "You should have called me."

    _____

12. He said to his wife, "I will call you."

    _____

13. He asked me, "Do you have any children?"

_____

14. He asked me, "Where are you from?"

_____

15. He asked me, "What time is it?"

_____

16. He asked me, "Did your father come home?"

_____

17. He asked me, "Where have you been?"

_____

18. He asked me, "Will you leave tomorrow?"

_____

19. He asked me, "What do you need?"

_____

20. He asked me, "Are you a student?"

_____

21. He asked us, "Can you help me today?"

_____

22. He asked us, "Who needs my help?"

_____

EXPANSION ACTIVITIES

CLASSROOM ACTIVITIES

1. Write questions you have about the topics in the readings of this chapter. Express your questions with "I wonder . . ." Compare your questions in a small group.

EXAMPLES:
> I wonder why parents spend so much less time with their children than they used to.
> I wonder why it is so hard to raise a child.

2. What advice did your parents, teachers, or other adults give you when you were younger? Write three sentences. Share them in a small group.

EXAMPLES:
> My mother told me to be honest.
> My grandfather told me that I should always respect older people.

_____

_____

_____

3. What advice or information did your teacher tell you at the beginning of this semester? Work in a small group and write three sentences to report what the teacher said.

EXAMPLES:
> She told us that we had to write five compositions.
> She told us to buy *Grammar in Context*.

_____

_____

_____

DISCUSSION

1. How is your philosophy of raising children different from your parents' philosophy or methods?

2. Do you think parents should or shouldn't hit children when they misbehave?

3. Did your parents read to you when you were a child?

4. Did you have a lot of toys when you were a child?

5. Do you think children today behave differently than when you were a child?

6. Is it hard to raise children? Why?

7. Read the following poem. Discuss the meaning.

> Your children are not your children.
> They are the sons and daughters of Life's longing for itself.
> They come through you but not from you,
> And though they are with you, yet they belong not to you.
> You may give them your love but not your thoughts.
> For they have their own thoughts.
> You may house their bodies but not their souls,
> For their souls dwell in the house of tomorrow, which you cannot visit,
>   not even in your dreams.
> You may strive to be like them, but seek not to make them like you.
> For life goes not backward nor tarries with yesterday.
> You are the bows from which your children as living arrows are sent
>   forth.
> . . .
> Let your bending in the archer's hand be for gladness;
> For even as he loves the arrow that flies, so He loves also the bow
>   that is stable.

Kahil Gibran (From *The Prophet*)

WRITING

1. Write a paragraph about an interesting conversation or argument that you had or that you heard recently.

EXAMPLE:

> Last week I had a conversation with my best friend about having children. I told her that I didn't want to have children. She asked me why I was against having kids. . . .

2. Write about an unpopular belief that you have. Explain why you have this belief and why it is unpopular.

EXAMPLES:

> I believe that there is life on other planets.
> I believe that schools shouldn't have tests.

3. Write about a belief you used to have that you no longer have. Explain what this belief was and why you no longer believe it to be true.

EXAMPLES:

> I used to believe that communism was the best form of government.
> I used to believe that marriage made people happy.

4. Write about a general belief that people in your native culture have. Explain what this belief means. Do you agree with it?

EXAMPLES:

> In my native country, it is said that it takes a village to raise a child.
> In my native culture, it is believed that wisdom comes with age.

5. Write a short fable or fairy tale that you remember. Include the characters' words in quotation marks. See the folk tale in Exercise 15 for an example.

6. Write about an incident from your childhood, like the one in Exercise 25.

1. Interview a classmate, coworker, or neighbor about his or her childhood. Find out about this person's family, school, house, activities, and toys.

2. Interview a friend, coworker, or neighbor who has a child. Ask him or her these questions:
   What's the hardest thing about raising a child?
   What's the best thing about raising a child?

Internet Activities

1. At a search engine, type in "parents" or "parenting" or "family." What kind of information can parents get about raising children from a Web site?

2. At a search engine, type in "homework." What kind of help can children get online with their homework?

3. For information about parenting and children, find these Web sites by typing in their names at a search engine:
   Zero to Three
   I am your child

Find some information about children that surprises you. Bring this information to class.

GRAMMAR

Unreal Conditions, Present and Past
Wishes

CONTEXT

Biotechnology
Legal Questions Raised by Science
Growing Older and Older and Older

LESSON FOCUS

An unreal condition is used to talk about hypothetical
or imagined situations.

We can use unreal conditions to talk about the present.

REALITY: I don't have a lot of money.

HYPOTHESIS: If I *had* a lot of money, I *would travel* around the
world.

We can use unreal conditions to talk about the past.

REALITY: I didn't study English when I was a child.

HYPOTHESIS: If I *had studied* English when I was a child, I *would
have learned* it more quickly.

Unreal situations can also be expressed after the word *wish*.

REALITY: I'm not rich.

WISH: I wish I *were* rich.

REALITY: I didn't see the movie.

WISH: I wish I *had seen* the movie.

1. Do you think a cure for cancer and other diseases is near?
2. What are some recent scientific discoveries that were unimaginable 25 years ago?

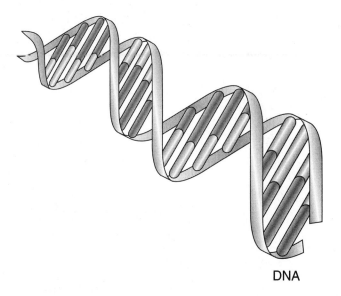

DNA

Read the following article. Pay special attention to unreal conditions.

Biotechnology

Biotechnology today is presenting possibilities that used to be the subject of science fiction. Organ transplants have become routine. Sheep, mice, and cows have been cloned. In June 2000, scientists announced that, after 10 years of research, they have mapped the 3.1 million units of the human DNA, which is the chemical "instruction book" of who we are. In the near future, scientists may be able to use this information to prevent diseases, such as cancer and Alzheimer's disease, or grow healthy tissue to replace diseased tissue. Genetic engineering may even allow parents to determine the hair color, intelligence, or personality of their child. By identifying diseased genes, scientists will one day be able to treat diseases before a baby is born.

In a survey,[1] Americans were asked if they **would use** genetic engineering to "design" their babies. Most Americans say that if they **could treat** or **prevent** a disease before a baby is born, they **would do** it. However, most Americans say they **would** not **try** to determine the sex of their babies. Just imagine: if everyone **chose** a son, who **would** these baby boys **marry** when they grew up?

Why **would** anyone want to clone a cow or other animal? Consider this:

[1] The survey was conducted by *Time* in 1999.

if a farmer **had** a cow that **produced** high quality meat or milk, he **would make** a lot of money if he **could make** many copies of this cow. But what **would** the world **be** like if we **could produce** another Michael Jordan, Elvis Presley, Albert Einstein, or Mother Teresa? What if we **had** a new Einstein and he **didn't show** any interest in science?

Even though brain transplants still belong only in science fiction, the idea raises some interesting questions. If you **had** the brain of another person, who **would** you **be**?

10.1 Unreal Conditions—Present

Examples	Explanation

If I **were** rich, I **would donate** money for medical research.
     (Reality: I **am** not rich.)
 	
If we **could** eliminate all diseases, the world **would be** a better place.
     (Reality: We **can't** eliminate all diseases.)
If I **didn't have to** study English, I **would have** more free time.
     (Reality: I **have to** study English.)
	For an unreal condition in the present, a past form is used in the *if* clause. *Would* + base form is used in the main clause.
	
	Use *could* as the past form of *can*.

If I **had** someone else's brain, I **might be** a lot smarter. If you **knew** English perfectly, you **could work** as a translator.	*Might* or *could* + base form can be used in the main clause.
If he **were living** in his native country now, he **wouldn't be studying** English. If I **were** a scientist, I **would be looking** for a cure for diseases.	To talk about a situation that is happening now, use *were* + verb *-ing* in the condition clause. Or use *would be* + verb *-ing* in the result clause.
If I **were** you, I **would buy** a new car. If I **were** you, I **would try** to find a better apartment.	We often give advice with the expression "If I were you . . ." *Were* is the correct form in the condition clause for all subjects. However, you will often hear people use *was* with *I*, *he*, *she*, and *it*.
I wouldn't marry you **even if** you were the last person on earth. I wouldn't join the army **unless** my country were at war.	You can use *even if* and *unless* in the condition clause.

LANGUAGE NOTES

1. All pronouns except *it* can be contracted with *would*.
   I'd   you'd   he'd   she'd   we'd   they'd
2. We use *what if* to propose a hypothetical situation.
   What if you could travel to the future?
   What if you were Einstein?
3. Notice that when the *if* clause precedes the main clause, a comma is used to separate the two clauses. When the main clause precedes the *if* clause, a comma is not used.
   If I were rich, I'd buy a house in Paris. (comma is used)
   I would buy a house in Paris *if I were rich*. (comma is not used)
4. Notice when we make a question with conditionals, the *if* clause uses statement word order.
   If *you had* the brain of another person, who would you be?

EXERCISE 1   Fill in the blanks with the correct form of the verb in parentheses.

EXAMPLE: If I ___*spoke*___ English perfectly, I ___*wouldn't be*___ in this class.
           (speak)   *(not/be)*

1. My parents aren't here. If my parents _____ here, my life
                                              (be)

   _____ better.
      (be)

2. He doesn't have a job. If he _____ a job, he _____
                                  (have)   *(be able to)*

   buy a new car.

3. If I _____ you, I _____ a new job.
         (be)   *(look for)*

4. He works all the time. If he _____ more time,
                                     (have)

   he _____ more.
          (read)

5. If she _____ more English, she _____ more Ameri-
            (know)   *(have)*

   can friends.

6. You usually get a B+ on the tests. You _____ get an A on every
                                             (can)

   test if you _____ a little harder.
                   (study)

7. I'm sorry to bother you. I _____ you if I
                                   (not/bother)

   _____ your help.
       (not/need)

8. I don't have much energy anymore. I _____ more energy
   (have)

   if I _____ younger.
      (be)

9. She needs more experience with computers. She _____
                                                    (be able to)

   find a better job if she _____ computer skills.
                              (have)

10. I really want to help you. If I _____ to help you, I
                                      (not/want)

    _____ my help.
       (not/offer)

11. I usually go to bed at 10 o'clock. I _____ to bed
                                            (go)

    much later if I _____ get up so early in the morning
                       (not/have to)

    for my job.

12. If I _____ the teacher, I _____ everyone an A.
           (be)   (give)

13. My family lives in Minneapolis. It's so cold there in the winter. If

    it _____ so cold there, I _____ there to be
          (not/be)   (move)
    with my family.

14. My sister loves being a social worker. She _____ it
                                                   (not/do)

    if she _____ it because she doesn't make a lot of
             (not/love)
    money.

EXERCISE 2 Make a list of things you would do if you had more time. You may share your sentences in a small group or with the entire class.

EXAMPLES: *If I had more free time, I'd read more novels.*

I'd visit my grandmother more often if I had more free time.

1. _____

2. _____

3. _____

EXERCISE 3   Make a list of things you would do differently if you spoke or understood English better. You may share your sentences in a small group or with the entire class.

EXAMPLES: *If I spoke English fluently, I wouldn't come to this class.*

I wouldn't be so nervous when I talk on the telephone if I

understood English better.

1. _____
2. _____
3. _____

EXERCISE 4   Complete each statement.

EXAMPLE: If I studied harder, *I would get better grades.*

1. If I were the President, _____
2. If I were the English teacher, _____
3. If I could live to be 200 years old, _____
4. If I could predict the future, _____
5. If I were rich, _____
6. If I could be a child again, _____
7. If I didn't have to work, _____
8. If I had the energy of a young person combined with the knowledge of an older person, _____
9. If people could "design" babies, _____
10. If I could change places with any other person in the world, _____
    _____

EXERCISE 5   Complete each statement.

EXAMPLE: The teacher would be surprised if *everyone got an A on the test.*

1. My life would be better if _____
2. I'd be learning English much faster if _____
3. I'd study more if _____

4. I'd travel a lot if _____

5. I'd be very unhappy if _____

6. I wouldn't borrow money from a friend unless _____

EXERCISE 6 Answer each question with *yes* or *no*. Then make a statement with an unreal condition.

EXAMPLES: Do you have the textbook?
Yes. If I didn't have the textbook, I wouldn't be able to do
_____
this exercise.
_____

Is this lesson easy?
No. If it were easy, we wouldn't have to spend so much time on it.
_____

1. Are you an American?

   _____

2. Do you know how to use the Internet?

   _____

3. Do you work on Sundays?

   _____

4. Do all the students in this class speak the same language?

   _____

5. Does the teacher speak your native language?

   _____

6. Are you taking other courses this semester?

   _____

7. Do you have a high school diploma?

   _____

8. Do you have a car?

   _____

9. Do you live far from school?

   _____

10. Do you have a job?

    _____

11. Do you own a house?

_____

12. Is today Saturday?

_____

13. Do you speak English perfectly?

_____

14. Do you have a computer?

_____

EXERCISE 7   Fill in the blanks with the correct form of an appropriate verb.

EXAMPLE: I don't travel much because I don't have time. I ___*would travel*___ more

if I ___*had*___ more time.

1. I don't have much money. If I _____ more money, I _____

_____ a new car.

2. All you do is complain about your job. If I _____ you,

I _____ a new job.

3. She doesn't make enough money, so she's going to quit her job. If

she _____ more money, she _____ her job.

4. She doesn't have a car, so she uses public transportation. If she

_____ a car, she _____ public transportation.

5. He doesn't get much exercise. If he _____ more exercise, he

_____ healthier.

6. My apartment is too small, so I'm going to move. If my present

apartment _____ bigger, I _____.

7. He doesn't have his glasses with him, so he isn't able to read the

small print. If he _____ glasses, he _____

_____ the small print.

8. She has three small children. She _____ more

free time if she _____.

9. It's raining. If it _____, the children _____

_____ outside.

10. I don't want to buy a car because owning a car is too expensive. If I _____ a car, I _____ gas, insurance, and repairs.

11. Nobody can travel to the past or future. If I _____ to the past, I _____ my ancestors and ask them about their lives.

12. I usually take a quick shower because I don't have much time. I _____ a slow bath if I _____ more time.

10.2 Implied Conditions

Examples	Explanation
I **would** never lie to a friend. **Would** you jump in the water to save a drowning person?	Sometimes the condition is implied, not stated. In these examples, the implication is "if you had the possibility" or "if the opportunity presented itself."
Would you **want** to meet the President? **Would** you **want** to travel to the moon? I **wouldn't want** to live in Alaska, **would** you?	*Would want* is used to present hypothetical situations.

EXERCISE 8 Answer these questions and discuss your answers.

beggar

1. Would you give money to a beggar?

2. Would you marry someone from another country?

3. Would you buy a used computer?

4. Would you lend a large amount of money to a friend?

5. Would you open someone else's mail?

6. Would you lie to protect a friend?

7. Would you tell a dying relative that he or she is dying?

8. Would you want to travel to the past or the future?

9. Would you want to live more than 100 years?

10. Would you want to visit another planet?

11. Would you want to live on the top floor of a hundred-story building?

12. Would you want to go on an African safari?

EXAMPLE: What would you do if a stranger on the street asked you for money?
I would say, "I'm sorry. I can't give you any."

1. What would you do if you found a wallet in the street with a name and phone number in it?

   _____

2. What would you do if you saw your sister's husband having dinner in a restaurant with another woman?

   _____

3. What would you do if you lost your money and didn't have enough money to get home by public transportation?

   _____

4. What would you do if you saw a man on the street hitting a woman?

   _____

5. What would you do if you saw a mother in a public place hitting a child?

   _____

6. What would you do if you saw a person in a public park picking flowers?

   _____

7. What would you do if a cashier in a supermarket gave you a ten-dollar bill in change instead of a one-dollar bill?

   _____

8. What would you do if you hit a car in a parking lot and no one saw you?

   _____

9. What would you do if you saw another student cheating on a test?

   _____

10. What would you do if your doctor told you that you had six months left to live?

   _____

11. What would you do if you lost your job and couldn't pay your rent?

   _____

12. What would you do if your best friend borrowed money from you and didn't pay you back?

_____

13. What would you do if your child brought home a street dog or cat and wanted to keep it?

_____

14. What would you do if your best friend told your secret to another person?

_____

15. What would you do if you married someone who didn't want to have kids?

_____

10.3   Real vs. Unreal Conditions

Examples	Explanation
My sister is pregnant. If my sister **has** a baby girl, she **will name** her Sarah, after our grandmother. I'm applying for a job in Toronto. If I **get** the job, I**'ll move** there immediately.	These are real possibilities and plans for the future.
He doesn't have any free time. If he **had** free time, he **would spend** it with his kids. If I **could fly**, I**'d feel** free.	These are not plans. They are just hypothetical situations.

EXERCISE 10 Fill in the blanks with the correct form of the verb in parentheses. Both real conditions and unreal conditions are used.

EXAMPLES: If I __*were*__ you, I __*would buy*__ a new car.
       (be)   (buy)

My sister is planning to get married on June 27. If the weather __*is*__ nice that day, the wedding __*will be*__ outdoors.
   (be)   (be)

1. If I _____ fluent in English, I _____ in this class.
      (be)   (not/be)

2. Linda hates Paul. She _____ (not/marry) him even if

    he _____ (be) the last man on earth.

3. My mother may visit me next week. If my mother _____ (come) here,

    I _____ (be) absent from class for a few days.

4. She loves her dog. She _____ (not/sell) her dog even if you

    _____ (pay) her a million dollars.

5. My boss will probably call this afternoon. If he _____ (call), tell him

    I'm not home.

6. She may get some money from her parents. If her parents _____ (send)

    her some money, she _____ (buy) some new clothes.

7. I live in Chicago. My brother lives in Detroit. If it _____ (be/not)

    so far, I _____ (drive) there every weekend.

8. It's raining now. If it _____ (not/rain), we _____ (go)

    for a walk.

9. My friend likes to parachute out of airplanes. I _____ (not/do) it

    even if you _____ (give) me a million dollars.

10. If I _____ (be) a child, I _____ (play) with video games all

    day.

11. If I _____ (pass) this course, I _____ (go) to the next level.

12. She's saving her money. If she _____ (have) enough money, she

    _____ (take) a vacation next year.

Before You Read
1. What are some options available to couples who are unable to have children of their own?
2. Do you think it is ethical, or morally correct, to pay a woman to have another person's child? Why or why not?

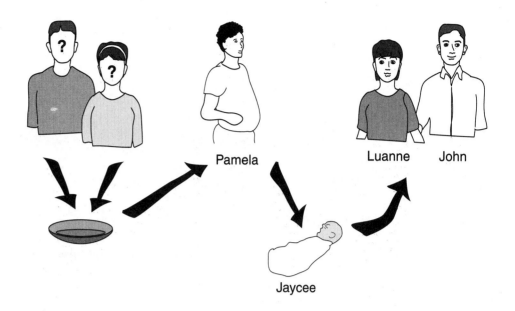

Pamela

Luanne   John

Jaycee

Read the following article. Pay special attention to unreal conditions.

Legal Questions Raised by Science

In 1978, the first "test tube" baby was born in England. Since then, more than 45,000 American babies have been born as a result of this procedure.[2] Many couples **would not have been able to have** children if they **hadn't used** this method. However, producing babies this way has brought up some legal and moral problems.

John and Luanne Buzzanca wanted to have a baby but couldn't. In 1994, they arranged to have a baby with an egg and sperm from anonymous donors implanted in a surrogate[3] mother, Pamela Snell. Pamela agreed to turn the baby over to the Buzzancas. However, a month before the baby, Jaycee, was born, John filed for divorce. He said he didn't want to pay child support because he wasn't the biological father. Luanne took John to court for child support. Pamela took Luanne to court, wanting to keep the baby. Pamela said that if she **had known** that there were going to be so many difficulties, she **wouldn't have agreed** to have the baby for the Buzzancas. She said that Luanne couldn't give the baby a stable home. The judge decided that Luanne should raise the little girl and that John had to pay child support. What **would** you **have done** if you **were** the judge?

---

[2] The correct term for this procedure is *in vitro fertilization*, or IVF.
[3] A *surrogate mother* is a woman who carries the child of another person.

Unreal Conditions, Present and Past; Wishes   **399**

10.4 Unreal Conditions—Past

For an unreal condition in the past, the past perfect is used in the *if* clause. *Would have* + past participle is used in the main clause.

If + Past Perfect	*Would Have* + Past Participle
If Pamela **had known** about the problems that were going to happen,	she **wouldn't have agreed** to have the baby.
If John and Luanne **hadn't gotten** divorced,	none of these problems **would have happened**.
If John **had agreed** to pay child support,	Pamela **wouldn't have tried** to keep the baby.

LANGUAGE NOTES

1. In the *if* clause, use *had been able to* for the past perfect of *could*.
   If the Buzzancas *had been able to have* children on their own, they *wouldn't have used* a surrogate mother.
2. *Could* or *might* can be used in the main clause.
   If you had told me about your problem, I *could* have helped you.
   If she had studied harder for the test, she *might* have passed it.
3. In informal speech, *have* after *could*, *would*, or *might* is pronounced like *of* or /ə/. Listen to your teacher pronounce the sentences above with fast, informal pronunciation.
4. In very informal conversational English, you often hear *would have* in both clauses.
   If I *would have known* about the problem, I *would have told* you. (INFORMAL)
   If I *had known* about the problem, I *would have told* you. (FORMAL)
5. A noun clause can be used within an *if* clause. Use past forms in a noun clause.
   If I had known that you *were going* to come to the party, I would have given you a ride.

EXERCISE 11 Fill in the blanks with the words in parentheses to complete the unreal condition in the past.

EXAMPLES: If I ___*hadn't come*___ to this city, I ___*wouldn't have met*___ you.
(not/come)   (not/meet)

1. Her life was hard when she was a child. If her family _____
(have)

_____ more money, her life _____ easier.
(be)

---

2. If we _____ alive 100 years ago, we _____
      (be)   (not/use)
   computers.

3. If we _____ lesson nine, we _____
         (not/do)   (not/learn)
   about Dr. Spock.

4. I _____ more English when I was younger if I
        (study)
   _____ it would be so useful.
        (know)

5. If I _____ English as a child, I _____
          (study)   (be able to)
   skip ESL courses and go into a regular English course.

6. I _____ you last night if I _____
        (call)   (not/lose)
   your phone number.

7. I didn't find your keys. If I _____ them, I _____
                                      (find)   (return)
   _____ them to you.

8. I didn't know that David was upset about what I said. If I _____
                                                                    (know)
   _____ that he was upset, I _____ to him.
                                             (apologize)

9. You missed a great movie. If you _____ it, you
                                          (see)
   _____ it very much.
        (enjoy)

10. A. I thought you moved.
    B. No, I didn't move. If I _____ I _____
                                  (move)   (tell)
    you about it.

11. Everybody who ate the fish got sick. I didn't eat any fish. If I
    _____ the fish, I _____
          (eat)   (get)
    sick too.

12. I took two years off from school to work. If I _____
                                                        (stay)
    in school, I _____ my degree by now.
                     (finish)

13. He didn't know she was dishonest. If he _____ how
                                                  (know)
    dishonest she was, he _____ her
                              (never/trust)
    with his money.

14. She was sleeping when the burglar entered the house. If she
    _____, she _____
         (not/sleep)   (hear)
    the burglar.

EXERCISE 12 Fill in the blanks with the correct form of an appropriate verb to complete the unreal condition in the past.

EXAMPLE: I yelled at my boss. As a result, I lost my job. If I ___*hadn't yelled*___ at my boss, I ___*wouldn't have lost*___ my job.

1. He went to a party and met his future wife there. If he _____ _____ to the party, he _____ his future wife.

2. Mary didn't study for the test. She failed it. If she _____ for the test, she _____ it.

3. He didn't know she didn't want to have kids when he married her. He _____ her if he _____ that she didn't want to have kids.

4. He told her his secret. He didn't know she was going to tell everyone. He _____ her his secret if he _____ that she was going to tell everyone.

5. They didn't want to get married without their parents' approval. They _____ married if their parents _____ of their marriage.

6. He left San Francisco because he couldn't find a job there. If he _____ a job in San Francisco, he _____ .

7. I found a lost wallet. I couldn't return it because there was no name in it. I _____ the wallet if there _____ a name or phone number in it.

8. I didn't know my friends were coming over. I didn't prepare any food. If I _____ that they were coming over, I _____ _____ some food.

9. The little boy broke the dish and lied to his mother about it, so his mother punished him. She _____ him if he _____ a lie.

10. I didn't know that you needed my help last Saturday. If I _____ _____ that you needed me, I _____ _____ you.

11. My friend didn't find a job, so he couldn't pay back the money he borrowed from me. If he _____ a job, he _____ me back last month.

12. You didn't ask your mechanic's opinion about buying that awful car. If you _____ for his opinion, he _____ that it was a lemon.[4]

13. Columbus discovered America in 1492. If he _____ America, another European _____ .

14. I didn't know that you sang so beautifully. If I _____ , I _____ you to sing at my last party.

15. John Kennedy, Jr. flew at night. His plane crashed. His plane might _____ if he _____ in daylight.

10.5 ## Mixed Tenses in Condition Statements

We can mix a present condition with a past result, or a past condition with a present result.

Present Condition (Use simple past)	Past Result (Use *would have* + past participle)
If you **were** the judge,	what **would** you **have decided**?
If I **were** you,	I **wouldn't have bought** that old car.
If I **had** a car,	I **would have taken** you to the airport last week.
If I **were** rich,	I **would have bought** a big house when I came to this city.

Past Condition (Use past perfect)	Present Result (Use *would* + base form)
If you **had read** the story,	you **would understand** what we're talking about now.
If she **hadn't come** to the U.S.,	she **would be living** with her parents now.
If she **hadn't lost** her job last month,	she **would be able** to take a vacation this summer.

[4] A *lemon* is a car that is defective.

EXERCISE 13 Fill in the blanks with the correct form of an appropriate verb. These sentences have mixed tenses.

EXAMPLE: She just came to the U.S., so she doesn't speak English perfectly. If she _____had come_____ here a long time ago, she _____would speak_____ English much better.

1. He invested a lot of money in a good stock, and now he's rich. If he _____ in that stock, he _____ rich today.

2. Luckily she didn't marry her high school boyfriend. If she _____ _____ him, she _____ happy now.

3. I passed the last course, and now I'm in this course. I _____ in this course if I _____ the last course.

4. The car you bought is terrible. If I _____ you, I _____ _____ that car.

5. She didn't see the accident, so she can't tell you what happened. She _____ what happened if she _____ the accident.

6. You didn't come to class yesterday, so you don't understand the teacher's explanation today. You _____ the teacher's explanation today if you _____ to class yesterday.

7. She has a lot of work to do, so she got up early. If she _____ _____ so much work, she _____ in bed all morning.

8. He's not living in his hometown, so he didn't graduate from college there. He _____ from college by now if _____ in his hometown now.

9. She doesn't have a car, so she didn't drive you to the hospital. If she _____ a car, she _____ you to the hospital yesterday.

10. I didn't learn English as a child. If I _____ English as a child, I _____ so many problems with it now.

EXERCISE 14 Complete each statement with a past or present result.

EXAMPLES: If I had taken the TOEFL® test last year, _I wouldn't have passed it._

If I hadn't brought my book to class today, _I wouldn't be able to do_ _this exercise._

1. If I hadn't taken this course, _____

2. If I hadn't taken beginning English, _____

3. If I hadn't come to class today, _____

4. If I hadn't studied for the last test, _____

5. If I hadn't paid last month's rent, _____

6. If I had been born 200 years ago, _____

EXERCISE 15 Complete each statement with a past or present condition.

EXAMPLES: I would have saved money if _I had bought a used book._

I would have studied last night if _we were having a test today._

1. I would have stayed after class yesterday if _____

2. I would have stayed home today if _____

3. I would have done better on the last test if _____

4. The teacher would have explained the last lesson again if _____

5. I would have taken an easier course if _____

6. I would have studied English when I was a child if _____

7. My parents would have been disappointed in me if _____

Fill in the blanks with the correct form of an appropriate verb. Some sentences have mixed tenses.

EXAMPLES: I took a wrong turn on the highway. I arrived at the meeting one hour late.
If I __*hadn't taken*__ a wrong turn on the highway, I __*would have arrived*__ at the meeting on time.

1. I forgot to set my alarm clock, so I didn't wake up on time. I _____ _____ on time if I _____ my alarm clock.

2. She didn't pass the final exam, so she didn't pass the course. If she _____ the final exam, she _____ _____ the course.

3. I didn't see the movie, so I can't give you any information about it. If I _____ the movie, I _____ you some information about it.

4. I don't like potatoes, so I didn't eat the potato salad. I _____ _____ the potato salad if I _____ potatoes.

5. He loves her, so he married her. If he _____ her, he _____ her.

6. She didn't hear the phone ring, so she didn't answer it. She _____ _____ the phone if she _____ it ring.

7. He left his keys at the office, so he couldn't get into the house. If he _____ his keys at the office, he _____ _____ into the house.

8. I don't have much money, so I didn't buy a new coat. I _____ _____ a new coat if I _____ more money.

9. He didn't take the medicine, so his condition didn't improve. If he _____ the medicine, his condition _____ .

10. I didn't have my credit card with me, so I didn't buy the computer I saw last week. I _____ the computer if I _____ my credit card with me.

EXERCISE 17 Complete each statement.

EXAMPLES: If I had a million dollars, _I would travel around the world._

If I had a computer, _I would have typed my last composition._

1. People would live longer if _____

_____

2. If I had lived in Italy as a child, _____

_____

3. The teacher would have skipped this lesson if _____

_____

4. I wouldn't have to work if _____

_____

5. If we had had a test on this lesson last week, _____

_____

6. If I could visit any country in the world, _____

_____

7. If everyone lived to be 150 years old, _____

_____

8. If I had lived in the nineteenth century, _____

_____

Before You Read
1. Do you wish you were a different age? What age?
2. Do you think the world would be better or worse if people lived to be 150 years old?

Read the following article. Pay special attention to the verbs after *wish*.

Growing Older and Older and Older

When you were a child, did you wish you **were** older? Most youngsters, especially teenagers, are in a hurry to grow up. They don't want their parents to make decisions for them. They wish they **could make** all their own decisions.

But as people age, they often wish they **were** younger. Or they wish they **could live** longer without looking or feeling old. Ponce de Leon, a Spanish explorer, came to America in the 1500s with hopes of discovering the fountain of youth. Until recently, however, wishing for youth or longer life has always been just a dream.

Recent research on aging shows promise that science will know how to give us a much longer, healthier life. In laboratory experiments, scientists have been able to double the life span of fruit flies from 70 days to 140 days. They have also been able to produce mice that live 30 percent longer than the average mouse. If these experiments worked in humans, that would mean that we would be able to live 100 to 150 years.

Do you wish you **could live** 150 years?

10.6 Wishes

Time	Real Situation	Wish Statement
Present	I **am** not young.	I wish I **were** younger.
	Teenagers **can't make** all their own decisions.	They wish they **could make** all their own decisions.
	I **am not working**.	I wish I **were working**.
Past	I **ate** too much, and now I feel sick.	I wish I **hadn't eaten** so much.
	I **didn't meet** you 10 years ago.	I wish I **had met** you 10 years ago.
	I **couldn't go** to the party last Saturday.	I wish I **could have gone** to the party last Saturday.

LANGUAGE NOTES

1. We often wish for things that are not real or true at the time of the wish. The verb after *wish* is like the verb in a clause of unreal condition. COMPARE:

   If my parents *were* here, I'd be happy. → I wish my parents *were* here.

   If I *had known* about the meeting, I would have attended it. → I wish I *had known* about the meeting.

2. If the real situation uses *could*, use *could have* + past participle after *wish*.

> I *couldn't* study English as a child. I wish I *could have studied* English as a child.

3. After *wish, that* can introduce the clause, but it is usually omitted.

> I wish (*that*) my parents were here.

4. With *be, were* is the correct form for all subjects. In conversation, however, you will often hear Americans use *was* with *I, he, she*, and *it*.

> FORMAL: I wish he *were* here.
> INFORMAL: I wish he *was* here.

5. In conversation, you often hear Americans use *would have* + past participle for past wishes.

> FORMAL: I wish you *had told* me the truth.
> INFORMAL: I wish you *would have told* me the truth.

EXERCISE 18 Fill in the blanks to make a wish about the present.

EXAMPLE: Today isn't Friday. I wish it ___*were*___ Friday.

1. You're not here with me. I wish you _____ here.

2. I have to work 60 hours a week. I wish I _____ work so much.

3. I can't speak English perfectly. I wish I _____ English perfectly.

4. I don't have a car. I wish I _____ a car.

5. You're going on vacation to Hawaii, but I can't go with you. I wish I _____ with you.

6. I'm not rich. I wish I _____ rich.

7. I have a lot of responsibilities. I wish I _____ so many responsibilities.

8. I don't have time to read much. I wish I _____ more time to read.

9. I'm not 18 years old. I wish I _____ .

10. I don't have the energy of a young person. I wish I _____ the energy of a young person.

11. Do you wish you _____ to be 150 years old?

12. I can't speak French. I wish _____ French.

EXERCISE 19 Fill in the blanks to complete each statement.

EXAMPLE: I wish I had ___*more time to spend with my family.*___

1. I wish I were _____
2. I wish I knew how to _____
3. I wish I didn't have to _____
4. I wish I had _____
5. I wish I could _____

EXERCISE 20 Fill in the blanks to make a wish about the past.

EXAMPLE: You didn't see the movie. I wish you ___*had seen it.*___

1. I didn't know it was your birthday. I wish I _____.
   I would have baked you a cake.

2. I didn't go to the concert. Everyone said it was wonderful. I wish
   I _____.

3. I didn't see the parade. I wish I _____ it.

4. I studied German in high school. I wish I _____
   _____ English instead.

5. I didn't see his face when he opened the present. I wish I _____
   _____ his face.

6. I lost my favorite ring. I was wearing it at the party. I wish I _____
   _____ it at home.

7. I told Larry my secret, and he told all his friends. I wish I _____
   _____ him my secret.

8. I forgot to bring my photo album when I moved to this city. I wish
   I _____ it.

EXERCISE 21 Name something.

EXAMPLE: Name something you wish had never happened.
             I wish the war had never happened.

1. Name something you wish you had done when you were younger.

2. Name something you wish you had studied when you were younger.

3. Name something your family wishes you had done differently.

4. Name something you wish you had known before you came to this city.

5. Name something you wish you had done when you were younger.

6. Name something you wish your parents had done or told you.

7. Name something you wish you had never done.

8. Name something you wish had never happened.

EXERCISE 22 Complete each statement with a wish about the present or past.

EXAMPLES: I'm not fluent in English. I wish I ___*were*___ fluent in English.

             I didn't prepare for the last test. I wish I ___*had prepared*___ for it.

1. I don't have a car. I wish I _____ a car.

2. I have to go to the dentist today. I wish I _____ go to the dentist.

3. I didn't have the opportunity to travel when I was younger. I wish I _____ the opportunity to visit other countries.

4. I'm in the U.S. My sister is in Poland. I wish we _____ together.

5. I can't type fast. I wish I _____ fast.

6. I bought a computer with a small memory. I wish I _____ _____ a computer with more memory.

7. My friend couldn't attend the concert with me last night. I wish she _____ the concert with me.

8. I didn't meet you ten years ago. I wish I _____ you ten years ago.

9. I didn't study English as a child. I wish I _____ English when I was young.

10. I don't know how to dance. I wish I _____ how to dance.

11. You can sing so beautifully, and I can't even carry a tune. I wish
I _____ as beautifully as you.

12. I couldn't help you last Saturday, and I know you needed me. I wish
I _____ .

10.7 *Wish* for Desired Changes

Examples	Explanation
I wish my neighbors **wouldn't make** so much noise.	I want them to make less noise.
I wish you **would visit** me more often.	I want you to visit me more often.
Your hair is too long. I wish you **would cut** it.	I want you to cut your hair.

LANGUAGE NOTES

Would + base form is used after *wish* to show that a person wants something different to happen. The speaker can wish for something good to happen or something bad to stop. *Wish* without *would* is not a desire for change but an expression of discontent with the present situation. Compare these sentences with *wish*.

I wish my parents *would visit* me. (I want them to visit me.)
I wish I *were* younger. (I'm unhappy that I'm not younger.)

EXERCISE 23 Fill in the blanks to show a desire that someone do something differently.

EXAMPLE: My parents are going back to my country. I wish they *would stay here.*

1. Are you leaving so soon? I wish you _____ for a few more hours.

2. My son doesn't want to clean his room. I wish he _____ his room.

3. My daughter wants to use the Internet all day. I wish she _____ _____ with her friends instead of sitting in front of the computer all day.

4. My apartment is too cold. I wish the landlord _____ more heat.

5. Some students are talking so loudly in the library that I can't think. I wish they _____.

6. My son's hair is so long. I don't like long hair on a boy. I wish he _____ his hair.

7. The teacher gives a lot of homework. I wish she _____ _____ so much homework.

8. My friend doesn't want to go to the party with me. I wish he _____ _____ to the party with me.

EXERCISE 24 Fill in the blanks to complete these statements. Your wish can include a desire for a change (by using *would*) or it can simply state that you're unhappy with the way things are right now.

EXAMPLES: I wish the class _*didn't have so many students.*_

I wish my parents _*would let me go out with my friends.*_

1. I wish my family _____

2. I wish the teacher _____

3. I wish my neighbors _____

4. I wish the government _____

5. I wish more people _____

6. I wish my apartment _____

EXERCISE 25 *Combination Exercise.* Two men are talking about a problem that one of them is having. Fill in the blanks to complete this conversation.

A. I have a problem. I need your advice.

B. What is it?

A. My wife's mother is going to come to visit for a month. A week's OK, but a month is too long.

B. If I _*were*_ you, I _____ tell her that she can visit, but
       (example)   (1)
    only for one week.

A. I wish I _____ tell her that, but my wife, Brenda, insists that
                     (2)
    she stay for a month.

B. What's so terrible about her?

A. Well, when she babysits for our kids, she tells them the opposite of what my wife and I tell them. For example, we tell the kids to go to bed at 9 o'clock. But she tells them that they can stay up as late as they like. I wish she _____ them the same rules we do.
(3)

B. At least you get a free babysitter. I wish my children _____ a
(4)
grandmother to babysit for them. But their grandparents live in Peru.

A. I wish my mother-in-law _____ in Peru. Unfortunately, she lives
(5)
in Minneapolis and visits twice a year.

B. I think you're making too much of the problem.

A. But there's more. The last time she was here, she gave the kids an expensive video game.

B. What's so bad about that?

A. We told the kids that they couldn't play video games. If she _____
(6 ask)

_____ us before buying them the game, we _____
(7 tell)

_____ her that we don't allow video games in our house. But she never asked us. The kids think that we're mean and that Grandma is nice.

B. Maybe she has nothing to do. If she _____ a life of her own,
(8)

maybe she _____ you so often.
(9)

A. The problem is that she isn't interested in anything, except interfering in our lives.

B. Can't she stay at a hotel while she's visiting?

A. Hotels are expensive. If I _____ a lot of money, I _____
(10)   (11)
definitely put her in a hotel.

B. I wish I _____ help you, but I can't.
(12)

A. I know. I just needed to talk to someone about it. If I _____
(13 know)

_____ that Brenda's mother was such a busybody,[5] I

_____ Brenda.
(14 not/marry)

B. I'm sure you don't mean that.

[5] A *busybody* is a person who interferes in other people's lives.

EXERCISE 26 *Combination Exercise.* Fill in the blanks to complete the conversation.

A. Are you happy you came to the U.S.?

B. Yes, I'm glad I'm here. But I wish I ___had come___ here when my
   (example)
   brother came here 15 years ago.

A. Why?

B. Well, now I'm 40 years old, and it's harder to learn English and find
   a good job. I didn't study English when I was a child. I wish I
   _____ it when I was younger.
   (1)

A. But your brother learned English quickly.

B. He was only 18 when he came here. Now he speaks English well, has
   a small business, and owns a big house. If I _____
   (2)
   here when he came here, I _____ successful
   (3)
   now. But now I have to start everything from the beginning. I wish I
   _____ to start so many new things at my age.
   (4)

A. Did your parents come here too?

B. No. My parents are alone in my country. I've asked them to come
   here. I wish they _____ here, but they're too old to make
   (5)
   such a big change. If they _____ here, they _____ have
   (6)   *(7)*
   to go to school to learn English. They're in their late seventies. If
   they _____ here, their life _____ much more difficult
   (8)   *(9)*
   than it is now.

A. There are a lot of things I wish _____ different in my life too.
   (10)

B. What, for example?

A. I got married when I was only 18. I wish I _____
   (11)
   married so young. And I had my first son when I was only 20. I think
   I _____ a better parent if I _____
   (12)   *(13)*
   _____ until I was older. I'm attending college
   now, and it's hard with so many family responsibilities. I wish I
   _____ to college when I was 18.
   (14)

B. It's too bad we can't go back and start our lives again. I wish I
_____ back and use the knowledge I have now to make
     (15)
better choices.

A. Who knows . . . we may live to be 150 years old and have time to
do all the things we wish we _____ do.
                                              (16)

B. If everyone _____ to be 150 years old,
                        (17)
the world _____ very crowded and there _____
                  (18)
_____ enough food or other resources for everybody.
     (19)

A. Maybe you're right. We should just do the best we can with the time
we have.

SUMMARY OF LESSON 10

1. Unreal Conditions—Present

Verb → Past	Verb → *Would/Might/Could* + Base Form
If I **were** you,	I **would quit** my job.
If she **didn't have** children,	she **would have** more free time.
If we **had** more time,	we **could go** to the movies more often.
If she **were living** in Paris,	she **would be** much happier.
If I **could** speak English perfectly,	I **might have** more opportunities.
If I **were** in Hawaii,	I **would be sitting** on a beach right now.

2. Unreal Conditions—Past

Verb → Past Perfect	Verb → *Would/Might/Could* + *Have* + Past Participle
If he **had seen** the accident,	he **would have reported** it to the police.
If you **had told** me about your problem,	I **could have helped** you.
If I **hadn't come** here,	I **wouldn't have met** you.
If you **had seen** the movie,	you **might have enjoyed** it.

3.   Mixed Tenses

Present Condition	Past Result
If she **were** rich,	she **would have sent** her kids to private school.
If I **had** your phone number,	I **would have called** you yesterday.
If I **were** you,	I **would have quit** my job a long time ago.

Past Condition	Present Result
If she **had married** him,	she **would be** very unhappy now.
If I **had stayed** home today,	I **wouldn't be reviewing** this lesson.

4.   Real Possibilities for the Future

Condition	Future Result
If you **need** my help next Sunday,	I **will help** you.
If she **is** late,	she **will miss** an important explanation.

5.   Wishes

Present	Past
I wish I **had** more money.	I wish I **had studied** English when I was younger.
I wish I **could fly**.	I wish you **had called** me.
I wish you **would turn** off the TV.	I wish I **hadn't spoken** so quickly.

EDITING ADVICE ✏

1. Don't use *will* with an unreal condition.

> If I ~~will be~~ ^{were} rich, I would buy a house.

2. Don't include *be* if you have another verb.

> If I knew more English, I would ~~be~~ find a better job.

3. Always use the base form after a modal.

> She would ~~has~~ ^{have} called you if she had your phone number.

4. Use the past perfect, not the present perfect, for unreal conditions and wishes.

> If she ~~has~~ ^{had} studied harder, she wouldn't have failed the test.
>
> I wish I ~~have~~ ^{had} seen that movie.

LESSON 10 TEST / REVIEW

PART 1 Find the mistakes with the underlined words, and correct them. Not every sentence has a mistake. If the sentence is correct, write **C**.

EXAMPLES: What ~~will~~ ^{would} you do if you had a million dollars?

I wouldn't be able to visit my friends if I <u>didn't have</u> a car.   C

1. I don't have much money. If I <u>have</u> a lot of money, I'd travel around the world.

2. I <u>will be</u> happier if my family were here.

3. I don't have any time. If I had time, I'd <u>help</u> my friend today.

4. If I <u>could meet</u> the President, I would tell him that he's doing a great job.

5. I'm unhappy because my daughter can't come here. I <u>will be</u> happy if my daughter could live with me.

6. I wish I <u>could speak</u> English perfectly.

7. If I <u>will be</u> you, I would buy a new car.

8. If I didn't have to study English, I <u>would be have</u> more free time.

9. I have a car. I wouldn't be able to find a job here if I <u>don't have</u> a car.

10. If she hadn't repaired the brakes on her car, she <u>might have had</u> an accident.

11. The teacher <u>would has explained</u> the grammar more slowly if she had had more time.

12. I came here when I was 40 years old. I wish I <u>had come</u> here when I was younger.

13. Can you help me?—Sorry. If I could, I <u>would</u>.

14. If I <u>would be</u> young, I would have more energy.

15. I'm sorry I didn't call you yesterday. I <u>would call</u> you if I hadn't been so busy.

16. I didn't know about the party so I didn't go. I wish I <u>have known</u> about it.

17. Mary hates Paul. She wouldn't marry him even if he <u>were</u> the last man on earth.

18. I wish you <u>would call</u> me more often.

19. What would you do if you <u>find</u> a wallet with a lot of money in it?

20. I got an invitation to my sister's graduation. I <u>wouldn't have been able to</u> go without the invitation.

21. I heard you saw a great movie last night. I wish I <u>have gone</u> with you.

22. If he <u>has been</u> more careful, the accident wouldn't have happened.

PART 2

Some of the following sentences contain real conditions; some contain unreal conditions. Write the letter of the correct words to fill in the blanks.

1. I _____ drive to Canada if I had a car.
   a. were   b. will   c. would   d. would be

2. I might go shopping next Saturday. If I _____ shopping next Saturday, I'll buy you a scarf.
   a. will go   b. went   c. would go   d. go

3. If I _____ you, I'd move to a different apartment.
   a. were   b. am   c. will be   d. would be

4. I can't help you. I would help you if I _____ .
    a. can   b. could   c. will be able to   d. would

5. I might have to work next Monday. If I have to work, I _____ be able to come to class.
    a. wouldn't   b. won't   c. weren't   d. wasn't

6. My life would be easier if I _____ more English.
    a. knew   b. know   c. will know   d. would know

7. She has three children. She has no time to study. If she _____ children, she would have more time to study.
    a. doesn't have   b. weren't have   c. wouldn't have   d. didn't have

8. It's raining now. If it _____ now, I'd go for a walk.
    a. isn't raining   c. weren't raining
    b. doesn't raining   d. wouldn't raining

9. She wouldn't tell you the secret even if you _____ her a million dollars.
    a. would be pay   b. paid   c. will pay   d. pay

10. If I could live in any city in the world, I _____ in Paris.
    a. will live   b. would have lived   c. would live   d. live

11. I don't have a house. I wish I _____ a house.
    a. had   b. will have   c. have had   d. have

12. I can't drive a car. I wish I _____ a car.
    a. could drive   b. can drive   c. would drive   d. will drive

13. If I had known how difficult it was to learn English, I _____ it when I was young.
    a. would study   c. would studied
    b. would had studied d. would have studied

14. He never exercised and was overweight. He had a heart attack and died when he was 50 years old. If he _____ better care of himself, he might have lived much longer.
    a. would take   b. took   c. had taken   d. will take

15. He needs more driving lessons before he can take the driver's license test. If he _____ the test last week, he would have failed it.
    a. were taken   b. would take   c. has taken   d. had taken

16. I didn't have time to call you yesterday. I _____ you if I had had more free time.
    a. would call   b. will call   c. would have called   d. would called

17. He was driving without a seat belt and had a car accident. He was seriously injured. If he had been wearing his seat belt, he _____ such a serious injury.
    a. might not have had   c. wouldn't had
    b. didn't have   d. hadn't had

18. Nobody told me we were going to have a test today. I wish someone _____ me.

    a. would tell   b. had told   c. would told   d. were told

19. Why didn't you tell me about your move last week? If you had told me, I _____ you.

    a. could have helped   c. could help
    b. could helped   d. could had helped

20. My roommate talks on the phone all the time. I wish he _____ on the phone so much.

    a. won't talk   c. wouldn't talk
    b. doesn't talk   d. wouldn't have talked

EXPANSION ACTIVITIES

CLASSROOM ACTIVITIES

1. Do you think the world would be better or worse if . . . ? Form a small group and discuss your reasons.

   a) If there were no computers?

   b) If everyone were the same religion or race?

   c) If everyone spoke the same language?

   d) If we could live to be about 150 years old?

   e) If people didn't have to work?

   f) If families were allowed to have only one child?

   g) If every job paid the same salary?

   h) If people decided on the sex (male or female), physical characteristics, or personality of their children?

2. Fill in the blanks. Share your sentences in a small group.

   a) If I could change one thing about myself (or my life), I'd change _____

   _____

   b) If I lost my _____, I'd be very upset.

   c) Most people would be happier if _____

   d) If I could travel to the past, _____

e) If I could travel to the future, _____

f) The world would be a better place if _____

g) I wish I were _____ years old.

3. Fill in the blanks and explain your answers.

   If I had known _____,

   I would (not) have _____.

EXAMPLE: If I had known that I needed computer skills in the U.S., I would have studied computers in my native country.

4. Fill in the blanks and explain your answer.

   I didn't _____, but I wish I had.

   I _____, but I wish I hadn't.

5. Write some sentences about your job, your school, your apartment, or your family. What do you wish were different? Share your answers in a small group.

EXAMPLES: I have to work on Saturdays. I wish I didn't have to work on Saturdays.
             My son watches TV all day. I wish he would play with his friends more.

6. On a piece of paper or index card, finish this sentence:

   I would be happier if _____.

   The teacher will collect the cards or papers and read each statement. The rest of the class has to guess who wrote it. (Many people will write "*if I were rich,*" so try to think of something else.)

DISCUSSION

1. If you could meet anyone in the world, who would you want to meet?

2. If you had the brain of another person, who would you be?

3. Since Albert Einstein's death in 1955, his brain has been kept in a jar for study. If it were possible to create a new Einstein from a brain cell, would it be a good idea to do so? Why or why not?

4. If you had the possibility of making a clone of yourself or a member of your family, would you do it? Why or why not?

5. If you could "design" your child—sex, hair color, intelligence, athletic ability, personality, attractiveness—would you do it?

6. If you adopted a child, would you tell your child that he or she is adopted?

7. In 1987, two families discovered that their children had been switched at birth. They discovered the mistake when, at the age of ten, one of the girls needed surgery. A blood test before the surgery revealed that she couldn't have been the biological child of her parents. The girl died, and later the family found their biological daughter. They went to court to determine where the girl should live. The judge decided to leave her with the family who had raised her. What would you have decided if you were the judge? What would you have wanted if you were the biological mother of the girl? What would you have wanted if you were the girl?

8. In Lesson Six, we read about Tim Berners-Lee, the creator of the World Wide Web. He has never made any money from the Web. Do you think he would have tried to make money on his idea if he had known how popular the Web was going to become?

9. In Lesson Five, we read about the death of President Kennedy. Do you think his death could have been prevented if he had had more security?

WRITING

1. Write about personality traits or bad habits you have. Write how your life would be different if you didn't have these traits or habits. (Or you can write about the habits or traits of another person you know well.)

EXAMPLES:

If I exercised, my health would be better.
If my son weren't so lazy, he'd be able to accomplish much more in his life.

2. Write about an event in history. Tell what the result would or might have been if this event hadn't happened.

3. Write about how your life would have been different if you had stayed in the same place your whole life.

4. Write about some things in your life that you are not happy about. How would you want to change your life?

OUTSIDE ACTIVITIES

1. Ask an American friend or classmate to answer the questions in the first classroom activity. Report this person's answers to the class.

2. Rent one of these movies: *Cocoon, Sleeper.*

Internet Activity

1. At a search engine, type in "human genome project." Find an interesting article. Bring it to class.

2. Who are James Watson and Francis Crick? Why are these names important? Find some information about these men on the Web.

3. At a search engine, type in "aging." Find an interesting article to bring to class.

Appendices

APPENDIX A

Noncount Nouns

The following groups of words are classified as noncount nouns.

Group A. Nouns that have no distinct, separate parts. We look at the whole:

air	coffee	oil	tea
blood	electricity	paper	thunder
bread	lightning	pork	water
butter	meat	poultry	wine
cholesterol	milk	soup	yogurt

Group B. Nouns that have parts that are too small or insignificant to count:

corn	popcorn	sand
grass	rice	snow
hair	salt	sugar

NOTE: Count and noncount nouns are grammatical terms, but they are not always logical. *Rice* is very small and is a noncount noun. *Beans* and *peas* are also very small but are count nouns.

Group C. Nouns that are classes or categories of things:

food (vegetables, meat, spaghetti)
furniture (chairs, tables, beds)
clothing (sweaters, pants, dresses)
mail (letters, packages, postcards, fliers)
fruit (cherries, apples, grapes)
makeup (lipstick, rouge, eye shadow)
homework (compositions, exercises, reading)
jewelry (necklaces, bracelets, rings)
housework (washing dishes, dusting, cooking)
money or cash (nickels, dimes, dollars)

(continued)

Group D. Nouns that are abstractions:

advice	fun	life	patience
art	happiness	love	pollution
beauty	health	luck	time
crime	help	music	trouble
education	information	nature	truth
energy	intelligence	noise	unemployment
experience	knowledge	nutrition	work

Group E. Subjects of study:

biology	geometry	history
chemistry	grammar	math (mathematics)*

*NOTE: Even though *mathematics* ends with *s*, it is not plural.

Notice the quantity words used with count and noncount nouns:

Singular Count	Plural Count	Noncount
a tomato	tomatoes	coffee
one tomato	**two** tomatoes	**two cups of** coffee
	some tomatoes	**some** coffee
no tomato	**no** tomatoes	**no** coffee
	any tomatoes (with questions and negatives)	**any** coffee
	a lot of tomatoes	**a lot of** coffee
	many tomatoes	**much** coffee (with questions and negatives)
	a few tomatoes	**a little** coffee
	several tomatoes	
	How many tomatoes?	**How much** coffee?

The following words can be used as either count nouns or noncount nouns. However, the meaning changes according to the way the nouns are used.

Count	Noncount
Oranges and grapefruit are **fruits** that contain a lot of vitamin C.	I bought some **fruit** at the fruit store.
Ice cream and butter are **foods** that contain cholesterol.	We don't need to go shopping today. We have a lot of **food** at home.
He wrote a **paper** about hypnosis.	I need some **paper** to write my composition.

(continued)

Count	Noncount
He committed three **crimes** last year.	There is a lot of **crime** in a big city.
I have 200 **chickens** on my farm.	We ate some **chicken** for dinner.
I don't want to bore you with all my **troubles**.	I have some **trouble** with my car.
She went to Puerto Rico three **times**.	She spent a lot of **time** on her project.
She drank three **glasses** of water.	The window is made of bulletproof **glass**.
I had a bad **experience** during my trip to Paris.	She has some **experience** with computer programming.
I don't know much about the **lives** of my grandparents.	**Life** is sometimes happy, sometimes sad.
I heard a **noise** outside my window.	Those children are making a lot of **noise**.

APPENDIX B

Uses of Articles

Overview of Articles

Articles tell us if a noun is definite or indefinite.

	Count		Noncount
	Singular	Plural	
Definite	**the** book	**the** books	**the** coffee
Indefinite	**a** book	**(some/any)** books	**(some/any)** coffee

Part A: Uses of the Indefinite Article

1. To classify the subject
2. To make a generalization
3. To introduce an indefinite noun into a conversation

To Classify the Subject

1. We use *a/an* after the verb *be* to classify, define, or identify a singular subject:

What's Chicago?[1]	It's **a city**.
What's Illinois?	It's **a state**.
Who was Abraham Lincoln?	He was **an American President**.
What's this? ★	It's **a star**.

(continued)

---

[1] Proper nouns (names) do not usually use articles.

2. We use no article after *be* to classify a plural subject:

What are Poland and Russia?	They're **countries**.
What are these? ♥ ♥	They're **hearts**.
Who were Lincoln and Washington?	They were **American Presidents**.

To Make a Generalization

To say that something is true of all members of a group:

1. With a count noun, use *a(n)* + singular form or no article + plural form:

A **dog** has sharp teeth.	**An elephant** has big ears.
OR	OR
Dogs have sharp teeth.	**Elephants** have big ears.

2. With a noncount noun, use no article:

Coffee contains caffeine.
Milk is white.
Love makes people happy.
Time passes quickly when you're having fun.
Money can't buy **happiness**.

To Introduce an Indefinite Noun into a Conversation

When we introduce a new noun into a conversation, the noun is indefinite. The speaker may or may not have something specific in mind, but the listener does not.

1. Use the indefinite article *a(n)* with singular count nouns. With plural nouns, you can use *some* or *any* to show an indefinite quantity.

   I had **a dog** when I was a child.
   I had **(some) turtles** when I was a child.
   Do you have **(any) questions** about this lesson?

2. You can use the indefinite quantity words *some/any* with noncount nouns.

   I have **(some) money** in my pocket.
   Do you want **(any) milk** with your lunch?

3. *There* + a form of *be* can introduce an indefinite noun into a conversation.

   Is there **an elevator** in this building?
   Are there **(any) public telephones** in this building?
   There is **(some) money** on the table.

NOTE: *Some* or *any* can be omitted before an indefinite noun.

Part B: Uses of the Definite Article

1. To refer to a previously introduced noun
2. When the speaker and the listener have the same reference
3. With certain familiar places
4. To make a formal, general statement

After an indefinite noun comes into the conversation, the speaker talks about it again by using the definite article.

1. COUNT NOUNS:

> I had a dog when I was a child. My father gave me **the dog** for Christmas.
> I had some turtles when I was a child. I kept **the turtles** in my room.

2. NONCOUNT:

> I need some sugar. I need **the sugar** to bake a cake.

> Did you buy any coffee? Yes. **The coffee** is in the cabinet.

The definite article shows that the speaker and listener have the same person(s) or object(s) in mind for one of these reasons:

1. The object is present:

> COUNT: **The dog** has big ears.
>   **The cats** are sleeping.
> NONCOUNT: **The milk** is sour. Don't drink it.

2. There is only one:

> **The sun** is not very bright in the winter.
> There are many problems in **the world**.
> Write your name on **the top** of the page. (The page has only one top.)
> Sign your name on **the back** of the check. (The check has only one back.)
> The Amazon is **the longest** river in the world.
> December is **the last** month of the year.

3. The speaker and listener share a common experience:

> Students in the same class talk about *the teacher, the textbook, the homework, the blackboard*, etc.
>   Did you do **the homework** last night?
> People who live together talk about *the house, the door, the windows, the light switch*, etc.
>   When you leave **the house**, please turn off **the lights**.
> People who live in the same country talk about *the President, the government, the flag*, etc.
>   Did you see **the President** on TV last night?

4. The speaker defines or specifies exactly which one:

> **The house on the corner** is beautiful.
> I spent **the money you gave me**.

1. We often use *the* with certain familiar places and people—*the bank, the zoo, the park, the store, the movies, the beach, the post office, the bus/train, the doctor*—when we refer to one that we habitually visit or use.

   I'm going to **the store** after work. Do you need anything?
   The bank is closed. I'll go tomorrow.

2. We omit *the* with some places after a preposition *(to, at, in)*.

   He's **in church**.
   I'm going **to school**.
   They're **at work**.
   I'm going **to bed**.

3. We say *go home* and *go downtown* without the article or the preposition.

   I'm going **home** now.
   Are you going **downtown** after class?

4. When we say *go to college* or *be in college*, this means to be a student at a college or university.

   Is your son in high school?

   No. He goes **to college** now.

   OR

   No. He's **in college** now.

1. We can use *the* with singular, count nouns to make a formal, general statement. We do this with the following categories:

   A. Species:

   The shark is the oldest and most primitive fish.
   The bat is a nocturnal animal. It hunts for food at night.

   shark   bat

   B. Inventions:

   The computer has changed the way Americans deal with information.
   Bell invented **the telephone**.

   C. Organs of the body:

   The heart is a muscle that has four chambers.
   The ear has three parts: outer, middle, and inner.

   D. In certain proverbs and sayings:

   The pen is mightier than **the sword**.
   The hand is quicker than **the eye**.
   Which came first, **the chicken** or **the egg**?

2. For informal generalizations, use *a* + singular noun or no article with a plural noun. Compare:

   The computer has changed the way Americans deal with information.   (FORMAL)
   Computers are expensive.   (INFORMAL)
   A **computer** is expensive.   (INFORMAL)

Part C: Special Uses of Articles

No Article	Article

Personal names:
    John Kennedy
    Michael Jackson
	The whole family:
	    the Kennedys
	    the Jacksons

Title and name:
    Queen Elizabeth
    Pope John Paul
	Title without name:
	    the Queen
	    the Pope

Cities, states, countries, continents:
    Cleveland
    Ohio
    Mexico
    South America
	Places that are considered a union:
	    the United States
	    the former Soviet Union
	    the United Kingdom
	Place names: the _____ of _____
	    the Republic of China
	    the District of Columbia

Mountains
    Mount Everest
    Mount McKinley
	Mountain ranges:
	    the Himalayas
	    the Rocky Mountains

Islands:
    Coney Island
    Staten Island
	Collectives of islands:
	    the Hawaiian Islands
	    the Virgin Islands
	    the Philippines

Lakes:
    Lake Superior
    Lake Michigan
	Collectives of lakes:
	    the Great Lakes
	    the Finger Lakes

Beaches:
    Palm Beach
    Pebble Beach
	Rivers, oceans, seas, canals:
	    the Mississippi River
	    the Atlantic Ocean
	    the Dead Sea
	    the Panama Canal

Streets and avenues:
    Madison Avenue
    Wall Street
	Well-known buildings:
	    the Sears Tower
	    the World Trade Center

Parks:
    Central Park
    Hyde Park
	Zoos:
	    the San Diego Zoo
	    the Milwaukee Zoo

Seasons:
    summer   fall
    spring   winter
    Summer is my favorite season.
NOTE: After a preposition, *the* may
be used.
    In (the) winter, my car runs
        badly.
	Deserts:
	    the Mojave Desert
	    the Sahara Desert

Directions:
    north   south
    east   west
	Sections of a piece of land:
	    the Southwest (of the U.S.)
	    the West Side (of New York)

(continued)

No Article	Article

School subjects:
   history
   math
	Unique geographical points:
	   the North Pole
	   the Vatican

Name + *college* or *university:*
   Northwestern University
   Bradford College
	The University (College) of _____
	   the University of Michigan
	   the College of DuPage County

Magazines:
   Time
   Sports Illustrated
	Newspapers:
	   the *Tribune*
	   the *Wall Street Journal*

Months and days:
   September
   Monday
	Ships:
	   the *Titanic*
	   the *Queen Elizabeth II*

Holidays and dates;
(month + day):
   Thanksgiving
   Mother's Day
   July 4
	The day of (month):
	   the Fourth of July
	   the fifth of May

Diseases:
   cancer
   polio
   AIDS
   malaria
	Ailments:
	   a cold
	   a headache
	   a toothache
	   the flu

Games and sports:
   poker
   soccer
	Musical instruments, after *play:*
	   the drums
	   the piano
	NOTE: Sometimes *the* is omitted.
	   She plays (the) drums.

Languages:
   French
   English
	The _____ language:
	   the French language
	   the English language

Last month, year, week, etc. = the one before this one:
   I forgot to pay my rent last month.
   The teacher gave us a test last week.
	The last month, the last year, the last week, etc. = the last in a series:
	   December is the last month of the year.
	   Summer vacation begins the last week in May.

In office = in an elected position:
   The president is in office for four years.
	In the office = in a specific room:
	   The teacher is in the office.

In back/front:
   She's in back of the car.
 	
	In the back/the front:
	   He's in the back of the bus.

The Verb *GET*

Get has many meanings. Here is a list of the most common ones:

- get something = receive

  I got a letter from my father.

- get + (to) place = arrive

  I got home at six. What time do you get to school?

- get + object + infinitive = persuade

  She got him to wash the dishes.

- get + past participle = become

get accustomed to	get dressed	get scared
get acquainted	get engaged	get tired
get bored	get hurt	get used to
get confused	get lost	get worried
get divorced	get married	

  They got married in 1989.

- get + adjective = become

get angry	get old
get dark	get rich
get fat	get sleepy
get hungry	get upset
get nervous	get well

  It gets dark at 6:30.

- get an illness = catch

  While I was traveling, I got malaria.

- get a joke or an idea = understand

  Everybody except Tom laughed at the joke. He didn't get it.

  The boss explained the project to us, but I didn't get it.

- get ahead = advance

  He works very hard because he wants to get ahead in his job.

- get along (well) (with someone) = have a good relationship

  She doesn't get along with her mother-in-law.

  Do you and your roommate get along well?

- get around to something = find the time to do something

  I wanted to write my brother a letter yesterday, but I didn't get around to it.

  (continued)

- get away = escape

  The police chased the thief, but he got away.

- get away with something = escape punishment

  He cheated on his taxes and got away with it.

- get back = return

  He got back from his vacation last Saturday.

- get back at someone = get revenge

  My brother wants to get back at me for stealing his girlfriend.

- get back to someone = communicate with someone at a later time

  I can't talk to you today. Can I get back to you tomorrow?

- get by = have just enough but nothing more

  On her salary, she's just getting by. She can't afford a car or a vacation.

- get in trouble = be caught and punished for doing something wrong

  They got in trouble for cheating on the test.

- get in(to) = enter a car

  She got in the car and drove away quickly.

- get out (of) = leave a car

  When the taxi arrived at the theater, everyone got out.

- get on = seat yourself on a bicycle, motorcycle, horse

  She got on the motorcycle and left.

- get on = enter a train, bus, airplane

  She got on the bus and took a seat in the back.

- get off = leave a bicycle, motorcycle, horse, train, bus, airplane

  They will get off the train at the next stop.

- get out of something = escape responsibility

  My boss wants me to help him on Saturday, but I'm going to try to get out of it.

- get over something = recover from an illness or disappointment

  She has the flu this week. I hope she gets over it soon.

- get rid of someone or something = free oneself of someone or something undesirable

  My apartment has roaches, and I can't get rid of them.

- get through (to someone) = communicate, often by telephone

  She tried to explain the harm of eating fast food to her son, but she couldn't get through to him.

  I tried to call my mother many times, but her line was busy. I couldn't get through.

- get through with something = finish

    I can meet you after I get through with my homework.

- get together = meet with another person

    I'd like to see you again. When can we get together?

- get up = arise from bed

    He woke up at 6 o'clock, but he didn't get up until 6:30.

APPENDIX **D**

Gerund and Infinitive Patterns

1. VERB + INFINITIVE:

	They need **to leave.** I learned **to speak** English.		
agree	claim	know how	seem
appear	consent	learn	swear
arrange	decide	manage	tend
ask	demand	need	threaten
attempt	deserve	offer	try
be able	expect	plan	volunteer
beg	fail	prepare	want
can afford	forget	pretend	wish
care	hope	promise	would like
choose	intend	refuse	

2. VERB + NOUN/OBJECT PRONOUN + INFINITIVE:

	I want you **to leave.** He expects me **to call** him.		
advise	convince	hire	require
allow	dare	instruct	select
appoint	enable	invite	teach
ask	encourage	need	tell
beg	expect	order	urge
cause	forbid	permit	want
challenge	force	persuade	warn
choose	get	remind	would like
command	help*		

*NOTE: After *help, to* is often omitted: "He helped me (to) move."

(continued)

3. ADJECTIVE + INFINITIVE:

> They're happy **to be** here.
> We're willing **to help** you.

afraid	disturbed	lucky	shocked
ashamed	eager	pleased	sorry
amazed	foolish	prepared	surprised
careful	fortunate	proud	upset
content	free	ready	willing
delighted	glad	reluctant	wrong
determined	happy	sad	
disappointed	likely		

4. VERB + GERUND:

> I enjoy **dancing**.
> They don't permit **drinking**.

admit	detest	miss	resent
advise	discuss	permit	resist
anticipate	dislike	postpone	risk
appreciate	enjoy	practice	stop
avoid	finish	put off	suggest
can't help	forbid	quit	tolerate
complete	imagine	recall	understand
consider	keep (on)	recommend	
delay	mention	regret	
deny	mind	remember	

5. EXPRESSIONS WITH GO + GERUND:

> He **goes fishing** every Saturday.
> They **went shopping** yesterday.

go boating	go hiking	go sightseeing
go bowling	go hunting	go skating
go camping	go jogging	go skiing
go dancing	go sailing	to swimming
go fishing	go shopping	

6. PREPOSITION + GERUND:

> Verb + Preposition + Gerund
> We talked about **moving**.
> I look forward to **having** my own apartment.

adjust to	concentrate on	forget about	refrain from
argue about	depend on	insist on	succeed in
believe in	(dis)approve of	look forward to	talk about
care about	dream about	object to	think about
complain about	feel like	plan on	worry about

> **Adjective + Preposition + Gerund**
> I'm fond of **traveling**.
> She's not accustomed to **eating** alone.

accustomed to	famous for	interested in	sure of
afraid of	fond of	lazy about	surprised at
appropriate for	good at	proud of	tired of
ashamed of	grateful to . . . for	responsible for	upset about
concerned about	guilty of	sorry about	used to
excited about	(in)capable of	suitable for	worried about

> **Verb + Object + Preposition + Gerund**
> I thanked him for **helping** me.
> I apologized to him for **forgetting** his birthday.

accuse . . . of	devote . . . to	prevent . . . from	suspect . . . of
apologize to . . . for	forgive . . . for	prohibit . . . from	thank . . . for
blame . . . for	keep . . . from	stop . . . from	warn . . . about

> **Gerund After Preposition in Certain Expressions**
> Who's in charge of **collecting** the papers?
> What is your reason for **coming** late?

need for	technique for	in charge of	in the middle of
reason for	interest in	in danger of	the point of
requirement for	impression of	in favor of	instead of

7. NOUN + GERUND:

> He has difficulty **speaking** English.
> She had a problem **finding** a job.
> She spent three weeks **looking** for an apartment.

Use a gerund after the noun in these expressions:

have a difficult time	have a hard time
have difficulty	have a problem
have experience	have trouble
have fun	spend time
have a good time	there's no use

8. VERB + GERUND OR INFINITIVE (with little or no difference in meaning):

> They like **to sing**.   I started **to read**.
> They like **singing**.   I started **reading**.

attempt	intend
begin	like
can't stand	love
continue	neglect
deserve	prefer
hate	start
hesitate	

Verbs and Adjectives Followed by a Preposition

accuse someone of	(be) familiar with	pray for
(be) accustomed to	(be) famous for	(be) prepared for
adjust to	feel like	prevent someone from
(be) afraid of	(be) fond of	prohibit someone from
agree with	forget about	protect someone from
(be) amazed at/by	forgive someone for	(be) proud of
(be) angry about	(be) glad about	recover from
(be) angry at/with	(be) good at	(be) related to
apologize for	(be) grateful to someone for	rely on/upon
approve of	(be) guilty of	(be) responsible for
argue about	(be) happy about	(be) sad about
argue with	hear about	(be) satisfied with
(be) ashamed of	hear of	(be) scared of
(be) aware of	hope for	(be) sick of
believe in	(be) incapable of	(be) sorry about/for
blame someone for	insist on/upon	speak about
(be) bored with/by	(be) interested in	speak to/with
(be) capable of	(be) involved in	succeed in
care about/for	(be) jealous of	(be) sure of/about
compare to/with	(be) known for	(be) surprised at
complain about	(be) lazy about	take care of
(be) concerned about	listen to	talk about
concentrate on	look at	talk to/with
consist of	look for	thank someone for
count on	look forward to	(be) thankful to someone for
deal with	(be) mad about	think about/of
decide on	(be) mad at	(be) tired of
depend on/upon	(be) made from/of	(be) upset about
(be) different from	(be) married to	(be) upset with
disapprove of	object to	(be) used to
(be) divorced from	(be) opposed to	wait for
dream about/of	participate in	warn someone about
(be) engaged to	plan on	(be) worried about
(be) excited about	pray to	worry about

Direct and Indirect Objects

1. The order of direct and indirect objects depends on the verb you use.

$$\overset{\text{IO}}{\text{his friend}} \quad \overset{\text{DO}}{\text{the answer}}$$

He told his friend the answer.

$$\overset{\text{DO}}{\text{the answer}} \quad \overset{\text{IO}}{\text{his friend}}$$

He explained the answer to his friend.

2. The order of the objects sometimes depends on whether you use a noun or a pronoun object.

```
S  V     IO       DO
He gave the woman the keys.
```

```
S  V    DO   IO
He gave them to her.
```

3. In some cases, the connecting preposition is *to;* in some cases, *for.* In some cases, there is no connecting preposition.

She'll serve lunch *to* her guests.
She reserved a seat *for* you.
I asked him a question.

Each of the following groups of words follows a specific pattern of word order and preposition choice.

Group I   **Pronouns affect word order.** The preposition is *to.*

Patterns: He gave a present to his wife. (DO to IO)
He gave his wife a present. (IO/DO)
He gave it to his wife. (DO to IO)
He gave her a present. (IO/DO)
He gave it to her. (DO to IO)

Verbs:	bring	lend	pass	sell	show	teach
	give	offer	pay	send	sing	tell
	hand	owe	read	serve	take	write

Group II   **Pronouns affect word order.** The preposition is *for.*

Patterns: He bought a car for his daughter. (DO for IO)
He bought his daughter a car. (IO/DO)
He bought it for his daughter. (DO for IO)
He bought her a car. (IO/DO)
He bought it for her. (DO for IO)

Verbs:	bake	buy	draw	get	make
	build	do	find	knit	reserve

Group III   **Pronouns don't affect word order.** The preposition is *to.*

Patterns: He explained the problem to his friend. (DO to IO)
He explained it to her. (DO to IO)

Verbs:	admit	introduce	recommend	say
	announce	mention	repeat	speak
	describe	prove	report	suggest
	explain			

(continued)

Group IV   Pronouns don't affect word order. The preposition is *for*.

Patterns: He cashed a check for his friend. (DO for IO)
He cashed it for her. (DO for IO)

Verbs: answer   change   design   open   prescribe
cash   close   fix   prepare   pronounce

Group V   Pronouns don't affect word order. No preposition is used.

Patterns: She asked the teacher a question. (IO/DO)
She asked him a question. (IO/DO)
It took me five minutes to answer the question. (IO/DO)

Verbs: ask   charge   cost   wish   take (with time)

APPENDIX G

Spelling and Pronunciation of Verbs

Spelling of the -*S* Form of Verbs

Rule	Base Form	-*S* Form
Add *s* to most verbs to make the -*s* form.	hope eat	hopes eats
When the base form ends in *s*, *z*, *sh*, *ch*, or *x*, add *es* and pronounce an extra syllable, /əz/.	miss buzz wash catch fix	misses buzzes washes catches fixes
When the base form ends in a consonant + *y*, change the *y* to *i* and add *es*.	carry worry	carries worries
When the base form ends in a vowel + *y*, do not change the *y*.	pay obey	pays obeys
Add *es* to *go* and *do*.	go do	goes does

Pronunciation of the -*S* Form
The -*s* form has three pronunciations.

A.   We pronounce /s/ if the verb ends in these voiceless sounds: /**p t k f**/.
hope—hopes   pick—picks
eat—eats   laugh—laughs

B. We pronounce /**z**/ if the verb ends in most voiced sounds.

live—lives	read—reads	sing—sings
grab—grabs	run—runs	borrow—borrows

C. When the base form ends in *s, z, sh, ch, x, se, ge,* or *ce,* we pronounce an extra syllable, /əz/.

miss—misses	watch—watches	change—changes
buzz—buzzes	fix—fixes	dance—dances
wash—washes	use—uses	

D. These verbs have a change in the vowel sound.

do /**du**/—does /**dʌz**/

say /**sei**/—says /**sɛz**/

Spelling of the *-ing* Form of Verbs

Rule	Base Form	*-ing* Form
Add *ing* to most verbs.	eat go study	eating going studying
For a one-syllable verb that ends in a consonant + vowel + consonant (CVC), double the final consonant and add *ing*.	p l a n | | | C V C s t o p | | | C V C s i t | | | C V C	planning stopping sitting
Do not double final *w, x,* or *y.*	show mix stay	showing mixing staying
For a two-syllable word that ends in CVC, double the final consonant only if the last syllable is stressed.	refér admít begín	referring admitting beginning
When the last syllable of a two-syllable word is not stressed, do not double the final consonant.	lísten ópen óffer	listening opening offering
If the word ends in a consonant + *e*, drop the *e* before adding *ing*.	live take write	living taking writing

(continued)

Spelling of the Past Tense of Regular Verbs

Rule	Base Form	-ed Form
Add *ed* to the base form to make the past tense of most regular verbs.	start kick	started kicked
When the base form ends in *e*, add *d* only.	die live	died lived
When the base form ends in a consonant + *y*, change the *y* to *i* and add *ed*.	carry worry	carried worried
When the base form ends in a vowel + *y*, do not change the *y*.	destroy stay	destroyed stayed
For a one-syllable word that ends in a consonant + vowel + consonant (CVC), double the final consonant and add *ed*.	s t o p | | | C V C p l u g | | | C V C	stopped plugged
Do not double final *w* or *x*.	sew fix	sewed fixed
For a two-syllable word that ends in CVC, double the final consonant only if the last syllable is stressed.	occúr permít	occurred permitted
When the last syllable of a two-syllable word is not stressed, do not double the final consonant.	ópen háppen	opened happened

Pronunciation of Past Forms That End in *-ed*

The past tense with *-ed* has three pronunciations.

A. We pronounce a /**t**/ if the base form ends in these voiceless sounds: /**p, k, f, s, š, č**/.

jump—jumped	cough—coughed	wash—washed
cook—cooked	kiss—kissed	watch—watched

B. We pronounce a /**d**/ if the base form ends in most voiced sounds.

rub—rubbed	charge—charged	bang—banged
drag—dragged	glue—glued	call—called
love—loved	massage—massaged	fear—feared
bathe—bathed	name—named	free—freed
use—used	learn—learned	

C. We pronounce an extra syllable /ə**d**/ if the base form ends in a /**t**/ or /**d**/ sound.

wait—waited	want—wanted	need—needed
hate—hated	add—added	decide—decided

Capitalization Rules

- The first word in a sentence: **My** friends are helpful.

- The word "I": My sister and **I** took a trip together.

- Names of people: **Michael Jackson**; **George Washington**

- Titles preceding names of people: **Doctor** (**Dr.**) **Smith**; **President Lincoln**; **Queen Elizabeth**; **Mr. Rogers**; **Mrs. Carter**

- Geographic names: the **United States**; **Lake Superior**; **California**; the **Rocky Mountains**; the **Mississippi River**

    NOTE: The word "the" in a geographic name is not capitalized.

- Street names: **Pennsylvania Avenue** (**Ave.**); **Wall Street** (**St.**); **Abbey Road** (**Rd.**)

- Names of organizations, companies, colleges, buildings, stores, hotels: the **Republican Party**; **Heinle and Heinle Publishers**; **Dartmouth College**; the **University of Wisconsin**; the **White House**; **Bloomingdale's**; the **Hilton Hotel**

- Nationalities and ethnic groups: **Mexicans**; **Canadians**; **Spaniards**; **Americans**; **Jews**; **Kurds**; **Eskimos**

- Languages: **English**; **Spanish**; **Polish**; **Vietnamese**; **Russian**

- Months: **January**; **February**

- Days: **Sunday**; **Monday**

- Holidays: **Christmas**; **Independence Day**

- Important words in a title: **Grammar in Context**; **The Old Man and the Sea**; **Romeo and Juliet**; **The Sound of Music**

    NOTE: Capitalize "the" as the first word of a title.

Plural Forms of Nouns

Regular Noun Plurals

Word Ending	Example Noun	Plural Addition	Plural Form	Pronunciation
Vowel	bee banana	+ s	bees bananas	/z/
s, ss, sh, ch, x, z	church dish box watch class	+ es	churches dishes boxes watches classes	/əz/
Voiceless consonants	cat lip month book	+ s	cats lips months books	/s/
Voiced consonants	card pin stove	+ s	cards pins stoves	/z/
Vowel + y	boy day key	+ s	boys days keys	/z/
Consonant + y	lady story party	ý + ies	ladies stories parties	/z/
Vowel + o	video radio	+ s	videos radios	/z/
Consonant + o	potato hero	+ es	potatoes heroes	/z/
EXCEPTIONS: photos, pianos, solos, altos, sporanos, autos, avocados				
f or fe	leaf knife	f + ves	leaves knives	/vz/
EXCEPTIONS: beliefs, chiefs, roofs, cliffs, chefs, sheriffs				

Irregular Noun Plurals

Singular	Plural	Explanation
man woman mouse tooth foot goose	men women mice teeth feet geese	Vowel change (NOTE: The first vowel in *women* is pronounced /I/.
sheep fish deer	sheep fish deer	No change
child person	children people (OR persons)	Different word form
	(eye)glasses belongings clothes goods groceries jeans pajamas pants/slacks scissors shorts	No singular form
alumnus cactus radius stimulus syllabus	alumni cacti OR cactuses radii stimuli syllabi OR syllabuses	us→i
analysis crisis hypothesis oasis parenthesis thesis	analyses crises hypotheses oases parentheses theses	is→es
appendix index	appendices OR appendixes indices OR indexes	ix→ices

(continued)

Singular	Plural	Explanation
bacterium	bacteria	um→a
criterion	criteria	ion→a
curriculum	curricula	on→a
datum	data	
medium	media	
memorandum	memoranda	
phenomenon	phenomena	
alga	algae	a→ae
formula	formulae OR	
	formulas	
vertebra	vertebrae	

APPENDIX J

Metric Conversion Chart

LENGTH

When You Know	Symbol	Multiply by	To Find	Symbol
inches	in	2.54	centimeters	cm
feet	ft	30.5	centimeters	cm
feet	ft	0.3	meters	m
yards	yd	0.91	meters	m
miles	mi	1.6	kilometers	km

When You Know	Symbol	Multiply by	To Find	Symbol
centimeters	cm	0.39	inches	in
centimeters	cm	0.32	feet	ft
meter	m	3.28	feet	ft
meters	m	1.09	yards	yd
kilometers	km	0.62	miles	mi

> NOTE:
> 1 foot = 12 inches
> 1 yard = 3 feet or 36 inches

AREA

When You Know	Symbol	Multiply by	To Find	Symbol
square inches	in²	6.5	square centimeters	cm²
square feet	ft²	0.09	square meters	m²
square yards	yd²	0.8	square meters	m²
square miles	mi²	2.6	square kilometers	km²

When You Know	Symbol	Multiply by	To Find	Symbol
square centimeters	cm²	0.16	square inches	in²
square meters	m²	10.76	square feet	ft²
square meters	m²	1.2	square yards	yd²
square kilometers	km²	0.39	square miles	mi²

WEIGHT (Mass)

When You Know	Symbol	Multiply by	To Find	Symbol
ounces	oz	28.35	grams	g
pounds	lb	0.45	kilograms	kg

When You Know	Symbol	Multiply by	To Find	Symbol
grams	g	0.04	ounces	oz
kilograms	kg	2.2	pounds	lb

NOTE:
16 ounces = 1 pound

(continued)

VOLUME

When You Know	Symbol	Multiply by	To Find	Symbol
fluid ounces	fl oz	30.0	milliliters	mL
pints	pt	0.47	liters	L
quarts	qt	0.95	liters	L
gallons	gal	3.8	liters	L

When You Know	Symbol	Multiply by	To Find	Symbol
milliliters	mL	0.03	fluid ounces	fl oz
liters	L	2.11	pints	pt
liters	L	1.05	quarts	qt
liters	L	0.26	gallons	gal

TEMPERATURE

When You Know	Symbol	Do This	To Find	Symbol
degrees Fahrenheit	°F	Subtract 32, then multiply by 5/9	degrees Celsius	°C

When You Know	Symbol	Do This	To Find	Symbol
degrees Celsius	°C	Multiply by 9/5, then add 32	degrees Fahrenheit	°F

Sample temperatures:

Fahrenheit	Celsius
0	−18
10	−12
20	−7
30	−1
40	4
50	10
60	16
70	21
80	27
90	32
100	38

APPENDIX K

Comparative and Superlative Forms

The chart below shows comparative and superlative forms.

	Simple	Comparative	Superlative
One-syllable adjectives and adverbs	tall fast	taller faster	the tallest the fastest
EXCEPTIONS:	bored tired	more bored more tired	the most bored the most tired
Two-syllable adjectives that end end in -y	easy happy pretty	easier happier prettier	the easiest the happiest the prettiest
Other two-syllable adjectives	frequent active	more frequent more active	the most frequent the most active
Some two-syllable adjectives have two forms.	simple common	simpler more simple commoner more common	the simplest the most simple the commonest the most common

NOTE: These two-syllable adjectives have two forms: *handsome, quiet, gentle, narrow, clever, friendly, angry.*

	Simple	Comparative	Superlative
Adjectives with three or more syllables	important difficult	more important more difficult	the most important the most difficult
-ly adverbs	quickly brightly	more quickly more brightly	the most quickly the most brightly
Irregular adjectives and adverbs	good/well bad/badly far little a lot	better worse farther/further* less more	the best the worst the farthest/furthest the least the most

*NOTE: *Farther* is for distances. *Further* is for ideas.

The Superlative Form

Subject	Verb	Superlative Form + Noun	Prepositional Phrase
Alaska	is	the biggest state	in the U.S.
California	is	the most populated state	in the U.S.

(continued)

The Comparative Form:

Subject	Linking Verb[1]	Comparative Adjective	*Than*	Noun/Pronoun
She	is	taller	than	her sister (is).
She	seems	more intelligent	than	her sister.

Subject	Verb Phrase	Comparative Adverb	*Than*	Noun/Pronoun
I	speak English	more fluently	than	my sister (does).
I	sleep	less	than	you (do).

Comparisons with Nouns:

Subject	Verb	Compartive Word + Noun		*Than*	Noun/Pronoun
I	work	fewer hours		than	you (do).
I	have	more time		than	you (do).

Equatives with Adjectives and Adverbs:

Subject	Linking Verb	*As*	Adjective	*As*	Noun/Pronoun
She	isn't	as	old	as	her husband (is).
She	looks	as	pretty	as	a picture.

Subject	Verb Phrase	*As*	Adverb	*As*	Noun/Pronoun
She	speaks English	as	fluently	as	her husband (does).
He	doesn't work	as	hard	as	his wife (does).

Equatives with Quantities:

Subject	Verb	*As Many/Much*	Noun	*As*	Noun/Pronoun
She	works	as many	hours	as	her husband (does).
Milk	doesn't have	as much	fat	as	cream (does).

Subject	Verb	*As Much As*	Noun/Pronoun
Chicken	doesn't cost	as much as	meat (does).
I	don't drive	as much as	you (do).

[1] The linking verbs are *be, look, seem, feel, taste, sound, seem.*

Equatives with Nouns:

Pattern A					
Subject	**Verb**	*The Same*	**Noun**	*As*	**Noun/Pronoun**
She	wears	the same	size	as	her mother (does).
She	isn't	the same	height	as	her brother (is).

Pattern B			
Subject & Subject	**Verb**	*The Same*	**Noun**
She and her mother	wear	the same	size.
She and her brother	aren't	the same	height.

Similarities using *Like:*

Pattern A			
X	**Linking Verb**	*Like*	**Y**
Sugar	looks	like	salt.
Regular coffee	tastes	like	decaf.

Pattern B		
X and Y	**Linking Verb**	*Alike*
Sugar and salt	look	alike.
Regular coffee and decaf	taste	alike.

APPENDIX L

Glossary of Grammatical Terms

- **Adjective** An adjective gives a description of a noun.

  It's a *tall* tree.   He's an *old* man.   My neighbors are *nice*.

- **Adverb** An adverb describes the action of a sentence or an adjective or another adverb.

  She speaks English *fluently*.   I drive *carefully*.

  She speaks English *extremely* well.   She is *very* intelligent.

- **Adverb of Frequency** An adverb of frequency tells how often the action happens.

  I *never* drink coffee.   They *usually* take the bus.

- **Affirmative** means *yes*.

- **Apostrophe** '

- **Article** The definite article is *the*. The indefinite articles are *a* and *an*.

    I have *a* cat.   I ate *an* apple.   *The* President was in New York last weekend.

- **Auxiliary Verb** Some verbs have two parts: an auxiliary verb and a main verb.

    He *can't* study.   We *will* return.

- **Base Form** The base form of the verb has no tense. It has no ending (*-s* or *-ed*): *be, go, eat, take, write*

    I didn't *go* out.   He doesn't *know* the answer.   You shouldn't *talk* loud.

- **Capital Letter** A B C D E F G . . .

- **Clause** A clause is a group of words that has a subject and a verb. Some sentences have only one clause.

    She speaks Spanish.

Some sentences have a **main clause** and a **dependent clause.**

MAIN CLAUSE	DEPENDENT CLAUSE (reason clause)
She found a good job	because she has computer skills.
MAIN CLAUSE	**DEPENDENT CLAUSE (time clause)**
She'll turn off the light	before she goes to bed.
MAIN CLAUSE	**DEPENDENT CLAUSE (*if* clause)**
I'll take you to the doctor	if you don't have your car on Saturday.

- **Colon :**

- **Comma ,**

- **Comparative Form** A comparative form of an adjective or adverb is used to compare two things.

    My house is *bigger* than your house.

    Her husband drives *faster* than she does.

- **Complement** The complement of the sentence is the information after the verb. It completes the verb phrase.

    He works *hard*.   I slept *for five hours*.   They are *late*.

- **Consonant** The following letters are consonants: *b, c, d, f, g, h, j, k, l, m, n, p, q, r, s, t, v, w, x, y, z.*

    NOTE: *y* is sometimes considered a vowel.

- **Contraction** A contraction is made up of two words put together with an apostrophe.

    He's my brother.   *You're* late.   They *won't* talk to me.
    (*He's* = *he is*)   (*You're* = *you are*)   (*won't* = *will not*)

- **Count Noun** Count nouns are nouns that we can count. They have a singular and a plural form.

  1 pen / 3 pens   1 table / 4 tables

- **Dependent Clause** See **Clause.**

- **Direct Object** A direct object is a noun (phrase) or pronoun that receives the action of the verb.

  We saw *the movie.*   You have *a nice car.*   I love *you.*

- **Exclamation Mark !**

- **Hyphen -**

- **Imperative** An imperative sentence gives a command or instructions. An imperative sentence omits the word *you.*

  Come here.   *Don't be* late.   Please *sit* down.

- **Indefinite Pronoun** An indefinite pronoun (*one, some, any*) takes the place of an indefinite noun.

  I have a cell phone. Do you have *one*?

  I didn't drink any coffee, but you drank *some.* Did he drink *any*?

- **Infinitive** An infinitive is *to* + base form.

  I want *to leave.*   You need *to be* here on time.

- **Linking Verb** A linking verb is a verb that links the subject to the noun or adjective after it. Linking verbs include *be, seem, feel, smell, sound, look, appear, taste.*

  She *is* a doctor.   She *seems* very intelligent.   She *looks* tired.

- **Modal** The modal verbs are *can, could, shall, should, will, would, may, might, must.*

  They *should* leave.   I *must* go.

- **Negative** means *no.*

- **Nonaction Verb** A nonaction verb has no action. We do not use a continuous tense (*be* + verb *-ing*) with a nonaction verb. The nonaction verbs are: *believe, cost, care, have, hear, know, like, love, matter, mean, need, own, prefer, remember, see, seem, think, understand, want*

- **Noncount Noun** A noncount noun is a noun that we don't count. It has no plural form.

  She drank some *water.*   He prepared some *rice.*   Do you need any *money*?

- **Noun** A noun is a person (*brother*), a place (*kitchen*) or a thing (*table*). Nouns can be either count (*1 table, 2 tables*) or noncount (*money, water*).

  My *brother* lives in California. My *sisters* live in New York. I get *mail* from them.

- **Noun Modifier** A noun modifier makes a noun more specific.

  fire department   *Independence* Day   *can* opener

- **Noun Phrase** A noun phrase is a group of words that form the subject or object of the sentence.

  A very nice woman helped me at registration.

  I bought *a big box of candy.*

- **Object** The object of the sentence follows a verb or a preposition.

  He bought *a car.*   I saw *a movie.*   She travels with *me.*

- **Object Pronoun** Use object pronouns (*me, you, him, her, it, us, them*) after the verb or preposition.

  He likes *her.*   I saw the movie. Did you see *it*?

- **Parentheses** ( )

- **Paragraph** A paragraph is a group of sentences about one topic.

- **Participle, Present** The present participle is verb + *-ing.*

  She is *sleeping.*   They were *laughing.*

- **Period** .

- **Phrase** A group of words that go together.

  Last month my sister came to visit.

  There is a strange car *in front of my house.*

- **Plural** Plural means more than one. A plural noun usually ends with *-s*.

  She has beautiful *eyes.*

- **Possessive Form** Possessive forms show ownership or relationship.

  Mary's coat is in the closet.   *My* brother lives in Miami.

- **Preposition** A preposition is a short connecting word: *about, above, across, after, around, as, at, away, back, before, behind, below, by, down, for, from, in, into, like, of, off, on, out, over, to, under, up, with.*

- **Pronoun** A pronoun takes the place of a noun.

  I have a new car. I bought *it* last week.

  John likes Mary, but *she* doesn't like *him.*

- **Punctuation** Period . Comma , Colon : Semicolon ; Question Mark ? Exclamation Mark !

- **Question Mark** ?

- **Quotation Marks** " "

- **Regular Verb** A regular verb forms its past tense with *-ed.*

  He *worked* yesterday.   I *laughed* at the joke.

- **Sense-Perception Verb** A sense-perception verb has no action. It describes a sense.

  She *feels* fine.   The coffee *smells* fresh.   The milk *tastes* sour.

- **Sentence** A sentence is a group of words that contains a subject[1] and a verb (at least) and gives a complete thought.

  Sentence: She came home.

  Not a sentence: When she came home

- **Simple Form of Verb** The simple form of the verb has no tense; it never has an *-s, -ed,* or *-ing* ending.

  Did you *see* the movie?

  I couldn't *find* your phone number.

- **Singular** Singular means one.

  She ate *a sandwich*.   I have one *television*.

- **Subject** The subject of the sentence tells who or what the sentence is about.

  My sister got married last April. *The wedding* was beautiful.

- **Subject Pronoun** Use subject pronouns (*I, you, he, she, it, we, you, they*) before a verb.

  They speak Japanese.   *We* speak Spanish.

- **Superlative Form** A superlative form of an adjective or adverb shows the number one item in a group of three or more.

  January is the *coldest* month of the year.

  My brother speaks English the *best* in my family.

- **Syllable** A syllable is a part of a word that has only one vowel sound. (Some words have only one syllable.)

  change (one syllable)   after (af·ter = 2 syllables)

  look (one syllable)   responsible (re·spon·si·ble = 4 syllables)

- **Tag Question** A tag question is a short question at the end of a sentence. It is used in conversation.

  You speak Spanish, *don't you?*

  He's not happy, *is he?*

- **Tense** A verb has tense. Tense shows when the action of the sentence happened.

  SIMPLE PRESENT: She usually *works* hard.

  FUTURE: She *will work* tomorrow.

  PRESENT CONTINUOUS: She *is working* now.

  SIMPLE PAST: She *worked* yesterday.

---

[1] In an imperative sentence, the subject *you* is omitted: *Sit down. Come here.*

- **Verb** A verb is the action of the sentence.

    He *runs* fast.   I *speak* English.

    Some verbs have no action. They are linking verbs. They connect the subject to the rest of the sentence.

    He *is* tall.   She *looks* beautiful.   You *seem* tired.

- **Vowel** The following letters are vowels: *a, e, i, o, u. Y* is sometimes considered a vowel (for example, in the word *mystery*).

APPENDIX M

Alphabetical List of Irregular Verb Forms

Base Form	Past Form	Past Participle	Base Form	Past Form	Past Participle
be	was/were	been	drive	drove	driven
bear	bore	born/borne	eat	ate	eaten
beat	beat	beaten	fall	fell	fallen
become	became	become	feed	fed	fed
begin	began	begun	feel	felt	felt
bend	bent	bent	fight	fought	fought
bet	bet	bet	find	found	found
bind	bound	bound	fit	fit	fit
bite	bit	bitten	flee	fled	fled
bleed	bled	bled	fly	flew	flown
blow	blew	blown	forbid	forbade	forbidden
break	broke	broken	forget	forgot	forgotten
breed	bred	bred	forgive	forgave	forgiven
bring	brought	brought	freeze	froze	frozen
broadcast	broadcast	broadcast	get	got	gotten
build	built	built	give	gave	given
burst	burst	burst	go	went	gone
buy	bought	bought	grind	ground	ground
cast	cast	cast	grow	grew	grown
catch	caught	caught	hang	hung	hung[1]
choose	chose	chosen	have	had	had
cling	clung	clung	hear	heard	heard
come	came	come	hide	hid	hidden
cost	cost	cost	hit	hit	hit
creep	crept	crept	hold	held	held
cut	cut	cut	hurt	hurt	hurt
deal	dealt	dealt	keep	kept	kept
dig	dug	dug	know	knew	known
do	did	done	lay	laid	laid
draw	drew	drawn	lead	led	led
drink	drank	drunk	leave	left	left

[1] *Hanged* is used as the past form to refer to punishment by death. *Hung* is used in other situations: She *hung* the picture on the wall.

Base Form	Past Form	Past Participle	Base Form	Past Form	Past Participle
lend	loaned/lent	loaned/lent	split	split	split
let	let	let	spread	spread	spread
lie	lay	lain	spring	sprang	sprung
light	lit/lighted	lit/lighted	stand	stood	stood
lose	lost	lost	steal	stole	stolen
make	made	made	stick	stuck	stuck
mean	meant	meant	sting	stung	stung
meet	met	met	stink	stank	stunk
mistake	mistook	mistaken	strike	struck	struck/stricken
pay	paid	paid	strive	strove	striven
prove	proved	proven/proved	swear	swore	sworn
put	put	put	sweep	swept	swept
quit	quit	quit	swim	swam	swum
read	read	read	swing	swung	swung
ride	rode	ridden	take	took	taken
ring	rang	rung	teach	taught	taught
rise	rose	risen	tear	tore	torn
run	ran	run	tell	told	told
say	said	said	think	thought	thought
see	saw	seen	throw	threw	thrown
seek	sought	sought	understand	understood	understood
sell	sold	sold	upset	upset	upset
send	sent	sent	wake	woke	woken
set	set	set	wear	wore	worn
shake	shook	shaken	weave	wove	woven
shed	shed	shed	weep	wept	wept
shine	shone/shined	shone/shined	win	won	won
shoot	shot	shot	wind	wound	wound
show	showed	shown/showed	withdraw	withdrew	withdrawn
shrink	shrank	shrunk	wring	wrung	wrung
shut	shut	shut	write	wrote	written
sing	sang	sung			
sink	sank	sunk			
sit	sat	sat			
sleep	slept	slept			
slide	slid	slid			
slit	slit	slit			
speak	spoke	spoken			
speed	sped	sped			
spend	spent	spent			
spin	spun	spun			
spit	spit	spit			

The past and past participle of some verbs can end in *-ed* or *-t*. Americans generally prefer the *-ed* form:

burn	burned or burnt
dream	dreamed or dreamt
kneel	kneeled or knelt
learn	learned or learnt
spill	spilled or spilt
spoil	spoiled or spoilt

The United States of America

AL	Alabama	IN	Indiana	NE	Nebraska	SC	South Carolina
AK	Alaska	IA	Iowa	NV	Nevada	SD	South Dakota
AZ	Arizona	KS	Kansas	NH	New Hampshire	TN	Tennessee
AR	Arkansas	KY	Kentucky	NJ	New Jersey	TX	Texas
CA	California	LA	Louisiana	NM	New Mexico	UT	Utah
CO	Colorado	ME	Maine	NY	New York	VT	Vermont
CT	Connecticut	MD	Maryland	NC	North Carolina	VA	Virginia
DE	Delaware	MA	Massachusetts	ND	North Dakota	WA	Washington
FL	Florida	MI	Michigan	OH	Ohio	WV	West Virginia
GA	Georgia	MN	Minnesota	OK	Oklahoma	WI	Wisconsin
HI	Hawaii	MS	Mississippi	OR	Oregon	WY	Wyoming
ID	Idaho	MO	Missouri	PA	Pennsylvania	DC*	District of Columbia
IL	Illinois	MT	Montana	RI	Rhode Island		

*The District of Columbia is not a state. Washington D.C. is the capital of the United States. Note: Washington D.C. and Washington state are not the same.

North America

Index